ENCYCLOPEDIA
OF THE
BLUES

■ Muddy Waters. *(Photograph © by Paul Harris; used with permission)*

ENCYCLOPEDIA
OF THE
BLUES

GÉRARD HERZHAFT

TRANSLATED BY BRIGITTE DEBORD

THE UNIVERSITY OF ARKANSAS PRESS ■ FAYETTEVILLE ■ 1992

This book was designed by Chiquita Babb using the Plantin and Revue typefaces.

The paper used in this publication meets the minimum requirements
of the American National Standard for Permanence of Paper for
Printed Library Materials z39.48-1984. ∞

LIBRARY OF CONGRESS CATALOGING-IN-PUBLICATION DATA

Herzhaft, Gérard.
    [Nouvelle encyclopédie du blues.   English]
    Encyclopedia of the blues / Gérard Herzhaft ; translated by
Brigitte Debord.
      p.   cm.
    Translation of: Nouvelle encyclopédie du blues.
    Includes bibliographical references and index.
    Discography: p.
    ISBN 1-55728-252-8. — ISBN 1-55728-253-6 (pbk.)
    1. Blues (Music)—Dictionaries.   I. Title.
ML102.B6H4313   1992
781.643′03—dc20   92-7386
                                                   CIP
                                                   MN

▪ CONTENTS

▪ PREFACE

From Mamie Smith, who recorded "Crazy Blues" in 1920, to rising young stars Robert Cray, Joe Louis Walker, and Kenny Neal; from the cotton fields of the American Deep South to the international festival scenes, the blues has had a long journey. All American music—and that of the South in particular—is related. Jimmie Rodgers, Bob Wills, and Hank Williams—big names of country music—weren't they blues musicians? Don't rockabilly and rock-and-roll come from, for the most part, the black blues as country singer and guitar player Merle Travis recognized in the mid-fifties? And isn't soul also largely inspired by the blues? Aren't rock artists, from the sixties to the present, from the Rolling Stones and the Yardbirds to ZZ Top and Dire Straits, strongly influenced by the blues? It is this itinerary our work explores, without leaving either main or secondary roads untraveled.

The trends, the movements, the major regions, the instruments, and, of course, the producers and musicians who made the blues are analyzed and depicted according to their importance and influence. The main blues figures, known or unknown, are designated with asterisks; those who played smaller roles are included in more general entries; and finally those who were part of the blues for only a brief period are cited and identified in the index.

The discographic choice within each article includes only album titles and the original label or the label that covered it. It is not possible, considering the abundance of countless reeditions on three formats, to give details of all recordings. To make it easier for the novice blues fan, we also include a choice of compact discs, but here, too, editions are being released so fast that we give titles and references with caution.

An appendix describes about three hundred famous blues titles and tries to trace them to their most probable origin. Many listeners and readers will be surprised to discover where some pieces originate.

The *Encyclopedia of the Blues* is the fruit of a long personal labor. It is impossible in these few lines to thank all those who, at some point, have offered their help, advice, knowledge, and kindness; those who welcomed us in their houses when we traveled in the U.S.; and those who were willing to play their music just for us. Above all, we want to acknowledge those whose help was crucial; in the U.S.: David Evans, Bill Ferris, Roy Ames, Amie Devereux, Frank Gillis, Sid Graves, Joe Hickerson, Tom Mazzolini, Bill Mitchell, Gerald Parsons, Barry Pearson, Louise Spear, Jose Yrraba, Mike Walters, Barry Jean Ancelet, A. E. Schroeder, and Jim Griffith; in France: Jean-Pierre Arniac, Alain Kaiser, Alain Gerber, Lucien Malson, Lise Brière de l'Isle, Jean Buzelin, Jacques Demêtre, Maurice Duffaud, Didier Gascon, Pierre Monnery, Philippe Grancher, Robert Sacré, Claudette Simonnet, Philippe Carles, Joel Dufour, Sebastian Danchin, Marc Radenac, and Paul Fournel, who allowed us to compose our blues in A minor!

And finally, we give special thanks to Jacques Périn, the tireless entertainer of *Soul Bag,* whose enthusiasm and generosity at the beginning of our undertaking has made this achievement possible. May the others, whom I cannot name, whom my memory can't find again, or who did not wish to be mentioned, be certain of my gratitude.

As for the readers, whose remarks, critiques, and suggestions have always been necessary stimuli to our work, may they continue to offer their comments to us.

This encyclopedia is before everything for them: the friends of the blues.

Gérard Herzhaft

ENCYCLOPEDIA
OF THE
BLUES

RAY AGEE

See California

DAVE ALEXANDER

(b. 1938 / vocals, piano)

Dave Alexander was one of the few blues artists to emerge during the sixties. Like many California artists, he was born in Texas and emigrated to the West Coast in 1955. There he learned piano, primarily by listening to records, which sets him apart from the majority of bluesmen, who learned by apprenticing themselves to other musicians.

Dave Alexander cites Albert Ammons* and Amos Milburn* as his principal influences; and for his chromatic style, Charles Brown.* Some of his compositions also reflect an interest in modern jazz piano players such as Horace Silver.

Gifted with an expressive voice and a virtuoso technique, original and seemingly effortless, he was one of the most sought-after seventies blues musicians for West Coast festivals and concerts, before his sullen nature alienated even his most ardent admirers. He appears on the superb anthology *Oakland Blues* (World Pacific) in the company of Albert Collins* and has been recorded on two excellent albums on which he is a featured player (*The Rattler:* Arhoolie and *The Dirt on the Ground:* Arhoolie). These albums reflect his originality and eclecticism, especially *The Dirt on the Ground,* on which he at times moves considerably away from the blues. One would hope that Dave Alexander, perhaps the best of the contemporary blues piano players, will someday record again.

TEXAS ALEXANDER

(Algier Alexander / ca. 1890–1954 / vocals)

Texas Alexander, known as "The Voice of Texas," had a voice that the state's black sharecroppers, small farmers, and prisoners identified with before it influenced regional singers such as Mercy Dee,* Lowell Fulson,* and Lightnin' Hopkins.*

Little is known about this itinerant musician: He went from town to town, accompanied by the best local guitar players, and is thought to have served time at the infamous Big Brazos Penitentiary, which he describes grippingly in the celebrated "Penitentiary Moan." Between 1927 and 1934, he made sixty-seven recordings. The most memorable are the first twenty on which he was accompanied by guitar player Lonnie Johnson.* One would have to be a musician of Johnson's stature to be able to follow Alexander's singing. This challenge had nothing to do with the blues, but with parts of the music that were much more primitive: the hollers that captured the sounds of cotton pickers or of penitentiary chain gangs, during which the singer threw out phrases with melodic lines that varied from one moment to the next. In addition to the extraordinary music produced by the combined talents of Johnson and Alexander, these hollers are exciting because they give rare recorded evidence of a musical form that prefigured the blues and because they suggest a link between songs that originated in Africa and the actual blues, the development of which seems to have been accelerated among blacks by the influence of recording in the early 1920s.

These pieces are available on the album *Texas Alexander, Vol. 1* (Matchbox). The remainder of his recordings are less original, although they present this powerful singer in varied musical contexts: with Texas guitar players Little Hat Jones, Carl Davis, and Willie Reed; and with jazz musicians Eddie Lang, King Oliver, and Clarence Williams. All of Alexander's works are available on the Matchbox label. Another source is *Texas Troublesome Blues* (Agram), which has a good selection of his titles.

Texas Alexander remained an itinerant musician through-out his lifetime. In 1947, he recorded a demo tape, which is still unedited, with Lightnin' Hopkins for the Aladdin label. In 1950 he recorded two titles for the small Freedom label on which he is no more than a shadow of his former self. This is the last we know about this great singer who apparently died in an unknown location around 1954.

LUTHER ALLISON

(b. 1939 / vocals, guitar, harmonica)

Coming to Chicago from the Deep South in 1952, Luther Allison mastered the guitar through his contacts with Freddie King* and Hound Dog Taylor.* Allison even took over King's small band before attracting the attention of Bob Koester, the producer of Delmark records, for whom he put together a 1967 anthology devoted to the "new" Chicago blues (*Sweet Home Chicago:* Delmark).

These recordings and his powerful performances in clubs in Chicago and Peoria led to tours of California, where he cut a number of albums as guitar player for Sunnyland Slim,* Shakey Jake,* and the blues/rock group Canned Heat.* After an outstanding performance at the Ann Arbor Festival in 1968, he recorded his first solo album, *Love Me Mama* (Delmark), on which the influences of B. B. King,* Otis Rush,* and Magic Sam* are particularly strong. On the strength of this album, he was able to cut a series of albums for Motown, including the remarkable *Luther's Blues* (Gordy), which remains his best album to date.

From 1976 on, Allison has been a regular on the European music scene where he is even more popular than in the United States. His dynamic performances, theatrical and animated, have gained him the reputation of a blues star with an eye on the rock audience. He has recorded prolifically, especially in France and England. The best of his recent albums is probably *Life Is a Bitch* (Encore).

Acclaimed for a short while as a major contemporary blues talent, the congenial and sensitive Luther Allison seems more a good emulator of the great creative geniuses of the West Side sound than a true originator himself.

AMERICAN FOLK BLUES FESTIVAL

In the late 1950s, two German jazz enthusiasts, Horst Lippmann and Fritz Rau, noted that European audiences were largely unfamiliar with the blues. Apart from Big Bill Broonzy,* who had just died and was considered to be the

■ Luther Allison. *(Photograph © by Anton J. Mikofsky. Courtesy of Anton J. Mikofsky and Archives and Special Collections, John Davis Williams Library, University of Mississippi)*

"last blues singer," the blues was recognized only as the source from which jazz had emerged. It was almost impossible to find a selection of blues records in Europe. However, in that era black clubs in America's big cities were host to countless quality bluesmen, and such greats as Muddy Waters,* Howlin' Wolf,* Jimmy Reed,* and John Lee Hooker* continued to enjoy a large commercial success at home.

Lippmann and Rau decided to produce a live blues extravaganza that would tour Western Europe in 1962. It featured John Lee Hooker, Memphis Slim,* Sonny Terry* and Brownie McGhee,* Willie Dixon,* Shakey Jake,* T-Bone Walker,* and Helen Humes.* The tour was a large commercial success. It attracted considerable interest not only from jazz fans, already numerous in Europe, but also from a newer, much younger audience, fans of rock-and-roll, who discovered via the tour one of the most obvious sources of the music they loved.

Encouraged by the success of the 1962 tour, Lippmann and Rau put together another tour in 1963 with Sonny Boy Williamson (Rice Miller),* Muddy Waters, Otis Spann,* Memphis Slim, Willie Dixon, Lonnie Johnson,* Big Joe Williams,* M. T. Murphy, and Victoria Spivey.* Once more, the enterprise was a total success. In addition, a 45 recorded by John Lee Hooker at the 1962 festival ("Shake It Baby") was a bestseller throughout Europe (more than one hundred thousand copies sold in France alone). The blues rapidly developed an audience that had begun to have its stars and its trends and which impatiently awaited the discovery of new faces.

Lippmann and Rau decided to make the American Folk Blues Festival an annual event: In 1964 Sonny Boy Williamson came back to Europe, with Howlin' Wolf, Hubert Sumlin,* Lightnin' Hopkins,* and Sleepy John Estes*; in 1965, John Lee Hooker—who had become a big star in Europe—was featured with Doctor Ross,* J. B. Lenoir,* Big Walter Horton,* Buddy Guy,* and singer Big Mama Thornton*; in 1966 Junior Wells,* Otis Rush,* Robert Pete Williams,* and Big Joe Turner* were introduced to European audiences; 1967 was the year for "country blues," with Skip James,* Son House,* and Bukka White,* as well as Little Walter* and Hound Dog

■ Helen Humes. *(Photograph © by Anton J. Mikofsky; used with permission)*

Taylor.* The festival was held for ten consecutive years, until 1972, when the event, which had begun with critical raves, ended by being generally panned. Among the problems it faced was the proliferation of competing festivals more responsive to the demands of an increasingly sophisticated blues audience.

In retrospect, one can assess the importance of these tours. Their historic significance is undeniable: The American Folk Blues Festival introduced Europe to the blues and influenced an array of young musicians. Not the least important was its effect on British performers who in part created English rock. Rock, in turn, reached many young white Americans who ultimately discovered the blues in their own back yard. The tours also brought the music to the attention of large numbers of young Europeans who became passionate devotees, with their own specialized magazines, their "schools" (country blues, Chicago, etc.), and their demand for records, thus creating a fairly important blues market in Europe.

On the debit side of this enterprise, the festival format hardly allowed the artists to perform at their best: Each made an appearance, played three or four numbers, and left. Even musicians with the ability to warm up an audience quickly— and they are rare—had to make way for the next in line without the time to develop their performances. Moreover, neither the very orderly European audiences nor the huge, often acoustically poor concert halls were well adapted to the blues. In clubs in the United States, there is a rapport between the artist and the audience that challenges, encourages, and pushes him to his very best. Europeans, on the other hand, listen to a blues concert as if it were a classical performance. Many bluesmen were surprised to learn that this reception, which they thought cold, was intended to be very appreciative of their talents. Finally, after several years, the tours, which had been conceived with enthusiasm, became static, lifeless events (and completely unorganized in the final years). The promoters did not understand that blues fans had become increasingly knowledgeable and that fans demanded something other than a procession of artists often well past their peak performance years.

Beginning in 1980, just when such tours seemed dead, the promoters revived the format. This time, however, with few big names and many of the same shortcomings as before, Lippmann and Rau's American Folk Blues Festival was met with general indifference.

ALBERT AMMONS

See Boogie-Woogie

PINK ANDERSON

See East Coast Blues

FERNEST ARCENEAUX

See Zydeco

ARCHIBALD

See New Orleans

BILLY BOY ARNOLD

(William Arnold / b. 1935 / vocals, harmonica)

This important innovator, too often unrecognized, started playing the harmonica at age twelve with his idol John Lee "Sonny Boy" Williamson.* At age sixteen, Billy Boy Arnold directed a band with guitar player Ellas McDaniel, who would soon be better known as Bo Diddley.*

Furthermore, he played an important role in the development of the distinct style of Bo Diddley (hypnotic and insistent, that would later influence reggae). He was also the harmonica player for most of the first records that Bo did for the Chess label.

Billy Boy chose to sign a contract in 1955 with a competing label, Vee-Jay. He had several hits, including the very rhythmical "I Wish You Would." He recorded about ten wonderful titles at Vee-Jay between 1955 and 1957. These recordings highlight the exceptional talents of his accompanists, piano player Henry Gray and guitar players Syl Johnson* and Jody Williams. They also bring out the personal qualities of Billy Boy, an outstanding composer of modern blues. The album *Crying & Pleading* (Charly) is a collection of these songs.

Vee-Jay's bankruptcy left Billy Boy without a record company and without a regular band. He then neglected music more and more, reappearing throughout the years only a few times, most often to go on European tours. In twenty years he cut only a handful of records of uneven quality. Nevertheless, two titles stand out: *Blues from the Southside* (Prestige), with a good Chicago band, in particular, the gifted guitar player Mighty Joe Young,* as well as a really interesting album of much more modern Chicago blues, *Ten Million Dollars* (Blue

Phoenix), enhanced by the elusive guitar player Jimmy Johnson.*

KOKOMO ARNOLD

(James Arnold / 1901–1969 / vocals, guitar)

Kokomo Arnold was one of the leading blues players to use a Hawaiian guitar. The Hawaiian guitar is placed flat on the knees while the left hand slides a steel pipe over the strings. Kokomo Arnold cleverly adapted this technique to his personality, combining the influence of Hawaiian guitar players, such as Sol Hoopi, and the influence of his fellow Georgians, Barbecue Bob* and Tampa Red.* Constantly playing in the high octaves and marking semitones, with his high-pitched tenor voice he created an immediately recognizable personal style of blues. This style made him popular in the African-American community. Within four years he made about a hundred recordings!

After moving to Chicago in 1929 he performed in the black clubs of the city, becoming increasingly popular. In 1930 he recorded under the name "Gitfiddle Jim" a 78 for RCA Victor (on *The Georgia Blues:* Yazoo). Only in 1934 did he really become a star. Indeed, that year the artist-producer from Decca, Joe McCoy,* noticed him and was impressed by his style and his original songs. McCoy persuaded him to record "Milk Cow Blues," a personal and new version of Sleepy John Estes's* blues, and "Original Old Kokomo Blues" that instantly became a national success. These two recordings continue to be appreciated by many artists.

The success of "Kokomo Blues" gave James Arnold his nickname. Between 1934 and 1940, Arnold took part in recording sessions as the featured player, or he accompanied with his particular guitar style other artists from Decca, such as Peetie Wheatstraw,* Roosevelt Sykes,* Mary Johnson, and Alice Moore. A great creator of lyrical blues larded with double meaning (some apparent, others hidden and often very erotic) that actually made blues poetry, Kokomo Arnold also managed several outstanding instrumental performances, among which "The Twelves" is one of the most impressive.

Similar to many blues stars of the thirties, Kokomo Arnold disappeared after the war. Only in 1959 did the French critic Jacques Demêtre find him in Chicago where he was a simple worker. Asked many times to record again, he seemed to have refused each time, although some persistent and contradictory rumors suggest that he recorded some albums for Willie Dixon* and Victoria Spivey.*

B

BABY TATE

See East Coast Blues

MICKEY BAKER

See New York

BARBECUE BOB

(Robert Hicks / 1902–1931 / vocals, guitar)

Between 1927 and 1930, Barbecue Bob was one of the most popular bluesmen of Atlanta, Georgia. A cook in that city (hence his nickname), he performed nights in black pubs. Although his tenor voice links him to other Georgia artists (Blind Willie McTell,* for instance), he nevertheless remained a musical anomaly: His highly rhythmical guitar style and his almost constant use of the bottleneck related much more to the rough blues of the Mississippi Delta than to the complex and delicate fingerpicking usually associated with the East Coast blues.

His guitar style was indeed unique: He rhythmically struck his guitar with his bottleneck, sliding it along the top strings. This style, primitive yet conducive to dancing, as well as his original numbers humorously and cynically describing the life of black farmers who came into town, made him extremely popular with Atlanta blacks. Within three years he recorded sixty titles for Columbia.

His early death from pneumonia put an end to this promising career. His simple, original style has been imitated by a few other artists: George Carter, Willie Baker, and especially Barbecue Bob's own brother, Charlie Lincoln, himself an excellent guitar player.

Chocolate to the Bone (Mamlish) is a good collection of Barbecue Bob's best titles.

DAVE BARTHOLOMEW

See New Orleans

BASS

In the blues the electric bass or double bass (stand-up bass) is essentially used to keep the beat and to provide the soloists some liberty. For instance, the guitar player can freely improvise in the upper registers without having to play the low notes at the same time. The blues bass player has to be both effective and discreet. Bass improvisations, common in jazz, are unusual in the blues.

Historically, the double bass is found in several of the first blues by the female blues singers, who actually recorded jazz songs. In the thirties, apart from the jug bands who used the washtub (a string attached along a broomstick placed on a boiler for washing laundry), more and more frequently a second guitar player would emphasize the bass notes of his instrument, often by significantly lowering the low strings of his guitar. After the years 1935–40 this form of imitating the double bass was replaced by the use of a real double bass. Following the war the use of the double bass became widespread in bands influenced by West Coast jazz (Johnny Miller) as well as Chicago jazz (Big Crawford).

In the early fifties the electric bass, an extension of the rare four-string guitar, became widespread, giving the bass notes a depth that had never been reached before. However, this was to the detriment of a flowing style compared to the double bass, whose effects are sometimes impossible to recreate on the bass guitar.

Almost all contemporary blues bands use electric bass. The

most famous blues bass players are, among others, Mac Thompson/Johnson, Dave Myers, Ernest Gatewood, Donald Dunn, Freddie Dixon, Snapper Mitchum, Aron Burton, Herman Applewhite, and Larry Taylor.

The peculiar sound of the double bass was, until recently, represented in Chicago by the late Willie Dixon,* who participated in hundreds of recording sessions and sometimes played solos on his instrument.

During the last few years the influence of soul/funk, where the autonomous bass dominates not only the rhythm but also the whole of the band, has become more and more significant for the blues.

CAREY BELL

(Carey Bell Harrington / b. 1936 / vocals, harmonica)

A furniture mover and a musician in the Chicago streets since 1956—especially at the Maxwell Street flea market—Carey Bell emerged during the late sixties when he set off on tours in Europe and made his first album (*Blues Harp:* Delmark) accompanied by the excellent guitar players Jimmy Dawkins* and Eddie Taylor.*

Bell then became part of the Muddy Waters* and Willie Dixon* bands before his own career had been established, making numerous albums for Bluesway, Alligator (*Big Walter with Carey Bell* and *Living Chicago Blues, Vol. 2*), and Spivey or Flying Fish. His appearance on the anthology *Just Off Halsted* is particularly striking.

A master of the difficult chromatic harmonica, he knows how to integrate the influence of great musicians, such as Big Walter Horton* and Little Walter,* with his personal innovations. This combination makes him one of the best blues harmonica players in Chicago. In the seventies, he participated in many recording sessions with bluesmen such as Eddie Clearwater,* Eddie C. Campbell,* and Buster Benton,* in which he showed talent and command of his instrument.

For the last few years, he has modernized his repertoire along with his approach to the blues and has been surrounded by a band of young musicians sometimes from his own family.

As a matter of fact, he has shared star billing with his son, Lurrie Bell, an excellent singer and guitar player, greatly influenced by Buddy Guy.* *Mellow Down Easy* (Blind Pig), recorded with his touring band, is his best recent album.

FRED BELOW

(1926–1988 / drums)

Until Fred Below, drums in the blues were a mere substitute for the washboard with the player pounding out the rhythm. Everything changed with Below: The rhythm is offbeat and underlines the previous musical phrase. The beat stimulates the rhythm, giving the other musicians further initiative. This is the famous Chicago beat, widespread in blues after 1955, that influenced rock music ever since the Beatles.

Born in Chicago, Fred Below graduated from the music school of Du Sable, specializing in percussion. An admirer of drummers Cozy Cole, Chick Webb, and Gene Krupa, he began his career as a jazz musician with Gene Ammons, Red Prysock, and Jack McDuff, with whom he recorded in 1947. When he got out of the army in 1951, he found it was easier to get a job as a blues drummer than as a jazz drummer. Since his friend Elgin Evans played the drums in Muddy Waters'* band, he got to know most of the Chicago bluesmen through him. He was hired by Junior Wells,* who was then playing with brothers Dave and Louis Myers.* They called their group the Aces, and they recorded first with Wells and later with Little Walter.*

Fred Below's particular style rapidly became appreciated on the Chicago blues scene, and he became a house drummer with the Chess* brothers. He took part in several recording sessions with Little Walter, Muddy Waters, Jimmy Rogers,* Sonny Boy Williamson (Rice Miller),* Eddie Boyd,* Etta James, and Chuck Berry.*

His fame continually grew among blues fans, and he went on many international tours before reuniting the Aces with the Myers brothers, again recording many albums.

He went into semiretirement for health reasons and died in 1988.

BUSTER BENTON

(b. 1932 / vocals, guitar)

Discovered by Willie Dixon★ in 1974 thanks to the superb blues tune "Spider in My Stew," Buster Benton had actually been living and active in Chicago for many years.

Born in Arkansas, Benton was deeply influenced by gospel, which he sang in church throughout his childhood. A great admirer of Sam Cooke and of B. B. King,★ in the fifties he undertook a bluesman's career under their influence. He moved to Chicago in 1959 where he accompanied many artists in all genres of black music, from John Lee Hooker★ to Tyrone Davis. He managed to record a few 45s for some obscure labels, and he appeared as a guitar player on several records of Jimmy Reed,★ Joe Tex, and Mighty Joe Young.★ He also recorded with G. L. Crockett, who imitated Jimmy Reed and who was successful with "It's a Man Down There" on which Benton has a solo.

His participation in Willie Dixon's blues band from 1971 on allowed him to display his talent fully. He appears on the album *Maestro Willie Dixon* (Spivey) and is featured on three songs with a vocal and instrumental style similar to B. B. King's, including an excellent version of "The Thrill Is Gone." In 1974 he became successful with "Spider in My Stew." He then made an album with the same title (*Spider in My Stew:* Ronn) accompanied by outstanding musicians, including Carey Bell.★ *Buster Benton Is the Feeling* (Ronn) is less successful, but is nevertheless excellent in some places.

Although he was obviously influenced by B. B. King and also by Bobby Bland★ and Albert King,★ Buster Benton has a personality of his own, which he demonstrates in his talent as a composer by augmenting original blues tunes with subtle lyrics in the tradition of the Delta blues. Benton successfully integrates all the modern derivations of black music: soul, disco, and funk. His elegant and efficient style on the guitar also owes a substantial amount to Wes Montgomery, whom Benton says he admires a lot.

After a car accident that resulted in his absence from clubs and recording studios for a few years, Buster Benton came back in peak condition, as proven on his albums on the Ichiban label.

CHUCK BERRY

(Charles Edward Berry / b. 1931 / vocals, guitar)

Chuck Berry is considered to be a pioneer of rock-and-roll. Indeed, by the age of ten, Berry was playing in a St. Louis blues band. In 1955 he went to Chicago, where one of his idols, Muddy Waters,★ at the peak of his popularity, introduced him to the famed record producers the Chess★ brothers. From 1955 onward Berry had contracts for a continuous succession of records that were regularly in the Top 10. His passionate style, an original combination of influences (blues, country, TexMex, and Caribbean), guaranteed his inclusion in the rock-and-roll movement that was sweeping America. He was a tremendous success and was one of the first black singers to appear in the white Top 40. His influence upon teen music of the sixties was significant, both in America and in Great Britain.

The spirit of the blues is always part of his work, which is often distinguished by comic, almost absurd lyrics ("Roll over Beethoven") such as are found in rockabilly. His exuberant way of playing the guitar captures the attention of his audience in a cascade of joyous notes. The best of his recorded work was produced by the Chess brothers between 1955 and 1965 with accompanists as talented as Otis Spann,★ Lafayette Leake, and Johnny Johnson on the piano, along with the flawless rhythm section of Willie Dixon★ and Fred Below.★ These works have been reissued many times with different covers, most recently on compact disc by MCA.

Since 1965 when he was charged with using drugs, Chuck Berry regained his popular success, but thereafter he did not always display the artistic gift that characterized his best records.

In seclusion much of the time, Chuck Berry comes out once in a while to appear at festivals and concerts or for the making of a movie in praise of him, the ever-slender figure of a rock-and-roll veteran. New and former fans graciously forgive him his mediocre accompanists or his humdrum performances. When you make history, one appearance and one famous "duck walk" are enough to live on.

BIG MACEO

(Major Merriweather / 1905–1953 / vocals, piano)

Big Maceo was one of the great innovators in blues history. Being a fantastic piano player, he knew how to adapt and modernize the barrelhouse style characteristic of blues piano players of the South, while at the same time adding his personal and original mark to it: rolling bass notes with the left hand. Although obviously inspired by Little Brother Montgomery★ and Roosevelt Sykes,★ he created a unique and immediately recognizable style on the piano. Despite his short career he influenced many Chicago piano players such as Otis Spann,★ Little Johnny Jones, Eddie Boyd,★ and Henry Gray. Relatively speaking, his role in the evolution of the blues piano after the war can be compared to that of B. B. King★ for guitar and Little Walter★ for harmonica. His husky voice and his recitative and impassive phrasing created a melancholy tune underlined by the bottleneck style of his guitar player and friend, Tampa Red.★

Big Maceo's life is easily summarized: Born in Georgia, he learned to play the piano at a very young age and left for Detroit in 1925 where he had a job in the auto industry. He performed in many black nightclubs, and his name became known in Chicago where Big Bill Broonzy★ and Tampa Red befriended him. They introduced him to producer Lester Melrose,★ who recorded him for Bluebird in 1941. With the help of Tampa Red he recorded "Worried Life Blues," an extraordinary version of "Someday Baby" by Sleepy John Estes.★ This version was a hit in Chicago and Detroit and later became a blues classic. Maceo was involved in several recording sessions and made many masterpieces: the poignant "Why Should I Hang Around," "Poor Kelly Blues," and the humorous "Maceo's 32-20," inspired by "44 Blues" by Lee Green and Little Brother Montgomery. He also penned several piano solos, among which was the surging boogie-woogie "Chicago

Breakdown," one of the best instrumental pieces in blues history.

At the peak of his fame Big Maceo had a stroke that left him paralyzed on one side, and the last records he made for Bluebird in 1947 were with the help of Eddie Boyd on the piano.

Bluebird did not renew his contract, and Maceo was unable to play in nightclubs. Without a record company or any financial resources, he recorded only two more times, but lacked his earlier brilliance: In 1949 for producer Art Rupe, accompanied by his student Johnny Jones; and in 1952 for the small Detroit company, Fortune, with guitar player John Brim. He died destitute after a second stroke in 1952.

His work for Bluebird is available in its entirety on *The King of Chicago Blues Piano, Vols. 1 & 2* (Blues Classics).

Among his closest disciples was unquestionably LITTLE JOHNNY JONES (1924–1964), who was an important figure in Chicago clubs for about fifteen years. He was the regular piano player for many artists, in particular Tampa Red★ and Elmore James.★

In fact, Little Johnny Jones was Big Maceo's replacement for Tampa Red in 1947. He shared a kind of leadership over the band of the great guitar player who was getting old, and he often sang the refrain. The recordings of Tampa Red accompanied by Johnny Jones are among the best Chicago blues of that period (between 1947 and 1952). Afterwards, he led his own band, which included the expressive saxophone player J. T. Brown. This band would accompany Elmore James when he went to Chicago. Including "Big Town Playboy," which knew a short-lived local success, Jones recorded only a handful of titles under his own name. They are available in diverse Chess and Atlantic anthologies, as well as on the album *Little Johnny Jones with Billy Boy Arnold* (Alligator).

BIG TIME SARAH STREETER

See Zora Young

BLACK ACE

(Babe Karo Turner / 1905–1975 / guitar)

Black Ace is one of the few blues guitarists to have played in the purest Hawaiian style, that is, with the guitar flat on the knees while the left hand moves a glass or metal slide along the strings (Black Ace used a small medicine bottle). The outstanding street musician Oscar Woods★ introduced Black Ace to this style during an encounter in Shreveport around 1930. Between 1935 and 1943 Black Ace was a professional musician playing in local bars, either alone or with Woods.

His particular style, as well as his talent for telling stories, allowed him to host a radio program from 1937 on called "The Black Ace," hence his nickname. The same year he made six beautiful records for Decca, in particular *Black Ace Blues,* whose success spread throughout Texas. He even began a movie career before he was called to active military duty in 1943.

After the war, the tastes of the black rural Texas audience switched to the electric blues of Lightnin' Hopkins,★ Lil' Son Jackson,★ and Smokey Hogg★ (a protégé of Black Ace). B. K. Turner gave up his musical ambitions and worked in a movie studio. Because of the reputation of Black Ace's 78s, the British musicologist Paul Oliver looked for him and found him in 1960 in Fort Worth. He recorded an excellent album (*Black Ace:* Arhoolie) on which one can hear his unique guitar style as well as several compositions never before recorded. Despite insistent requests by his audience and by blues fans, he refused to give up his regular job for an uncertain new musical career.

SCRAPPER BLACKWELL

See Leroy Carr

BLIND BLAKE

(Arthur Phelps / ca. 1880–1935 / vocals, guitar)

Like Blind Lemon Jefferson★ in Texas and Charlie Patton★ in the Mississippi Delta, Blind Blake may rightly be considered one of the great founders of the East Coast blues (or Piedmont blues), a particular style that first spread to southern states along the Atlantic Ocean (the Carolinas, Georgia, the Virginias, and Florida) before reaching New York and the North.

Contrary to the raw music of the Mississippi, this East Coast blues is characterized by its cool elegance and the instrumental mastery of its players. These terms perfectly describe the music of Blind Blake, who had a good natural voice and who was an extraordinary guitar player. His skill and subtlety are still admired by devotees of fingerpicking.

The origin of his particular style of fingerpicking is obscure: It is undeniably a transposition of "ragtime" piano, very popular at the beginning of the century, to the guitar. One can also feel the influence of the Negro music of the Caribbean; as a matter of fact, Blind Blake mentions specifically this part of the world in the spoken introduction of "Southern Rag," one of his most famous pieces.

Despite his present fame—which goes far beyond blues fans—Blind Blake remains a mysterious figure: Little is known of his life, except that he lived near Atlanta before he went to Chicago to record for Paramount. He presumably stayed there until his death; the date of his death is uncertain (probably between 1933 and 1940). He recorded about one hundred titles between 1926 and 1932; he was so popular that Paramount released at least one and sometimes several new records under his name every month! Moreover, he accompanied Gus Cannon,★ Ma Rainey,★ Leola Wilson, and piano player Charlie Spand on several of their records; and he influenced many East Coast guitar players, black and white, in particular Blind Boy Fuller,★ the Reverend Gary Davis,★ Buddy Moss,★ and Bill Williams.★ He even influenced much younger bluesmen, such as John Jackson★ and Larry Johnson.★ His influence on country music guitar player Merle Travis, considered to be the main popularizer of fingerpicking (or Travis style), currently used by thousands of guitarists around the world, is acknowledged by Travis himself.

Blind Blake's recording works are very consistent; almost all of the tracks he cut are important. They are easily available

■ Bobby "Blue" Bland. *(Photograph © by Burnham Ware. Courtesy of Burnham Ware and Archives and Special Collections, John Davis Williams Library, University of Mississippi)*

on Biograph albums, and the double album *Ragtime Guitar's Foremost Fingerpicker* (Yazoo), acoustically exceptional, includes some of his best work.

BOBBY "BLUE" BLAND

(Robert Bland / b. 1930 / vocals)

For a long time this singer from Tennessee has been an idol of the black public, in particular, women. His singing, soft, enthralling, and terribly sensual, made him one of the best crooners of American pop music. It also explains why he distanced himself from the blues of his early years to take on with a mixed success the genre of the langorous ballad.

Bland began his career singing in churches in Memphis. He was an admirer of the great B. B. King,* working as his chauffeur and servant for several years. Moreover, his vocal style is influenced by B. B. King as is his stage presence and his corpulence! He recorded as early as 1951 with Ike Turner,* Earl Forest, Roscoe Gordon, Johnny Ace, and the superb singer and harmonica player Junior Parker.* Parker, who was then very popular, got him a contract with the Texas label Duke, for which Bland recorded several albums between 1952 and 1972. Accompanied by great guitar players, like Clarence Holliman and Wayne Bennett, Bland established himself as one of the great stars of black music. From very sophisticated blues to ballads and love songs, Bobby Bland's repertoire allowed him to remain in the Top 40. "Cry Cry Cry," "Hold Me Tenderly," and "Pity the Fool" are some of his greatest hits. The totality of that prolific period can be found on several albums, including the collections *Memphis Original Blues Brothers* (Ace), which features his first recordings; *Woke Up Screaming* (Ace); *Blues in the Night* (Ace); and *Foolin' with the Blues* (Charly).

After 1972 the takeover of Duke by ABC was hardly favorable to Bland. He became less a bluesman and more a pop singer, and soon he became a very poor disco singer. Here and there his talent reappeared intact, in particular on two albums recorded with B. B. King (*Together for the First Time:* MCA and *Together Again:* MCA). In 1992, Bland was inducted into the Rock-and-Roll Hall of Fame.

The recent revival of soul and of the genuine blues in the South allowed Bland to return to his real calling: that of a bluesman full of feeling and emotion. The Malaco label, for which he currently records, gives him the opportunity to once more attain the quality of his early years (*Members Only:* Malaco, *After All:* Malaco, or *The Best of Bobby Bland:* Malaco).

MIKE BLOOMFIELD

See White Blues

LITTLE JOE BLUE

(Joseph Valery, Jr. / 1934–1990 / vocals, guitar)
The bluesman's place among his fans is sometimes so important and his message is so strong that he creates not only emulators, but also imitators. Thus Leroy Carr,★ Blind Boy Fuller,★ and Elmore James,★ among others, had exact replicas, while others, such as Muddy Waters, Jr., or Howlin' Wolf, Jr. (Little Wolf), are still performing in Chicago.

But in the whole history of the blues, B. B. King will probably remain the most copied bluesman: His presence, his originality, his style, and especially his tremendous and constant success earned him an impressive number of imitators. For the most part mediocre, they strained their voices to excess to reach the register of their model, which was itself already at the limit; they mimicked his style, his way of dressing, and his stage mannerism to the point of ridicule!

Little Joe Blue was different from the others. Without apparent effort, without affectation or mannerisms, his admiration for his idol was so big and so old that he succeeded in being more than just a second B. B. King; he was instead a first Little Joe Blue. Furthermore, he tried constantly to be original within his limits. He used a little of his mentor's repertoire, and he created and composed a few pieces with skilled texts. These pieces were directed to the black rural southern audience, where Little Joe Blue came from and where he obviously stayed, if not physically, then at least musically. Born Joseph Valery in Vicksburg, on the border of

Mississippi and Louisiana, he became, at a young age, "Little Joe Blue" by constantly playing the famous traditional "Little Boy Blue" on his harmonica. After meeting B. B. King in 1949, he fell beneath his spell, and King urged him to become a blues singer. He moved to Detroit in 1950, then to Reno, where he formed his first band without much success. A prolific and very personal composer, he managed to record for several companies from 1961 on, among them Kent and especially Jewel, a label in Shreveport with which he was mainly successful among the blacks of the Deep South. In "Southern Country Boy" Joe Blue proudly claimed his southern peasants' roots. This became a standard in the regional bluesmen's repertoire for a while. The vocal style and arrangements are taken from B. B. King; they are modeled on the first stage of his career, before any excessive sophistication (in *Blue's Blues:* Charly).

In the late sixties Little Joe Blue, who had only strummed away on his guitar, decided to seriously learn that instrument; he turned to Lafayette Thomas,* one of the best and most original California talents. Thanks to this outstanding teacher Little Joe Blue progressed rapidly; and without being a great guitarist, he was able to play some beautiful musical phrases similar to Thomas's and the Texas trend, and significantly far from B. B. King. It seemed that Little Joe Blue progressed constantly. He cut several albums and singles for a local audience —the sensitive "Give Me an Hour in the Garden" deserves to be remembered. He remained active on the West Coast and in southern states; he also went on two tours in Europe. His recent album on the Evejim label shows that he was strong to the end.

Little Joe Blue is not a great name in blues history; but his sincerity, his constant concern for improvement, his fidelity to his roots, and his talents as a composer deserve mention as the best of the many musical sons of B. B. King.

BLUES

In general, the blues is defined according to several technical features. In part, it is poetic singing for twelve measures in the scheme AAB as follows: *A telephone is all right to have hangin' on your wall; a telephone is all right to have hangin' on your wall; but a telephone is no good when you have no one to call.* The basic harmonic structure follows the chord progression: tonic, subdominant, dominant, tonic. For example, in the key of C the progression would be C for four measures, F two measures, C two measures, G one measure, F one measure, then back to C for two. These measures are very irregular, allowing space for a response from the instrument. Furthermore, the scales often have flatted or natural third and seventh scale degrees which produce the "blues" air and which are known as the "blue notes."

The interaction between the singing and the instrumental part is another characteristic of the blues. The instrument prolongs or imitates human voice. The bluesman is not really accompanied by his instrument, he sings with it. Therefore, the metrical precision, the accuracy of the notes used, and the melody of the whole are less important than the inflections coming from the instrument, the sounds obtained, and the emotional intensity of the musician as he is playing (feeling). To learn the blues, then, is less a matter of practice than a way of life.

Although there are possible important variations (there are many blues with eight or sixteen measures), the blues is nevertheless a music relatively rigid and limited, which often gives the impression to an uninformed listener that "all blues sound the same." Of course, they do not, but one blues is often different from another according to the feeling of the artist.

A "technical" definition of the blues does not take into account the role of the bluesman in the lives of blacks living in segregated America. The black community asked the bluesman to compose, to improvise, to be a poet, to be a collector, to arrange traditional themes, to be a singer, to be an instrumental virtuoso, to entertain, to be a sociologist . . . Furthermore, the bluesman also had a therapeutic role for himself and his audience, for whom this music had a cathartic effect.

Much better than a long musicological exegesis, the title of a famous blues tune summarizes everything that the blues represents:

"The blues ain't nothing but a good man feeling bad."
See also White Blues

BLUES REVIVAL

Around 1960 a considerable interest for all folk sources of American music evolved among students in the Northeast, and it soon spread to the whole country. This revival consisted of turning away from the music of the crooners of "Tin Pan Alley" in New York or Las Vegas as well as the electric sounds of rock-and-roll. At first limited to the traditional repertoire of American folk songs gathered around the review *Sing Out* and expressing itself at the Newport Folk Festival, this movement soon became interested in other sources such as bluegrass, ragtime, and the blues, specifically acoustic country blues, which was not commercially promoted after WWII.

The acoustic blues revival allowed numerous artists rediscovered on that occasion to begin a new career, in particular some blues giants of the Delta: Son House,★ Skip James,★ Mississippi John Hurt,★ Bukka White,★ and the fantastic New York guitar player Reverend Gary Davis.★ Other bluesmen whose careers were at a standstill for several years vis-à-vis the black public jumped onto the blues-revival train and adapted their style to the musical demands of their new public: Lightnin' Hopkins,★ John Lee Hooker,★ and Big Joe Williams★ gave up the electric guitar; Memphis Slim,★ Sonny Terry,★ Willie Dixon,★ and Brownie McGhee★ gave up their bands, which had become useless, to perform in solo or duo. They claimed that this style of performance was the only one that ever suited them. Finally, several new rural bluesmen who had never recorded were made known to this new public; the most important discoveries of the blues revival were Mance Lipscomb,★ Fred McDowell,★ and Robert Pete Williams.★ The Prestige/Bluesville label specialized in that blues form, and between 1960 and 1964 it released around a hundred albums. Its producers—Chris Strachwitz, Mack McCormick, and Kenneth Goldstein—went through the southern states with a fine-tooth comb.

Record companies sprang up which then catered to this

new public, for the most part young and white. Arhoolie, created in California by Bob Koester, and Testament created in Los Angeles by Pete Welding were among the blues-revival record companies.

Very soon these new blues devotees realized that there was an obvious relationship between the Delta blues of Son House and the electric blues of Muddy Waters* in Chicago. Trying to give an acoustic definition of the blues was a mere aberration. In 1965 the excellent series of albums produced by. Sam Charters *Chicago / The Blues Today, Vols. 1, 2 & 3* (Vanguard) firmly introduced the electric Chicago blues to this blues-revival public. An important factor was that the series was extensively commented on by the review *Sing Out,* which from then on ran a regular column for every kind of blues, written by the well-informed harmonica player Tony Glover.

From that point, the popularity of the blues mushroomed, (the English began that trend with their remarkable review *Blues Unlimited*) and a more and more real and total appreciation of the blues developed: The number of fans increased constantly and constitute today an international movement. It is true that this movement is relatively limited in number; nevertheless, it is impressive in its universality (Western Europe, Japan, United States, Australia, Scandinavia, and also Asia and Eastern Europe).

What can one say about this blues revival? Any judgment has to be subjective. Some, who discovered the blues through the blues revival, later criticized it, asserting that an artist cut off from the public of his early years was no longer able to give the best of himself. Numerous albums (especially those at the beginning of the blues revival) rang false, and by presenting a bluesman out of his usual context these albums sounded as "fabricated" as some of the commercial productions against which they supposedly reacted. However, to compare the music which came out of the blues-revival phenomenon with the commercial productions is intellectual snobbery. A white person—whether European or American—in touch with a musical culture not his own (that of black Americans stemming from slavery) finds in it something other than what the people, from whom the music comes, were looking for. A perfect example of that is the relative lack of interest shown until recently by the entire white public toward the great black stars of the thirties: Peetie Wheatstraw,* Walter Davis,* and Jazz Gillum,* whose lyrics full of sexual allusions delighted blacks of the time for whom the blues was above all a poem, preferably satirical, and secondarily an instrumental exercise.

Finally, with few exceptions, most blues recordings of the seventies and eighties were directed to a primarily white public, which had for a long time become the major consumer of that music and its commercial look-alikes.

The blues-revival phenomenon should be considered with its best and worst moments as a homogeneous whole that constitutes the latest phase in blues history: that of its international recognition, and in a way, the end of its limited anchorage in the black American community.

BLUES SHOUTERS

Around 1935 the great swing bands gave the black bourgeoisie a civilized, urban, and lively music that was all the rage. To sing blues and ballads most of the bands had a singer whose essential quality—in order to be heard by the public over the brass—was power. These singers had nothing in common with rural blues singers: They dressed neatly and seldom played an instrument, and they favored the ballad or the folk melody to the blues that they interpreted as a vocal part of an orchestral piece.

Although the archetype of these blues shouters is Big Joe Turner* and their favorite city is Kansas City, one cannot say that it is a school, but rather a style that lasted about fifteen years and that developed among all the swing bands and then rhythm-and-blues bands, whether they came from New York, Kansas City, Los Angeles, or New Orleans. From 1950 on, it was too expensive to maintain these big bands, and they could not fight against the competition of both the small combos and the jukeboxes. Only a few renowned bands survived, such as Count Basie's or Lionel Hampton's, directed more and more exclusively to jazz fans. In general the blues shouters disappeared because the big bands to which they belonged disappeared as well. Some, like Jimmy Witherspoon,★ Jimmy Rushing,★ or Louis Jordan,★ had very fruitful personal careers. Others tried to follow their example, with less success.

The Texan WALTER BROWN (1917–1956) is especially known as the co-author with his conductor, piano player Jay McShann,★ of the famous "Confessin' the Blues" that became a blues classic, interpreted by many artists. He recorded several tracks with McShann that were collected on the album *Confessin' the Blues* (Affinity). He then tried in vain to pursue a solo career before disappearing from the musical scene.

Also born in Texas, the saxophone player EDDIE VINSON (1917–1988) first belonged to Cootie Williams' band before being fairly successful around 1950 with a cocky style close to that of Louis Jordan and with humorous compositions such as "They Call Me Mr. Cleanhead." After a long absence from the stage, Eddie Vinson made a comeback in 1967 on the Johnny Otis★ show and figured in many blues and jazz festivals. Some of his best recordings of the fifties appeared on *Back in Town* (Charly). Among the numerous recordings he made after his comeback were the important *Kidney Stew* (Black & Blue/Delmark), *I Want a Little Girl* (Pablo) in which the guitar player Cal Green★ is fantastic, and *The Clean Machine* (Muse).

SONNY PARKER (1925–1957), perhaps the most powerful of these blues shouters, was the regular singer in Lionel Hampton's band for a long time, and he appears on numerous Hampton albums. He too tried a solo career, but he died soon afterward.

SCREAMIN' JAY HAWKINS (b. 1929) is a blues shouter like Big Joe Turner, who succeeded in rock-and-roll for a while, with oddities like "Feast of the Mau-Mau" and the famous "Constipation Blues." His eccentricities on stage made him famous, but too often they hide his talents as a powerful and hearty singer and as a truly gifted pianist. His best cuts, recorded with guitar player Tiny Grimes, are on the excellent album *Screamin' the Blues* (Red Lightnin').

WYNONIE HARRIS (1915–1969) started in Lucky Millinder's band, and he created the juicy "Who Threw the Whisky in the Well?" After the war, his extreme cool, his strong stage presence, and his preference for thrilling rhythms allowed him to have a fruitful career whose best moments are on the albums *Rock Mr. Blues* (Charly), *Good Rockin' Blues* (Gusto), *Mr. Blues Is Coming to Town* (Route 66), and *Playful Baby* (Route 66).

MYRON "TINY" BRADSHAW (1905–1959) is less known, but he was nevertheless a powerful singer and a delightful composer. He started as a drummer for several jazz bands and then recorded a series of very good titles for Decca (e.g., "Bradshaw Boogie" and "The Blues Came Rolling Down"), which placed him among the best blues shouters (listen to the album *Breakin' up the House:* Charly).

NAPPY BROWN (b. 1929) made a few witty and humorous recordings for Savoy. He reached the charts with "Don't Be Angry," "The Night Time" (which Ray Charles★ also covered), and "I Cried Like a Baby" (on the albums *That Man: Mr. R&B* and *Don't Be Angry:* Savoy). After a long hiatus, Nappy reappeared to record several albums, among which the best is *Something Gonna Jump out of the Bushes* (Black Top) accompanied by some brilliant musicians, such as Anson Funderburgh, Earl King,★ Ronnie Earl, and Ron Levy.

With a style between rock-and-roll and the blues, H-BOMB FERGUSON (b. 1929) is a good piano player and singer with a surprising range. He too was successful for a few years around New York before disappearing from the musical scene. The revival of interest toward rhythm and blues has allowed him to make a comeback, which we hope will be successful.

An excellent anthology, *The Shouters* (Savoy), presents some of these artists along with lesser-known names, such as Carl Davis and Gatemouth Moore.

WELDON "JUKE BOY" BONNER

(1932–1978 / vocals, guitar, harmonica)

This imitator of Jimmy Reed★ had an essential quality: He was a blues poet of exceptional originality who dealt equally with the condition of blacks, the riots in Houston, and with his own health.

A street singer in Houston, Austin, and San Francisco from

early on, "Juke Boy" Bonner recorded two titles in 1958 that imitated Jimmy Reed, helped by the guitar player Lafayette Thomas* (on *Oakland Blues:* Arhoolie). The records, produced in Louisiana by Eddie Schuler in 1960, attracted particular attention from blues fans, especially from the publisher of the English review *Blues Unlimited,* Mike Leadbitter. Beyond the music, which does not really differentiate itself from other bluesmen of the area, there is a real creator, poet, and humorist, rich in intelligence and sensitivity.

Leadbitter led a passionate campaign for Juke Boy, who was then seriously sick, and raised enough money to finance the production of a 45. In 1968 Bonner, cured of this illness, triumphed in England and again in Europe the following year at the American Folk Blues Festival.

An important personality in blues between 1968 and 1974, Juke Boy unfortunately was incapable of taking advantage of the opportunities offered to him at the Montreux, Ann Arbor, and Nancy festivals. He died sick, alcoholic, and disillusioned. His musical legacy remains interesting: *Going Back to the Country* (Arhoolie), *The Struggle* (Arhoolie), *Juke Boy Bonner* (Sonet), as well as a strange album (*Authenticity:* Home Cooking) made by the excellent Texas producer Roy Ames.

BOOGIE-WOOGIE

One of the most important innovations in contemporary music, the boogie-woogie, created by black piano players of the United States, is characterized by the continuous pounding of the left hand as it plays eight bass notes a measure, creating a sustained impression of marching in step (walking bass). The right hand, meanwhile, improvises endless variations according to the rhythm or against it. When this music is played well, an intense swing emanates from it, a swing which strongly influenced jazz, modern blues, and rock-and-roll.

Boogie-woogie was probably born at the beginning of the century in the barrelhouses in the southern United States. The piano player had first to cover the noise from the customers' conversations and then to entertain them. Besides the actual blues reserved for after-hours, the customers requested dance music. The boogie-woogie—some critics think its origin was the imitation of a train noise—was the answer to the dancers' requests. Contrary to ragtime, a lighter music that dominated the Southeast from the beginning of the century on, boogie-woogie, powerful and aggressive, developed in the Deep South (Mississippi, Alabama, and Louisiana). It then reached—according to the usual itinerary of the blues—St. Louis, Kansas City, and Chicago.

Most blues and jazz piano players cut numerous boogie-woogie recordings in their careers, but some specialized in them:

CLARENCE "PINETOP" SMITH (1904–1929), born in Alabama, moved to Chicago in 1920. Pinetop Smith is the supposed inventor of the boogie-woogie. Although some pianists before Smith (e.g., Wesley Wallace, Charles Avery, and Hersel Thomas) played similar pieces, the term "boogie-woogie" appeared for the first time with "Pinetop's Boogie-Woogie," an insistent and powerful piece, cut in 1928, that became one of the great blues and jazz classics. Besides "Pinetop's Blues," another remarkable boogie, the other pieces recorded by Smith ("I'm Sober Now") show a real impregnation by vaudeville music. Moreover, Smith had gone on several vaudeville tours, accompanying in particular the famous black duo Butterbeans and Susie in 1918. A short time after the recording of his famous "Pinetop's Boogie-Woogie," Clarence Smith was killed by a stray bullet during a fight.

CHARLIE "COW-COW" DAVENPORT (1894–1955) was also at the source of the boogie-woogie. He was a very original pianist and singer as shown by the particular structure of his "Cow Cow Blues" (1928), which was played by other piano players almost as much as "Pinetop's Boogie-Woogie." Like Smith, he went on vaudeville tours; for many years he performed with singer Dora Carr. After his brilliant recordings of the twenties he recorded prolifically in an urban jazz/blues style before he fell into oblivion.

JIMMY YANCEY (1898–1951) was born in Chicago where he lived until his death. He was among the most remarkable singers and piano players in blues and jazz history. Although he created marvelous boogie-woogies, his talent extended beyond that genre. His work was filled with a pervasive Spanish influence. His particularly expressive style gained him the admiration of other musicians whom he influenced and who named him "the father of boogie-woogie." Shy and reserved, he did not record as much as his talent deserved.

CRIPPLE CLARENCE LOFTON (1896–?) was one of those old hands of the barrelhouses. He created boogies with rolling bass lines in a powerful style comparable to Davenport's. Some of his creations ("Strut That Thing" and "Streamline Train") gained him a certain success; but as a whole he recorded very little, and he seems to have died in poverty sometime in the fifties.

PETE JOHNSON (1904–1967), a piano player from Kansas City, is the greatest contributor of boogie-woogie to the rich piano tradition of that city (e.g., Jay McShann* and Count Basie). As he played each passage, the theme seemed nearly to vanish, then it would suddenly spring to life again. Pete Johnson was a brilliant and surprising musician with a constant creative verve, and at his best he cut many boogie-woogie masterpieces: "Dive Bomber," "Death Ray Boogie," "Basemen Boogie," and more. A regular piano player at Piney Brown's Café, there he met the singer Joe Turner,* whom he stayed with for many years. In 1937 he was invited to the famous "Spirituals to Swing" concert presented in Carnegie Hall by John Hammond. He recorded many times until 1954, when he became paralyzed by a stroke.

MEADE "LUX" LEWIS (1905–1964) lived with Albert Ammons in the same building as Pinetop Smith, who taught him the boogie-woogie. Lewis was also influenced by Jimmy Yancey. In his early years Lewis was a brilliantly inventive piano player as revealed in his famous creations "Honky Tonk Train Blues," "Celeste Blues," and his delicate interpretation of "Yancey Special." He recorded in solo, in duo with his friend Ammons, in trio (with Ammons and Pete Johnson), and with numerous jazz bands. Then his music toned down; at the end of his career, he was famous in high-society bars playing cocktail music.

ALBERT AMMONS (1907–1954), a co-tenant with and friend of Lewis, was a direct heir to Pinetop Smith. All the illuminations of Lewis and the subtleties of Yancey were foreign to him: He was without doubt the most powerful and direct pianist among the great interpreters of boogie-woogie. Although he shared his time between his musical career and his job as a cab driver, he recorded numerous times, either alone or in trio or with his own band, until his death.

ARTHUR "MONTANA" TAYLOR (1903–1954) lived in Indianapolis. Although he recorded very little, the few available titles show a powerful and original piano player, much less influenced by Smith and Yancey than others. "Detroit Rocks" and "Indiana Avenue Stomp" are his masterpieces. Taylor was rediscovered in 1946, and he recorded a few astonishing titles for the small Solo Art label before he disappeared for good.

A few other names are worth mentioning: Romeo Nelson, author of the brilliant piece "Head Rag Hop"; Speckled Red (Rufus Perryman / 1892–1973), a limited piano player but maybe the composer of the famous shocking blues "The Dirty Dozen," later covered by several artists; speckled Red's brother, Piano Red (Willie Perryman), who had a fruitful career, encompassing all genres through many recordings; and Cleo Brown, the first to cover "Pinetop's Boogie-Woogie" with an interpretation full of subtlety. Of course, piano players like Memphis Slim,★ Big Maceo,★ Jay McShann, Otis Spann,★ Little Brother Montgomery,★ and Champion Jack Dupree★ also composed or interpreted many boogie-woogies, but their careers were not dominated by that musical form.

Most of the great titles in the history of boogie-woogie are available on numerous albums. The Oldie Blues label specialized more particularly in that type of music.

We recommend Albert Ammons: *King of Boogie Woogie* (Blues Classics) and *Boogie Woogie & the Blues* (Commodore); Clarence "Pinetop" Smith: *Piano in Style* (MCA); *Cow Cow Davenport* (Oldie Blues); Cripple Clarence Lofton: *Clarence Blues* (Oldie Blues); Pete Johnson: *Boogie Woogie Mood* (MCA) and *Pete's Blues* (Savoy); Meade Lux Lewis: *Tell Your Story* (Oldie Blues); Montana Taylor: *Montana Blues* (Oldie Blues); *The Boogie Woogie Masters* (Affinity); and *Boogie Woogie* (Murray Hill).

BOOGIE WOOGIE RED

See Detroit

BOTTLENECK OR SLIDE GUITAR

Originally produced by a sawed-off bottleneck that the guitar player slipped on one finger of the left hand (often the little finger) and slid along the top of the strings, the sound of a bottleneck or slide guitar is one of rare beauty. Any round metal object can be substituted for the bottleneck; currently music dealers sell the slide, a metal or glass tube used by many blues, rock, and folk guitarists, as a sophisticated replacement for the bottleneck.

Bottleneck guitar was likely an adaptation of the Hawaiian guitar—popular at the beginning of the century—by rural bluesmen, although some sources prove the existence of that technique much before that period. Other manifestations of this sound occur in the lap steel guitar, the dobro or National Steel guitar, and the pedal steel guitar of country music.

A great many blues guitar players occasionally use this technique but others specialize in it. Son House,★ Fred McDowell,★ Tampa Red,★ Robert Nighthawk,★ and Muddy Waters★ played bottleneck note by note. On the other hand, Elmore James★ and his disciples alternated that method with sliding effects on the whole chord, with the guitar in an open tuning (e.g., Hound Dog Taylor,★ J. B. Hutto,★ and Homesick James★). This technique, by creating a climate of strong confusion between the notes and the chords of the minor and major scales, multiplies the blue notes, and it is particularly characteristic of the blues.

EDDIE BOYD

(b. 1914 / vocals, piano)

Eddie Boyd, an urbane and sophisticated singer, has little to do with the Chicago tradition, although he was one of its main bluesmen after the war. Sometimes a brilliant pianist, in the line of Big Maceo,★ Boyd is a former student of Big Maceo's;

he is an especially good blues composer. The famous "Five Long Years" has become a classic, recorded many times by dozens of musicians.

Like many others Eddie Boyd came from Mississippi to Chicago via Memphis in 1941. He was hired by RCA in 1947 to substitute on the piano for his mentor Big Maceo, who was paralyzed on one side. Maceo, still extremely popular, remained unable to recapture his past vigor, and RCA decided to replace him with Boyd. That was a mistake: Maceo's style was as powerful and direct as Eddie Boyd's music was flowing and chromatic. After about ten unsuccessful records for RCA, Eddie Boyd struggled along for a few years in Chicago clubs hoping for new opportunities. Producer Len Chess* rejected Boyd when he came to audition for him, and finally it was the small JOB label that recorded in 1952 "Five Long Years," one of the rare pure blues to reach and maintain the top of the charts. But, as expected, Boyd soon found his way to the Chess studios. He recorded prolifically for this label in the following years, with several new successes such as "24 Hours," "Third Degree," and "I'm a Prisoner." All his recordings radiate a sophisticated and jazzy atmosphere in the mood of the West Coast more than in the mood of the Chicago blues.

After 1958 Eddie Boyd's popularity faded. Chess did not renew his contract and Boyd recorded for several small labels (Bea & Baby) before he finally emigrated to Scandinavia. The best album of his "European" period is the excellent *Five Long Years* (L+R) recorded with guitar player Buddy Guy.* Nevertheless, his work for Chess needs to be released in a quality reedition someday.

TINY BRADSHAW

See Blues Shouters

BILLY BRANCH

See Chicago

LONNIE BROOKS

(Lee Baker, Jr. / b. 1933 / vocals, guitar)

This native of Louisiana began his career around 1958 with a series of rock-and-roll songs influenced by his fellow Louisianans Fats Domino* and Guitar Slim, produced by the Goldband label under the stage name Guitar Junior. One of his titles, "Family Rules," was rather successful in the Southwest (on *The Crawl:* Charly).

Brooks then moved to Chicago where he recorded unsuccessfully for different small labels, as well as for Chess and Mercury. He also accompanied Jimmy Reed* and harmonica player Little Mack Simmons.

Little by little his style, at first very much inspired by Guitar Slim, became harsher and took on the tones of the Chicago blues. Traces of Albert King's* and Otis Rush's* guitar styles can be found in his best pieces on the Alligator label's anthology *Living Chicago Blues, Vol. 1.*

The albums *Bayou Lightning, Turn on the Night,* and *Hot Shot* (Alligator), produced by Bruce Iglauer, prolong these qualities, with some fragments of gospel but with more rock. It is to this last area that he seems to be turning more and more, with, in particular, the addition of a rhythm section strongly influenced by hard rock.

BIG BILL BROONZY

(William Lee Conley Broonzy / 1897–1958 / vocals, guitar)

Thirty years after his death, Big Bill Broonzy's reputation remains intact, due to the quality and longevity of his career as much as to his reputation as the "last blues singer alive," which he was able to create for himself and to exploit to the fullest.

Indeed, he came from the South to Chicago at an early age, and he recorded his first 78 as early as 1926. In 1928, his "Big Bill Blues" was extremely successful, and it provided him a reputation that was to last until his death. Gifted with a powerful voice, he used the vocal style of gospel singers to express his blues with words often full of humor and double meanings.

■ Big Bill Broonzy *(center)*. *(Photograph © by Margo Bruynoghe. Courtesy of Margo Bruynoghe and Archives and Special Collections, John Davis Williams Library, University of Mississippi)*

However, more than his talents as a singer, it is his guitar style that most holds the attention of today's fans: In fact, Big Bill was one of the great innovators with his instrument. He was as comfortable fingerpicking as he was in flat-picking, which was later to become widespread with the electric guitar. Big Bill always showed his richness, his inventiveness, the fluidity of his fingering technique, and his particularly inventive style with the difficult C scale. His style dominated the blues until the Second World War. His only known rival then was another great innovator, Lonnie Johnson.★

From 1928 on Big Bill made more than three hundred recordings as the featured artist, and he recorded as many as an accompanist for artists like Lil Green,★ Washboard Sam,★ Jazz Gillum,★ and John Lee "Sonny Boy" Williamson.★ He made records for all the big companies of the time: Okeh, Vocation, Bluebird, ARC, Columbia, Mercury, and Chess. His immense talent, coupled with an exceptionally open personality, made him popular among the blacks in Chicago; and he was the lord of the city's clubs. He used this influence to help many young artists record; Washboard Sam, Gillum, Williamson, Memphis Slim,* and even Muddy Waters* owed him a lot.

After the war, his style, which had become more refined, was abandoned for a harder, more electrified blues. He recorded a few more times (especially for Chess) but without success. He was one of the first bluesmen to go to Europe in 1951, thanks to Hugues Panassié. He was welcomed there with curiosity and enthusiasm by jazz fans for whom the blues was only a nearly extinct ancestor of jazz. With a flair for business, Big Bill understood what he could gain from that: He gave up his electric guitar and his rhythm section, he dug out old southern folk tunes, which he had never interpreted in Chicago, and he introduced himself as a "black southern farmer" and the "last blues singer alive." From 1951 to 1958 he traveled over Western Europe and recorded prolifically in this folk vein. Despite the total absence of authenticity in his performances, he played a major role in introducing the blues to Europe. When he died in 1958, he was sadly forgotten in Chicago, but acclaimed by the European press, although the blues had never been so alive and popular in the black ghettos of the U.S.

The best collection of recordings by Big Bill is available on the album *Big Bill's Blues* (Portrait). Also of interest are *Big Bill Broonzy, 1932–42* (Biograph), *The Young Big Bill* (Yazoo), and *Do That Guitar Rag* (Yazoo). The "European" cuts featuring the acoustic guitar are available on several compilations on the Vogue label.

ANDREW BROWN

(1937–1985 / vocals, guitar, organ, tenor saxophone)

An original emulator of Albert King,* spending his life in Chicago clubs, Andrew Brown was an excellent guitar player and a multi-talented artist able to express himself with ease in all genres of black music (from blues to gospel to jazz). What may have held the most attention was his powerful and warm voice, particularly effective in slow blues where it seemed to float above a gentle sea of brass. He called to mind the great Albert King, as well as B. B. King★ and Little Milton.★

Born in Jackson, Mississippi, Andrew Brown was submerged in music at an early age. All his close relatives played one or several instruments. He moved to Chicago in the mid-fifties where he was close to Earl Hooker,★ Magic Sam★—he always kept something from the West Side sound—and Freddie King.★ Albert King's success, particularly with "Don't Throw Your Love on Me So Strong," persuaded Brown to take up a career as a professional musician. At that time Brown's strong build also allowed him to do physical work. Often playing in cocktail lounges, he was known as a jazz guitarist. On a few records he accompanied Baby Face Willette and Dave Cortez. Nevertheless, the handful of 45s he succeeded in recording for different small Chicago labels were all modern blues, with many arrangements borrowed from soul. Despite the high quality of these titles ("You Better Stop" and "You Ought to Be Ashamed"), these records did not sell well, and they brought Andrew Brown neither money nor fame. Disenchanted, he contemplated giving up music, when back problems forced him to stop his manual labor and to rely on his bluesman's talents to live.

Being more active in Chicago clubs, he was noticed by producer Bruce Iglauer, who recorded him for the anthology *Living Chicago Blues, Vol. 5* (Alligator). He appeared in great shape with his own compositions, full of feeling and force. He recorded an excellent album, *Big Brown's Chicago Blues* (Black Magic), that included the remarkable piece "Mary Jane." A few years later and despite health problems, he was aided by producer Dick Shurman in recording an extraordinary album of modern blues—one of the great successes of the eighties, *On the Case* (Double Trouble). This success will remain our major legacy from Brown; he died soon after.

BUSTER BROWN

See New York

■ Clarence "Gatemouth" Brown. *(Photograph © by Renato Tonelli. Courtesy of Renato Tonelli and Archives and Special Collections, John Davis Williams Library, University of Mississippi)*

CHARLES BROWN

(b. 1924 / vocals, piano)

Born in Texas, he moved to California where he taught classical piano. He tried to make a name for himself by imitating the langorous style of jazz and pop star Nat King Cole. But "Driftin' Blues," recorded in 1945 with the band of guitar player Johnny Moore,★ made him famous. His vocal style, almost bombastic, and the subtle mingling of guitar and piano evoked the darkness in which inconsolable sorrow would dissolve. The response of young black girls to that explicit offer was extraordinary between 1945 and 1953. Charles Brown became one of the great names of rhythm and blues: Besides "Driftin' Blues," "Black Nights," "My Heart Is Mended," "Merry Christmas," and later, "Gloria" were extremely successful.

Numerous piano players—for example, Amos Milburn,★ Floyd Dixon,★ Little Willie Littlefield,★ and Ray Charles★—

were influenced by Charles Brown. After recording prolifically for Aladdin, Exclusive, Imperial, King, and Atlantic, Brown experienced a tough time away from the stage. He tried, with moderate success, to regain the devotion of the black public by turning his already very sweet blues into totally indigestible confection. In 1968 he did find the vigor of his early years with an excellent album, *Legend* (Bluesway), recorded with some great guitarists like Earl Hooker* and Mel Brown. Among his recent recordings the best is certainly the low-key *All My Life* (Bullseye).

He was neglected for a long time by blues fans because they found him too sophisticated. Charles Brown is today rightly recognized as one of the founders of the West Coast blues.

His "classic" cuts are available on three albums: *Driftin' Blues* (Aladdin), *Sunny Road* (Route 66), and *Race Track Blues* (Route 66).

CLARENCE "GATEMOUTH" BROWN

(b. 1924 / vocals, guitar, fiddle, harmonica)

Clarence "Gatemouth" Brown was for a long time forsaken by blues fans who assumed that he was a mere imitator of T-Bone Walker.*

As a matter of fact, this Texan had been very popular in the period 1948 to 1958 with a rhythm-and-blues style which was largely dominated by T-Bone's influence. But his records demonstrate that he is also an extremely quick and expressive guitarist, a composer full of humor, with predominant musical phrases borrowed from jazz. (The great trombone player Al Grey belonged to his band for a long time.) "Ookie Dokie Stomp," "Gate's Salty Blues," "She Winked Her Eye," and "Boogie Uproar" are a few pieces whose swing is irresistible.

Disappointed by show business, Clarence Brown gave up music in the mid-sixties, but in 1971 he accepted an invitation to a European tour. The European public discovered an artist with great presence, a warm and cocky singer, and an extraordinary virtuoso of the guitar and the fiddle, as much at ease in blues or jazz as in country music.

After participating in numerous festivals in America and

in Europe (the Montreux Festival, in particular), and after having asserted himself as a major blues and jazz musician, Gatemouth Brown seemed to turn successfully to country music. He cut many albums in that style, among them *Makin' Music* (MCA), recorded with the great guitar player Roy Clark. This album should not be disregarded.

A few years ago, he recorded under contract with the Rounder label for which he cut excellent albums: *Alright Again* (Rounder), *One More Mile* (Rounder), and *Real Life* (Rounder). Also impressive is *Pressure Cooker* (Alligator), which is much more jazzy, as well as the very good *Standing My Ground* (Alligator). Some of his best tracks of the fifties are on *The Original Peacock Recordings* (Rounder).

NAPPY BROWN

See *Blues Shouters*

ROY BROWN

(1925–1981 / vocals)

Roy Brown, a powerful singer, was extremely successful between 1948 and 1955; he remained almost constantly on the national charts.

Born and raised in New Orleans, a gospel singer since he was twelve, Brown began his musical career by imitating his idols: Bing Crosby and Frank Sinatra. But, being black, he could only hope to capitalize on his talents by singing the blues. He did it in the style of the Kansas City blues shouters, such as Big Joe Turner.* The church, the crooners, the blues shouters—all these influences are to be found in that expressive, melodious, and sophisticated singing that made him successful. In 1947 his success at the Drew Drop Inn in New Orleans enabled him to record for DeLuxe, a small local label, "Good Rockin' Tonight," which was soon covered by Wynonie Harris* and Jimmy Witherspoon.* It was a tremendous national success and enabled Brown to tour across the Southwest and California with his band, the "Mighty Men." The following years, Roy Brown triumphed with "Hard Luck

Blues," "Boogie at Midnight," "Love Don't Love Nobody," and "Butcher Pete." Along with his exceptional vocal qualities, Brown was an outstanding composer. The tone of his blues or of his ballads fluctuated between a caustic irony, a really macabre humor, and a sensitive lyricism full of imagery. His success decreased after 1954; despite efforts to change, Roy Brown failed to get on the fruitful train of rock-and-roll, to which his friends Joe Turner and Fats Domino* were able to cling. After 1960, Brown lived almost entirely away from the music business despite an appearance in Monterey in 1970.

A serious revival of interest toward Brown was apparent shortly after his death. Roy Brown appears today as one of the founders of the urban blues of New Orleans.

Some of his best titles can be found in the collections *Boogie at Midnight* (Charly), *Hard Luck Blues* (King), and *Saturday Night* (Mr. R&B).

RUTH BROWN

See New York

WALTER BROWN

See Blues Shouters

ROY BUCHANAN

See White Blues

BUCKWHEAT

See Zydeco

BUMBLE BEE SLIM

(Amos Easton / 1905–1968 / vocals, guitar)

Bumble Bee Slim was extremely popular for a short time between 1934 and 1937, during which time he recorded more than 150 songs.

As a singer he was somewhat monotonous, but as a composer he was an inspired and humorous storyteller.

Born in Georgia, he moved to Indianapolis in 1928. Influenced by the famous local duo of Leroy Carr* and Scrapper Blackwell,* Slim created his own style. After Carr died, Bumble Bee appeared as a natural successor to the bluesman. Soon he went to Chicago where he recorded for Decca and Bluebird. He was not only a guitarist, but also a comedian and an actor; nevertheless, he focused on his singing, relying on the great quality of his accompanists, such as Big Bill Broonzy,* Memphis Minnie,* and the brilliant Casey Bill Weldon.* The piano accompaniment, usually major, was entrusted to his friend Myrtle Jenkins.

Similar to countless blues stars of the thirties, Bumble Bee Slim sank into oblivion after the war, despite a few recordings in California for Specialty and a really weak album in 1962, with jazzmen Les McCann and Joe Pass on the Pacific Jazz label.

EDDIE BURNS

(b. 1928 / vocals, guitar)

Eddie Burns is one of the rare bluesmen of Detroit to have succeeded in making a name for himself. Deeply influenced by Tommy McClennan* and John Lee "Sonny Boy" Williamson,* he became known first as a harmonica player in Detroit nightclubs. John Lee Hooker* noticed him and took him under his wing in 1948. By day a mechanic, at night a musician, Burns managed to record a certain number of songs for several labels (on *Treat Me Like I Treat You:* Moonshine). After learning to play the guitar in the late fifties he accompanied John Lee Hooker on the album *The Real Folk Blues* (Chess). In the same session he recorded several unreleased titles as the featured player.

In spite of a financially lackluster career, Eddie Burns never gave up. He was able to tour in Europe and be in several U.S. festivals. He is still active in Detroit, as shown by his excellent participation on the anthology *Detroit Blues Factory* (Blues

Factory) and *Eddie Burns: Detroit* (Blue Suit), one of only two albums in Burns's long career.

R. L. BURNSIDE

(Rural Burnside / b. 1926 / vocals, guitar)

The Mississippi Delta is a constant source of musicians, and the blues remains the favorite music of the small black rural communities scattered along this flat and desolate region. The Delta blues tradition lives on in many juke joints, always electrified and usually influenced by other sounds like the Chicago blues—its direct heir—but also by soul music, disco, and funk.

R. L. (Rural) Burnside is one of the best representatives of the modern Delta blues. Born in Oxford, Mississippi, he was very early on immersed in music. He sang in several bands but learned the guitar in 1953 with his neighbors Ranie Burnette and Fred McDowell* as teachers. Long stays in Chicago and Memphis from 1947 on also influenced his music: He admired Muddy Waters,* John Lee Hooker,* Little Walter,* Howlin' Wolf,* and Lightnin' Hopkins.* In 1959 when he went back to Mississippi to get married and take care of a small holding, Burnside—as much because he liked it as because he needed it—opened a small bar where he played his music and sold his homemade whiskey. His band was formed with several musicians from the area—among them McDowell, harmonica player Johnny Woods, and guitarist-drummer Napoleon Strickland—until his many children were big enough for him to form an all-family band. These youngsters introduced the current styles to Burnside's music, such as he now plays around Coldwater.

In 1967, the ethnomusicologist George Mitchell, looking for bluesmen, discovered Burnside without a guitar or an amplifier—both were at the pawnshop—and lent him his own acoustic guitar to record him. That day he recorded wonderful songs that built Burnside's reputation among Delta blues fans: *Mississippi Delta Blues, Vol. 2* (Arhoolie). Still very much influenced by African music, Burnside expressed himself largely in a rhythmic way and on only one chord. He also beat the wood of his guitar in the fashion of Charlie Patton* and Bukka White.* Due to overwhelming financial burdens, Burnside missed many opportunities to appear in concerts in the U.S. and abroad. Only in 1979 did he really emerge: He was rediscovered by David Evans, and he often played in Memphis, toured in America and Europe, and finally fulfilled his dream of buying a plot of land thanks to his music. However, he never stopped playing for his neighbors and friends; it is only when he does that, that he feels most comfortable and at his best, giving performances of an intensity unheard of in European concerts. In that atmosphere he recorded the excellent *Sound Machine Groove* (Vogue), on which, surrounded by his regular band, Burnside plays superbly and sings with his deep and expressive voice an eclectic, modern/primitive repertoire that authentically represents the present Delta blues. Recorded in the Netherlands, *Sings the Mississippi Delta Blues* (Swingmaster) and *The Blues of R. L. Burnside* (Swingmaster) present Burnside alone on guitar.

The Clarksdale region where Burnside lives abounds in talented bluesmen who are finally starting to be recorded: Jessie Mae Hemphill,* Lonnie Pitchford, Boyd Rivers, and Othar Turner, to name a few.

JAMES "SON FORD" THOMAS (b. 1926), like Burnside, is a kind of local "star." He appeared at several festivals and concerts, and he recently found, thanks to harmonica player Walter Liniger, the necessary support for a national career. A limited guitarist (but very faithful to the Delta tradition) and a passionate singer, he made several quality recordings for Swingmaster, Black and Blue, and Flying High. Perhaps his best album is *Highway 61 Blues* (Southern Culture) issued by the University of Mississippi.

Another neighbor of R. L. Burnside, JOHNNY WOODS (1917–1990) is an extraordinary harmonica player uncommonly devoid of any urban influence. Difficult to accompany, he appears on several recordings of Fred McDowell's (*Kings of Country Blues, Vol. 2:* Arhoolie) and recently cut a solo album, the captivating *Blues of Johnny Woods* (Swingmaster).

PAUL BUTTERFIELD

See White Blues

■

C

CALIFORNIA

Blacks really began to settle on the West Coast only after the start of the Second World War, in a migratory current from the rural Southwest (Texas, Louisiana, and Oklahoma). No noticeable musical tradition existed there before that, except for the obvious Mexican influence in the southern part of the state. The blues created in California is then an extension and an urbanization of the Texas blues. Moreover, a great number of West Coast artists lived in Texas, while they regularly recorded and performed in California.

Right away there were two distinct trends: Around Los Angeles and Hollywood a very sophisticated blues arose, directed toward the chic clubs of the city, often tending toward the ballad and influenced by piano players Nat King Cole and Charles Brown.★ On the other hand, the San Francisco Bay area seemed to have attracted a more rural black population, and it developed a blues style much closer to its roots. The influence of the producers might have also been an important factor: Bob Geddins, a blues promoter in San Francisco, was himself a black from the rural Southwest, and he discovered and recorded the artists he liked.

The differences between both forms of blues must not be exaggerated. In both cases, the California blues are different from others in the mellowness of the electric instruments on which the voice seems to float. In general it is a very urban and delicate blues, often bordering on jazz or the ballad, which reflects a certain gentle way of life in that region.

Several great California blues artists became known in the forties: Charles Brown, T-Bone Walker,★ Lowell Fulson,★ Roy Milton,★ PeeWee Crayton,★ Johnny Fuller,★ Percy Mayfield,★

and Jimmy McCracklin.* Producers like J. R. Fullbright, Maxwell Davis, and Bob Geddins played an important role, creating a multitude of small record companies that enabled these artists to be discovered. Through their advice and choice, they helped to create the California blues, producing a number of recordings.

FLOYD DIXON (b. 1929), an excellent singer and piano player, uses a style inspired directly by Charles Brown and Amos Milburn.* His "Hey Bartender" was covered by Koko Taylor* and the Blues Brothers. Rediscovered in the seventies, his second career was not as promising as his first efforts. They are available on the collections *Opportunity Blues* (Route 66), *Houston* (Route 66), and *Empty Stocking Blues* (Route 66).

JOE LIGGINS (1920–1987), piano player and singer, had big hits in the late forties: "Honeydripper" and "Pink Champagne" recorded in a style that successfully mixed jazz, blues, and pop (on *Joe Liggins and His Honeydrippers:* Specialty).

His brother JIMMY LIGGINS (1924–1984), guitar and harmonica player, was also successful with "Drunk" and "Saturday Night Boogie-Woogie Man." His recording *I Can't Stop It* (Route 66) made his reputation on the West Coast.

Singer JIMMY WILSON (1923–1965) is the author of a famous version of "Tin Pan Alley," originally a blues from Curtis Jones,* a great commercial and artistic success, evocative of disreputable street dives with a muted atmosphere typical of the California blues. Wilson, unable to exploit this masterpiece, died totally forgotten (*Trouble in My House:* Diving Duck).

Piano player LLOYD GLENN (1909–1985) shared his time between blues and jazz. Except for a few sides cut as the featured player, he is especially known as the superb accompanist of Lowell Fulson, B. B. King,* and T-Bone Walker.

ROY HAWKINS is a mysterious figure of California blues. He recorded many blues and ballads, in particular "The Thrill Is Gone," which was covered successfully by B. B. King in 1969. His recorded work is extremely consistent (*Highway 59*: Ace).

JOHNNY and OSCAR MOORE were among the first guitar

players to use the electric guitar. Oscar was a member of the famous Nat King Cole Trio for a long time, and Johnny founded his own band, which included Charles Brown on the piano. Their sound is distinguished by an extreme sophistication that marked all black music of that region: blues, jazz, and pop.

T.V. SLIM (Oscar Wills / 1916–1976) was a TV repairman, a singer, a guitar player, a fiddle player, and a producer; he recorded a series of original blues, from the purest Texas country blues to a furious, New Orleans style, rock-and-roll. "Flatfoot Sam" was his only commercial success.

The guitar player LAFAYETTE THOMAS (1932–1977), nephew of Texan Jesse Thomas,* his teacher, recorded little under his own name. He mainly accompanied multiple artists such as Jimmy McCracklin, Jimmy Wilson, Little Brother Montgomery,* Juke Boy Bonner,* Memphis Slim,* and Sammy Price. His guitar style was totally original: He adapted and developed the characteristic style of his uncle and added flawless technique. It was an important creation—parallel to that of T-Bone Walker—which did not have the desired effect, probably because Thomas was so reserved. However, he influenced the guitar players of the West Coast, especially Johnny Heartsman*—a name equally important and often forgotten—as well as Albert Collins.*

LITTLE WILLIE LITTLEFIELD (b. 1931), a piano player with a powerful swing, is the author of the famous "Kansas City" covered by a great number of blues and rock-and-roll singers. Unfortunately, he was never a success despite his talent. In the eighties he recorded a series of albums that were far from being as good as his first efforts.

JOHNNY "GUITAR" WATSON (b. 1935) is a famous name in soul music and disco, although at first he was an excellent singer and guitar player in the Texas tradition of his uncle and mentor, Frankie Lee Sims.* His biting guitar style is original and efficient. His first sessions are available on *Gonna Hit the Highway* (Ace) and *I Heard That* (Charly).

RAY AGEE (b. 1930) is the creator of an excellent version of "Tin Pan Alley," in which a performance on guitar by Johnny Heartsman adds to the alarming mood of this blues. A good singer, inspired by gospel and soul, Ray Agee is also a remarkable composer whose prolific career did not earn him the credit he deserved. *Black Night Is Gone* (Mr. R&B) and *I'm Not Looking Back* (Mr. R&B) perfectly summarize his work.

The singer AL KING (Alvin K. Smith / b. 1926) also does not have the place he merits. Influenced as much by the blues shouters as by Lowell Fulson, in the fifties and sixties he recorded with Johnny Heartsman a whole series of superb blues with a muted, nostalgic tone, enhanced by the incomparable quality of the lyrics. In fact, pieces like "My Money Ain't Long Enough," "Think Twice before You Speak," and the extraordinary "High Cost of Living" are destined to be classics (*On My Way:* Diving Duck).

The piano player and singer GUS JENKINS (1931–1985) first recorded in Chicago for the Chess label with Big Walter Horton* before he moved to the West Coast. An imitator of Howlin' Wolf,* an emulator of Lowell Fulson and Charles Brown, and a player of dance music in the Ramsey Lewis style, he is nevertheless a convincing interpreter (*Cold Love:* Diving Duck).

The singer JIMMY NELSON (b. 1928) had a hit in 1951 with "T 99," later a classic of California blues. Labeled a one-hit wonder, Nelson deserves better, as shown on the collection *Watch That Action* (Ace).

Others deserving mention are James Reed, Honeyboy Frank Patt, Ernest Lewis, Guitar Slim Green, Saunders King, Al Simmons, King Solomon, Luke "Long" Miles, Sidney Maiden, Ace Holder, and the Carter Brothers.

Numerous anthologies illustrate California blues: *Oakland Blues* (Arhoolie), *Alla Blues* (Muskadine), *Unfinished Boogie* (Muskadine), *Bay Area Blues Blasters* (Ace), *Blues around Midnight* (Ace), *The Jake Porter Story* (Ace), and *West Coast Winners* (Moonshine).

Although California blues never really went into decline, particularly around the Bay area which is studded with clubs, since the late sixties California blues has been renewed by a generation of new artists. They added to the traditional style of that region the influence of Chicago blues (especially with the success of Canned Heat,* Charlie Musselwhite,* and their emulators) and the imported sound of rock music, often inspired by the blues, as played by Jefferson Airplane and Hot Tuna.

The present scene of California blues is led by several excellent musicians: Robert Cray,* Phillip Walker,* Sonny Rhodes,* Joe Louis Walker,* Hi-Tide Harris, Little Joe Blue,* Smokey Wilson, Troyce Key, Ron Thompson, Isaac Scott, Freddie Robinson, Freddie Roulette, Little Charly and Rick Estrin, Mark Hummell, Doug McLeod, Chuck Norris, Dave Alexander,* and J. J. Malone*; singers Little Frankie Lee, Sugar Pie Desanto, and Margie Evans*; harmonica players Rod Piazza, Johnny Dyer, Curtis Salgado, and Gary Smith. Unfortunately, traditional artists like Robert Lowery, Charles Conley, and Sonny Lane did not record more.

Despite the efforts of local critic Tom Mazzolini, organizer of the annual San Francisco Blues Festival, and despite the presence of several record companies like Arhoolie and Hightone, California has yet to be recognized for what it may be: one of the most important sources for blues at the end of the twentieth century.

EDDIE C. CAMPBELL

(b. 1939 / vocals, guitar)

A motorcyclist and karate champion, Eddie C. Campbell sprang from the West Side of Chicago in the seventies to renown as one of the best bluesmen of the new generation.

From Clarksdale to Chicago, his journey is not unique: a kid from Mississippi who grew up in the ghetto of the blues capital, who adored Muddy Waters,* and who played in the streets with Luther Allison* and Magic Sam.* An obscure guitar player playing in local small clubs, he accompanied a great number of "stars": Howlin' Wolf,* Freddie King,* Jimmy Reed,* Little Johnny Taylor,* and Percy Mayfield.* He took from each an idea, a song, a guitar effect, a voice inflection. He recorded under his own name for the small Hawaii label. But it was when he joined Willie Dixon's band in the mid-seventies that he was exposed to the public. At that time, with Dixon's musicians (Carey Bell* and Lafayette

Leake, in particular) he cut the superb *King of the Jungle* (Rooster Blues), an album that has been reissued several times and acclaimed by critics as one of the best recordings of modern Chicago blues. Eddie Campbell's dominant qualities are creativity, originality, humor, and dynamism.

He cut three other excellent albums: *Let's Pick It* (Black Magic), *Mind Trouble* (Double Trouble), and *The Baddest Cat on the Block* (JSP).

Eddie Campbell is a major talent of Chicago blues.

CANNED HEAT

See White Blues

LEROY CARR AND SCRAPPER BLACKWELL

(1905–1935 / vocals, piano) and (1906–1962 / vocals, guitar, piano)

The increasing number of piano-guitar duos in the thirties was a major point in the transformation of blues from a rural and primitive art into an urban and civilized one. The piano player pounded out the rhythm, and the guitar player was then able to improvise along a melodious line: The whole development of modern blues is based on this innovation.

The creators of that trend—or at least the first to have recorded in that pattern—were piano player Leroy Carr and guitar player Scrapper Blackwell.

Leroy Carr moved to Indianapolis, and in the black taverns there he developed a simple but efficient piano style, stressing the beat with a rolling bass which provided rhythmic support to his bittersweet singing.

In one of these taverns in 1928, the producer Guernsey, an English immigrant, noticed him. A few days later, as he was looking for new talents, Guernsey discovered Scrapper Blackwell, who was then making money selling moonshine, playing only occasionally in the taverns of Indianapolis. After having recorded Carr and Blackwell separately, Guernsey got the idea of combining their talents: Blackwell's rich, clear guitar style of alternating chords with note-by-note playing perfectly complemented Leroy Carr's style. They were immediately successful: From 1928 on, the duo was at the top of all record sales at the time and accumulated successes in Nashville, Cincinnati, Chicago, St. Louis, and New York. Between 1928 and 1934, they recorded about a hundred titles, for the most part composed by Blackwell.

Most of the time they were melancholic blues, although sometimes there was a quick, swinging piece. Blackwell revealed himself to be inventive, original, and brilliant; he was one of the best guitar players in blues history. In April 1935 Leroy Carr died from cirrhosis of the liver at age thirty. In a few years he had built a considerable reputation, and his tragic fate added to his legend. His imitators were numerous (Bumble Bee Slim* and Little Bill Gaither,* in particular) and the late Champion Jack Dupree,* who was much inspired by Carr's vocal style, was very popular. Several of the numbers sung by Leroy Carr have become classics: "Prison Bound," "How Long Blues," "In the Evening," "Mean Mistreater," and "I Believe I'll Make a Change" have been covered by dozens of artists.

After his partner died, Scrapper Blackwell more or less withdrew from show business; however, he kept on playing for fun. He was rediscovered shortly before his death (he was murdered in an alley) in 1958, and he recorded a few albums, among which was *Mr. Scrapper's Blues* (Ace). His influence went beyond the narrow frame of Indianapolis to which he had limited himself. His work is available on the collection *The Virtuoso Guitar of Scrapper Blackwell* (Yazoo).

The best recordings by the duo Carr and Blackwell can be heard on the albums *Blues before Sunrise* (Portrait) and *Naptown Blues* (Yazoo).

GUS CANNON

See Memphis

CANNON'S JUG STOMPERS

See Memphis

BO CARTER

See Mississippi Sheiks

JOHN CEPHAS

(b. 1932 / vocals, guitar)

This carpenter from Washington, born in Bowling Green, Virginia, had been playing for a long time for his own pleasure and for a local audience when he was discovered in 1979 by the German producer Axel Kustner, which led to several European tours.

In fact, John Cephas had recorded tapes on several occasions for the Library of Congress, and he was central to the little country blues scene in Washington, with John Jackson,★ Flora Molton, and Archie Edwards, where he remained attached to the tradition of the East Coast blues. His guitar style, a delicate fingerpicking, owes a great deal to Blind Boy Fuller,★ Buddy Moss,★ as well as to some white guitar players of that area. His expressive but tense singing is reminiscent of Tarheel Slim.★

John Cephas cut several albums with harmonica player Phil Wiggins, including the remarkable *Dog Days of August* (Flying Fish) on which his clear and graceful style did wonders. His repertoire covered the whole range of the East Coast blues tradition, from very old pieces like "Going down the Road Feeling Bad" and "Chicken" to the instrumental of Sylvester Weaver and Leon McAuliffe, "Guitar Rag," to more modern rhythmical pieces.

Not a major bluesman, Cephas, nevertheless, has major qualities. His discovery has attracted attention to the blues of the Washington, D.C., area, where, like in other big cities, there is an underground network of bluesmen deserving popular and critical acclaim.

RAY CHARLES

(b. 1930 / vocals, piano)

For some a genius, for others a pure product of American show business, Brother Ray is probably one of the most controversial figures of African-American music in all genres—blues, rhythm and blues, rock, soul, jazz, country, and pop.

Born in Georgia and raised in Florida in a school for the-blind, he began his professional career very early. After several attempts, he went to the West Coast and became the piano player for Lowell Fulson,* thanks to whom he recorded as early as 1948 on the small California Swing Time label. During that time, Ray imitated Nat King Cole and Charles Brown,* then local idols. From 1951 on, Ray Charles's association with the Atlantic label allowed him to demonstrate the extent of his talent. The first recordings for Atlantic (in particular, the wonderful "Losing Hand") all are blues or ballads in the pure West Coast tradition, revealing Charles as a sensitive piano player and a fascinating singer with an expressive, husky, and sensuous voice. In the fifties he integrated more and more of the phrasing, the frenzy, and the band arrangements of gospel, adding a group of female singers, the Raelets, who, after the fashion of a gospel chorus, underlined his profane preaching or responded in counterpoint. The commercial success of some excellent titles in this style (e.g., "I Got a Woman," "Hallelujah I Love Her So," and "Talkin' about You") is nevertheless nothing compared to that of his 1959 hit "What'd I Say."

Ray Charles signed then with the giant ABC, for which he recorded several beautiful pieces that were written by Percy Mayfield* during their short-lived association: "I Wonder," "Hit the Road, Jack," "Georgia on My Mind," and "The Danger Zone." From the sixties on, Ray Charles—whose name has become legendary—gave up little by little the style he had created for other horizons, especially country music, which he is said to have always loved (he cut beautiful renditions of the famous "I Can't Stop Loving You" by Hank Williams and "Born to Lose," the honky-tonk classic by Ted Daffan). In 1968 he founded his own labels, Tangerine and then Crossover. He then softened his style to the point of appearing essentially as a crooner, following the examples of Sammy Davis, Jr., and Harry Belafonte.

His influence has been very important on such singers as Stevie Wonder and Otis Redding. By moving in the fifties from the traditional patterns of rhythm and blues, by using forcefully the sounds and manners of the gospel in profane music, he played an undeniable role in the future emergence of soul music.

SAM CHATMON

See Mississippi Sheiks

C. J. CHENIER

See Zydeco

CLIFTON CHENIER

(1925–1987 / vocals, accordion, harmonica)

Clifton Chenier was the biggest popularizer of zydeco, the blues style particular to French-speaking black Louisiana. This great singer and accordion player, rightly nicknamed the "Zydeco King," played tirelessly in the bayous for forty years, before he achieved national and international fame. His musical perfection and surprising professionalism (for a music that is not always so) and his contagious dynamism and good humor, increased his own success in particular and that of zydeco in general each time he performed.

Chenier was accompanied by a flawless band, which included through the years his brother Cleveland on the washboard, his son C. J. Chenier,* saxophone player John Hart, piano player Elmore Nixon, and guitar players Lonesome Sundown* and Phillip Walker.* Chenier sang for several decades, with a powerful guttural voice enhanced by an accordion style hard to equal in the zydeco world, a repertoire that included rock-and-roll, blues, waltzes, and two-steps, mixing English and French in the purest Acadian tradition.

After a difficult beginning, Chenier recorded for Imperial, Chess, and Specialty. He attracted the attention of producer Chris Strachwitz. Because of his stubbornness, Chris, who had fallen under the spell of this type of music and its main interpreter, succeeded in promoting Clifton and his records all around the world. Chenier cut his best records with this

■ Clifton Chenier. *(Photograph © by Gerard Robs. Courtesy of Archives and Special Collections, John Davis Williams Library, University of Mississippi)*

producer; the Arhoolie albums are outstanding. *Louisiana Blues and Zydeco* (Arhoolie); his first album for Strachwitz, *Black Snake Blues* (Arhoolie); *King of the Bayous* (Arhoolie); and especially *Bogalusa Boogie* (Arhoolie) and *Out West* (Arhoolie) are exceptional.

CHESS (PHIL AND LEN)

Muddy Waters,* Little Walter,* Chuck Berry,* Sonny Boy Williamson (Rice Miller),* Bo Diddley,* Jimmy Rogers,* Eddie Boyd,* Howlin' Wolf,* Elmore James,* Otis Rush,* and Buddy Guy*—all the great founders of the Chicago blues after 1945—recorded the best of their work for the Chess record label.

Brothers Phil and Len Chess, Polish immigrants, came to Chicago in 1937 and started a liquor business. By the end of the war they owned a small chain of stores and taverns. The most prosperous ones, like the Macomba Club, were located in the black district of Chicago and featured blues and jazz bands. The Chess brothers were amazed that most popular artists, like the young Muddy Waters, were not recorded by the big companies, RCA, Columbia, or Decca, which preferred the more civilized style of the performers from before the war (Jazz Gillum,* Washboard Sam,* and Tampa Red*).

It led them to create their own record company, Aristocrat, which from 1947 to 1948 recorded a great number of musicians newly arrived from the South. They expressed themselves in a style that was sometimes electrified and close to the country blues of the Delta, translating the preoccupations of their fellow travelers who had come en masse to work in the North during the war.

Muddy Waters, with Memphis Slim's* bass player, Big Crawford, achieved commercial success in Chicago, Detroit, and also Memphis and the southern states. The Chess brothers decided to record the Chicago bluesmen. Soon Len Chess traveled a lot in the South to promote his records and to discover new talents. In 1952, Aristocrat became the Chess and Checker labels, with the addition later on, of Argo and Cadet. In 1954, with the help of promoter and disc jockey Alan

Freed, the Chess "products" covered half of the places on the rhythm-and-blues charts. They established Chess among the big companies.

The music and artists of the Chicago blues are analyzed in other sections of this book, but it is important to underline here the importance of the producer. Indeed, Phil and Len Chess and their "producers," Gene Barge, Ralph Bass, and Willie Dixon,* not only recorded the greatest black artists of that period, but thanks to their management and promoting, they also made stars out of them. Their advice and their musical arrangements brought out the best in their artists. The conversations between Sonny Boy Williamson and Len Chess recorded on the album *Bummer Road* (Chess) document the patience and care and the perfect flair necessary to produce hundreds of records that rank among the best of the blues.

The Chess brothers were instrumental in the creation and expansion of the Chicago blues, and also in the history of contemporary music as a whole, considering the influence of that style on the rock of the sixties. In addition to their contribution to the blues, Chess successfully produced many jazz, gospel, rock-and-roll, soul, folk, and country music records.

After 1965, the enterprise's dimensions became colossal. That, combined with the withdrawal of Len Chess, led to artistic and commercial decline of the company. The label was producing too many mediocre albums and finally was sold in 1970.

After years of oblivion and indifference by the series of owners of all its masterpieces, Chess records—recognized worldwide for their true worth—are today marketed in the U.S. by MCA, their new owner.

CHICAGO

By the beginning of the twentieth century Chicago had become a great industrial center and had become a favorite place to emigrate to for the tenant farmers of the Mississippi Delta drawn to the appeal of city life.

This is how, as early as 1920, blacks of the Deep South brought their music to Chicago. This tendency was reinforced by the proximity of modern recording studios. The Paramount company brought some bluesmen, such as Blind Lemon Jefferson★ and Blind Blake,★ to Chicago to record them.

However, it was not until 1928 that a characteristic Chicago blues style emerged: a mixture of the declining classic blues, born from vaudeville, and country blues, a southern traditional music, which was directed at an urban black public trying to be refined and looking for a good time, without excluding certain aspects of their previous life in the South. This new music was represented by the Hokum Boys: guitar player Tampa Red★ and piano player Georgia Tom Dorsey. They were tremendously successful with light pieces like "It's Tight Like That."

The birth of the Chicago blues before 1945 is above all the work of the white producer LESTER MELROSE. This businessman, crazy about jazz, producer of King Oliver and Jelly Roll Morton, played an active role in the transformation— some said the sweetening—of the rural southern blues into an urban blues that was strongly tinted with jazz. After the Hokum Boys, Melrose discovered and recorded Big Bill Broonzy★ in 1930. During the next decade, Melrose ruled supreme over the Chicago blues, producing the black catalogs of Columbia and RCA/Bluebird. This Bluebird beat is obvious in the recordings of Broonzy, Tampa Red, Jazz Gillum,★ Washboard Sam,★ and John Lee "Sonny Boy" Williamson★— the stars of Chicago clubs. He also recorded musicians who had different styles: Walter Davis,★ Roosevelt Sykes,★ Big Joe Williams,★ Tommy McClennan,★ Bukka White,★ and, later the Big Three Trio of Willie Dixon★ as well as Doctor Clayton, an African black originally, an eloquent composer, and the object of a brief admiration (he died in 1946) from the black public. Although he was criticized by blues fans, Lester Melrose left behind a work largely positive, as a producer and as a discoverer of new talents.

The Second World War witnessed a massive flow of southern black immigrants who did not find their music in the Bluebird beat. Melrose himself seemed unable to understand the change in taste of this public: He recorded Muddy Waters★ as early as 1946, but he did not recognize any original talent, and these recordings were to remain unreleased until 1971. At that time, Chicago was a melting pot rich with creation, and the decade 1947 to 1957 was the "golden age of blues" par excellence. A vast number of outstanding artists started in the streets of the Maxwell Street flea market or the South Side clubs. Some—John Brim, Moody Jones, Blue Smitty, and Arthur Spires—disappeared after a few remarkable records. Others—Johnny Young,* Snooky Pryor,* J. B. Hutto,* and Homesick James*—more persistent and luckier, were rediscovered by the blues-revival public fifteen years later and were then recorded abundantly. Others—Muddy Waters, Howlin' Wolf,* Little Walter,* Sonny Boy Williamson (Rice Miller),* Elmore James,* and Jimmy Rogers*—became stars.

After the war, record sales of the established artists decreased regularly, and around 1948, the big companies— RCA and Columbia—abandoned the blues almost entirely. Blues remained prosperous in Chicago clubs, but it was not the civilized and mellow Bluebird blues but rather an intensified blues that maintained the harshness and the drama of the Delta blues. There, a few small independent companies took over. They recorded the artists who had newly arrived in Chicago and who were successful in the city clubs. Chess was the most famous company; it discovered Muddy Waters, Little Walter, Jimmy Rogers, and others; but Vee-Jay, founded by Vivian Carter and Jim Bracken, was the first big record company exclusively managed by blacks. Vee-Jay was then the only true competitor of Chess for the blues, with such artists as John Lee Hooker,* Jimmy Reed,* Memphis Slim,* and Billy Boy Arnold* under contract.

Aside from these two "big" independent companies, a vast number of small ones tried to follow the example of Chess and Vee-Jay. Some survived only a few years: Ora-Nelle, Chance, Sabre, and Parrot. Others maintained themselves with an occasional hit: For instance, Eddie Boyd,* an artist with JOB, reached number one on the charts with "Five Long Years" in 1952; but he used that success to sign a contract with Chess, which had superior distribution. On the artistic level, the production from these small companies was remarkable: JOB recorded artists like J. B. Lenoir,* Johnny Shines,* Otis

Spann,* and Floyd Jones.* Robert Nighthawk and Junior Wells cut their best records for United/States; the Cobra label, managed by Eli Toscano, discovered Otis Rush* and Magic Sam,* thus playing a major role in the evolution of the Chicago blues from 1958 on.

At that time indeed, the Chicago blues made way for a new generation of musicians from the West Side, the poorest ghetto in the city. These musicians, who in general had come to Chicago at a young age, added to the influence of Delta blues that of B. B. King*; they introduced strong gospel sounds, in particular the abundant use of the minor scale. This West Side sound showed a real Chicago blues renewal that is still alive today through such musicians as Jimmy Dawkins,* Magic Slim,* Eddie Campbell,* Jimmy Johnson,* Luther Allison,* and Lonnie Brooks.*

From 1963 on, the Chicago blues declined: Vee-Jay disappeared for management reasons, and Chess turned more and more to rhythm and blues, soon to be called soul. The young black public was no longer interested in the blues, and the white fans were not numerous enough to constitute a sufficient market. The seventies were the darkest years for the blues, in Chicago and elsewhere. Only the old blacks and the young whites were interested in it. The blues could be found only in the poorest and most sordid districts or on college campuses. Independent record companies (e.g., Alligator and Delmark) recorded bluesmen, but they aimed at a public for the most part white and sometimes exclusively European. Black music radio stations did not broadcast soul any more but rather disco and funk.

For the past few years though, this appalling situation has been changing: The Chicago blues is now recognized by the official establishment of the Windy City which has assigned it to a special place in the culture of the city. At the same time, a new generation of both black and white listeners are turning to the blues. A renewal developed that took advantage of the comeback of white bluesmen like Johnny Winter* and Roy Buchanan* and also took advantage of the success of Robert Cray* and the renewal of southern soul. The Chicago blues is universally appreciated and even if it becomes a "historical" music, like Dixieland in New Orleans, the sound of electric guitars, harmonicas, and walking bass lines clings today almost everywhere in the city by the lake, drawing in new aficionados, tourists, and more and more local clientele.

Several young musicians came to the fore in Chicago clubs:

BILLY BRANCH (b. 1951) is an excellent harmonica player from Los Angeles who came to the blues because of Paul Butterfield. After he moved to Chicago, Billy rapidly adopted the harmonica style of the city. He belonged to Willie Dixon's* band, and he recorded in numerous sessions as an accompanist before he was able to create his own group with the singer-guitarist J. W. Williams: The Sons of the Blues. Their best album is *Where's My Money* (Red Beans). But Billy can do better.

LIL' ED (Ed Williams / b. 1955) is a nephew of J. B. Hutto* from whom he borrowed the slide guitar style and a good deal of his vocal inflections. Very dynamic on stage, his records have a lot of punch (*Roughhousin:* Alligator and *Chicken, Gravy and Biscuits:* Alligator) although they lack somewhat in feeling.

JOHNNY B. MOORE (b. 1952) played a great deal in clubs as a member of the bands of Koko Taylor,* Willie Dixon, and Eddie Taylor.* His albums reflect a strong Delta flavor that is refreshing in the present blues scene, dominated by rock or funk overtones (*Hard Times:* Blues).

MAURICE JOHN VAUGHN (b. 1953) is an excellent singer and guitar player as well as a good saxophone player. Trained by Phil Guy and A. C. Reed, Maurice recorded the good album *Generic Blues* (Alligator).

JOHN WATKINS (b. 1954), another guitar player, also belonged to Willie Dixon's band before setting out on his own. Particularly good in slow and rhythmic blues, Watkins may someday record the good album that he now needs.

The old hand BYTHER SMITH (b. 1933) belongs to another generation; he emerged only recently with two superb albums: *Tell Me How You Like It* (Razor) and *Gritty Soul* (Razor). A cousin of J. B. Lenoir, he is very much appreciated in Japan and Europe.

Other names are worth mentioning: Dion Payton, Professor

Eddie Lusk, Michael Coleman, Johnny Dollar, Johnny Christian, Melvin Taylor, and such young female singers as Valerie Wellington* and Zora Young.* Without being sensational, this Chicago blues renewal is nonetheless real. It still needs to provide masterpieces in order to distinguish it. The anthology *The New Bluebloods* (Alligator) offers several of these artists.

There are numerous collections that make it possible to hear the Chicago blues from its origins to the present: *Chicago Blues* (RCA/Bluebird), *Chicago / The Blues Today, Vols. 1, 2 & 3* (Vanguard), *Living Chicago Blues* (Alligator; 6 volumes), *Chicago Bluesmasters, Vols. 1, 2 & 3* (Charly), *Chicago Ain't Nothing but a Bluesband* (Delmark), *Sweet Home Chicago* (Delmark), *King Cobras* (Flyright), *Fishing in My Pond* (Flyright), *World of Trouble* (Flyright), *Windy City Blues* (Nighthawk), *Chicago Slickers, Vols. 1 & 2* (Nighthawk), and *Harmonica Blues Kings* (Pearl). The Chess anthologies are indispensable.

CHICAGO BOB

(Robert Lee Nelson / b. 1944 / vocals, harmonica)

Born in Louisiana, Chicago Bob was a student of Lazy Lester* and Slim Harpo.* He created his harmonica style through his contact with the great bluesmen of Chicago (Buddy Guy,* Howlin' Wolf,* and J. B. Hutto*) when he spent the summer with his aunt who lived there. Muddy Waters* gave him the nickname of Chicago Bob.

Around 1965 in Boston, Chicago Bob met Luther Johnson,* with whom he became partners for about ten years, performing in Boston clubs and in some festivals, like Newport. A short stint in John Lee Hooker's* band in 1977 left Bob in Atlanta looking for a job. He became a part of the local underground blues scene. Noticed by local producer George Mitchell, Bob recorded several albums with an Atlanta band, the Heartfixers, in which he became the singer. *Just Your Fool* (High Water), cut in 1987 with guitar player J. T. Speed, gave recognition to Chicago Bob in the field of contemporary blues.

His desire to continue in the Chicago blues tradition of the fifties, as well as his strong Louisiana influences ("Call My Landlady"), his good harmonica style, and his hearty voice distinguish Chicago Bob from his contemporaries.

OTIS CLAY

See Soul

EDDIE CLEARWATER

(Edward Harrington / b. 1935 / vocals, guitar)

The eclectic dabbler Eddie Clearwater is an unlikely but important bluesman. His journey relegated him to the margins of the genres he approached. A dishwasher, a bouncer, a cab driver, an educator, a record producer and editor, but always a musician, Eddie Harrington's road has been a rough one.

Born in Mississippi, Eddie was first influenced by local bluesmen and gospel singers, in particular the splendid Sister Rosetta Tharpe. He was soon attracted by the rhythm and blues of Louis Jordan★ and by country singer Hank Williams. He arrived in Chicago in 1950, where he was taken under the wing of his uncle, Houston Harrington, an extraordinary character (a preacher and also an inventor of many crazy objects, such as a flying submarine) who managed the tiny label Atomic-H, which produced the 45s of Morris Pejoe, Sunnyland Slim,★ JoJo Williams, J. T. Brown, and others. Eddie was thus very quickly at the core of the Chicago blues. Having learned the guitar, he met Muddy Waters★—even imitated him by changing his name to Clear Waters then Clearwater—and Chuck Berry,★ of whom he became a faithful admirer. He created his own band in 1957 and was able to perform simultaneously in black (blues) and white (country music) clubs, a rare exploit in the Chicago of that time! He recorded several 45s for his uncle, aiming at diverse publics. In particular, the wild *Hillbilly Blues* showed the diversity of his talents. The rise of the dramatic and enthralling West Side sound of Magic Sam★ and Otis Rush★ in the late fifties did not go unnoticed by Clearwater, and he included this new style in his repertoire and cut the excellent "A Minor Cha Cha." Some of these sides are collected on the very good anthology *Chicago Ain't Nothing but a Blues Band* (Delmark).

Practicing all the genres for different audiences and integrating soul and country music in his huge repertoire, Eddie Clearwater was able to remain active in the sixties and seventies, although a good number of blues bands were disappearing from the Chicago clubs.

Clearwater is a dynamic artist who has a rare mastery on stage. His eclecticism is after all his best quality: it enables him to perform with zest a varied repertoire. His powerful singing, substantially influenced by gospel, and his guitar style with cascades of notes in the fashion of Chuck Berry or the harmonic demonstrations of Magic Sam are also very convincing.

Clearwater recorded several interesting albums, in particular *Two Times Nine* (Charly) that deals with all the genres of American folk music and *The Chief* (Rooster), a much "bluesier" album in which the harmonica player Carey Bell* is outstanding. *Flimdoozie* (Rooster) also gives the opportunity to hear Otis Rush* at his best.

WILLIE COBBS

See Calvin Leavy

GARY "B. B." COLEMAN

(ca. 1950 / vocals, guitar, harmonica, piano, bass)

Mystery still surrounds Gary Coleman, who seemed to have sprung from nowhere around 1986 with a few southern hits with "One-Eyed Woman" and "Watch Where You Stroke."

Both a singer and an instrumentalist, this "B. B." is also producer, arranger, and talent scout for John Abbey and for his Ichiban label, a major player in the southern blues and soul revival.

Coleman was born in Paris, Texas. The owner of a club and a record store in Jackson, Mississippi, he became quite popular locally. His music, sometimes incredibly simple—even crude—and relaxed, seems to be at the opposite extremes of the usual black hits. His popularity among blacks in the South demonstrate the return to the "good old blues" in the region where he was born.

Although B. B. Coleman shows nothing of the brilliance of his idols B. B. King* and Albert King,* his albums nevertheless have a certain charm and warmth: *Nothing but the Blues* (Ichiban), *If You Can Beat Me Rockin'* (Ichiban), and *One Night Stand* (Ichiban).

As a producer for Ichiban records, Coleman has discovered many southern artists who were thus able to make their recording debuts: harmonica players Blues Boy Willie and Thomas "Snake" Johnson, singers Roshell Anderson and Dwight Ross, guitar player Travis "Moonshine" Haddix, and the talented Trudy Lynn. He is also responsible for the comeback of veterans like Clarence Carter, Little Johnny Taylor,* and Chick Willis.

ALBERT COLLINS

(b. 1932 / vocals, guitar)

It was only at the end of the seventies that Albert Collins received the international recognition he deserved. Indeed, this Texas guitar player, a great innovator, remained for a long time in obscurity despite the active support that the band Canned Heat* gave him for a while.

Collins lived near Dallas and began playing the guitar at an early age under the guidance of the larger-than-life Frankie Lee Sims.* Moreover, it is as the guitar player of Sims's son, the singer Little Frankie Lee, that he started as a professional musician. He developed a personal style: short, clear, and high notes springing from a thick background of bass and a systematic use of minor scales. His guitar style shows traces of the traditional economical Texas style and even some features of Lowell Fulson* and Lafayette Thomas.* But he is especially close to Johnny "Guitar" Watson,* a nephew of Frankie Lee Sims, who was inspired by the same musical sources.

He recorded a series of instrumental pieces in the late fifties that were local successes: "Deep Freeze" and "Frosty," a

■ Albert Collins. *(Photograph © by Jerry Hausler. Courtesy of Jerry Hausler and Archives and Special Collections, John Davis Williams Library, University of Mississippi)*

succession of precise and tight notes, creates an elegant and "icy" atmosphere that forever remains the mark of Albert Collins. His records (see *The Cool Sound:* Crosscut) became minor classics in the sixties, adored by fans, especially the critics in the British review *Blues Unlimited*. But it was Bob Hite and Canned Heat who did the most to promote him: Collins appeared at Filmore East where he was compared (wrongly) to Jimi Hendrix. He cut a series of albums for Imperial, Blue Thumb, and Tumbleweed. He was not confident about his vocal talents—he certainly is not a great singer but his acrid voice is not unpleasant. Collins stuck to instrumental pieces, suitable for dancing, but too light to be hits. His participation in recording sessions for Dave Alexander* and Ike and Tina Turner* is much more impressive.

The seventies were very disappointing for Albert Collins. Surrounded by an aura of legend among a handful of fans and musicians of the West Coast, but unrecognized by the general public, he vegetated, spending his life humbly and passively in

Houston and San Francisco clubs. He would still be there if, at the end of the seventies, one of his most ardent admirers, producer Bruce Iglauer, had not made him come to Chicago to record on his Alligator label. Surrounded by excellent local musicians that were to provide the mainstay for his regular band (saxophone player A. C. Reed,* bass player Aron Burton, and drummer Casey Jones), Albert Collins recorded several albums on which he showed the durability of his talent. *Ice Pickin'* (Alligator), *Frostbite* (Alligator), *Don't Lose Your Cool* (Alligator), and *Cold Snap* (Alligator) were well produced, and they enabled Collins to reveal his musical ideas in a favorable context, while his accompanists added the solidity of the Chicago blues to the refined suppleness of Collins' style. The latter added more and more elements of contemporary black music to his ever-dominant California/Texas roots.

Frozen Alive (Alligator) caught a little of the energy that Collins put into his stage shows. *Showdown* (Alligator) grouped around Collins two of his most gifted students: the veteran Johnny Copeland* and the young blues prodigy, Robert Cray.*

JOHNNY COPELAND

(b. 1937 / vocals, guitar)

Like Jimmy Johnson,* Johnny Copeland is another soul singer who came back to the blues in the seventies. This Louisiana native and son of tenant farmers was influenced as a child by B. B. King,* Sonny Boy Williamson (Rice Miller),* and the radio broadcast of country music, "Louisiana Hayride." Reaching Houston in 1950, he became a bootblack, while at the same time learning to play guitar in the black clubs of the city.

He soon became good enough to play with T-Bone Walker,* Bobby Bland,* and Big Mama Thornton* and to go on a tour with singer Clarence Samuels with whom he cut a 45, "Chicken-Hearted Woman," a small hit in the South. This further enabled him to record under his own name for several local labels, among which was Duke, then for national labels like Mercury and Atlantic. "Down on Bending Knees" and especially "Sufferin' City," in a firm soul style, were somewhat

■ Johnny Copeland. *(Photograph © by Paul Harris; used with permission)*

successful. After that Copeland, who had made something of a name for himself in soul music, toured with Otis Redding and Eddie Floyd. He continued to record sporadically in the sixties. The sudden popularity of disco forced him to go back to his first love, the blues, and to cut for the producer Huey Meaux the album *Johnny Copeland Sings the Blues* (Crazy Cajun), an album that showed that he was comfortable in several genres, from acoustic country blues to southern soul. But, in the mid-seventies, the blues scene in Houston that had formerly been flourishing was changing dramatically; the black districts of the city were becoming little by little populated by Mexican immigrants. Johnny Copeland decided then, in 1975, to move to New York where he created a new band.

Finally, he recorded several excellent albums for the Rounder label that enabled him to appear as one of the great "revelations" of the blues in the eighties: *Copeland Special*, *Make My Home Where I Hang My Hat*, and *Texas Twister.* He appeared as a vehement and powerful singer, influenced by Sam Cooke and Johnny Ace, as well as a guitarist who was faithful to the Texas tradition, being inspired by Clarence "Gatemouth" Brown,★ Johnny "Guitar" Watson, and also Freddie King.★ But Albert Collins★ may be his most obvious influence, as shown on *Showdown* (Alligator) which brought them together along with the young Robert Cray.★

Several collections put the first recordings of Copeland together. Between soul and the blues, he was often hesitant, looking for an assertive identity: *Houston Roots* (Ace), *The Copeland Collection* (Home Cooking), and *Dedicated to the Greatest* (Kent).

Bringing It All Back Home (Rounder) is a strange album, recorded in Africa, that featured Copeland with African musicians.

JAMES COTTON

(b. 1935 / vocals, harmonica)

This excellent harmonica player was very young when he was directly influenced by Sonny Boy Williamson (Rice Miller),★ whom he followed in his peregrinations across the South of

■ James Cotton. *(Photograph © by Anton J. Mikofsky; used with permission)*

the United States. In the early fifties he moved to Memphis, which then was a real musical culture medium in which a very particular current of electric blues developed with Howlin' Wolf,★ Junior Parker,★ Rufus Thomas,★ Joe Hill Louis,★ and others around the astonishing Sun record producer, Sam Philips.★

He recorded his first titles for Sun, which were regional hits: "Cotton Crop Blues" and "Hold Me in Your Arms." But his real growth occurred during the nearly ten years he was a member of Muddy Waters'★ band. He replaced Little Walter★ and Junior Wells★ as Muddy's harmonica player. At first it seemed that he was uneasy with the lingering presence of his predecessors, but, little by little, he developed a very personal style on the harmonica, midway between the swinging approach of Little Walter and the rawness of Sonny Boy. In fact, his style never stopped evolving, and after he left Muddy's band, with which he recorded many songs, James

Cotton—who had become a confirmed leader of his own band—managed to combine successfully soul, rock, Chicago blues, and jazz.

Active for nearly forty years, Cotton recorded many albums, of which very few are still available. *The Blues Never Die* (Ace) and *Chicago/The Blues Today, Vol. 2* (Vanguard) date from the time when he was still a sideman for Muddy Waters; they are excellent. *From Cotton with Verve* (Black Magic) is also commendable. *High Compression* (Alligator), *Live from Chicago* (Alligator), and the excellent *Mighty Long Time* (Antone's), his most recent performances, show that Cotton was able to evolve without denying his roots. Nevertheless, although his talents on the harmonica are intact, his voice has become excessively harsh and has lost its flexibility.

COUSIN JOE

(Pleasant Joseph / b. 1907 / vocals, piano)

Not well known outside New Orleans, Cousin Joe is nonetheless an important figure in blues history. Raised in the Crescent City, Joe learned music in church choirs, then in New Orleans taverns, in which he progressively became one of the favorite piano players.

In 1942 Joe moved to New York and mixed with the jazz specialists who abounded there. He performed in Harlem clubs, and there he recorded his first titles. "Lightnin' Struck the Poorhouse," "You Ain't So Such a Much," and "Evolution Blues" made him an important name of black music. They were masterpieces with a devastating humor, the signature of Cousin Joe.

Tired of the hectic New York life, Joe went back to New Orleans in 1948 and continued to record for local labels like De Luxe and Imperial. He became one of the favorite bluesmen of the French Quarter. Joe rarely left the Quarter, only venturing away for a European tour.

His tracks in the forties and fifties, on which Earl Hines, Al Casey, Jimmy Shirley, Sidney Bechet, and Sammy Price stood out, are not often reissued. The same is true for his superb album recorded in the seventies for Bluesway (*Cousin Joe of New Orleans*), cut with the excellent guitar player Justin Adams.

One will have to be contented with the delicious *Relaxin' in New Orleans* (Great Southern) on which Cousin Joe sings his memories solo.

IDA COX

See Female Blues Singers

JAMES "SUGAR BOY" CRAWFORD

See New Orleans

ROBERT CRAY

(b. 1953 / vocals, guitar)

From 1985 on, the tremendous success of Robert Cray, in blues (he holds the record for W. C. Handy★ Awards) as well as in rock (a regular place on the charts), underlined the comeback of the blues to the fore of the musical scene after a long commercial lapse.

It is true that Cray is criticized by a lot of experts who deny his music is really "blues." But could the blues of the nineties be that of Muddy Waters★? And could today's bluesman do something other than claim and take responsibility for this inheritance while modernizing it at the same time?

The son of a serviceman, juggled from Georgia to Germany and finally to the West Coast, Robert Cray, as did many Americans his age, grew up with the psychedelic sounds of rock before discovering the blues through the records of Magic Sam,★ B. B. King,★ Albert King,★ and Howlin' Wolf.★

After taking some guitar lessons and playing in several teen bands, Cray decided to be a real musician when he met Albert Collins,★ who gave a concert at the University of Tacoma (Washington) which Cray was attending. An incredible

■ Robert Cray. *(Photograph © by G. Michael Wall. Courtesy of Archives and Special Collections, John Davis Williams Library, University of Mississippi)*

admiration and a real friendship were born from this meeting. Collins' guitar style remains the dominant influence on Robert Cray's music.

He formed a band with childhood friend Richard Cousins, a supple and efficient bass player, with whom he moved to Oregon. The addition of harmonica player Curtis Salgado, the meeting with the intelligent producer Bruce Bromberg and co-producer Dennis Walker, and a lucky small role in the movie *Animal House* enabled Cray to record his first album *Who's Been Talkin'* (Tomato/Charly) in 1980. It was already possible to appreciate the beautiful warm voice of Cray, strongly influenced by Otis Redding and Sam Cooke, and his flowing guitar style that wraps around all the pieces he interprets, even the powerful blues of Howlin' Wolf, Sammy Myers,* and Willie Dixon.*

A few years later his second album (*Bad Influence:* Hightone), produced by Bromberg, showed an important step in Cray's career, revealing him as a composer of lyrics full of gravity and depth. The powerful "Phone Booth" was covered by Albert King, and the beautiful ballad "Bad Influence" was covered by Eric Clapton. This album established Cray as a significant blues artist.

Although compared more often to Mark Knopfler than to Howlin' Wolf, Cray never stops asserting himself as the prototype of the new bluesman, who articulates his music on several levels without ignoring its debt to the Texas-California blues. Albert Collins, Johnny Copeland,* and Robert Cray were together on the excellent *Showdown* (Alligator).

But nothing that Cray recorded is to be ignored, whether it be *False Accusations* (Hightone), a collection of ballads about adultery, or *Strong Persuader* (Mercury). Being careful not to record too many albums, composing most of his own pieces, and managing his success cleverly, Robert Cray has become a trendsetter.

Whichever course Cray will take in the future, it is comforting to see an artist of that quality emerge, mixing tradition and modernity so successfully.

PEEWEE CRAYTON

(Connie Crayton / 1914–1985)

Like many Texas bluesmen, PeeWee Crayton moved, in 1935, to California. But it was only later (during the war) that he learned to play the guitar under the influence of Charlie Christian and T-Bone Walker,★ who took him under his wing. He incorporated stylistic features particular to T-Bone and Lowell Fulson,★ and played in small Oakland clubs with Ivory Joe Hunter's and Jimmy Witherspoon's★ bands before recording two guitar solos in 1949: "Blues after Hours" and "Texas Hop," which were big hits among the blacks of Los Angeles and San Francisco and which, despite their simplicity, have become archetypes of the West Coast guitar style, particularly for the cascade of notes on prolonged riffs.

Encouraged by this success, PeeWee recorded constantly for several labels (Modern, Imperial, and Vee-Jay) in this California rhythm-and blues-style that devotes a lot of room to brass and to romantic ballads for which Crayton's warm voice was particularly suited.

Between 1958 and 1968, PeeWee Crayton went through a low period because of personal problems. At the same time the musical taste of the black population was changing. Moreover, the very urban blues style that he embodied was not much appreciated by the first blues-revival fans.

It is only because of the efforts of his friend Johnny Otis★ that he came back to the fore in 1970 with his participation in the Monterey Jazz Festival.

Unfortunately, despite a few appearances at festivals, a handful of albums for Vanguard, Blues Spectrum, and Murray Brothers (the excellent *Make Room for PeeWee:* Murray Brothers), and a few sessions as Big Joe Turner's★ sideman, the blues boom of the eighties did not really profit PeeWee. His first tracks, very consistent, are today largely available on the collections: *Memorial Album* (Ace), *Rockin' down on Central Avenue* (Ace), and *Blues before Dawn* (Imperial).

ARTHUR "BIG BOY" CRUDUP

(1905–1974 / vocals, guitar)

Arthur Crudup was nicknamed the "Father of Rock and Roll." More than his declamatory singing and his simple and very rhythmic guitar style, this nickname suggests especially the influence he had on Elvis Presley. The first record by Elvis which contributed to his fame was "That's All Right," an old hit by Crudup. Shortly afterward, he did it again with two other popular songs by Crudup: "My Baby Left Me" and "So Glad You're Mine." A talented composer, he wrote many blues classics including, "Mean Old Frisco," "Dig Myself a Hole," and "Rock Me Mama." A favorite of the black public, Crudup was appreciated for the very particular atmosphere on his records: a tenor voice with a powerful rhythmic support (electric guitar, bass, and drums). It is in a way the modernization of the Mississippi country blues which prefigured as early as 1940 what Muddy Waters★ or Jimmy Rogers★ were going to do. The rhythmic beat created by bass player Ransom Knowlin and drummer Judge Riley is often irresistible, particularly in the fast pieces. It is quite obvious that it influenced rockabilly.

Crudup was a musician full of energy, whose work, however, was sometimes monotonous (he almost always used the same melody lines), but he was a mediocre businessman, and he was unable to manage his career. He moved to Chicago in 1936, where he was discovered by producer Lester Melrose,★ who recorded him for RCA/Bluebird. Big Boy accumulated hits, and he is one of the rare Bluebird artists to have continued to record for Trumpet and Chess under several pseudonyms, including that of Elmer James. It seems that Crudup never made a penny on the royalties of the many blues songs he composed. "That's All Right" would have been enough to sustain him in his old age, but he never got the money he was entitled to. He died in near-poverty after having recorded a few poor albums, directed at the blues-revival public.

His work is easily available on these collections: *Give Me a 32-20* (Crown Prince), *Star Bootlegger* (Krazy Kat), *I'm in the Mood* (Krazy Kat), and *Crudup's Rockin Blues* (RCA).

■ Arthur "Big Boy" Crudup. *(Photograph © by Anton J. Mikofsky; used with permission)*

D

LARRY DALE

See New York

CHARLES "COW COW" DAVENPORT

See Boogie-Woogie

BLIND REVEREND GARY DAVIS

(1896–1972 / vocals, guitar, banjo, harmonica, piano)

Along with Blind Blake★ and Blind Boy Fuller,★ Blind Reverend Gary Davis is one of the founders of the East Coast blues, also called Piedmont blues.

Born in South Carolina, Gary Davis showed extraordinary musical talents. By the age of seven he played harmonica, banjo, and guitar. As early as 1910, he belonged to a string-band, and he traveled with it all over the southeastern U.S.

Following a tragic event, Gary became blind and turned to religion. He started to preach in the streets, and he sang sermons in southern cities before moving to Harlem, where he became popular.

Although he recorded only a little before the war, both solo and with Blind Boy Fuller, his influence on East Coast guitar players was significant. This is not surprising considering Gary Davis's virtuosity: His ease with chording, his complete knowledge of his instrument, his perfect fingerpicking, and the extraordinary speed and precision are stupendous. Gary Davis is undeniably one of the best guitar players in music history. Besides the ingenuity and the humor of his "sermons," his superb declamatory singing as a street preacher made him a wonderful interpreter of this inspired sound, that is called Holy blues.

Singing and playing in Harlem streets, the Reverend Gary Davis was eventually able to attract the attention of record producers and, from 1954 on, he recorded numerous outstanding albums. In the wake of these albums, many guitarists-apprentices found in him a benevolent and caring teacher; Stefan Grossman,* Sweet Papa Stovepipe, and Larry Johnson,* among others, were his students for a long time. Through the intermediation of Grossman, Gary Davis became one of the people who popularized ragtime guitar.

Reverend Gary Davis (Yazoo) includes all the recordings that this artist made between 1935 and 1940. His talents were already considerable, but, in our opinion, he cut his best albums between 1959 and 1969 for the Prestige/Bluesville label: *When I Die I'll Live Again* (Fantasy), *Pure Religion* (Prestige), and *The Guitar and Banjo of Reverend Gary Davis* (Prestige).

LARRY DAVIS

(b. 1936 / vocals, guitar, drums)

It took Larry Davis a long time to reemerge and confirm the hope that the blues world had for his young talent.

Indeed, raised in Little Rock, Larry began very early to play drums and to sing in city clubs with Driftin' Slim, Sunny Blair, Sammy Lawhorn, and guitar player Fenton Robinson,* with whom in 1956 he created a band that accompanied the bluesmen who came through town. This is how the singer Bobby Bland* noticed the band and persuaded them to come to Houston in 1958 to record for the Duke label. In a vocal style influenced by gospel, by B. B. King,* and by Bland himself, Larry Davis cut some beautiful and successful records ("Texas Flood" and "Angels in Houston"), which remain as small blues classics, covered by many artists (on *Angels in Houston:* Rounder). But Davis was unable to capitalize on this success: He moved to St. Louis—a city devoid of a real record company—where he gravitated around the bands of Ike Turner,* Oliver Sain, and in particular Albert King* (who taught him basic guitar).

During the sixties, he recorded sporadically in St. Louis and Los Angeles, and later in Memphis in 1973. Although he recorded a few interesting titles, without any real distribution and promotion he became disillusioned about a musical career. A serious traffic accident forced him to an early retirement in Little Rock. But because of the reputation of his Duke albums, in the early eighties several collectors pushed him to resume a career as a bluesman. This fresh start took him back to the clubs of St. Louis and Chicago and enabled him to go on tours in Europe and in Japan.

In 1982 the album *Funny Stuff* (Rooster Blues) won him a certain recognition for his talent with a W. C. Handy★ Award. Produced in St. Louis by Oliver Sain, surrounded by old hands, this Larry Davis recording appeared in a different light from his first records, cut a quarter of a century earlier. He was still a wonderful singer, with a soft tenor voice and a guitar style between those of B. B. and Albert King.

Unfortunately, it was only in 1989 that he recorded a new album, *I Ain't Beggin' Nobody* (Pulsar), but it was not as good as the first one. Meanwhile, the Ace label dug up a few titles from the sixties, which are his best ones so far, and released them as the excellent anthology *Blues around Midnight* (Ace).

WALTER DAVIS

(1912–1964 / vocals, piano)

Walter Davis was one of the most popular blues singers of the thirties. He recorded constantly for RCA/Bluebird, for which he cut close to 160 records. A primitive but expressive piano player, with an irregular rhythm, Davis was unappreciated for a long time by blues fans who did not understand why he was successful among blacks. In fact, as several specialists have noted, it was not the brilliant instrumentalist that the black public was looking for in the blues singer but rather a poet who could translate their concerns into words and music. And Davis—like Peetie Wheatstraw,★ another artist neglected for too long—knew how to do that with brio. His songs humorously and derisively told of the misfortunes of his people. He was also one singer who could deal skillfully with double entendres, which were then widespread in the blues, to describe, in an apparent innocent way, erotic situations or ways the whites behaved. Some titles (e.g., "Think You Need a Shot" and "Let Me in Your Saddle") are in themselves evocative.

Walter Davis's career was simple: Born in the South, he settled in St. Louis in 1924, and Roosevelt Sykes,★ then a talent scout for RCA, noticed him and recorded him in 1930. His first title, "M & O Blues," already had the qualities mentioned above; it was a great success. From then on, Davis took part in many recording sessions, at first with such musicians as Roosevelt Sykes, Big Joe Williams,★ and the outstanding guitar player Henry Townsend★ and then alone on the piano. After the war, his blues style—typical for most stars of the thirties—was out of date, and he gave up music to become a preacher before he died forgotten by all, although his influence is still noticeable among younger artists like Memphis Willie Borum and Jimmy McCracklin.★

There are not many albums that gather the considerable work recorded by Walter Davis for RCA/Bluebird. *Bullet Sides* (Krazy Kat) includes the last songs cut by Davis between 1949 and 1952 for a small label in Nashville.

JIMMY DAWKINS

(b. 1936 / vocals, guitar)

Discovered at the end of the sixties and omnipresent during the seventies, Jimmy Dawkins is today somewhat on the fringe of the blues, which is unfortunate considering his talent.

A professional musician in Chicago since 1957, he barely survived by playing his music. Nevertheless, Jimmy Dawkins managed, through his perseverance and talent, to be internationally recognized. So far he has recorded a dozen albums, and he has gone on numerous tours in Europe, especially in France where he enjoys a solid reputation among the connoisseurs.

After years of working unrecognized in Chicago clubs, Dawkins attracted attention in 1968 with his brilliant guitar work behind the duo Johnny Young★ and Big Walter Horton★ on their remarkable album *Chicago Blues* (Arhoolie). One

■ Jimmy Dawkins. *(Photograph by Jim Fraher, © 1989 Chicago Sun Times. Courtesy of Jimmy Dawkins and "Leric Music")*

performance at the Ann Arbor Festival in 1970 enabled him to record his first album, the excellent *Fast Fingers* (Delmark), which led to tours and regular engagements in Chicago.

Deeply introverted and pessimistic, sometimes to the point of despair, Dawkins—following the Delta blues tradition from which he stemmed—exorcized his fears in his music. His personality is evident through these tortured blues. Dawkins is also one of the rare bluesmen to be earnest about the quality of his music. He made constant improvements and managed to develop a guitar style rooted in the West Side sound of Magic Sam,* but also deeply personal.

Dawkins's blues added to his dramatic guitar style—an economical use of notes with tremolo, interspersed with full chords, often in the minor scale—a singing apparently detached but in reality rich in contained emotion. The result is often outstanding: a tough, bitter, tense, and deeply moving music.

Jimmy Dawkins recorded a dozen good albums. Unfortunately, many are no longer available. *Blisterstring* (Delmark) has a good version of the moving "Welfare Blues," but his best album so far, *Hot Wire* (Isabel), is hard to get.

DELTA BLUES

The Mississippi Delta stretches between the Yazoo River and the Mississippi River south of Memphis; it is said to have been the cradle of the blues. Although this statement may vary—different forms from the Delta blues were born in Texas and on the East Coast, maybe because of local adaptations of the Delta blues—it is certain that the Delta region with its black majority, its long held, deeply felt segregationist attitudes, and its desolate, strange, and almost frightening landscape caused the creation of the most poignant and moving blues possible.

The Delta blues singer is so totally involved in his music that he creates in the act of performing. He and his audience look for a catharsis to their troubles. The singing is generally tense and vehement; the verse is full of metaphors fit into each other without any obvious logic, but they weave a poetic framework that is highly evocative. The guitar style (with a few exceptions like John Hurt's*) is not very sophisticated but rather, very often, imaginative and complex, using all the resources of the instrument. The bottleneck is used often. Above all, the Delta blues is characterized by its powerful bass notes and an insistent rhythm that came directly from its African origins. These low notes and syncopated rhythm are found, beyond the individual styles, among all the great blues-men of the Delta: Skip James,* Charlie Patton,* Son House,* Tommy Johnson,* Robert Johnson,* Big Joe Williams,* Bukka White,* and Tommy McClennan.*

The influence of Delta blues on postwar electric blues was considerable. Chicago, the first blues city after 1945, was flooded with black migrants from this region. The Chicago blues of the fifties is, in fact, an extension and an electri-fication of the Delta blues. The Delta blues also went beyond its narrow geographic boundaries, influencing the blues of the neighboring southern states: Louisiana, Arkansas, Alabama, and Georgia.

This blues form, probably more primitive and much more ethnic than that of the other regions, was for a long time the only one to be recognized by the white blues-revival fans; thus it influenced rock music after 1960. Today, the Delta blues is surprisingly still very much alive among the black communi-ties of small towns and villages of that region.

The Delta blues is particularly well represented on albums; each important artist has one or several under his own name. Moreover, a great number of anthologies cover several charac-teristic sides of that region, but several have the same titles and one has to choose among them.

We recommend *Mississippi Blues* (Yazoo), *Mississippi Moaners* (Yazoo), *Lonesome Road Blues* (Yazoo), *Mississippi Delta Blues, Vols. 1 & 2* (Arhoolie), *Walking Blues* (Flyright), *Mississippi Blues Festival* (Black & Blue), *South Mississippi Blues* (Rounder), *Goin' up the Country* (Rounder), *Mississippi Folk Voices* (Southern Culture), and *Bothered All the Time* (Southern Culture).

DETROIT

Detroit attracted black migrants from the beginning of the century, and by the twenties an important black community had settled there.

At that time there was an important number of taverns fea-turing black musicians near Hastings Street. But, unlike Chicago, Detroit had no recording studios. In the thirties and forties, artists such as piano players Charlie Spand and Big Maceo★ managed to record in Chicago because of their local fame, but other bluesmen, who must have been numerous, sank into oblivion.

After World War II, advanced recording techniques enabled many small record companies to spring up all across the country. In Detroit, independent producers began to record the many bluesmen of the city. The two main producers were the Brown brothers, who created the Fortune label, and the enterprising Joe Von Battle, the owner of a record store on Hastings Street. Von Battle built a small recording studio behind his store, recording an incredible number of bluesmen for the labels JVB, Von, and Battle.

However, not only were the recordings made in Detroit of mediocre technical quality, but these small producers were also financially incapable of distributing records on a national scale.

As a result, bluesmen in Detroit recorded very little, and most disappeared from the scene by the end of the fifties. The blues, out-of-date when compared to the sophisticated music of the Tamla/Motown productions, could not sustain its artists. Today, only a handful of Detroit blues artists remain. John Lee Hooker,★ whose extraordinary originality gave him a large following, was the only one to succeed nationally and even internationally. Eddie Burns★ and Eddie Kirkland,★ by their tenacity, were able to gain recognition, though of small consequence.

In the seventies the harmonica player LITTLE SONNY (Aaron Willis / b. 1936) benefited from a special promotion by Isaac Hayes's label, Enterprise, for which he made three successful albums; nevertheless, these albums are now difficult to find.

Between 1948 and 1960 other Detroit artists produced music similar to the original Delta blues, predominantly through the use of the amplified harmonica, influenced by Sonny Boy Williamson (Rice Miller).★ The differences between the Chicago blues and the Detroit blues lie in the lack of producers, like the Chess★ brothers, and the lack of personalities with the stature of Muddy Waters.★

BOBO JENKINS (1917–1984), singer and guitar player, knew a certain success in 1954 with his political "Democrat Blues" recorded for Chess. Toward the end of his life, he created his own production company, Big Star; he was then able to record a few albums under his own name.

BABY BOY WARREN (Robert Warren / 1919–1977), also a singer and a guitar player, recorded about ten 78s that were representative of Detroit blues. He was an eloquent composer who expressed himself in a vocal style similar to that of John Lee "Sonny Boy" Williamson.

For many years, Warren's friend BOOGIE WOOGIE RED (Vernon Harrison / 1925–1985), a former piano player for John Lee Hooker, was one of only a few musicians devoted to the piano tradition of Detroit.

The city harbored other talented bluesmen: harmonica players Sam Kelly, Robert Richard, and Walter Mitchell; guitar players Calvin Frazier (a cousin of Robert Johnson★), L. C. Green, and Henry Smith; the curious Washboard Willie; and piano player Detroit Count. These names appear on some excellent anthologies: *Detroit Blues* (Blues Classics), *Detroit Ghetto Blues* (Nighthawk), and *Blues for Big Town* (Chess). Recently, guitar player Robert Noll produced the interesting album *Detroit Blues Factory* (Blues Factory), which featured veterans like Eddie Burns, guitar player Willie D. Warren, and a few new names (e.g., Harmonica Shaw, the Butler Twins, and Yard Dog Jones) who provide surprising durability to the Detroit blues.

DETROIT JUNIOR

(Emery Williams, Jr. / b. 1931 / vocals, piano)

Because of the ever-decreasing number of active blues piano players in Chicago, several old hands resurfaced at the end of the seventies: Pinetop Perkins,★ Lovie Lee, and Detroit Junior in particular.

From Arkansas to Detroit—a short stay that gave him his name—then to Chicago, the itinerary of Emery Williams, Jr., is not very different from most bluesmen of his generation.

The years as an apprentice spent in the southern juke-joints influenced his piano style which is powerful and straight, without subtleties, as well as his voice: His laconic tone enhances the grating humor of most of his compositions.

Taken under the wing of Eddie Boyd★ as soon as he arrived in Chicago in the fifties, Detroit Junior rapidly came to spend all his time in the Chicago clubs. He belonged to the bands of Morris Pejoe and Lefty Dizz before he teamed with harmonica player Little Mack Simmons and recorded on the Bea & Baby label for the producer Cadillac Baby. The very funny "Money Tree," recorded in 1960, was a local hit (and remains a Chicago blues classic); it enabled Detroit Junior to create his own band. He then recorded a series of albums, mostly in the same humorous style, for several labels (e.g., Chess, CJ, and Palos) before he made his biggest hit in 1965, the hilarious "Call My Job." But the Chicago blues scene was in crisis in those years, and only the big names managed to survive professionally. Detroit Junior is not one of the survivors; he resumed his role as a piano player for several bands, in particular that of Howlin' Wolf.★ The blues revival touched him only lightly, despite an excellent album in 1971, *Chicago Urban Blues* (Antilles), produced by Al Smith, on which Detroit Junior was in a great shape, accompanied by the subtle Mighty Joe Young.★ In 1980 Detroit Junior recorded new songs as the featured player: His eloquence is intact on four excellent songs that he sang on the anthology *Living Chicago Blues, Vol. 6* (Alligator). Since then, he has continued to scour the clubs of Chicago, often with the singer-guitar player L. C. Roby. It is surprising that Detroit Junior, an original talent, one of the last active piano players in Chicago and an excellent showman, is no longer present on the national and international blues scene and that he no longer records.

BO DIDDLEY

(Othas Ellas Bates or Ellas McDaniel / b. 1928 / vocals, guitar)
Considered a "pioneer of rock-and-roll," Bo Diddley was quite obviously inspired by the blues. Born in Mississippi, he

■ Bo Diddley. *(Courtesy of Archives and Special Collections, John Davis Williams Library, University of Mississippi)*

did not develop his original style in Chicago until after 1950. That style is a mixture of the Chicago blues, the zest of Louis Jordan,* singing influenced by gospel, and an African-Cuban rhythm section. He performed in the streets of Chicago with a small band, in which harmonica player Billy Boy Arnold*—who may have played a major role in the making of the Bo Diddley sound—and percussionist Jerome Green distinguished themselves. He convinced the Chess* brothers to record him in 1955; his first record was an instant hit. The release of *Bo Diddley* gave him his stage name and would be covered by several rock groups, particularly British ones; the declamatory "I'm a Man" gave rise to a whole new current in the Chicago blues, that even reached Muddy Waters,* who included this title (under the name of "Mannish Boy") in his repertoire. Most of his titles recorded for Chess between 1955 and 1960 were excellent and truly eloquent, marked with humor and verve. Bo Diddley's music is still appreciated by rock-and-roll fans who are nostalgic for the "golden age of rock"; nevertheless, it seems to have lost many of its essential qualities, even though his stage shows remain interesting. It is necessary to stress that the sound, totally innovative, created by Bo Diddley and Billy Boy Arnold—a kind of new blues of Chicago's South Side—was not popular among blacks and did not give rise to any musical trend. On the other hand, this surprising style *did* influence the English bands of the early sixties (the Rolling Stones, the Animals, and even the Beatles) and, through them, a considerable part of present-day rock.

In retrospect, the Bo Diddley sound seems to have been a precursor of the reggae. Several Chess collections have the best sides recorded by Bo in the years 1955–65.

FLOYD DIXON

See California

WILLIE DIXON

(1915–1992 / vocals, bass, guitar)
"I am the blues," claimed Willie Dixon in one of his most famous titles. And this peremptory statement summarizes the reality—if we add ". . . in Chicago."

This professional boxer, who switched to music in 1940,

played the double bass and sang with his deep voice for the group The Five Breezes, performing in the clubs of Chicago. This jazzy and cool music, suited to early evening dances, was a real success at that time among rich blacks. Encouraged by that experience, Dixon and piano players Gene Gilmore and Leonard Caston created the Big Three Trio, recording a mixture of jazz/pop/blues for Columbia in 1947.

But Willie Dixon's exceptional musical flair was already apparent: In 1950, he understood that the arrival en masse of black immigrants from the Deep South did much to change public taste. He met the Chess* brothers in 1951 and produced for them the wonderful pieces of Robert Nighthawk,* proving his extraordinary ability to adapt himself and his great talents as an arranger-composer. From 1954 on, he became one of the house producers at Chess, producing and arranging dozens of recording sessions in which he usually played bass: Muddy Waters,* Howlin' Wolf,* Sonny Boy Williamson (Rice Miller),* Little Walter,* Chuck Berry,* Buddy Guy,* Otis Rush,* and others benefited from his advice and his presence. Because he had a hand in several small companies, he was omnipresent on the Chicago blues scene from 1955 to 1965, nearly replacing the departed Lester Melrose.* He played a major role in the making of the West Side sound, assisting Eli Toscano and Shakey Jake* for the Cobra label and producing many of the records of Otis Rush.*

Although he was sometimes criticized for his melodramatic lyrics, and a tendency toward the emphatic homily, Willie Dixon was a clever composer, able, with unique arrangements, to transform an indistinct blues into a tune impossible to forget ("My Babe" by Little Walter and "Row Your Boat" by Charles Clark). The theatrical effects of Howlin' Wolf ("Goin' Down Slow") and Otis Rush ("I Can't Quit You Baby") became big hits. Nobody can deny Dixon's talents as a witty and inventive lyric writer. The list of his successes is impressive: "I Just Want to Make Love to You," "I'm Ready," and "The Same Thing" (for Muddy Waters); "Close to You" (for Sonny Boy Williamson); "300 Pounds of Heavenly Joy," "Hidden Charms," "I Ain't Superstitious," and "Backdoor Man" (for Howlin' Wolf); "Wang Dang Doodle" (for Koko

Taylor); and "The Red Rooster," "The Seventh Son," and "Flaming Mamie."

Although his deep voice may have been effective, he recorded relatively little under his own name: "Walkin' the Blues" and "Crazy about My Baby" are his most famous titles. After 1960, anticipating the blues revival, he became Memphis Slim's* partner for a while; they performed folk duos at the Newport Festival, in the white clubs of Greenwich Village in New York, and in Europe. This led him to take part in the first European tours of the American Folk Blues Festival (1962, 1963, and 1964). After 1967, he created a regular band, the Chicago Blues All Stars, whose composition changed drastically throughout the years; nevertheless, it included remarkable musicians: guitar players Johnny Shines,* Lee Jackson, Eddie Campbell,* and Buster Benton*; piano players Lafayette Leake and Sunnyland Slim*; harmonica players Big Walter Horton,* Carey Bell,* Billy Branch, Snooky Pryor,* and Sugar Blue*; his son, bass player Freddie Dixon; and drummer Clifton James. These musicians exhibited great talents as accompanists, and they shared the vocals with their leader, thus creating one of the most homogeneous groups of contemporary blues.

As well as being manager of his band, Dixon was also a producer, composer, and editor. He tried to promote new artists (e.g., Little Wolf and Margie Evans), and he managed his own record company (Yambo).

Regrettably, a great number of the albums Dixon recorded in the seventies with the Chicago Blues All Stars have been withdrawn from catalogs, in particular the superb *Peace* (Yambo), his best LP. Still available are *I Am the Blues* (Columbia), *Willie's Blues* (OBC/Prestige), and his "revivalists" albums *Songs* (Folkways) and *At the Village Gate* (Folkways). His last album, *Hidden Charms* (Capitol), showed that in spite of his age, Willie Dixon was still a great singer and a smart composer.

His Chess period is particularly well represented by *Willie Dixon* (Chess), and one can listen nostalgically to the *Big Three Trio: I Feel like Steppin' Out* (Dr. Horse).

■ Fats Domino. *(Photograph © by Paul Harris; used with permission)*

FATS DOMINO

(Antoine Domino / b. 1929 / vocals, piano)

This rock-and-roll pioneer is one of many talented blues singers that New Orleans produced. The blues of that city evolved from Dixieland, Creole and Mexican music, music from the Caribbean, and, after the war, the music of the Kansas City swing bands. To the traditional piano were added numerous brass instruments over a Latin rhythm (rhumba, mambo, and cha-cha). This exuberant blues style found its main representative in Fats Domino.

Using his roundness with jollity and raciness, Antoine "Fats" Domino—born in Cajun country and locally claimed with pride—plays a tonic and joyful music, with sometimes an incursion into poignant blues, as shown on his beautiful interpretation of John Lee Hooker's★ "Trouble Blues."

Born and raised in New Orleans, Fats Domino is a singer with a melancholic and chromatic voice and a piano player who mixes the subtlety of Professor Longhair* and the power of Amos Milburn.* With sax player Dave Bartholomew's* small band, Fats Domino recorded under his own name in 1949 "The Fat Man" for the local Imperial label, which was then making its first recording attempts. This warm blues, strongly inspired by Professor Longhair, was, against all expectations, a big hit, quickly selling a million copies. It helped Imperial to prosper and gave Domino his nickname, while at the same time opening the way for a vast number of local singers expressing themselves in a similar style (e.g., Archibald,* Smiley Lewis,* and Fats Matthews). After "The Fat Man," Domino recorded constantly. Until 1955, he produced a stunning series of blues and ballads that made him one of the big names among black Americans: "Don't You Lie to Me," "Hey La-Bas," and "Going Home." At that time most successes by black artists were covered by whites who capitalized on them for the white public, but Fats Domino broke the color barrier and made the hit parades reserved for whites with "Ain't That a Shame," opening the way for the many who were to follow.

Since then, Fats has clung to the fruitful rock-and-roll train; he leads the luxurious life of a superstar, touring incessantly across the United States and appearing on television and in movies. He collected hits such as "Blueberry Hill," "I'm in Love Again," "Blue Monday," and "I'm Ready," but as he increased his audience, his music weakened. Despite a few hits, like the superb ballad "Walking to New Orleans," after 1962 and despite his leaving Imperial, he seldom regained the fire of his early years. With the vogue of rock-and-roll diminishing, he started a new career in the tradition of the crooners, such as Dean Martin and Frank Sinatra. Except for a few entries in the hit parades (as with his version of "Lady Madonna" by the Beatles), he never entirely regained the popular success he had in the fifties. Today he performs mostly for a nostalgic public.

His most creative work (1949–63) is regularly reissued under different presentations, creating a discographic maze difficult to disentangle.

K. C. DOUGLAS

(1913–1975 / vocals, guitar)

K. C. Douglas was the only bluesman of the West Coast who came from Mississippi and who maintained and developed in California the Delta style he faithfully represented.

Indeed, he was well acquainted with Tommy Johnson,* one of the big creators of the Delta blues, who taught him a great deal before he left during the war for the shipyards of Vallejo in California. Accompanied by the harmonica player Sidney Maiden, Douglas created a small band successful enough to attract the attention of producer Bob Geddins for whom he recorded "Mercury Boogie" in 1948. It was one of the first blues with a truly rural style cut in California.

In 1955, then in 1960, noticed by folk singer Barbara Dane, Douglas recorded a total of three good albums directed to the new blues-revival public. The authenticity of his performances was largely appreciated (*Big Road Blues:* Ace).

From the sixties on, his audience increased considerably. Douglas, along with his new partner, harmonica player Richard Riggins, became a popular figure in numerous blues concerts and festivals in the San Francisco area. After a brilliant 45 for the Galaxy label, he cut a superb album, *Country Boy* (Arhoolie), on which the young slide guitarist Ron Thompson is outstanding. "My Mind's Going Back in 1929" is probably the best recording made by K. C. Douglas.

DRUMS

As with the bass, the drums asserted themselves in the blues only after the end of the thirties and especially after the war when the black population, attracted en masse to northern cities by the paying jobs of a war or reconstruction industry in full gear, wanted an electric music with strong tempos that reflected the new day-to-day life. The drums then became an essential element of the blues band; with the bass, it constituted the rhythmic foundation of the band.

Before, this function was often accomplished by the washboard. In the blues, the solidity of the rhythm is often more important than virtuosity, and rarely are improvisations left to the drummer. The drummers who influenced the blues history are not many, and it is precisely this capacity to assume efficiently a small but essential role that is praised among musicians like Judge Riley, Fred Williams, Bill Stepney, Willie Smith, Odie Payne, and Frank Kirkland. Many jazz drummers flirted for a long time with the blues, thus adding another element to the genre: Panama Francis and Earl Palmer, for instance, often were the determinant between a recording session's failure and success.

However, the greatest creator on this instrument in the blues is unquestionably Fred Below.* It is important also to mention Alvino Bennett, Ray Allison, Dino Alvarez, Casey Jones, Ike Davis, and Joe Hicks.

CHAMPION JACK DUPREE

(1910–1992 / vocals, piano)

Long stays in Europe are usually not very profitable from an artistic viewpoint for bluesmen who, cut off from their roots, end up by repeating themselves constantly. However, although he lived in Europe from 1959 to his death, Jack Dupree was able, on a good day, to switch from the most moving blues to pieces with devastating humor.

Born in New Orleans and raised in the same orphanage as Louis Armstrong, Dupree attempted careers in music and in boxing. As a singer, he was influenced by Leroy Carr*; his piano style, without nuance but strong and precise, evoked the long years he spent playing in barrelhouses, cheap clubs, and hotels, with a rhythmic style borrowed from his childhood friend, Professor Longhair.*

As a boxer he acquired a certain reputation that enabled him to play as far away as Indianapolis (the city of his idol Leroy Carr), where a stronger than usual knockout turned him forever away from this sport. He then devoted himself to music. For a while, he even teamed with Scrapper Blackwell,* guitar player for the late, but still popular, Leroy Carr.

■ Champion Jack Dupree. *(Photograph © by Paul Harris; used with permission)*

In 1940 he was at last noticed by the producers of the Okeh label, who recorded in Chicago more than twenty sides under his name between June 1940 and November 1941. Among these, the somber "Chain Gang Blues," the funny "Cabbage Greens," and the furious "Dupree Shake Dance" are small hits. At the death of his first wife in 1944, Dupree settled in New York where he became a dominant figure of the city's blues scene. He recorded for Harlem labels a vast number of superb songs with some of the best local musicians: Sonny Terry,★ Brownie McGhee,★ Mickey Baker,★ and Larry Dale.★

In 1953, he switched to the King label, for which he also made excellent recordings, again with Mickey Baker as well as harmonica players George Smith★ and Papa Lightfoot. "Walking the Blues," "Stumbling Block," and "Me and My Mule" are commercial successes that led Dupree to sign a contract for RCA. With Larry Dale, Mr. Bear, and Pete Smith, he cut his most beautiful tracks, available today on the excellent album *Shake, Baby, Shake* (Detour).

In the same style, he recorded a wonderful album for Atlantic in 1958. *Blues from the Gutter* was wrapped in an intensely depressive atmosphere, and the ferocious vocals of Dupree are enhanced by the brilliant guitar style of Larry Dale.

At that time Jack chose to expatriate himself definitively, and he successfully undertook a new career in Europe. There, Dupree accumulated several albums, none of which equaled the level of his American performances. Some are nevertheless highly commendable, in particular, those on which he was again with his old accomplice (who still lives in Europe) Mickey Baker: *The Tricks* (Vogue) and *Death of Louis Armstrong* (Vogue).

Besides the Detour collection, his first tracks are today largely reissued: *Blues for Everybody* (King), *Rub a Little Boogie* (Krazy Kat), and *Junker Blues* (Travelin' Man).

Before his death, Dupree recorded two very moving discs for the Bullseye label (*Back Home in New Orleans* and *Forever and Ever*), proving that, to the very end, he was still a champion of the blues.

E

SNOOKS EAGLIN

See New Orleans

EAST COAST BLUES

(also sometimes: Piedmont Blues)

In the southeastern United States, along the Appalachian Mountains (Carolinas, Virginias, Georgia, Kentucky, and part of Tennessee), a relaxed form of the blues developed, favoring instrumental virtuosity rather than depth of feelings, contrary to blues in the Delta or in Texas (with noticeable exceptions, such as Mississippi John Hurt,* who expressed himself in a style similar to that of the East Coast).

Several explanations were given: Racial separation was less strong there than elsewhere, and blacks enjoyed a life relatively easier than that which existed in the strongholds of segregation, which would explain the nonchalance of that music as well as the intermingling of the traditional black and white musical repertoires, forming a common background. The colonization was also much more dense and structured in the coastal Old South than in the Deep South. In any case, the East Coast blues include adaptations of ragtime from the beginning of the century. Ragtime guitar, now widespread (e.g., Stefan Grossman* and Marcel Dadi) was probably born in that region. The great creator of that music was Blind Blake,* who influenced blues history on the East Coast in particular, and the history of the guitar in general. Following him, several musicians recorded in a similar style: Luke Jordan, Sylvester Weaver, Josh White,* Blind Gary Davis,* Curley Weaver, Fred McMullen, Buddy Moss,* and, around Atlanta, Blind Willie McTell,* whose role of regional "leader" was considerable.

But it is really Blind Boy Fuller* who set the rules and the blues repertoire of that region. The tremendous success of his records between 1935 and 1940 encouraged musicians to express themselves in the East Coast style, which still today remains surprisingly alive.

WILLIE TRICE (1910–1977), for example, was strongly inspired by Fuller. He recorded two sides in 1937 and played incessantly until his death, perfecting his guitar style and creating many new blues (*Blue and Ragged:* Trix)

PINK ANDERSON (1900–1974) was a regular of the medicine shows. His considerable repertoire was recorded in part on albums: *Carolina Medicine Show* (Folkways) and *Carolina Blues Man* (OBC).

With a similar experience and a fantastic talent as a harmonica player, PEG LEG SAM (Sam Jackson / 1911–1977) continued until his death to perform in concerts and festivals with eloquence and a devastating humor (*Medicine Show Man:* Trix).

Guitar player BILL WILLIAMS (1897–1974) was a fellow traveler of Blind Blake, from whom he borrowed style and repertoire. *Low and Lonesome* (Blue Goose) pays homage to his talent.

FRANK EDWARDS (1909–1990), who plays guitar and harmonica simultaneously, clings less to the East Coast style. In fact, his highly rhythmic music and most of his compositions are unique. He recorded a handful of sides between 1940 and 1949 and an album in 1972: *Done Some Traveling* (Trix).

In a style similar to Josh White's, the superb guitar-mandolin-fiddle player CARL MARTIN (1906–1979) recorded substantially in the thirties before going to Chicago. There, surprisingly enough, he did not embrace the electric blues of that city, preferring to perform his own way for private gatherings. He cut several albums in the seventies, the best of which is *Barnyard Dance* (Rounder).

LARRY JOHNSON (b. 1938), a student of Gary Davis, an excellent guitar player and sometimes a good harmonica player, stubbornly perpetuates the blues tradition of the East Coast in New York City (*Fast and Funky:* Blue Goose).

BABY TATE (1916–1977) underwent the influence of both Blind Boy Fuller and Lightnin' Hopkins.* He was able to mix them both in an original ensemble.

One can also feel this double influence among several guitarists-singers: Carolina Slim, in particular, who remains a mysterious name but who cut more than fifty sides for Savoy and other labels; Henry Johnson; Pernell Charity; Roy Dunn; and Nyles Jones, the creator of an excellent album in the seventies.

Georgia is a somewhat different musical field, although it is included in the East Coast blues movement. It is necessary to mention Willie Guy Rainey, the surprising William Robertson, Guitar Shorty, J. B. Williams, and John Lee Ziegler. On the borders of Alabama, the important names to remember are Dan Pickett, the superb imitator of Tampa Red,* and Albert Macon.

Numerous anthologies exist: before the war, *Atlanta Blues 1933* (JEMF), *The Atlanta Blues* (RBF), *Georgia Blues* (Yazoo), and *East Coast Blues* (Yazoo); and after the war, *Sugar Mama Blues* (Biograph), *Georgia Blues* (Rounder), and *Georgia Blues Today* (Flyright).

FRANK EDWARDS

See East Coast Blues

HONEYBOY EDWARDS

(David Edwards / b. 1915 / vocals, guitar, harmonica)

Although he is one of the rare authentic Delta bluesmen still active, Honeyboy Edwards never received the attention that others, less interesting, obtained. Naturally shy and reserved, he has lived in Chicago since 1954 without really modernizing his style.

Honeyboy Edwards was born in the middle of the Delta (in Itta Bena, Mississippi); he traveled with the great Robert Johnson* and Big Joe Williams,* and his style is a compromise between those of both these great figures. Moreover, he played with all the big names of the Delta blues: Charlie Patton,* Son House,* Tommy McClennan,* Tommy Johnson,* and Robert Petway.* Honeyboy probably would have been recognized as an important figure of this musical current, if fate had not decided otherwise.

■ Honeyboy Edwards. *(Photograph © by Mauro Presini. Courtesy of Mauro Presini and Archives and Special Collections, John Davis Williams Library, University of Mississippi)*

In 1941, he was at Stovall's plantation when Alan Lomax, who was looking for a successor to Robert Johnson, had just recorded Muddy Waters★ for the Library of Congress. Honeyboy too was interviewed for a long time and recorded, but some technical flaws make these beautiful tapes only an exciting document. All the commercial pieces that could be exploited are gathered on the superb *Walking Blues* (Flyright). Honeyboy then went off to Texas where he recorded a wonderful disc for an obscure local label (*Juke Joint Blues:* Blues Classics), then he went to Memphis where he recorded two titles, one of which is a powerful electric version of "Sweet Home Chicago" for the Sun label of Sam Phillips.★ These tracks remained unedited for more than twenty years, and even then they were absurdly attributed to piano player Albert Williams!

Honeyboy's bad luck continued when he went to Chicago. His vehement singing and his electrified bottleneck attracted the attention of Len Chess,★ who recorded him but decided, so as not to compete with his star Muddy Waters, not to promote these titles (*Drop Down Mama:* Chess). And again, Edwards was with Fred Below★ and the Myers brothers when they formed the Aces, but he left them right before they recorded. He was there, in 1963, at the beginning of the blues revival, and he took part in many recording sessions which, again, remained unedited. He was also in the Chess studios in 1969 with Fleetwood Mac, Big Walter Horton,★ Willie Dixon,★ and Otis Spann,★ but a sound engineer accidentally erased the two titles on which Honeyboy was the featured singer!

Finally, the same year, he succeeded in cutting four titles on the anthology *Really's Chicago Blues* (Adelphi), and his remarkable contribution drew the attention of the fans. In the mid-seventies he recorded at last a few albums, entirely acoustic, on which he showed his authenticity and the depth of his roots. On *Mississippi Delta Bluesman* (Folkways) and especially *I've Been Around* (Trix), Honeyboy was accompanied by Big Walter Horton and guitar player Eddie Ell. But Honeyboy, who has been playing for thirty years in several electric bands in the style of the early postwar years of the Chicago blues, recorded very little in that context (a few titles on *Old Friends:* Earwig).

QUEEN SYLVIA EMBRY

(b. 1941 / vocals, bass)

Many female singers gave up the blues—or the blues did not want them—but after the Second World War there was a comeback of female blues voices. Queen Sylvia is one of the most interesting of these blueswomen: She is creative, composing many of her own blues, self-willed, and an excellent bass player. At first she was a singer with a somewhat limited but powerful voice, obviously influenced by gospel with some strange inflections, trailing off, even dying, similar to Lucille Spann, another excellent singer who unsuccessfully tried to make a blues career in the seventies.

Going from Arkansas to Chicago through Memphis, from

the local church choir to teen idols like Chuck Berry* and Lloyd Price,* Sylvia Embry might not have been a professional musician if she had not met Johnny Embry, an outstanding guitar player in the style of Buddy Guy* (although unfortunately Johnny Embry is seldom recognized). Johnny took Sylvia for his wife and also for a singer and bass player in the combo he led. At the end of the seventies Sylvia performed in the clubs of Chicago's West Side, and she recorded with Johnny the excellent *After Work* (Razor), drawing the critics' attention.

Separated from Johnny Embry—in life and on stage—she played bass with guitar player Lefty Dizz before she created her own group, with which she regularly played in Chicago. She recorded four pieces that are on the anthology *Living Chicago Blues, Vol. 6* (Alligator), which shows her range. She started to enjoy a certain international fame when she suddenly decided to give up music. Let's hope that her decision is not forever.

SLEEPY JOHN ESTES

(John Adam Estes / 1904–1977 / vocals, guitar)

"Sleepy" John Estes was one of the first prewar musicians to acquire considerable fame among blues fans. The fifty titles or so that he recorded between 1929 and 1941 had an impressive quality: John Estes's dying voice expressed in short bursts of incredibly evocative lines, accompanied with a counterpoint on the harmonica or the mandolin that reinforced the plaintive side of the piece. This primitive music, with a regular rhythm and extremely personal, has a rare emotional power. As many critics have said, Sleepy John Estes does not sing the blues, he "cries" it. Because of these qualities, his success was considerable. Estes toured incessantly around Memphis, in the North, and in Chicago, where he was still popular after the war. In 1948 he returned to Memphis, long enough to record a few sides for Sun, the new label of Sam Phillips.* Most of his compositions are original pieces and "Diving Duck Blues," "Milk Cow Blues," "Someday Baby," and "Drop Down

■ Sleepy John Estes. *(Photograph © by Anton J. Mikofsky; used with permission)*

Mama," among the most famous ones, have become classics; they resisted time through adaptations by Kokomo Arnold,★ Walter Davis,★ Big Maceo,★ Muddy Waters,★ B. B. King,★ and Taj Mahal.★ Some of these are on the album *Down South Blues* (MCA).

Moreover, Estes was the creator of a regional style that developed around him and around Brownsville, where he lived, near Memphis.

Among his main followers, it is important to mention HAMMIE NIXON, an original and inventive harmonica player; the singers and guitar players HAMBONE WILLIE NEWBERN, creator of the famous "Rollin' and Tumblin," and

SON BONDS, who recorded fifteen titles on Decca and Bluebird in a style similar to Estes before he was murdered in front of his home; and finally the mandolin player Yank Rachell.*

Another of Estes's "satellites," CHARLIE PICKETT, recorded only four titles. "Down the Highway" was one of the most beautiful successes of the thirties.

Sleepy John Estes also influenced one of his neighbors, the young John Lee Williamson (the future "Sonny Boy"*), who, with his cousin James Williamson (who later became "Homesick" James*), accompanied him in his peregrinations. A great part of the vocal manners that gained Sonny Boy success came directly from the way that Sleepy sang. His love for the harmonica was inspired by Hammie Nixon, who introduced him to that instrument. Indirectly through Sonny Boy, Sleepy John Estes's influence on the postwar Chicago blues was substantial.

In 1957, when asked about Sleepy John Estes, Big Bill Broonzy* said he had seen him in his childhood sing in the camps for the railway workers. He thought he was twenty years older than he himself was, and he believed he was dead. The surprise of blues fans was total when John Estes was rediscovered in 1961, at only fifty-eight! Blind, he was then living in utter misery. Producer Bob Koester quickly introduced him at several concerts and festivals (Newport, in particular), and he went on two tours in Europe with the American Folk Blues Festival. From the many albums recorded by John Estes after his "rediscovery," his first, *The Legend of Sleepy John Estes* (Delmark), is the best, with an especially moving composition on his recent misery: "Rats in My Kitchen." *Broke & Hungry* (Delmark) and *Brownsville Blues* (Delmark) also have good moments but, on the recent records, Estes sounded tired, without that vocal power and constant creativity that were part of his style.

Despite these last efforts and because of his originality, his invention, his poetic flair, and the influence he had on a great number of musicians, Sleepy John Estes is one of the most important artists in blues history.

MARGIE EVANS

See Soul

■
F

FEMALE BLUES SINGERS

A long time before the earliest bluesmen—Blind Lemon Jefferson,★ Blind Blake,★ and Lonnie Johnson,★ for example—first set foot in recording studios, a vast number of female blues singers were already tremendously successful among the black public. Between 1920 and 1930, the vocal blues was considered to be an essentially feminine art, and from Bessie Smith★ to Ma Rainey★ the blues had its "Empress" and its "Mother" without mentioning the "Queens" and "Princesses!"

Although these singers came from different regions and social contexts, they all had in common the fact that they came from vaudeville tours, those itinerant shows of the beginning of the century that offered small theatrical plays, circus numbers, comic skits, and songs. The parts that were sung were composed of music-hall pieces of the time, and, in the evening, they were blues pieces that made the listeners cry. These tours were often the only entertainment for months for the small towns that they visited. Consequently, their popularity there was exceptional.

Thus, these female singers who had generally lived their childhood in a rural blues environment adapted to the music-hall habits of the time: clear diction, sophisticated vocal effects, even cries and loud moaning between the choruses. The accompaniments for the singing came from jazz that was essential to the popular musical background of the times. Besides, with the exception of Ma Rainey, these singers did not see themselves as blues specialists, and their repertoire included all the music-hall themes. Finally, they were professional performers, often acting in plays on the Chicago or New York stages, or in the studios of Hollywood.

■ Alberta Hunter. *(Photograph © by Anton J. Mikofsky; used with permission)*

The lives of these singers could, during their brief successful years, be compared to those of the white stars of the silent
movies and of the white singers: a luxurious lifestyle, a tumultuous love life, and, in general, a miserable end to those who
were lucky for a while but who did not know how to keep their
good fortune.

Except for the use of the twelve blues bars, these "classic"
singers had little in common with their male counterparts who
would follow them—the music having by then a real social and

■ Anton Mikofsky, Sarah Dash, Little Brother Montgomery, Barbara Dane, and Edith Wilson. *(Photograph © by Anton J. Mikofsky; used with permission)*

psychological function—and whose creations were going to defy time; today they enjoy international recognition.

The identification of these female singers with the turn-of-the-century music-hall world is the reason for their neglect in blues history. Moreover, the poor quality of the recordings (often made before the invention of electric recording) does not favor an objective appreciation. However, the historic importance of these singers is undeniable, for they created a series of records for the black clientele that included many masterpieces. Without them we would have had to wait much longer for the blues to be recorded and for great successes of that art to have been kept on records. Besides the great Bessie Smith and Ma Rainey and the superb Victoria Spivey,★ some others—not as well represented on records—deserve more attention than they have been given.

MAMIE SMITH (1883–1946) is the singer who cut the first blues in recording history: "Crazy Blues" in 1920. Very popular in Harlem as early as 1914, she was taken under the wing of composer and conductor Perry Bradford, who, after many difficulties, convinced the record company Okeh to record Mamie. "Crazy Blues" was obviously the answer to the request of the black public, since Okeh sold seventy-five thousand records the first month they were issued! Mamie then began a fruitful career: She had cut about a hundred records by 1931. She was the target of gossip columns regarding her love affairs with big jazz names. She also had parts in a series of musical films at the beginning of the talkies, but she died in misery, forgotten by the public. Despite some strong vocal affectations, she interpreted several beautiful blues.

LUCILLE HEGAMIN (1897–1970), the *Supreme,* recorded her first hits in 1920. She was already appreciated in Chicago, Los Angeles, and New York, where her talents as a singer, a comedienne, and a dancer had made her popular. Thus it was natural that several record companies competed to record her. Her recordings often showed the strong influence of years of vaudeville and cabaret. They seemed outdated, but she cut several excellent pieces, among them the famous "Aggravatin' Papa" and "Downhearted Blues," and her greatest hit, the very funny "He May Be Your Man but He Comes to See Me Sometimes."

EDITH WILSON (1906–1981) lived for music. A powerful and expressive singer, her repertoire always favored jazz; nevertheless, she cut several very good blues, in the same ironic vein, with excellent jazzmen like Fats Waller and Louis Armstrong. After the commercial decline of "classical blues," she undertook a career as a comedienne in films, then on radio and TV. She recorded an excellent album with Little Brother Montgomery★ and the subtle guitar player Ikey Robinson: *He May Be Your Man* (Delmark).

The soft voice of ROSA HENDERSON (1898–1968) gained her tremendous success between 1923 and 1931, when she recorded for a great number of labels. Despite the excellence of some of her work ("Penitentiary Bound Blues"), it was in general typical of the shortcomings of vaudeville; her singing seemed very affected, in addition to the multiple sound effects of her accompanists.

IDA COX (1889–1967), the "Queen without a Crown" was often introduced as the equal of Bessie Smith or Ma Rainey. In fact, her compositions were extremely personal ("Coffin Blues" and "Moanin' the Blues"). Her exceptional flair when she surrounded herself with remarkable jazz musicians placed her above most other singers. T-Bone Walker* and Victoria Spivey* acknowledged her influence on their music. Her unusually long record career lasted from 1923 to 1940 and was renewed in 1961. From her first recordings that belonged entirely to vaudeville to the gloomy and moving "Last Mile Blues," cut in 1940, Ida Cox followed the evolution of the different currents that pervaded black music, while at the same time maintaining her own style.

CLARA SMITH (1895–1935) was, in her lifetime, a major rival of Bessie Smith, with whom she recorded several vocal duets. Her moving voice and her melancholic themes made her a more authentic blues singer than most of her rivals. "Salty Dog," "I've Got Everything a Good Woman Needs," and "Mean Papa Turn Your Key" are excellent blues pieces. She was often accompanied by talented guitarists, such as the brilliant Lonnie Johnson.*

SIPPIE WALLACE (1899–1986) performed continuously in blues and jazz festivals until her death. She directly influenced rock singers like Bonnie Raitt. She too stemmed from the vaudeville circuit, and she was able to produce several superb blues, among which was the classic "Suitcase Blues." With Bonnie Raitt she recorded the excellent album *Sippie Wallace* (Atlantic) in 1983.

ALBERTA HUNTER (1895–1984) had an extraordinary career as a singer for nearly seventy years. With vaudeville, jazz, and blues, Alberta easily played all sorts of roles, from the provocative pin-up of the twenties to the good old grandma wisely advising the youth of the whole world, who religiously came to hear that "living legend." Her best tracks from before the war are on the album *Young Alberta* (Jass), but the excellent *Amtrak* (Columbia) was cut half a century later.

Other singers also deserve mention: Bertha "Chippie" Hill, who recorded the first version of "Trouble in Mind," accompanied on piano by Richard M. Jones, the composer of that famous theme; Trixie Smith, who with Louis Armstrong and Sidney Bechet, cut the fiery "The World's Crazy" and the gloomy "My Daddy Rocks Me with a Long Steady Roll"; the gorgeous Viola McCoy, Maggie Jones, Martha Copeland, Sara Martin, Bessie Tucker, and more.

This style so popular at the beginning of the blues disappeared little by little. Nevertheless, it influenced the jazz and blues singers of the thirties and forties, among which were of course the famous Lil Green★ and Billie Holiday.

Today, some singers still sing in a similar style, for example, Jeanne Carroll, Jeanne Chatham, and Olive Brown.

LINDA HOPKINS (b. 1925) was a comedienne, a piano player, and a gospel and jazz singer. As she grew older, she became more and more involved in the preservation of the female blues singers' tradition, as can be heard in her beautiful interpretation of Bessie Smith in the piece "Me and Bessie." Her album *How Blues Can You Get* is recommended, but we would like to see the dynamism she has on stage and on the screen (in *Honky Tonk Man*) on record.

It is a must to listen to *Wild Women Don't Have the Blues* (Rosetta), *When Women Sang the Blues* (Blues Classics), *Mean Mothers* (Rosetta), *Women's Railroad Blues* (Rosetta), *Red, White, and Blues* (Rosetta), *Big Mamas* (Rosetta), *Super Sisters* (Rosetta), *Sweet Petunias* (Rosetta), and *Street Talking Blues* (Stash).

H-BOMB FERGUSON

See Blues Shouters

FIDDLE

The fiddle, a dominant instrument of the rural string bands of the beginning of the century, has retained its importance in white traditional music (bluegrass and country and western) but has almost completely disappeared from the blues.

However, the adaptable use and the flexibility of its strings favorable to the blue notes could have made it an important instrument of the blues. It seems that in the twenties it was in competition with the harmonica, which has a similar musical register and which is easier to handle, cheaper, and more bluesy. As a result, the cohabitation of the fiddle and the harmonica in the blues bands of the twenties did not last long, and the harmonica quickly became the essential blues instrument. Several excellent black fiddle players (e.g., Carl Martin★ and Lonnie Johnson★) abandoned that instrument for the guitar.

In the postwar blues, the only fiddle players still sporadically active came mainly from Texas, the western-swing state dominated by the white fiddle player Bob Wills, whose impact among blacks and bluesmen should not be underestimated: L. C. Robinson,★ Gatemouth Brown,★ Papa John Creach, and the eclectic Don Sugarcane Harris.

FIELDSTONES

This Memphis band of five musicians was one of the great discoveries of the early eighties. Singer-guitar player Willie Roy Sanders, guitar player Wordie Perkins, keyboard player Bobby Carnes, bass player Lois Brown, and drummer-singer Joe Hicks—and also sometimes guitar player Clarence Nelson—created the Fieldstones. They were all trained by guitar player Leroy Hodges, father of the Hodges Brothers, pillars of the Memphis sound of the sixties and seventies. In fact, they were all deeply attached to the Memphis blues sound, modernizing it and at the same time perpetuating it. Thus, the guitar duos of Willie Roy Sanders and Wordie Perkins evoked those of the twenties and thirties between Frank Stokes★ and Dan Sane or Memphis Minnie★ and Joe McCoy.★ Both band singers shared the tasks in two different directions: Sanders with his piercing voice was influenced by gospel, and he began to sing soul music; Joe Hicks had a deeper tone of voice, and he was much more attached to the Delta blues of Mississippi, where he came from. Furthermore, Hicks was a remarkable drummer who used polyphonic techniques he learned during his long stay with the fife-and-drum orchestra of Napoleon Strickland, who still plays around Como.

The repertoire of the Fieldstones was thus extremely varied: They could master the latest hit or give an excellent rendition of the classic "Saddle My Pony" by Charlie Patton.* They were formed in the mid-seventies, when the Memphis sound showed the way. Most of the musicians had sporadically taken part in recording sessions, such as Joe Hicks in 1964 with the Binghampton Blues Boys. Regularly playing around West Memphis for an exclusively black public, the Fieldstones were discovered by specialist David Evans, who, living in Memphis since the mid-seventies, progressively played a central role in the reemergence of the Memphis blues. Two good 45s for his High Water label enabled Evans to offer numerous engagements to the Fieldstones, away from the small black clubs, in festivals and concerts. *Fieldstones: Memphis Blues Today* (High Water), issued in 1983 but completed over several years, is an excellent album that shows both the durability of the Memphis blues and the intrinsic qualities of the Fieldstones.

FRANK FROST

(b. 1936 / vocals, harmonica, guitar, organ)

Frank Frost's part in the movie *Crossroads* directed by Walter Hill helped this excellent Delta artist recover from the unjust oblivion he had sunk into.

Near Clarksdale, Frank Frost has been leading one of the best blues bands, the Nighthawks, for almost thirty years. The Nighthawks was Robert Nighthawk's* band; Nighthawk's son, Sam Carr, is the drummer.

Frost is an instrumentalist and a talented singer with a drawling accent, an imitation, more or less, of Jimmy Reed.* But there are more than just traces of Sonny Boy Williamson's (Rice Miller's)* influence in his music. He became part of the blues legend when in 1962 he recorded a superb album for Sam Phillips,* *Hey Bossman* (Charly), one the lastest productions of "down-home blues" directed to the black public. After that album, Frost cut several beautiful sides for Jewel, some of which were reissued on *Ride with Your Daddy Tonight* (Charly). Besides Frost, we can hear the excellent harmonica player Oscar Williams, who succeeded in injecting new life into such hackneyed pieces as "Got My Mojo Working."

Frost had to wait for more than ten years before going back to the studios for *Rockin' the Juke Joint Down* (Earwig) and *The Oil Man* (Earwig). On this album, eclectic guitar player Big Jack Johnson was at last the featured player. Frost's most recent record, *Midnight Prowler* (Earwig), is also a worthwhile effort.

BLIND BOY FULLER

(1903–1940 / vocals, guitar)

If Blind Blake★ is the historic creator of the East Coast blues, Blind Boy Fuller is the founding father. In fact, his blues identify themselves in the repertoire of local musicians, who even went as far as to take his name.

For a few years (1935–40), he recorded prolifically (about 150 sides), and his records were commercially successful among the black public, who found a representative in this short and puny man with a loud voice and a powerful guitar style (he used a "National," a steel guitar with a strong resonance). Whereas Blind Blake was a very urban and sophisticated musician, who wanted to be cut off from his rural origins, Fuller was a countryman, whose compositions revolved around the daily worries of black tenant farmers and also their bitter confrontation with big cities in the East, like New York. On the instrumental level, Fuller was inspired by the guitar style of his friend Gary Davis,★ although he never had the ease or the invention of his model. Fuller's style emphasized the bass notes and gave his music a rhythmic character, completely absent in Blake or in Davis. On the other hand, his inspirations were seldom adventurous, and Fuller stuck to a few patterns he adapted depending on the circumstances. In fact, Blind Boy Fuller often had talented accompanists on whom he could count to inject his blues with the instrumental eloquence and invention they otherwise lacked: It is this role that guitar players Brownie McGhee★

and Blind Gary Davis, harmonica player Sonny Terry,* and the picturesque washboard player Oh Red/Bull City Red played.

Besides these stylistic considerations, the career and life of Blind Boy Fuller can be quickly summarized: He was an amateur musician working in tobacco factories in the Carolinas when a jealous woman blinded him with a mixture of vitriol and perfume. To live, he depended entirely upon his music; he played at dances and at dinners, along the cities of the "tobacco belt," Winston-Salem, Greensboro, and others. There, the producer J. B. Long noticed him and signed him for the Okeh label. Several years later, at the peak of his popular success, Blind Boy Fuller died of pneumonia. His sudden disappearance left a void that several musicians, inspired by his style, tried to fill: Brownie McGhee (under the name Blind Boy Fuller #2), Willie Trice,* Dipper Boy Council, and Ralph Willis* are among the best-known ones. The best collections of songs by Fuller are *Blind Boy Fuller* (Blues Classics), *Blind Boy Fuller* (Travelin' Man), and also *Truckin' My Blues Away* (Yazoo). *Blind Boy Fuller* (CBS/Sony) is an excellent twenty-track CD.

JESSE FULLER

(1896–1975 / vocals, guitar, harmonica, kazoo)

With his "San Francisco Bay Blues," recorded in 1955 and covered by dozens of folk artists, including Peter, Paul, and Mary, who made a big hit out of it, Jesse Fuller, in his sixties, became an overnight blues-revival star.

Before that, he had done many different jobs, including being an extra in Hollywood (in *The Thief of Bagdad*). He struck up a friendship with Douglas Fairbanks, who got him a concession stand right in front of the studios. However, his taste for travel always brought him back to his favorite activity: playing in the streets where his act as a one-man band and his glibness enabled him to attract the attention and the money of passers-by.

His style announced the birth of the blues, but he was comfortable in all genres of American folk music. An extroverted musician, he based his performance on a rhythmic style that revealed a contagious good humor. Nevertheless, he was able to play superb slow blues, as well as to play guitar in the style of East Coast guitar players.

Several albums from Jesse Fuller are more or less available. Generally, they all are of high quality, but maybe the best one is *Frisco Bound* (Arhoolie), one of his first albums that encompasses all aspects of his great talents.

JOHNNY FULLER

(1929–1985 / vocals, guitar)

Although he came from Mississippi, Johnny Fuller seems not to have been significantly influenced in music before he went to California in 1945. The nearly twenty blues records he cut for producer Bob Geddins in 1954 are classics of the California-Texas blues: very low electric guitar, faint voice similar to that of Charles Brown,* and revealing or bitter lyrics, in the real tradition of that region. The superb "Back Home"; the subtle "Buddy" with its nice fall away at the end, worthy of a good poet; the enraged "Train, Train Blues"; and "First Stage of the Blues" are only the first brilliant peaks of a promising career.

At that time Fuller's talents were often focused on genres other than the blues: gospel, rhythm and blues, rock-and-roll, and country. He thus obtained an honorable place on the charts with "Haunted House." Despite this eclectism, he was not able to keep his black audience, and because of that he was neglected by blues-revival fans. From 1960 on, he progressively disappeared from the recording studios as well as from important local or national contracts.

He worked in a garage until the end of his life, although the excellent *Fuller's Blues* (Diving Duck) recorded with Phillip Walker* clearly showed the years had not erased the quality of his music.

Although his best records are no longer available, a selection of his titles from the fifties is available on the compilation *Fool's Paradise* (Diving Duck).

■ Lowell Fulson. *(Photograph © by Paul Harris; used with permission)*

LOWELL FULSON

(sometimes known as Lowell Fulsom / b. 1921 / vocals, guitar)

Born on an Indian reservation in Oklahoma, Lowell Fulson soon became established in Texas where he came into contact with the rich blues tradition of that region. Blind Lemon Jefferson,★ Lonnie Johnson,★ and Little Hat Jones were his youth idols; he fashioned his guitar style after them. By 1940 he was talented enough to replace guitar player Funny Papa Smith★ as sideman to traveling singer Texas Alexander.★

As did many of his compatriots, during the war he moved to California, where he became a professional musician. His voice—veiled, nonchalant, and very expressive—as well as his guitar style, influenced by Lonnie Johnson, quickly made him popular in the clubs of the San Francisco Bay area. Along with T-Bone Walker,★ he is the creator of modern California blues. He is still close to his rural roots, although he borrows many inflections from jazz and the ballad.

This variety of influences is well represented in the recorded works of Fulson. As early as 1946 he began an uninterrupted discographic career for several small California companies. His early records were in the popular jazz-blues style of the region. But in the face of a tremendous commercial success of some Texas singers, much more primitive, such as Lightnin' Hopkins* and Smokey Hogg,* he was able to record in 1949 a series of titles in the same style as theirs. Accompanied only by his guitar and that of his brother Martin, Lowell Fulson recorded some of the most beautiful postwar rural blues. A deep and moving voice and a nostalgic sadness, with the flawless rhythm of Martin Fulson and the staccato notes of Lowell, create an impressive blues atmosphere (*Lowell Fulson:* Arhoolie).

The following year he began working with the great piano player Lloyd Glenn,* with whom he recorded "Everyday I Have the Blues," "Blues Shadows," and "Low Society Blues," all national successes.

In 1954 he signed a contract with the Chess brothers. They worked together ten years, profitting on all levels, commercial and artistic. Fulson was then head of a rhythm-and-blues band of rare homogeneity, characteristic of the West Coast swing-blues. Besides Glenn, there were the saxophone players Eddie Chamblee and Earl Brown and the perfect bass player Billy Hadnott. Fulson was performing at his peak, and the songs he recorded were then among the best of the postwar blues: "Reconsider Baby," a great modern blues classic; the gloomy "Tollin' Bells"; "That's All Right"; "I Want to Know"; and "Hung Down Head."

In 1964 Fulson changed to the Kent recording company. He had two national hits: "Tramp," covered by Otis Redding, and the classic "Black Nights." In spite of some heavy-handed orchestral arrangements, the quality of the titles recorded by Fulson during that time remains significant, as shown in the collection *Blue Days, Black Nights* (Kent). The first sides recorded by Lowell have been largely reissued on *Lowell Fulson* (Blues Boy), *Lowell Fulson* (Chess), *Hung Down Head* (Chess), and *The Blues Got Me Down* (Diving Duck).

After 1970 Fulson's success among black Americans weakened, and he tried to attract the attention of the increasing number of white blues fans whom his jazzy style had put off. The results were moderate, although his records for Jewel were not insignificant (*Man of Motion:* Charly).

Roaming from small recording companies to festivals, Lowell Fulson went through hard times. However, he eventually came to the front of the blues scene again: In 1978, his album *Lovemaker* (Big Town) had an astonishing version of "My Mind Is Trying to Leave Me Too" written by Percy Mayfield★; and his appearance at the San Francisco Blues Festival was noticed. Finally, in 1988, excellently produced by Ron Levy's team, Fulson recorded one of the best albums of the eighties: *It's a Good Day* (Rounder). He thus showed that he is still a major artist of contemporary blues. Nevertheless, his past works already guarantee him his place in blues history.

■

G

BOB GADDY

See New York

ROY GAINES

See Joe Hughes

LITTLE BILL GAITHER

(b. 1905–? / vocals, guitar)

In the thirties and forties record companies recorded imitators of the big bluesmen in order to capitalize on their names: Robert Lee McCoy,★ an accompanist for Peetie Wheatstraw,★ recorded under the stage name Peetie's Boy; Sunnyland Slim★ used the name "Doctor Clayton's Buddy"; and Bumble Bee Slim★ kept his own name, although his music was extremely close to that of Leroy Carr.* As for Little Bill Gaither, he specialized as an imitator. He began his career in 1935 when he recreated with the excellent piano player Honey Hill the duo Leroy Carr–Scrapper Blackwell* under the name "Leroy's Buddy"; he then went on to imitate almost perfectly Lonnie Johnson,* Johnny Temple,* Big Bill Broonzy,* Joe Pullum, and finally Big Maceo* (the brilliant piano player Joshua Altheimer had the difficult instrumental role of Maceo).

This formula was certainly profitable to Gaither, for in six years he cut 118 records for Decca and Okeh. On the artistic level, an imitation (as perfect as it can be) cannot, of course, be compared to an original creation. Moreover, it is important to underline that the imitations were of the style and seldom of the songs. In most instances Gaither proved to be an excellent composer, as shown in the poignant "Pains in My Heart" or the evocative "Rocky Mountain Blues" that Lightnin' Hopkins* incorporated into his repertoire. Little Bill Gaither's records display his musical character, but during his whole career he stuck to his formula of a perfect "copier," just as a talented painter might prefer for financial reasons to reproduce the work of a master rather than create his own.

CECIL GANT

(1915–1951 / vocals, piano)

Although Cecil Gant has been nearly forgotten, between 1945 and 1951 he was one of the most popular artists of the West Coast, and his first huge success "I Wonder" opened the commercial way for the sophisticated blues ballad identified with the California style.

Whereas most black artists of that region came from Texas, Gant was born in Nashville, Tennessee. He went to the West Coast only because he was mobilized to Los Angeles during the war. An excellent piano player, he was first influenced by the great musicians of boogie-woogie (Albert Ammons* and Meade Lux Lewis,* especially) from whom he got the prodigious swing of the left hand and the economy of manner in his right hand. While in the army, he was influenced by the jazz singer and piano player Nat King Cole, then very popular in California.

He performed regularly in the army and in Los Angeles nightclubs. His increasing success enabled him to record as early as 1944 for the small company Gilt Edge under the humorous name of Cecil Gant, "The G.I. Sing-Station!" After the success of "I Wonder," he did not stop recording until his death. In Los Angeles and then in New York and New Orleans, he cut more than 150 titles without losing the support of his black audience. The formula for his success was simple: He coupled a furious boogie-woogie with a sentimental and witty ballad, which created a varied record. A great performer who wanted only to entertain, Cecil Gant was also able to compose beautiful slow blues for which his harsh voice was perfect, much better than for his ballads that lacked the suggestive force of a Nat King Cole or of a Charles Brown.*

Rock the Boogie (Krazy Kat) is the best existing collection of blues and boogies recorded by Gant.

CLARENCE GARLOW

See J. D. Miller

PAUL GAYTEN

See New Orleans

CLIFFORD GIBSON

See St. Louis

LACY GIBSON

(b. 1936 / vocals, guitar)

Lacy Gibson developed a reputation in Chicago, moving around from club to club and from band to band. Finally, in the eighties, he emerged on the national scene. Born in South Carolina, Lacy learned to play the guitar at an early age. As a child he was strongly influenced by gospel and by country music. These influences were always present in his music. He moved to Chicago in 1949 and became acquainted with jazz and blues, with a definite preference for the subtleties of T-Bone Walker* and Kenny Burrell. The regular company of the Chicago guitar players, such as M. T. Murphy, Lefty Bates, and Wayne Bennett, enriched him. Thanks to them he became a complete and eclectic guitar player. Eventually, he developed a large and varied repertoire after long stays with numerous bands, many recording sessions, and performances in Chicago nightclubs. He recorded a few titles for Chess; then, for his brother-in-law, Sun Ra, he recorded two interesting 45s as well as an appalling failure, which is better forgotten.

During the seventies Lacy, who had always been more a guitar technician than a true bluesman, drifted further from the blues until a succession of fortunate events brought him back to Son Seals'* band. He went on several tours in the U.S. and in Europe, opening the show with a few hits. His warm baritone and slightly husky voice, influenced by that of Little Milton,* along with his instrumental virtuosity and his professionalism, made Lacy Gibson the surprise hit of these concerts. He participated then on the anthology *Living Chicago Blues, Vol. 5* (Alligator) in which he confirmed his qualities though without quite living up to his reputation. The album *Switchy Titchy* (Black Magic), recorded in 1983, brought due recognition to his talents. His ease and virtuosity were remarkable on it, going easily from an intense B. B. King* style blues to jazzy instrumentals and even to pieces close to rockabilly, revealing his many sources of inspiration.

JAZZ GILLUM

(William McKinley Gillum / 1904–1964 / vocals, harmonica)

Jazz Gillum was the best representative of the Bluebird beat, that form of blues created by producer Lester Melrose* in Chicago in the thirties that dominated this music for ten years. It was characterized by a polite, detached voice (so as not to reveal the rural origins), a monolithic bass guitar rhythm section, and the intensive use of the piano as lead instrument. For years the fans kept away from that music, which for a long time may have seemed stereotypical, favoring instead other forms of less emotional blues (the Delta blues, in particular). However, the black public of the big cities raved about this style, and Gillum was famous between 1934 and 1947 by dealing in this urban manner with traditional themes ("Outskirts of Town") or personal compositions, some of which became famous, especially the great classic "Key to the Highway." He recorded a total of one hundred tracks for RCA/Victor/Bluebird; after the war they became more and more rhythmical and electrified, trying to sound like the powerful blues of Muddy Waters.* But the task was impossible, and after a few attempts to return to the forefront of the musical scene Jazz Gillum disappeared. There was a brief and unconvincing comeback in 1960–61 for the white public of the blues revival.

It is easy to understand that this passionless singer, a mediocre harmonica player, lacking subtlety in his improvisations, suffered in comparison to his contemporary John Lee "Sonny Boy" Williamson.* However, a better knowledge of the artist is necessary to find his many musical qualities: his compositions are full of that double-meaning wit that is itself the essence of the blues. His accompanists are among the best musicians of the time: in particular, piano players Joshua Altheimer and Blind John Davis and guitar players Big Bill Broonzy* and Willie Lacey. Contrary to the current style, blacks of that time primarily wanted their bluesmen to tell them stories, to move and entertain them, with instrumental brio being largely secondary. Jazz Gillum gave them what they wanted.

A vigorous reedition of the Bluebird records of this artist would be great. In the meantime, the good anthology *Jazz Gillum, 1938–47* (Travelin' Man) will do.

LLOYD GLENN

See California

CAL GREEN

See Joe Hughes

LIL GREEN

(1919–1954 / vocals)

This wonderful singer who was famous for a short time in the early forties is today unjustly forgotten. Although her fame was short, it was nonetheless important. Born in Mississippi, Lil Green moved with her parents to Chicago in 1929. She began her career at a young age, singing in Chicago nightclubs. Her soprano voice lacked some power; however, being acidic, insinuating, and mischievous, it was extremely erotic, probably one of the most sensuous female voices in blues history, and there were many such voices! This, intensified by her extremely attractive figure, brought her attention, and she recorded for producer Lester Melrose★ when she was only eighteen years old. Between 1939 and 1944 she recorded for Bluebird a whole series of records that were almost all commercially successful, making her a favorite of the black public of that time: "My Mellow Man," "What's the Matter with Love?," and "Romance in the Dark" showed her accompanied by Big Bill Broonzy★ at his best. Another special piece, in a minor key, "Why Don't You Do Right?," written by Joe McCoy,★ was incredibly sensuous. A masterpiece that became a classic, it was covered by a great number of male and female singers, such as Peggy Lee, who made it her first success.

Unfortunately, Lil Green did not maintain her popularity with the black audience of the big cities, which, at the end of the war preferred both the electrified rural blues and the powerful rhythm and blues, two genres that Lil Green's sophistication, fragility, and sensitivity obviously could not handle. After a triumph in the Apollo Theater of New York, her career stalled, and after 1944 she tried in vain to become a jazz singer in the manner of Billie Holiday. She recorded in this style for Aladdin in 1949 and for Atlantic in 1951. Then she disappeared from the musical scene. Unable to deal with her failure, she drifted for a few years and then died of pneumonia in 1954.

Really neither a blues singer nor a jazz singer, but rather a pop singer, Lil Green has not been claimed by any group. However, her music remains extremely consistent: light and mischievous and very moving.

Lil Green: Chicago, 1940–47 (Rosetta) is a fine collection, but Lil Green recorded many sides that should be reissued.

STEFAN GROSSMAN

See White Blues

GUITAR

Introduced in the U.S. by Mexican vaqueros working in Texas, the guitar is the blues instrument par excellence. The guitar became popular and cheap right at the time when the first bluesmen were recorded; the increased use of this instrument coincided with the spread of the blues. However, the guitar quickly became essential in blues, contrary to rural white music where the banjo and the fiddle were as important as the guitar. The most primitive black rural musicians (e.g., Gus Cannon* and Papa Charlie Jackson*) also expressed themselves with the banjo, but the guitar's flexibility easily allowed the making of blue notes, the characteristic alterations of the scale that are the true essence of the blues.

The low cost and ease with which it could be used, with a wide range of effects, played an important role in the domination of the guitar among black musicians. The guitar was soon used in different ways, moving farther from the use in classical music, with which the black musicians usually were unfamiliar. This is how they adapted almost simultaneously fingerpicking in which the melody is interwoven among the alternating bass notes (as Blind Blake* and Blind Lemon Jefferson*) as well as flatpicking, a real revolution in the art of the guitar. In blues flatpicking, the musician plays the melody line, note by note, with a pick. This technique, probably invented by Lonnie Johnson,* is used with a backup band. Previously, in this context the guitar was only a rhythm instrument. Johnson removed it from that unrewarding function and transformed it into a solo instrument comparable to the trumpet or the clarinet.

If fingerpicking is the origin of the present "folk" guitar, the flatpicking technique had yet more universal results. Indeed, it found its logical outcome with the electric guitar, which enabled guitar players to express themselves without being concerned with the weak sound of their instruments. The first jazz electric guitar players, Charlie Christian and Floyd Smith, and the first blues electric guitar players, T-Bone Walker* and B. B. King,* were very much inspired by Lonnie Johnson, whose reputation was tremendous before the Second World War. They in turn influenced a great number of guitar players. It is evident that the genius of Lonnie Johnson was the source of the present electric guitar, whether in modern blues, in jazz, or in rock.

BUDDY GUY

(b. 1936 / vocals, guitar)

This native of Louisiana is said to have been influenced by local bluesmen Lightnin' Slim,* Slim Harpo,* and Guitar Slim.* He moved very early to Chicago and quickly assimilated the musical style of the city. He was one of the main artisans with Otis Rush* and Magic Sam* of the West Side sound in the late fifties, which melded the rhythm and tension of the Chicago blues, many elements of gospel, and the guitar style of B. B. King.* King was always the dominant influence, although Guy created his own style.

Buddy Guy's music is one of the most successful in modern blues: a tension caused by an oppressive rhythm section, made still heavier by melodramatic singing, soothed by virtuoso flashes of the guitar solos. Under the rule of producer Eli Toscano, Buddy Guy recorded two remarkable 45s, in 1958 with Ike Turner,* Otis Rush, and Willie Dixon,* although the young Buddy Guy was obviously still looking for his way in life (on *Fishing in My Pond:* Flyright). Thanks to these records, he became the house guitar player for Chess records, sitting in on many recording sessions with Muddy Waters,* Big Walter Horton,* Sonny Boy Williamson (Rice Miller),* and more. At the same time, he recorded under his own name several remarkable 45s between 1960 and 1964, collected on *Buddy Guy on Chess, Vols. 1 & 2* (Chess).

He then joined forces with Junior Wells,* bought a club in Chicago, and went on numerous tours in Africa, Asia, and

■ Buddy Guy. *(Photograph © by Paul Harris; used with permission)*

Europe, especially with the Rolling Stones. The Buddy Guy–Junior Wells' band remained, through inevitable changes, one of the most accomplished bands in Chicago. The music, though, having become somewhat softer, lost part of its dramatic tension. In spite of that, the albums that Buddy Guy recorded between 1964 and 1970, *Man and the Blues* (Vanguard), *This Is Buddy Guy* (Vanguard), and *Hold That Plane* (Vanguard), are among the best ones that Chicago produced during that period. They then put out a good album featuring guitar player Eric Clapton (*Junior Wells and Buddy Guy Play the Blues:* Atlantic). Buddy Guy subsequently went through a decade of doubt, "a living legend" for the blues fans, taking part in festivals and concerts but without any recording contract and without any substantial income. He turned bitter and became disillusioned about his future musical career, knowing that he would never be the star he thought he could be. At the beginning of the eighties Buddy Guy went again to the studios for a series of albums, unfortunately inept, in which he indulged in the worst vocal and instrumental excesses in order to please—so he thought—the rock audience.

Amid this desolation, *Stone Crazy* (Alligator) appears to be a success, but this mediocre album is far from the quality of his previous work. And although Buddy Guy has benefited from the media exposure created by the current blues boom, his *Damn Right I've Got the Blues* (Silvertone), although well crafted, is very rock-oriented.

H

JOHN HAMMOND, JR.

See White Blues

MAJOR HANDY

See Zydeco

W. C. HANDY

(William Christopher Handy / 1873–1958)

This black musician who came from a middle-class family was the creator of the famous "Memphis Blues," "St. Louis Blues," and "Beale Street Blues" and for a long time was considered by some to be the "inventor of the blues." In actuality, as co-owner of a music publishing company in Memphis then in New York at the beginning of the twentieth century, he was the first to come up with the idea to transcribe blues songs and publish them.

His role as guardian, promoter, and publisher of the blues should not be ignored, even if his legend, depicted in the 1958 film *St. Louis Blues,* in which Nat King Cole played the lead, went beyond reality.

The city of Memphis, undoubtedly a "cradle of the blues," immortalized W. C. Handy by giving his name to a park, erecting a statue, and, since 1980, giving out the W. C. Handy Awards, the annual recognition of achievement in the field of blues music. Although criticized by a great number of fans because of their commercialism, these awards have been successful year after year in displaying a "positive" image of the blues to a number of organizations, sponsors, and individuals who often know nothing of the musical richness of their own country.

Any recognition of the blues, any promotion of the blues-men, is a good thing.

HARLEM HAMFATS

See Memphis Minnie

HARMONICA

In no other musical genre does the harmonica hold such an important place. Even more than the bottleneck guitar, the harmonica is the characteristic instrument of the deepest blues.

Several reasons seem to explain that surprising predominance: first, the price, which favored its adoption by very poor rural musicians; its apparent simple use—it is one of the rare instruments on which one can play a tune after a few days of practice; and last, the blues harmonica players knew how to make that basic instrument (only the diatonic scale exists) coincide with the demands of the blues. In fact they use a harmonica whose key is different from that of the other instruments (for instance: the F harmonica for a piece in C), hence they get the indispensable blue notes. This use of the instrument is the essential characteristic of the blues harmonica; country music or folk harmonica players generally follow the melody more.

Some recent research shows that at first the fiddle had the place that the harmonica took in the small string bands in the South.

From exclusive soloists like Alfred Lewis, De Ford Bailey, and Freeman Stowers to the first harmonica players of Memphis, Will Shade, Noah Lewis, Hammie Nixon—who express themselves within a band and are the real creators of the blues harmonica—the harmonica became more and more prevalent before World War II to finally becoming with the great innovator John Lee "Sonny Boy" Williamson* one of the dominant blues instruments after the war. Although the virtuosity of the New Yorker by adoption, Sonny Terry,* is legendary, it is particularly along the Mississippi-Chicago current that the harmonica found its greatest innovators: Big Walter Horton,* Little Walter,* and Sonny Boy Williamson (Rice Miller)* took that instrument, by amplifying it electrically, to the peak of complexity, virtuosity, and sophistication, unequaled to this day. It is also necessary to mention the simple but extremely influential style of Jimmy Reed.*

Besides these big names, others could have become more prevalent in blues history if they had recorded more: Jaybird Coleman, the superb innovator of the twenties, with a small following; and George "Papa" Lightfoot, an extreme virtuoso of the Natchez region to whom we owe the amazing "When the Saints Go Marching In."

At present, the best active blues harmonica players are, in Chicago, James Cotton,* Junior Wells,* Carey Bell,* the astonishing Sugar Blue* (a great technician), Lester

Davenport, and Billy Branch*; in New York, Bill Dicey and Paul Oscher (Brooklyn Slim); in California, Rod Piazza, Curtis Salgado, Johnny Dyer, Gary Smith, and the remarkable Charlie Musselwhite*; in the South, Jerry McCain, Willie Cobbs,* Chicago Bob,* Eugene Ray, and Kim Wilson. Also of significance are the followers of the late Paul Butterfield*: Madison Slim, Jerry Portnoy, and Dimestore Fred.

PEPPERMINT HARRIS

(Harrison D. Nelson / b. 1925 / vocals, guitar, piano)

Although Peppermint Harris recorded substantially for several labels, for a long time he was considered to be a secondary name in blues history. Maybe this Texas bluesman was too difficult to classify or his fluctuating itinerary and his versatility too disconcerting. More likely, since he (like other bluesmen of the South) did not take advantage of the blues revival and did not tour Europe nor record any album directed to this new public, Peppermint Harris simply faded from the forefront of the blues scene.

Neither a leader nor a great innovator, Peppermint is above all an original: tempted for a while by a career in sports, he entered the University of Texas where he got a degree in speech. During his years in college, Harris became much more interested in music than in anything else: he spent whole nights in the ghetto of Houston listening to Lightnin' Hopkins* and Gatemouth Brown,* his two main influences. In 1948 he had already played enough in the blues clubs for Hopkins to present him to producer Bill Quinn, who recorded him in a mammoth session where everybody (musicians and technicians) was soaked in alcohol. This did not prevent his tracks, very close to electric rural blues, from being high quality. Peppermint revealed himself as a sensual singer and an expressive guitar player, playing the flowing and precise note by note of the Texas-California style, but he seemed always to be between two whiskeys. It was in that atmosphere of undecided grief that would dissolve slowly in alcohol that "Rainin' in My Heart" was bathed, his first big success. Peppermint then went on tours in the South with Lowell Fulson,* Ray

Charles,★ and Amos Milburn.★ It was in a similar style to that of Milburn that Harris recorded "I Got Loaded" for the Aladdin label; he had a major success which made him a star of some importance. Then Harris composed a real alcoholic saga ("Have Another Drink") full of humor that met with approval of the black public. In the same way he also created many slow blues, increasingly more arranged and sophisticated, in which the lyrics were often remarkable. But at the end of the fifties Harris had difficulties in maintaining his commercial momentum. He recorded for several labels (RCA, Checker, and Duke), but he had to write more and more blues for other artists (and sell them the rights) in order to survive. Thus Junior Parker,★ Bobby Bland,★ Etta James, Amos Milburn, Guitar Slim, Clifton Chenier,★ Albert King,★ Elmore James,★ B. B. King,★ and others took advantage of Peppermint's talents as a composer. Harris too tried in vain to follow the commercial tastes of the black public by trying multiple musical formulas. In the meantime, he also appeared as an artist much too modern to please the white fans of the blues revival. His association with Jewel provided a few more beautiful recordings, but the seventies saw him progressively fade away from the musical scene, playing sporadically around the shrinking Houston blues scene and recording a few 45s, sometimes excellent, for several small labels. His best efforts are to be found on the albums *I Got Loaded* (Route 66), *Peppermint Harris* (Charly), and *Sittin' in with Peppermint Harris* (Mainstream).

WYNONIE HARRIS

See Blues Shouters

WILBERT HARRISON

See New York

SCREAMIN' JAY HAWKINS

See Blues Shouters

ROY HAWKINS

See California

JOHNNY HEARTSMAN

(b. 1937 / vocals, guitar, organ, flute)

This gifted performer, arranger, conductor, and lyricist lived in the shadow of all the great California bluesmen whom he often accompanied on stage and on record and whose style he often enhanced.

Born in California, Heartsman developed an early interest in blues and jazz. In the fifties he was in the San Francisco Bay area with producer Bob Geddins taking part in recording sessions behind Jimmy Wilson,★ Johnny Fuller,★ Al King,★ Tiny Powell, Sugar Pie Desanto, Big Mama Thornton,★ Ray Agee,★ Jimmy McCracklin,★ Rodger Collins, Jesse James, Joe Simon, and others.

His unique guitar style, at first inspired by Lafayette Thomas★ and T-Bone Walker★ and also jazzmen like Billy Butler—a mesh of notes and chords and a plaintive effect obtained by manipulating the volume control—is instantly recognizable. It became one of the prime characteristics of the San Francisco blues. Several generations of artists including Robert Cray★ and Joe Louis Walker★ have been inspired by it.

This should have gained Heartsman fame, but, a modest musician and no showman, not prone to singing, cutting very few records under his own name, Heartsman flirted with diverse musical trends (the bossa nova, for example) before he settled down in Sacramento and contented himself with contracts in local clubs.

Only after a long crusade launched by Tom Mazzolini in 1977 did Johnny Heartsman appear at last in the spotlight. The indispensable album *Sacramento* (Crosscut) cut in 1989 was a great success and without doubt a revelation for many listeners.

Heartsman's talent is indeed too great to limit itself to only one success. One of the founders of the Bay blues, he is also a major artist of contemporary blues who has much to say. Now signed on a major label, Heartsman has added the worthwhile *The Touch* (Alligator) to his meager discography.

LUCILLE HEGAMIN

See Female Blues Singers

JESSIE MAE HEMPHILL

(b. 1934 / vocals, guitar, drums)

The Deep South and the Mississippi Delta in particular still abound in talented bluesmen (and blueswomen) who are totally immersed in the tradition. And Jessie Mae Hemphill is packed with talent: A superb singer in the passionate Delta style with a curious nasal phrasing and a slightly acid tone; a somewhat limited guitar player but with a hypnotic style; a powerful blues composer often autobiographical and evocative, she is undisputably one of the major discoveries of the eighties.

Born in Senatobia, in the heart of the Delta, Jessie Mae belongs to a long tradition of musicians. Her father, Sid Hemphill, and her aunt, Rosalie Hill, recorded sporadically. A cleaning lady struggling along with her music, she needed all the energy of David Evans of Memphis State University to make her aware of her potential. Under his influence, she decided to write new lyrics, to polish her guitar style, and to record in 1979. Produced a few years later thanks to André Clergeat, the album *She-Wolf* (Vogue) is a wonderful collection of rural, modern, and traditional blues that puts Jessie Mae Hemphill in the great tradition of the creators of Delta blues.

Because of that album, Jessie Mae was able to escape the isolation she was living in. She now tours the U.S. and Europe, attends a greater number of concerts, and has received a W. C. Handy⋆ Award.

She recorded several titles for High Water (the wonderful *Feelin' Good*) and Black & Blue. She has enough original material to fill several eagerly awaited albums.

ROSA HENDERSON

See Female Blues Singers

Z. Z. HILL

(Arzee Hill / 1935–1984 / vocals)

This old hand of Texas soul reappeared surprisingly in 1982 with a series of albums containing a great number of blues, such as "Down Home," a big hit among southern blacks, which established the reputation of Z. Z. Hill as a "blues singer."

Raised in Dallas, Z. Z. Hill was first influenced by church choirs, then by Sam Cooke, Little Willie John (the creator of *Fever*), and Otis Redding, who became his main inspiration. He began as a soul singer in Dallas clubs and then in Los Angeles, where he recorded between 1963 and 1971 many tracks for several labels. His main successes are "You Were Wrong" and "I Need Someone to Love," sentimental ballads without much character, and "Don't Make Me Pay for His Mistakes," a really beautiful blues, remarkable for its insistent bass style.

The decline of soul in the seventies left Hill adrift. He tried his hand at disco, rock, and country without any commercial or artistic success.

A producer in Jackson, Mississippi, Dave Clark, director of Malaco records, decided early in the eighties to put Hill back in his environment. The albums *Z. Z. Hill* (Malaco), *Down Home* (Malaco), *The Rhythm & the Blues* (Malaco), *I'm a Bluesman* (Malaco), and *Bluesmaster* (Malaco) all show the same successful mix of ballads and rhythm pieces in the southern soul tradition, as well as many blues reminiscent of Little Johnny Taylor.* These recordings, deliberately directed toward southern blacks whose hearts always remained faithful to blues and soul, met with a big local success. They contributed largely to the return of these styles to the foreground. Z. Z. Hill's warm, generous, enthralling, and sensuous voice should have been heard many more years if a premature and senseless death had not prevented him from enjoying a late but deserved success.

In Memoriam (Malaco) gathers some of his best blues.

HIP LINKCHAIN

See Magic Slim

SILAS HOGAN

See J. D. Miller

SMOKEY HOGG

(Andrew Hogg / 1914–1960 / vocals, guitar)

Right after the Second World War three singer-guitarists from Texas (Lightnin' Hopkins,* Lil' Son Jackson,* and Smokey Hogg) made a hit among the black communities of the West and the Southwest by amplifying the sound of their guitars in a style directly inspired by Blind Lemon Jefferson* and his immediate followers. Before he reached the charts with "Too Many Drivers" and "Little School Girl," Smokey Hogg led a difficult life as a rural singer going from town to town, from balls to railroad campsites, in order to entertain his fellow men. These long years of learning had a positive impact on his music: To the traditional influences of the Texas blues (accentuated bass interspersed with scattered notes), he added those of Peetie Wheatstraw* and Big Bill Broonzy,* whose records were very popular, as well as the influence of his friend, the strange guitar player Black Ace.* He was also an original bluesman, a regional rarity having assimilated the sounds of his famous contemporaries of the big northern cities. He recorded his first two titles in 1937 for Decca (thanks to Black Ace), then more consistently after 1947.

Very unstable and a heavy drinker, Smokey Hogg alternated between Los Angeles and Texas, where he performed regularly in black taverns. He was extremely popular for his rhythmic style, his modernization of traditional themes, and the quality of those who accompanied him, in particular the piano player Skippy Brooks. Always short of money, he used his fame to convince the record companies to record him. Between 1947 and 1954, he recorded about two hundred tracks for a dozen competing companies. However, the success of his formula (electrification of traditional themes and styles) did not last past 1954; his simple and direct blues left the way open, according to the preferences of his public, to more elaborate forms of rhythm and blues. Sick, prematurely old because of alcohol abuse, Smokey Hogg died in 1960 forgotten by all.

Appreciated very late in his life, he was criticized for his lack of subtlety. But if Hogg's music seems lighter compared to the deep blues of fellow Texan Lightnin' Hopkins, there is also a freshness, a joy of playing, and a dancing rhythm that everybody liked. Smokey Hogg aimed only at entertaining his public: The commercial success that he achieved for years proves that he did just that.

Goin' Back Home (Krazy Kat) and *Jive You Woman* (Grown Prince) are nice collections of his best tracks.

EARL HOOKER

(1930–1970 / vocals, guitar)

This cousin of John Lee Hooker's* was undeniably a virtuoso among guitar players. As a matter of fact, his musical range went beyond the blues toward country, jazz, and pop. His main sources of influence were country music guitar players Merle Travis, Les Paul, and especially Joe Maphis (Hooker's famous double-neck guitar was modeled on that of Joe Maphis, the inventor of that double guitar).

When he interpreted the blues, he was largely indebted to Robert Nighthawk* for the smoothness of his bottleneck, along with a good part of his repertoire. After 1952 Earl Hooker recorded, first around Memphis then in Chicago, a few tracks under his own name, often with a very rhythmic side, great for dancing. His mastery of the guitar and his unease as a singer enabled him to accompany many Chicago artists without obtaining real success. His reputation among the musicians of Chicago was considerable, but it was only after 1968 that he recorded a series of albums. The best one, *Don't Have to Worry* (Bluesway), cannot be found; it contained the excellent "You Got to Lose," which later became the first success of George Thorogood. *Two Bugs and a Roach* (Arhoolie) and *Hooker & Steve* (Arhoolie) contained a few beautiful pieces such as the smooth "Anna Lee" and "The Moon Is Rising" that naturally reminded listeners of the subtle Robert Nighthawk. After his early death from tuberculosis, it was unfair for Earl Hooker to be left in oblivion. *Play Your Guitar, Mr. Hooker* (Black Magic) and the excellent work that his faithful exegete Sebastian Danchin dedicated to him recall what a superb musician he was.

JOHN LEE HOOKER

(b. 1920 / vocals, guitar)

He may be the most prolific bluesman in blues history, having recorded more than five hundred tracks and dozens of albums. Since his first records in 1948 his commercial success has been assured. He gained a new public each time the last one left him; he always knew how to be on center stage.

Born in Vance, about thirty miles from Clarksdale, Mississippi, Hooker learned the guitar from his stepfather. Although he might have played professionally in the South, what is certain is that at the time he came to work in Detroit during the war his style was already mature. A primitive and extremely limited guitar player, he uses the electrification of his guitar to compensate for technical weaknesses. More than with other bluesmen, his guitar prolongs his deep and expressive voice: Each note, parsimoniously played, stretched or muffled, endlessly vibrating or cracking drily, is a lyric. Thus he managed to create a style and a sound that are among the most original of black music, immediately recognizable after the first notes of any piece. His compositions can be divided into two groups: furious, primitive boogies, in which his extraordinary rhythmic sense, the clicking of the hob-nailed shoes, the flight of his notes in staccato, establishes the beat for the whole band; and slow blues, with such a thick atmosphere it takes a knife to cut through, deeply expressive blues,

■ John Lee Hooker. *(Photograph © by Paul Harris; used with permission)*

which move the listener inexplicably. His best works are among the most expressive emotional experiences that the blues can offer. Finally, the intensity of the message delivered by John Lee Hooker lies entirely in his sincerity and his personal involvement when performing.

His commercial career really began in 1948 with the recording of "Boogie Chillen" and "Wednesday Evening Blues" that were huge hits in the Chicago and Detroit ghettos. Alone with his amplified guitar or with Eddie Kirkland,★ Hooker recorded many titles in the same vein for several labels: Spontaneity, freshness, and sincere emotion dominate his early career. Because of his omnipresence and his deep-rooted nature, he succeeded in overcoming the big handicap of not having appropriately equipped studios in Detroit at his disposal. His fame became so that he recorded for King and Chess before becoming one of the great stars of the prosperous Chicago company, Vee-Jay.

With Vee-Jay he was able to enjoy a flawless rhythm section led by Eddie Taylor★ and drummer Tom Whitehead. The adaptation of John Lee Hooker's personal style to the rules of the Chicago beat was superb. Despite a few uneven arrangements, the records produced by Hooker at the time may be

JOHN LEE HOOKER   143

considered his most successful: "Time Is Marching," "Dimples," "Trouble Blues," "I'm Mad," and "Want Ad Blues" are masterpieces of movement and power executed with brio by Hooker, who was in peak form, shouting his blues above an irresistible rhythm.

Around 1959, while continuing to record rhythm-and-blues pieces on Vee-Jay for the black audience, Hooker was one of the first to get on the blues-revival wagon. With just an acoustic guitar, he recorded several albums full of the atmosphere of Clarksdale. They introduced him to a white public looking for "authentic" bluesmen, meaning at the time "acoustic" (on *Black Snake Blues:* Fantasy). As early as 1960 he participated in the Newport Festival, and in 1962 he was the star of the first European tour of the American Folk Blues Festival. During that tour, he recorded "Shake It Baby," which became an astonishing commercial success throughout Europe. Hooker's reputation was then huge; he influenced various English groups, such as the Animals, the Yardbirds, the Spencer Davis Group, and the Groundhogs, with whom he recorded a mediocre album in 1965. That was one of the first times a black bluesman and an English group played together on a recording.

Although he continued to record numerous albums with blues musicians, Hooker tried more and more to concentrate on rock. With his particular business sense, he managed, even after the age of fifty, to thrive in the pop music world without changing his style. In 1970 he recorded a double album with Canned Heat,★ thus identifying himself almost completely with rock.

After a few years of rather excessive presence in the recording studios (especially for ABC), John Lee Hooker was content with his public image as the "father of the boogie" and as a living legend, entertaining audiences with his coast-to-coast blues band that included musicians more oriented toward California rock rather than the deep blues.

During the early nineties John Lee Hooker climbed again to the top of the charts, without compromising his personal style. *The Healer* (Chameleon) and *Mr. Lucky* (PointBlank/ Charisma) are good albums and million-sellers.

Among all the original editions, reissues, and new presentations of old titles are the very strong and the very weak. Everything that Hooker did for Modern and Chess is high quality. One can say almost the same thing of his work for Vee-Jay, with the exception of a few flops. Then he alternated between the very good and the very weak. For now, we recommend *House of the Blues* (Chess); *Plays and Sings the Blues* (Chess); *Boogie Chillen* (Official); *Mad Man Blues* (Chess); *Sittin' Here Thinkin'* (Muse); *This Is Hip* (Charly); *Everybody's Rockin'* (Charly); *Moanin' the Blues* (Charly); *Solid Sender* (Charly); *The Real Folk Blues* (Chess); and, among his most recent albums, *Back Home* (Black & Blue); *Lonesome Mood* (MCA), accompanied by Earl Hooker★; and *Never Get Out of These Blues Alive* (ABC).

LINDA HOPKINS

See Female Blues Singers

SAM "LIGHTNIN'" HOPKINS

(1912–1982 / vocals, guitar)

Lightnin' Hopkins was rightly considered one of the most creative and influential postwar bluesmen. He was famous in Europe after a single visit to that continent. He has authored many albums and was honored by Houston, his hometown.

His style was deeply rooted in the Texas blues with a subtle arpeggio alternated with accented bass notes. Lightnin' Hopkins, as well as many other guitar players of that region, was influenced by Blind Lemon Jefferson,★ whom he supposedly accompanied on his tours in the late twenties. Eventually, he created his own style: a sharp manner of playing the electric guitar, and strained singing, heavy with emotion, creating an almost magical, enthralling atmosphere. Lightnin' gave everything he had to his music. One met his whole personality when listening to him: unstable and whimsical, boasting and fragile, at times ironic and biting, and other times serious and moving, or brilliant and happy, then suddenly depressed and pathetic. He was a good guitarist who often limited himself

■ Sam Lightnin' Hopkins. *(Photograph © by Anton J. Mikofsky; used with permission)*

voluntarily to a few basic patterns to which he added witty lyrics that were usually improvised on the spot depending on the situations. Listening to Lightnin' Hopkins requires a special receptivity to go beyond voice inflections and instrumental improvisations to a musical experience that is very uncommon.

After years of wandering, alone or with Texas Alexander,* playing in workers' camps or for country parties, Lightnin' went to Houston in 1940 and led a precarious life of fights, violence, exhausting jobs, and time at Big Brazos Penitentiary. However, in 1946 his blues talents enabled him to record several songs accompanied by piano player "Thunder" Smith. After 1946, his caustic and moving blues and his use of the electric guitar (this full sound was new for the period) put him at the top of the charts several times. Pieces like "Short-Haired Woman," "Lonesome Home," "Tim Moore's Farm" (an avenging blues against a white farmer who gave Lightnin' some trouble), "Coffee Blues," and "Hello Central" all had a considerable impact upon the black public. Soon his reputation was national, and he influenced musicians of the Southwest (e.g., Lightnin' Slim* and Silas Hogan*), of California (e.g., L. C. Robinson,* Johnny Fuller,* and Phillip Walker*), and even of the East Coast (e.g., Baby Tate, Carolina Slim, and Tarheel Slim*).

He recorded prolifically until 1953 when the audience turned again to a more sophisticated blues. Lightnin' then lived off his local reputation and was rediscovered in 1959 by the ethnomusicologists Mack McCormick and Sam Charters. Turned into a "folkloric" artist, Lightnin' quickly became one of the key figures of the blues revival. As a matter of fact, he filled the gap left open by the absence of Big Bill Broonzy,* the place of the mythical "last blues singer alive."

Lightnin' Hopkins was everywhere: festivals; concerts; clubs; in universities and colleges; and appearances in New York, Houston, Chicago, and Los Angeles. He also spent a lot of time in recording studios. Between 1959 and 1966 he recorded intensively but irregularly several albums for more than ten different companies, at times recording as many as three albums in one week.

Anyone else might have drowned in that ocean of records, but despite a few notable "flops," the quality of that abundant collection is remarkably high. Moreover, it contained relatively few repetitions, especially of the lyrics.

Little by little, this blues revival became tiresome to Hopkins, and once his reputation was secure he willingly abandoned the revival in 1966 and limited himself to Houston and its neighboring area. He had a fear of planes and several times refused to go on tours in Europe and in Japan. Except for a few brief appearances in the East and in California, until his death he played exclusively in Texas and recorded irregularly for his friend, producer Chris Strachwitz.

Similar to John Lee Hooker,* the overabundant, edited, reedited, and changed record production of Lightnin' Hopkins does not make an easy choice. We recommend *L.A. Burning* (Arhoolie), *Early Recordings, Vols. 1 & 2* (Arhoolie), *Houston's King of the Blues* (Blues Classics), *Texas Bluesman* (Arhoolie), *Move on Out* (Jewel/Charly), *How Many More Years* (Fantasy), *Blue Lightnin'* (Jewel), and *Got to Move Your Baby* (Prestige).

BIG WALTER HORTON

(sometimes known as Shakey Horton or Mumbles / 1918–1981 / vocals, harmonica)

Though much less known than the big postwar harmonica players Sonny Boy Williamson (Rice Miller)* and Little Walter,* Walter Horton might have been superior to them considering his talent. The complexity of his solos was equaled only by their virtuosity and their breathtaking invention. Whether it stayed in the low notes only to end in a rush of high staccato notes or whether it was built on a musical phrase in the mid-range, a Big Walter Horton solo was still astonishing. He was responsible for some of the most beautiful harmonica work in blues history. From his first efforts, recorded with guitar player Jimmy DeBerry ("Little Boy Blue" or "Easy") to his accompaniments of Fleetwood Mac, through his classic solos of the fifties with the bands of Jimmy Rogers* and Muddy Waters,* the number of instrumental masterpieces that he

■ Big Walter Horton. *(Photograph © by Anton J. Mikofsky; used with permission)*

recorded was impressive. His harmonica saved a great number of albums from mediocrity.

Solitary and withdrawn, Big Walter Horton never was as successful as his prodigious talent should have guaranteed him. He moved to Memphis very early on and learned to play the harmonica from Will Shade and Hammie Nixon. He was often in Handy Park where he played with Memphis Minnie,* Big Joe Williams,* Little Buddy Doyle, Floyd Jones,* Eddie Taylor,* and Jimmy DeBerry, with whom he recorded some superb titles in 1951 for Sam Phillips.*

He followed Eddie Taylor to Chicago in 1953 and joined Muddy Waters' band for a few months. Then his exceptional talents enabled him to take part in numerous recording sessions for many Chicago labels; he also belonged to several bands, including Willie Dixon's,* with whom he traveled several times to Europe. He recorded very few records under his own name: He did not trust his voice, which had become harsh, and his repertoire remained limited to a few oft-repeated titles.

The end of Horton's life was marked by disenchantment. He was almost poverty stricken, ignored by record companies and radio stations, without a regular band or a regular income, although recognized as one of the greatest blues harmonica players.

Big Walter Horton did not record the remarkable album that his huge talent deserved. His early songs are gathered on *Mumbles* (Ace) and the compilation *Sun Records: The Blues Years* (Sun Box). *The Soul of Blues Harmonica* (Chess) is interesting; it showed Horton with Buddy Guy* and Willie Dixon. His best albums are *Big Walter Horton with Carey Bell* (Alligator) and *Fine Cuts* (Blind Pig). However, perhaps his best harmonica solo is the one he played behind Jimmy Rogers in the breathtaking "Walking by Myself," recorded for Chess in 1956.

SON HOUSE

(1902–1988 / vocals, guitar)

In 1967 during the Parisian concert of the annual tour of the

American Folk Blues Festival, the microphones suddenly quit working, and Son House found himself alone with his guitar in front of five thousand people. He was so engrossed in his "Preachin' Blues" that he did not even notice the technical incident that deprived him of volume. He kept on vehemently singing his passionate song, punctuated with furious phrases marked by the bottleneck of his steel guitar. Once his performance was over, the entire audience gave him the most incredible standing ovation ever received by a blues artist in a European room. That was only fair: The public had just witnessed the performance of a true bluesman who delivered his message without worrying about the contingencies of the world.

Son House did not exude the instrumental virtuosity and mature tenderness of Mississippi John Hurt,* but rather he was a man of the Delta, alone with his blues, moving the listener with his incredible emotional power. Son House was one of the great creators of the Delta blues, influencing Robert Johnson* and Muddy Waters. He recorded only a few songs in 1930 for Paramount. In 1941–42 John Lomax went through the Delta region with a fine-tooth comb for the Library of Congress; Lomax recorded Son House singing, performing, and talking about his life. This superb document was edited as *Son House: The Library of Congress Sessions* (Folklyric) and *Walking Blues* (Flyright).

In 1943 he left for Rochester, New York, where he got several jobs and led a quiet life. Around 1960, at the time of the blues revival, his records had such a reputation among the collectors that some of them—in particular, the future harmonica player for Canned Heat,* Al Wilson—started looking for him. After several years searching, they found Son House in 1964, who thought it was a bad joke!

Despite his age and his relative musical inactivity, Son House's talents were at their peak, as he proved when he stunned the audiences of the Newport Festival, the American Folk Blues Festival, and numerous American and European tours. As he felt his talents weaken, Son House retired quietly in 1971 after a triumphant series of concerts in Great Britain.

His first recordings are available in the collection *Son*

House/Blind Lemon Jefferson (Biograph). The best album he ever recorded after his rediscovery is without doubt *Father of the Folk Blues* (Columbia).

HOWLIN' WOLF

(Chester Burnett / 1910–1976 / vocals, harmonica, guitar)

Born in the Delta, Chester Burnett divided his life between farm work and music. He was inspired by great bluesmen Charlie Patton★ and Tommy Johnson,★ who would forever leave their mark on his music. His success in the South was due mainly to his dramatic acting, to his incredible vocal power, and to his ability to imitate a wolf howling, hence his nickname. A subdued guitar player but with a good bottleneck style, he learned the harmonica from his brother-in-law, Sonny Boy Williamson (Rice Miller).★

After World War II, Howlin' Wolf found a job as a disc jockey in Memphis, and he led his own band, which included guitar player Willie Johnson, very much influenced by be-bop. His style was then that of the Memphis blues: almost saturated with electrified instruments. The whole gave an impression of vitality and force on the verge of chaos. Howlin' Wolf howled his lyrics above the fray and punctuated them with a rapid, brief, and insistent chorus on the harmonica. His music was both powerful, rough, and primitive and very effective. After 1948 he recorded for Sam Phillips,★ who gave his songs to the Bihari brothers, owners of the Modern label, and to the Chess★ brothers in Chicago. "Moaning at Midnight" and "Riding in the Moonlight," inspired by Tommy Johnson, were big commercial hits which used a formula that Howlin' Wolf repeated endlessly (e.g., "I Asked for Water," "Smokestack Lightnin'," and "No Place to Go").

Howlin' Wolf's records, radio shows, and personal appearances allowed him to enjoy an immense popularity in the South and to finally sign an exclusive contract with Chess. He settled in Chicago where he stayed until the end of his life.

There, after a few trials and errors, Howlin' Wolf managed to renew his music almost entirely. His own temperament was

■ Howlin' Wolf. *(Photograph © by Anton J. Mikofsky; used with permission)*

in perfect harmony with the deep blues of the Chicago ghettos. His association after 1955 with superb guitar player Hubert Sumlin,* as well as his work with some of the best musicians in Chicago (piano players Henry Gray and Johnny Jones* and bass player Willie Dixon,* who became his regular composer), produced in the sixties a series of masterpieces of the Chicago blues: "Who's Been Talking?," "Spoonful," "The Red Rooster," "I Ain't Superstitious," "Going Down Slow," "Hidden Charms," and more.

Although Howlin' Wolf's primitive blues style, much rooted in the southern tradition, was gradually neglected by blacks who turned to a more sophisticated music, he was suddenly discovered by young European musicians, namely the Rolling Stones, who covered several of his hits and who introduced him in their shows to the British public in 1964. From then on it was toward the white public that Howlin' Wolf turned.

He recorded many albums in which Chess experimented, unsuccessfully, with several new formulas: rock, psychedelic, and soul ballads. Sick and old, Howlin' Wolf seemed to be indifferent to these sessions. Only when Chess finally understood that it was impossible to adapt such a wonderful talent to any genre did he create the excellent *Back Door Wolf.*

A great creator of postwar blues, he never stopped performing in the Chicago clubs, in which he was among the most outstanding personalities. Several artists (e.g., Little Wolf, The Highway Man, and Tail Dragger) tried to follow his style.

His work remains considerable. His first recordings, made in Memphis, were often reissued and are today available on several labels (Rounder, Bear Family, and Charly). We recommend *Cadillac Daddy* (Rounder). His Chess titles also were reissued many times. Now, the compact discs *Rocking Chair* (Chess), *The Real Folk Blues* (Chess), *More Real Folk Blues* (Chess), and the great boxed set *Howlin' Wolf: The Chess Years* (Chess) comprise the best of his works.

Recorded in his best years with Eric Clapton, a few members of the Rolling Stones, Steve Winwood, and Ringo Starr, *The London Howlin' Wolf Sessions* (Chess) is charming.

JOE HUGHES

(b. 1937 / vocals, guitar)

For a long time neglected for the Chicago and Delta blues, the Texas blues has recently enjoyed the success of Robert Cray,★ Johnny Copeland,★ and Albert Collins★ and met with a general revival of popularity. Subtle, smooth, caressing, very jazzy, the Texas guitar style was elaborated on by T-Bone Walker,★ Lowell Fulson,★ and Lafayette Thomas,★ and also by rural bluesmen such as Lil' Son Jackson,★ Frankie Lee Sims,★ and the great Lightnin' Hopkins.★

Born in Texas, Joe Hughes came out of the dark after years spent scouring the clubs of big cities. He created a small band with one of his neighbors, Johnny Copeland. Influenced by T-Bone Walker, whose records he listened to as a child, Joe did not neglect the lessons of Clarence "Gatemouth" Brown.★

In 1958 Hughes recorded his first 45s for the tiny Kangaroo label, which enabled him to be hired by saxophone player Grady Gaines, formerly with Little Richard,★ who had suddenly become religious. This relatively prosperous group—the Upsetters—gave Joe Hughes the chance to play throughout the Southwest, to record a few records, and to accompany a great number of blues and soul musicians, from Howlin' Wolf★ to Diana Ross.

Hughes finally succeeded in accompanying his idol, T-Bone Walker, during a memorable concert at the Apollo Theater in New York. He played in the bands of Bobby Bland★ and of Al "TNT" Braggs before being "found" by Texas blues specialist Alan Govenar. At last he recorded his first albums.

The excellent CD *Craftsman* (Double Trouble) reveals the extent of his talent and enabled Hughes, the perpetuator of Texas blues, to undertake the international career he deserves.

Other guitar players from Houston recently profited by this renewal of interest in their music.

The singer and guitar player ROY GAINES (b. 1937) was also influenced by T-Bone Walker and Gatemouth Brown. He recorded many tracks in New York and Los Angeles, less under his own name than as a studio musician. He played backup for Roy Milton,* Chuck Willis, the Everly Brothers, the Supremes, Bobby Darin, Stevie Wonder, Gladys Knight, and others. Despite the quality of some of his pieces for such labels as Chart, DeLuxe, Groove, and RCA, Roy Gaines was really noticed by the general public only recently (he had a small role in the film *The Color Purple*). He sang and played guitar accompanied by his brother, saxophone player Grady Gaines, on the remarkable *Full Gain* (Black Top).

PETE MAYES (b. 1938) underwent the same influences, the shadow of the great T-Bone flying over the rare (and very good) tracks he recorded for Mercury, Ovide, and Black & Blue. The album *I'm Ready* (Double Trouble) did him a little justice, but Mayes can undeniably do better.

CAL GREEN (b. 1937) is often mistaken for his late brother Clarence, who was also a good guitar player. He accompanied an incredible number of musicians from Texas, and he only recorded under his own name sporadically. Green's style mixed the usual Texas influences with those of George Benson and Wes Montgomery. In the album *White Pearl* (Double Trouble), recently released, Cal Green appeared with impressive eclecticism and virtuosity.

Other guitar players deserve more attention and could take advantage of the publicity directed toward postwar Texas blues: Texas Johnny Brown, Clarence Holliman, Wayne Bennett, Long John Hunter, ZuZu Bollin, Lester Williams, and Goree Carter.

HELEN HUMES

See American Folk Blues Festival

ALBERTA HUNTER

See Female Blues Singers

MISSISSIPPI JOHN HURT

(1894–1966 / vocals, guitar)

Mississippi John Hurt's quiet dignity, suave humor, superb

guitar style, and his tender and expressive voice made him the most popular artist of traditional country blues rediscovered by the young white public in the sixties.

Mississippi John Hurt was not a real bluesman. He was a collector of popular songs who arranged them to his own style and played them to entertain his neighbors on Saturday evenings. Before radios were commonplace, each small American town had its "walking victrola."

Hurt never pursued success. In 1928 a mobile unit of the Vocalion company came to Avalon, Mississippi, to look for new talents. The "natives" naturally led that team to their Saturday night entertainer. An audition in Avalon resulted in Hurt being called several months later to go to New York for a recording session under the direction of Lonnie Johnson.* The economic depression led to a significant reduction in the pressing of records, and because Hurt stayed in Avalon, he stopped recording and lived quietly on his farm with his fourteen children. But the six 78s issued under the name of Mississippi John Hurt would, without the author knowing about it, take an important place among the most demanded pieces by blues and folk fans and by admirers of the acoustic guitar. Indeed, Hurt's perfect manner of fingerpicking was, along with his regularly accented bass notes, a regional abnormality; this style was much more common on the East Coast than in the Delta. Nevertheless, he showed in that region, considered to be the birthplace of the blues, the existing black tradition that prefigured the blues which was very close to styles found elsewhere, in Carolina and in Texas.

Guided by the words of one of the titles recorded in 1928 by Hurt, "Avalon, My Home Town," the folklorist Tom Hoskins decided in 1963 to go to that small place in Mississippi. Hoskins met with John Hurt, who was befuddled to see that somebody remembered his meager record production done thirty-five years before and that had brought him only twenty dollars a song.

John Hurt's new career lasted only three years, but at the Newport Festival, on college campuses, and in the folk clubs of Washington, he displayed his talents as storyteller, entertainer, and singer. He overwhelmed the public with his outstanding mastery of the guitar, which had inspired numerous musicians such as Doc Watson, John Fahey, and Stefan Grossman.*

Mississippi John Hurt died in 1966. Fortunately, there are many recorded testimonies of his great talent: *1928 Sessions* (Yazoo) is unique and gathers his first recordings; *Today!* (Vanguard) and *The Immortal Mississippi John Hurt* (Vanguard) are the best albums made after he was rediscovered.

J. B. HUTTO

(Joseph Benjamin Hutto / 1929–1983 / vocals, guitar)

J. B. Hutto was among the many Chicago bluesmen to have recorded a few songs that became fifties classics. He went to Chicago from Georgia after the war, and he and his group, the Hawks, scoured the clubs of Chicago. There he created his style: an amplified guitar, a dominant use of the bottleneck, a tense and harsh singing, influenced by Elmore James,* and an extraordinarily dynamic performance on stage. Moreover, many of his compositions revealed a talented poet; he was particularly brilliant at double entendres (e.g., "Pet Cream Man").

He recorded a few remarkable songs in 1954 for the small Chance label, but despite their high quality these records were not successful. Thanks to his own perseverance, Hutto finally was noticed by producer Sam Charters, who in 1965 arranged for his appearance on the anthology *Chicago: The Blues Today, Vol. 1* (Vanguard). Hutto's dynamism and imagination as well as the remarkable presence of drummer Frank Kirkland made these pieces the best moments of that interesting anthology.

J. B. Hutto did not stop playing in the Chicago clubs. He recorded several good albums, although they did not equal his previous ones: *Hawk Squat* (Delmark), very uneven but containing the outstanding "Too Much"; and *Masters of Modern Blues* (Testament), his best album, recorded in 1966.

Upon the death of Hound Dog Taylor,* J. B. Hutto—so advised by some of his fans—hired Taylor's musicians and tried to renew the commercial success that Hound Dog enjoyed before he died. The results were generally disappointing, for Hutto seemed to be cramped in a role he was unable to play and that he probably did not enjoy very much.

Despite everything, *Slideslinger* (Varrick) has good moments, and *Slippin' and Slidin'* (Varrick), recorded a few months before his death, abounds in feeling. His nephew, Lil' Ed,★ took up his style and part of his repertoire and is successful to a degree that J. B. never reached.

J

PAPA CHARLIE JACKSON

(ca. 1890–1950 / vocals, banjo)

Although the first artists who recorded blues were exclusively female "classic" singers (e.g., Ma Rainey★ and Edith Wilson★) accompanied by jazz bands, little by little the record companies recognized the commercial potential of male singers whose rural origins were deeply rooted in the southern community they represented. Papa Charlie Jackson was one of those artists made known through the recording studio. The singers and guitarists Sylvester Weaver (November 1923) and Ed Andrews (April 1924) were recording several months before him, but Papa Charlie Jackson was in fact the first country blues performer to enjoy tremendous commercial success.

Little is known about his life. Born in New Orleans, he played in several traveling shows. His primitive style was influenced by ragtime, that jazz music that was expressed on a four-string banjo, an instrument with limited possibilities. Nevertheless, by doubling some notes, he made the most of that instrument.

In August 1924 in Chicago he recorded a 78 that included "Papa's Lawdy Lawdy Blues" and "Airy Man Blues," whose sexual metaphor gained him notoriety among black communities. From 1924 to 1934 he recorded about seventy tracks for Paramount and Okeh, among which were the first-known versions of "Spoonful" (a standard that Charlie Patton★ and then

Howlin' Wolf★ covered) and "Salty Dog" (a southern folk classic), the intelligent and funny "Salt Lake City Blues," and the furious ragtimes "Skoodleumskoo" and "Shake That Thing." He accompanied Ma Rainey★ and Ida Cox,★ and in 1929, with guitar player Blind Blake,★ he recorded his best pieces. Commercially, he survived the economic crisis that greatly affected record production, but after 1934 he disappeared from the musical scene without a trace.

Fat Mouth (Yazoo) and *Papa Charlie Jackson* (Biograph) are two good albums despite a somewhat mediocre sound.

FRANKIE "HALF PINT" JACKSON

See Kansas City

JIM JACKSON

See Memphis

JOHN JACKSON

(b. 1924 / vocals, guitar, banjo)

John Jackson is a small star in Washington, D.C., among country blues fans. Although he never gave up his job as a gravedigger in Fairfax, Virginia, his guitar style, rooted in the purest tradition of the East Coast blues, won him international fame.

He is deeply inspired by Blind Blake,★ Josh White,★ Blind Boy Fuller,★ and also by the great country music singer Jimmie Rodgers.★ As adept at ragtime as at the ballad, as at ease in the blues as in a dance tune, Jackson is an excellent fingerpicker. Maybe if he had been more available or had had a more adventurous temperament, he would have had a larger public.

In spite of his relative obscurity these past years, he is still a pillar of the blues in Washington, along with John Cephas,★ Phil Wiggins, Flora Molton, and Archie Edwards.

He recorded five quality albums, among which the best

may be *John Jackson in Europe* (Arhoolie) and *Step It Up and Go* (Rounder).

LIL' SON JACKSON

(Melvin Jackson / 1916–1976 / vocals, guitar)

Lil' Son Jackson, very popular in the South between 1948 and 1953, was along with Lightnin' Hopkins,* Frankie Lee Sims,* and Smokey Hogg* one of the great modern perpetuators of traditional Texas blues. Indeed, his guitar style (continuous bass notes interspaced with arpeggios) came directly from Blind Lemon Jefferson.* But his stingy use of high notes and his singing, apparently detached but also charged with a contained passion, enabled him to create an insistent atmosphere that was deeply despairing and extremely personal.

Only after the war did Jackson think about a musical career. A demo record, sent to producer Bill Quinn, enabled him to do a series of recordings between 1948 and 1950 for the Gold Star label. These great records stressed all the qualities of the singer-guitarist. Unfortunately, they were only parsimoniously reissued.

Encouraged by the popular success of his records, he was hired in 1950 by the big Imperial label of New Orleans, for which he recorded over fifty songs between 1950 and 1954. Although some recording sessions were partly spoiled by a tenor saxophone which unfortunately covered Jackson's voice and guitar, many of these Imperial sides are excellent, for example, "Disgusted," "Thrill Me Baby," and "Rockin' and Rollin'," from which originated B. B. King's* big hit "Rock Me Baby."

Involved in a serious car accident and slightly disenchanted by life as a professional musician, Lil' Son Jackson gave up music and became a mechanic after 1955. However, he recorded a few more albums for Roy Ames and a good album for Chris Strachwitz (*Lil' Son Jackson:* Arhoolie).

His influence has been acknowledged by a great many musicians, from Joe Hughes* to Robert Lowery on the West Coast.

ELMORE JAMES

(1910–1963 / vocals, guitar)

Nearly thirty years after his death Elmore James is still the object of a cult of other bluesmen who adopted his style (e.g., Joe Carter, John Littlejohn,* and Homesick James*), of numerous blues lovers, and also some rock guitar players.

Elmore was indeed one of the great creators of modern blues. Moreover, when alive, he was extremely popular among the blacks of the South and of Chicago. His biggest hit, "Dust My Broom," recorded in 1952, was covered by a great number of blues and rock musicians.

Born in Canton, Mississippi, on a small plantation, Elmore James was early on strongly impressed by some Hawaiian guitar players on tour who played their instrument with a metallic tube. He quickly became expert in that manner of playing. He led the life of an itinerant musician; he toured in Mississippi and Arkansas with Sonny Boy Williamson (Rice Miller)* and Robert Jr. Lockwood.* He greatly admired Lockwood, who then played exclusively like his grandfather, the legendary Robert Johnson.*

Johnson's influence upon Elmore James's music always remained powerful: his falsetto voice, almost shrill, and the intensive use of the "walking" bass notes of boogie-woogie; furthermore, several pieces of James's repertoire were borrowed from Johnson (e.g., "Dust My Broom," "Ramblin' on My Mind," and "Crossroads"). However, Elmore James's originality lay in his powerful style with the bottleneck: whereas his contemporaries Muddy Waters* and Robert Nighthawk* use their metallic tube softly to get a smooth sound, James furiously attacked his amplified guitar with it. That, along with his declamatory but slightly muted voice, produced one of the most exciting sounds in blues history.

After his formula on "Dust My Broom" was used up by numerous variations, Elmore James proved himself to be a powerful lyrical composer; "The Sky Is Crying," "Twelve Years Old Boy," and "Hand in Hand" are some superb slow blues, imaginative and evocative. He left his imprint on all the themes he borrowed from others, so much that "It Hurts Me

Too," "Everyday I Have the Blues," and "Anna Lee" became Elmore James pieces. Overall, Elmore James was one of the most personal, most accomplished, and most influential blues musicians.

His career was relatively brief: after the extraordinary success he had in 1952 with the small Trumpet label, thanks to the insistent riff of "Dust My Broom," he enjoyed a few years of fame and recorded a lot for several companies. Because of his poor health he seldom went to New Orleans or Chicago (where he was extremely popular). He performed then with the regular band of Tampa Red,* which included the subtle piano player Little Johnny Jones and the powerful saxophone player J. T. Brown.

After 1958 his record sales decreased dramatically, and he had to play more often in Chicago clubs in order to survive. It was only because of producer Bobby Robinson, one of his ardent admirers, that he was able to continue recording. This time of commercial decline for Elmore James was, however, his most creative. Modern and aggressive, sensitive and fierce, this last period of Elmore James's work has its place among the great moments in blues history. It partly overshadowed his first records which, in comparison, appear only as rough work.

Elmore James died of a heart attack in 1963 without realizing the popularity he already had in Europe and especially in Great Britain, where his influence on rock groups of the time was tremendous.

Almost all of Elmore James's work is available today on different formats: compact disc, cassette, and albums. Ace reissued all of his first records cut for Meteor and Flair: *Let's Cut It* (Ace), *The Original Meteor and Flair Sides* (Ace), and *Whose Muddy Shoes* (Chess). His second and best period for Bobby Robinson is available in its entirety on Charly: *Got to Move, One Way Out,* and *Shake Your Moneymaker.*

HOMESICK JAMES

(James Williamson or John Henderson / b. 1910 / vocals, guitar)

A cousin of John Lee "Sonny Boy" Williamson* from whom he learned music in their native Tennessee, James Williamson also played substantially with Yank Rachell,* Sleepy John Estes,* and Walter Horton.*

In 1939 he moved to Chicago with Sonny Boy and became a regular of the small clubs of the city. He became friends with Memphis Minnie,* whose shrill and drawling vocal style he imitated. Despite the fact that he played Chicago taverns for a long time, it was only in 1952 that he had the opportunity to record for the small Chance label. Elmore James* was extremely popular at that time, and James Williamson played the guitar in a style that was obviously influenced by him. From that recording session only three songs were produced, among which "Homesick" was a local hit and it gave James his nickname. He took advantage of that to pretend to be Elmore James's cousin, thus hoping to benefit from that supposed relation.

Homesick recorded a few more titles for some obscure labels and finally played regularly with Elmore James, whose repertoire he absorbed little by little. When the latter died in 1963, Homesick was better suited than anyone to fill his shoes. The legend created around Elmore as well as the constant presence of Homesick in the Chicago clubs was at last profitable. In 1964–65 he recorded a good album for Sam Charters, *Blues on the South Side* (Prestige/Ace), and he had a key role on the anthology *Chicago/The Blues Today, Vol. 2* (Vanguard).

The following years were the best ones for Homesick. Almost totally unknown in Chicago, he was recognized as a major bluesman in Europe where he often went on tours. His stage presence, the purity of his bottleneck style, and the conviction of his interpretations gave him the success he deserved. He recorded without being very picky about what he was given. But it is outrageous that two great achievements such as *Ain't Sick No More* (Bluesway) and *Homesick James/Snooky Pryor* (Caroline/Big Bear) are impossible to find today. Homesick James, as well as his accompanist, harmonica player Snooky Pryor,* was truly brilliant on them.

The ever-young Homesick James has been somewhat abandoned by the organizers of concerts, along with the record companies, although in the early eighties he recorded a beautiful album of acoustic blues (*Going Back Home:* Trix), which showed the reality of his roots.

SKIP JAMES

(Nehemiah James / 1902–1969 / vocals, guitar, piano)

Unlike Son House,* Bukka White,* or John Hurt,* it was only by chance that Skip James was rediscovered in 1964. At that time he was in a hospital in Tunica, Mississippi, when his friend, guitar player Ishman Bracey, who was being pressured in vain by Bill Barth and John Fahey to resume performing, gave them his address.

Skip James accepted this return to music, and a few weeks later his first performance before the public of the Newport Festival was one of the great moments in blues-revival history. Almost totally unknown by the public, Skip James was a great revelation: it was the totally personal and original music of an introverted man that the public, entirely convinced of his talent, could enjoy for a few years after his rediscovery. Listening to one of his records is an experience that requires constant attention; moreover, the listener needs to be open to the difficult and closed world of Skip James. The effort is worthwhile, for James was a unique talent, and his music came from deep within, without the least compromise to commercial tastes and fashions.

Born in the town of Bentonia (in the Mississippi Delta), Skip James is said to have been influenced by several local guitar players—especially Henry Stuckey—but his falsetto vocal style, his predeliction for the blues in minor keys played on the guitar in a jerky manner (first hesitant and followed by a flow of scattered notes) produced one of the strangest musics, clearly influenced by the Celtic music of Irish colonists. That music was unique among bluesmen of the Delta and elsewhere. An individual creation? The only known testimony of a very localized tradition? What is certain is that in 1931, when living in Jackson, Skip James impressed Paramount producer H. C. Spears, who immediately sent him to recording studios in the North. Skip James recorded there seventeen songs (among which four are on the piano). Then he returned to Jackson where he never again heard about his records until he was rediscovered in 1964. However, his "Devil Got My Woman," while failing to sell well among blacks, sufficiently influenced Johnny Temple,* who made it his hit a few years later under the title "Evil Woman Blues."

In spite of a difficult second career after 1964—this character and this strange music were not particularly well adapted to the great concert halls—Skip James recorded several beautiful albums. *Today!* (Vanguard) and *Devil Got My Woman* (Vanguard) are outstanding.

His work of 1931 was collected in its entirety on *Skip James: The Complete 1931 Sessions* (Yazoo), which is indispensible. Also of note is the fact that one of his compositions, "I'm So Glad," adapted by Eric Clapton and Cream, sold millions of copies. When Skip James died from cancer, a collection was taken among his admirers to pay for the burial.

His music gave birth to a micro-style of the Delta blues around Bentonia, whose principal follower was Jack Owens.

BLIND LEMON JEFFERSON

(ca. 1897–1930 / vocals, guitar)

Blind Lemon Jefferson, street singer, born blind, was with Texas Alexander,* the founder of the Texas blues. He played a music that was already in existence, but the blues was not yet a tradition. Through the influence of the records of that first generation of bluesmen (Jefferson in Texas, Blind Blake* on the East Coast, Charlie Patton* in Mississippi) the blues became set, codified, and developed.

Jefferson's high, clear voice, developed from the singing style of the cotton workers, and his guitar style that alternated very marked bass notes with arpeggios—inspired by the flamenco patterns introduced in Texas by the Mexican vaqueros—influenced the other musicians of the region: Ramblin' Thomas, Little Hat Jones, Lightnin' Hopkins,* and Lowell Fulson.*

Though he had been scouring Texas for several years, Jefferson was discovered by a bazaar merchant of Dallas who was looking for new black talents. He recorded him and sent a demo record to the A&R director of Paramount records, Mayo Williams. After that, Blind Lemon Jefferson made many trips to Chicago studios where he recorded more than eighty songs between 1926 and 1929. His popularity seems to have been huge; even country music guitarist Chet Atkins is said to have been impressed by Blind Lemon's records that he had heard in his childhood. He recorded numerous songs that became famous: "Jack of Diamonds," "Matchbox Blues," "Broke and Hungry," and especially "See That My Grave Is Kept Clean," which became one of the most interpreted pieces of the American folklore from Lightnin' Hopkins to Bob Dylan to the rock group Jefferson Airplane, who took their name in his honor.

During the winter of 1929–30 he came to Chicago one more time to record. He attended a reception at some friends' house and left late into the night. Hampered by densely falling snow, he got lost in the streets of the big city and froze to death there. Blind Lemon Jefferson's reputation is such that nearly all his recorded work is available on LPs, a surprising special treatment for an artist who made his last recordings more than sixty years ago. Furthermore, his memory is the object of a small cult: In 1967 a foundation collected a significant sum in order to find where his corpse was and to erect there a memorial, thus being careful to "keep his grave clean," as Blind Lemon wished for in his famous blues.

Jefferson's work was amply reissued on Milestone and Biograph. However, it is difficult to listen to because of the poor quality of the retaping of the original 78s. The contribution of the Yazoo label, with the double album *King of the Country Blues* (Yazoo), offers not only an exceptional selection of his best titles but also very high sound quality.

BOBO JENKINS

See Detroit

GUS JENKINS

See California

JIMMY JOHNSON

(Jimmy Thompson / b. 1928 / vocals, guitar)

Unlike his brothers Mac, bass player for a number of record-ing sessions, and Syl Johnson,* a singer and guitar player who made a name for himself in soul music, Jimmy Johnson remained anonymous for a long time. Born in Mississippi and influenced by blues and gospel, Jimmy began his career in Chicago in the bands of Slim Willis, Freddie King,* and Magic Sam,* who left a lasting impression on him. He con-stantly vacillated between soul and the blues. In fact, during the sixties he played in the soul genre and recorded a few 45s for some obscure labels; he also accompanied soul artists such as Otis Clay* and Denise LaSalle.*

With the sudden decline of soul in the seventies, Jimmy Johnson returned to the blues. He was the second guitar player in the bands of Jimmy Dawkins* and Otis Rush.* From then on, he drew his inspiration largely from Otis Rush in his extremely tense singing as well as in his superbly expressive guitar style. In 1975, almost fifty, he at last created his own blues band and recorded before a live audience for Marcelle Morgantini *Ma Bea's Rock* (MCM), an album of unequaled value. It displayed the possibilities of Jimmy Johnson, with a superb version of Otis Rush's "So Many Roads."

His 1978 contribution to the anthology *Living Chicago Blues, Vol. 1* (Alligator) revealed Jimmy Johnson's talent: on the four titles that he recorded as the featured player he appeared as a wonderful stylist similar to Otis Rush and Magic Sam of Chicago's West Side sound. His tenor voice, along with his fantastic guitar style, flows freely, creating an intense and dra-matic climate. The same qualities made the album *Johnson's Whacks* (Delmark) a big hit; the years spent in the dark enabled Jimmy Johnson to polish several original pieces whose quality of the text equaled that of the arrangements. It is indeed a major album of contemporary blues, justly rewarded in the U.S. Jimmy Johnson mixes blues and gospel with soul and even disco in an ensemble that is incredibly harmonious and efficient, thus continuing the great tradition of the West Side sound. His second American album, *North/South* (Delmark), includes excellent moments, although it does not reach the quality of the previous one.

The excellent *Bar Room Preacher* (Alligator), his last effort, was made in 1983. Since then, Jimmy Johnson has not made his way back to the studio.

LARRY JOHNSON

See East Coast Blues

LONNIE JOHNSON

(1894–1970 / vocals, guitar, piano)

Django Reinhardt and Charlie Christian drew their inspiration from Lonnie Johnson for their creation of jazz guitar. T-Bone Walker* and B. B. King,* creators of the modern blues, always recognized his influence on their style; Robert Johnson* used his name to make it seem they were brothers; Henry Townsend,* Clifford Gibson,* and Skip James* ("I'm So Glad," in particular), to mention the most remarkable ones, copied his style and his repertoire on several occasions.

And the achievements of Lonnie Johnson did not stop there: In the twenties he recorded with the great jazzmen Eddie Lang, Louis Armstrong, Johnny Dodds, and Duke Ellington, then with the famous blues artists Texas Alexander,* Victoria Spivey,* Clara Smith,* and Roosevelt Sykes*; he went on tours (and also had a brief affair) with Bessie Smith.* He was undeniably the creator of the guitar solo (played note by note with a pick), successful in jazz, blues, country, and rock; only the obscure guitar player Nick Lucas had recorded a folk ballad in a similar style a few months before him. His wonderful guitar style, with incredible clarity and accented and prolonged blue notes followed by quick arpeggio, opened the way for hundreds of guitar players who without him would certainly not have used their instruments in that manner.

Born in New Orleans, he traveled a lot. He stayed for long periods in New Orleans, St. Louis, Texas, New York, and Chicago, leaving his mark on the different blues and jazz styles, from all these regions. Moreover, Lonnie Johnson made 130 recordings between 1925 and 1932. He suffered a lapse because of an argument with the powerful producer Lester Melrose,* but he recorded a lot again between 1937 and 1942. He came to the forefront again after the war with a series of hits on his electric guitar, but his popularity lasted only until 1953. Tampa Red* alone can say that his popularity lasted that long among the black public. Finally, he was rediscovered in 1959 working as a porter in a Philadelphia hotel. He then went on many tours in the U.S. and Europe, and he bewildered the blues-revival audience with his extraordinary talents as a guitar player. He remained musically active until his death.

As the inventor of the guitar solo, Lonnie Johnson created an approach to that instrument which revolutionized the history of jazz, blues, and popular music in general. Considering that extraordinary influence, Johnson should have reaped the favors of the blues fans. He did not.

Why that incredible indifference? The exclusively white public of the sixties first favored the ethnic qualities of the blues. Lonnie Johnson was an educated black, born and raised in a big city; he could not be characterized as "picturesque." Moreover, he never considered himself as a blues singer because that music, suddenly appreciated by the whites, seemed suspect to him. His repertoire included blues, ballads, guitar pieces, and popular songs from before the war, and their charm was outdated. His bitter voice that prolonged the phrases with a vibrato effect obviously belonged to the musical world of the thirties. Even his deepest blues carried a sophistication and an urban touch which set his music apart from that of Big Joe Williams,* Muddy Waters,* and Lightnin' Hopkins.*

Several collections are indispensable examples of his work: *Mr. Johnson's Blues* (Mamlish), *Eddie Lang and Lonnie Johnson,*

Vols. 1 & 2 (Swaggie), and *The Originator of Modern Guitar* (Blues Boy). Also interesting are *Blues by Lonnie Johnson* (Prestige/OBC) and *Tears Don't Fall No More* (Folkways) that were recorded at the end of his life.

LUTHER JOHNSON

(1934–1976 / vocals, guitar)

He is today completely forgotten to the benefit of his name-sake, Luther Johnson, Jr.★; Luther was nevertheless an interesting Chicago bluesman who belonged to Muddy Waters'★ band for a long time. Born in Georgia, Luther moved to the North at the end of the war. There, he was a passionate admirer of Sonny Boy Williamson (Rice Miller),★ Little Walter,★ and especially Muddy Waters, who became his idol and whose repertoire he quickly learned. In 1967 Muddy needed a guitar player; he hired Luther Johnson. Until 1970, Luther played with Muddy's band. He appeared on several records and anthologies with the band, which included piano player Otis Spann★ and harmonica player Mojo Buford. His warm, soft voice and the reliability of his guitar style allowed him to perform even more as the featured player. He recorded several interesting albums for Muse (with Muddy Waters' blues band) and for Black & Blue, whose superb *Born in Georgia* (Black & Blue) needs to be reissued. *Lonesome in My Bedroom* (Black & Blue), recorded at the end of his life, finds Luther in a moving and unusual introspective mood.

LUTHER JOHNSON, JR.

(b. 1939 / vocals, guitar)

In 1973 Luther Johnson, Jr., joined Muddy Waters'★ band—only a short time after Luther Johnson★ had left it. One could have thought it was a gag or one of those patronymic borrowings common for the blues. In fact, it was nothing of the sort: His real name is Luther Johnson, Jr., and he is a musician quite different from his namesake.

Born in Itta Bena, Mississippi, he began to play a makeshift guitar just like many young local blacks, worshiping Sonny Boy

Williamson (Rice Miller)★ and especially Robert Nighthawk,★ whom he still considers his master. A brief stay in Memphis enabled him to meet the excellent Floyd Murphy, a guitar player for Sun studios, who opened Luther to the subtleties of modern guitar. When he arrived in Chicago, it was not hard for him to find a job as a guitar player in Tall Miton's band, and in 1962 he joined Magic Sam,★ who influenced him deeply. After that time Luther played in the clubs of the West Side, adding more and more elements of the West Side sound to his style, especially that characteristic succession of chords interspersed with flowing musical phrases.

But Luther Johnson, Jr., was also open to numerous other influences. When he joined Muddy Waters in 1973, he had the opportunity to use his many talents; the album *Unk in Funk* (Chess), in particular, revealed to the public his great qualities as a guitar player. Strictly defined, concise, elegant, and powerful, Luther Johnson, Jr.'s, style crossed some of Magic Sam with some of T-Bone Walker,★ Hubert Sumlin,★ and Freddie King,★ from whom Luther adopted his attack as well as his effects. Thanks to his long stay with Muddy Waters' band, Luther polished his style, became familiar with the big international stages, and attracted the attention of blues fans. He often played superb solos and sang a few blues with a voice devoid of subtlety but rather strong.

He recorded several albums for Black & Blue and Adelphi with the Nighthawks: *Jacks and Kings, Vols. 1 & 2* (Adelphi) and recorded his best work under his own name for Bruce Iglauer on the anthology *Living Chicago Blues, Vol. 6* (Alligator). The more modern and aggressive album *Doing the Sugar Too* (Rooster Blues), on which he was accompanied by Roomful of Blues, is also very good. *I Want to Groove with You* (Bullseye) is a good recording of modern blues, but Luther Johnson, Jr., a musician full of feeling and power, can obviously do better still.

Luther "Houserocker" Johnson, a fine bluesman himself and a recording artist for the Ichiban label, is neither Luther "Georgia Boy" Johnson nor Luther Johnson, Jr. His style is more rooted in the southern down-home blues tradition.

PETE JOHNSON

See Boogie-Woogie

ROBERT JOHNSON

(1914–1938 / vocals, guitar)

If there is a blues singer who deserves to be called legendary, it is Robert Johnson. His tragic life, his poignant poetry, and his guitar innovations impressed his contemporaries (e.g., Son House,* Muddy Waters,* Johnny Shines,* and Honeyboy Edwards*) and changed blues history. Robert Johnson influenced a great number of musicians, black and white, from Elmore James* to Eric Clapton. The sales figure for *King of the Delta Blues Singers, Vols. 1 & 2* (Columbia) attests to his lasting popularity. This figure remains one of the highest for the blues.

All the testimonies about Robert Johnson describe him as a tormented, unstable, and quarrelsome individual, always looking for affection, which he usually found in the wives of others. Son House, who seemed to have been his only source of moral influence, said that he warned Johnson against these particularly dangerous tastes.

In 1936 and 1937 Johnson recorded around thirty tracks in Texas for a traveling studio sent by the ARC company. At the beginning of 1938 the producer John Hammond, impressed by Johnson's records, looked for him to perform in his famous program "From Spirituals to Swing" at Carnegie Hall. However, Johnson had been killed by a jealous husband only a few weeks before.

His work, although short, has great artistic value. The intense poetry coming from his blues was the object of several detailed studies (e.g., in *Blues Unlimited*). The heartbreaking voice of Robert Johnson gave his performances an incredibly emotional intensity. Apparently, Johnson lived his music totally, and the records offer us a sense of this tortured life.

Robert Johnson's original compositions "Dust My Broom," "Sweet Home Chicago," "Ramblin' on My Mind," and "Walkin' Blues" were covered by many blues and rock artists.

He was the first-known guitar player to have used the marked walking bass line of boogie-woogie. That particular emphasis on the rhythm was the basis for the Chicago blues that would be created ten years later by some black musicians of the South who came to Chicago during and after the war. Robert Johnson also used the bottleneck in a remarkably modern manner, freely inspired by Son House (in "Preachin' Blues" and "Ramblin' on My Mind").

The boxed set *Robert Johnson: The Complete Recordings* (CBS/Sony), with an accompanying booklet, is a valuable addition to every blues library.

SYL JOHNSON

(Syl Thompson / b. 1938 / vocals, guitar)

Syl Johnson, the most famous of the three Johnson/Thompson brothers (Mac and Jimmy Johnson★ are the others), appeared marginally and sporadically as a bluesman—his career was in soul music.

Born in Mississippi where he learned early to play the guitar, he moved to Chicago in 1952. Syl Johnson made his musical debut with Muddy Waters,★ Howlin' Wolf,★ Eddie Boyd,★ and Junior Wells.★ His elder brother, Jimmy, introduced him to Magic Sam★—the great stylist of the West Side sound. That association would have a lasting influence upon Johnson's guitar style and his singing; he had a beautiful tenor voice, deeply marked by gospel sounds. He made his recording debut as a guitar player: If his participation in several sessions with Jimmy Reed★ was mediocre, his guitar style as backup for Billy Boy Arnold★ (and other artists of the Vee-Jay label) attracted attention. A modern and aggressive sound and a precise and melodic line, interspersed with chords, revealed that the lessons from Magic Sam were well learned.

Despite his abilities, Syl Johnson did not record under his own name until some years later. In the early sixties, he recorded a few sides for King in a style influenced by soul music. After that he recorded as a soul singer for the Hi label for Memphis producer Willie Mitchell. "C'mon Sock It to Me," "Is It Because I'm Black?," and "I'm Still Here" were big hits, followed by "We Did It" and "Back for a Taste of Love," both number-one hits of black music. These titles—rhythmic pieces and ballads—were not blues, but they often had a "bluesy" atmosphere common in Chicago soul music (e.g., the music of Tyrone Davis and Denise LaSalle*). Years of apprenticeship in Chicago clubs obviously left quite a mark on Syl Johnson.

From 1974 to 1977 there was a decline in soul music. Syl Johnson, an ex-star of soul, found himself without a record company, without a contract, and, soon after, without a band. The example of his brother Jimmy—who had turned successfully to the blues—convinced Syl Johnson to go back to his first love. The blues had a small black public, but for a long time it was also popular among the young whites of colleges and universities and among underground radio stations. At that time Syl could be found in Chicago clubs accompanied by Lonnie Brooks,* harmonica player Little Mack Simmons, or Phil Guy. In 1980, after a triumphant tour in Japan, he recorded his first blues album. Despite a few disappointments, *Brings out the Blues in Me* (Shama) is an interesting album, deeply rooted in Chicago's West Side sound. After a few years of half-successes (especially the interesting "Ms. Fine Brown Frame") and an association with harmonica player James Cotton,* Syl Johnson seems now to be coasting along. He is a wonderful singer and a talented guitar player who has the potential to record a great album of contemporary blues.

TOMMY JOHNSON

(1896–1956 / vocals, guitar)

Tommy Johnson is undeniably the most exemplary of all the great Delta bluesmen, for he demonstrates all the qualities of that style: dramatic intensity of the singing (with an astonishing use of the falsetto effects); compositions full of superb allegories; a guitar style with syncopated bass notes, and an unrestrained personal life that ended miserably. He recorded only fourteen titles between 1928 and 1930, but these influenced his contemporaries so much that almost all of his compositions became classics and were covered by a great number of bluesmen in the South and in Chicago: for example, "Maggie Campbell," "Big Fat Mama," "Big Road Blues," "Cool Drink of Water," and "Slidin' Delta." One of them, "Canned Heat," even gave its name to a popular blues-rock group.

His guitar style (freely inspired by Charlie Patton★) and his way of singing influenced many artists: Ishman Bracey, Roosevelt Holts, Floyd Jones,★ Howlin' Wolf,★ Houston Stackhouse, Big Boy Spires, Tommy Lee Thompson, Robert Nighthawk,★ Muddy Waters,★ and K. C. Douglas.★ Sixty years later, his recorded work remains so alive around Jackson, Mississippi, that many blues artists (e.g., Boogie Bill Webb, Roosevelt Holts, and Arzo Youngblood) express themselves in his style, perpetuating his repertoire.

Tommy Johnson was born near the small town of Crystal Springs near Jackson. He spent most of his life in that region. Very early on he was inclined to drink and was attracted to women. He eloped when he was eighteen. When he returned two years later he was an accomplished guitar player and singer. Members of his family who are still alive today say that his sudden talent could only have come from a pact with the devil (cf: David Evans, work cited). Nevertheless, Johnson became the main bluesman in the region; he played particularly with his brothers and his neighbors Ishman Bracey, Charlie McCoy,★ and the Mississippi Sheiks.★ When in 1928 H. C. Spears, talent scout for RCA/Victor, tried to record some good bluesmen, he was naturally led to Tommy Johnson's group. Spears was so impressed by them that he rented a bus to take them to the studios in Memphis. During that unforgettable session, Johnson recorded his best works, followed by some excellent pieces by Bracey and McCoy.

His records were hits in the South, especially the evocative "Big Road Blues." For a while Johnson led the life of a star. He recorded a few more wonderful songs the same year (1928). In 1930 he left for Chicago for a few weeks and then went back to Mississippi for good. He was very unstable and was unable to build his career. He wasted his money; he even gambled away the fruitful rights to his "Big Road Blues." For twenty years he led a miserable life as an alcoholic, with a few stays in jail. Because he always played around Jackson he remained a constant and major influence for all the bluesmen of the region. He died because of his alcoholism in 1956.

His superb work is available in its entirety on *Tommy Johnson* (Wolf). *Jackson Blues* (Yazoo), *Roosevelt Holts and His Friends* (Arhoolie), and *Goin' up the Country* (Rounder) show Tommy Johnson and those he influenced in a regional context.

BLIND WILLIE JOHNSON

(1890–1947 / vocals, guitar)

Although he was strictly an interpreter of negro spirituals and not a real blues singer, Blind Willie Johnson, a street preacher after the fashion of the Reverend Gary Davis,* was different from the bluesmen only because of the sacred nature of his repertoire. A powerful singer with a low, rough voice, who was entirely absorbed in his sermon, he was also a wonderful guitar player, particularly brilliant with the slide, which was in his case a pocketknife he used with a virtuosity seldom equaled. Contrary to other slide guitar players, Blind Willie Johnson did not draw his inspiration from the Hawaiian guitar players. Because he was isolated he tried—with no money—to imitate the sound of the fiddle, an instrument he would have liked to have owned. As he sang, he played a constant and difficult melody, with frequent solos played note by note, with more or less continual intensity. The resonance produced by his pocketknife alternated quickly between low and high notes. Some of his musical phrases are still difficult to equal for the folk guitarist candidates for whom Johnson became an inspiration.

Born in a small Texas town, isolated from big cities, Willie Johnson was blinded with vitriol by his father's second wife when he was seven. From then on, his only means of making a living was to sing in the streets. He became a Baptist preacher and performed around Dallas and Waco with his wife. In 1927, he was recorded by Columbia, which was looking for religiously inspired singers. His first recording session included the classics "Jesus Make Up My Dying Bed" and

"Motherless Children." It was successful enough to enable him to record several times in New Orleans and in Atlanta. Between 1927 and 1930 he recorded thirty tracks with an important number of masterpieces of extraordinary dramatic intensity and instrumental virtuosity.

Johnson did not record after 1930, choosing instead to make his living by playing in the streets of Waco. In 1947 a fire destroyed his home; he lay down in the ashes and died of pneumonia after the hospital refused to treat him, assuming he was uninsured because of his blindness.

His most famous records deeply influenced the bottleneck style of several bluesmen, for example, Mance Lipscomb★ ("Motherless Children") and Fred McDowell★ ("Keep Your Lamp Trimmed and Burning").

The best of his work is available on the album *Praise God, I'm Satisfied* (Yazoo). *Sweeter as the Years Go By* (Yazoo) contains the remainder of his recorded work and, although not indispensable, is nevertheless worthwhile.

CURTIS JONES

(1906–1973 / vocals, piano, guitar)

Curtis Jones is representative of the powerful piano style of Texas, his native state: emphasis on the bass notes and arpeggio with the right hand. After a difficult beginning when he played in disreputable bars, he went on tours with the Georgia Strollers, a company of traveling musicians. He styled his piano playing after the tradition of the Texas blues, through his contact with the older Alex Moore. In 1937 he recorded for Vocalion the classic title "Lonesome Bedroom Blues," which was to become a national hit. To capitalize on this first success he recorded about one hundred unsuccessful titles for Vocalion, Bluebird, and Okeh between 1937 and 1940. Some of these tracks, on which he was usually accompanied by outstanding musicians (e.g., guitar players Willie Bee and Hobson Johnson, drummer Fred Williams, and harmonica player Jazz Gillum★), have been reissued on the album *Blues and Trouble* (Oldie Blues).

After the war Jones, who settled in Chicago despite the fact that he never felt quite at home there, recorded a few tracks for several labels on which he developed a dark and chromatic blues style, which linked him strongly to other pianists of the West Coast. Then, he sank into oblivion, and in 1959 the French blues critic Jacques Demêtre found him in a Chicago slum. His active comeback meant several tours in England, Poland, and France and in Morocco where he lived for several years. But his lack of stage presence, his shyness, and his crazy stubbornness to play the guitar, an instrument he did not master, did not gain him the favor of the European public.

Among his recorded albums, *Curtis Jones in London* is a must, cut with the guitarist Alexis Koerner, which included the moving version of "Dust My Broom" in homage to Elmore James, who had just died.

FLOYD JONES

(1917–1990 / vocals, guitar)

Influenced by Tommy Johnson,* Floyd Jones played an important though somewhat unknown role in the creation of postwar Chicago blues. He was indeed one of the very first to electrify the insistent Delta sound that was to become the symbol of the Chicago blues after 1945. However, although Jones had been present in the studios as early as 1947 and although he had recorded several classics of the Chicago blues ("Stockyard Blues," "Schooldays," "Dark Road," and "On the Road Again" [covered by Canned Heat*]), he recorded only fourteen titles before 1966. They can be found on the albums *Baby Face Leroy / Floyd Jones* (Flyright) and *Drop Down Mama* (Chess).

In 1966 at the time of the blues revival, he missed an opportunity to address a larger audience, fond of his style of down-home blues. Nevertheless, he recorded half of a superb album *Floyd Jones/Eddie Taylor: Masters of Modern Blues* (Testament). Bad luck struck again when the master of an album that he judged excellent and that he had recorded for ABC/Bluesway disappeared in the seventies. Jones performed irregularly in Chicago clubs, where his introverted and primitive style became less and less popular.

LOUIS JORDAN

(1908–1974 / vocals, alto saxophone)

Blues? Jazz? Rhythm and blues? Rock-and-roll? Pop? Louis Jordan's music cannot be classified; it is situated at the confluence of all the genres he practiced with the same good humor and the same swing. After a long apprenticeship with many great jazz bands (e.g., Jungle Band, Leroy Smith, and especially Chick Webb) Louis Jordan created his own group, the Tympany Five, with whom he recorded prolifically after 1938.

His cocky humor, his constant use of puns, his use of words to stress the beat, and especially the furious rhythm he produced with his band placed him quickly at the top of the hit parades. "Choo-Choo-Ch-Boogie," "Saturday Night Fish Fry," "Ain't Nobody Here but Us Chickens," "Caldonia," and "Let the Good Times Roll" are incredible hits. During the forties Louis Jordan was at the top of the sales of 78s in the U.S. His popularity was huge among blacks and whites who appreciated his extraordinary stage performances; he toured the United States regularly. He continued the tradition of the swing orchestras of the thirties; he created and interpreted several blues and was respected by many bluesmen (e.g., Clarence "Gatemouth" Brown,★ Sonny Boy Williamson [Rice Miller],★ and Muddy Waters★).

Although now somewhat forgotten by the general public, he was still playing regularly around Los Angeles at the time of his death.

Louis Jordan's work is an endless repertoire of gags and inventions as well as moving moments. Much of his work is available today. His best moments are on the compilations *The Best of Louis Jordan* (MCA), *Louis Jordan's Greatest Hits, Vols. 1 & 2* (MCA), *Rockin' and Jivin,' Vols. 1 & 2* (Bear Family), and *Rock and Roll Call* (Bear Family). The CD *I Believe in Music* (Black & Blue) that he recorded toward the end of his life should not be neglected either.

KANSAS CITY

After 1925 Kansas City, Missouri, became the home of a simple and direct jazz, very much inspired by the blues, with artists such as Count Basie, Jay McShann, and Andy Kirk, who have all interpreted many blues numbers and introduced new blues singers in their bands.

The Kansas City style is characterized by an accentuation of the rhythm, the central place of the piano in a rather big band, the use of continuous riffs upon which improvisations are built and especially the perpetual bounce between the beats (the Kansas City bounce), which is the real dominant feature of this style. With these elements, it is naturally a happy music, great for dancing, dominated by an unbridled swing. The big swing bands from all across the country imitated those from Kansas City and dominated American popular music in the thirties.

It is difficult in Kansas City to separate blues artists from jazz artists as we can see with the singers Joe Turner★ and Jimmy Rushing★ and the wonderful piano player Pete Johnson,★ who are archetypes of the jazz-blues of that region, which is a combination of both fields.

Before these artists the Kansas City blues scene was dominated by female singers such as Lottie Beaman, a huge woman whose singing was generally accompanied with whistling which imitated bird songs.

FRANKIE "HALF PINT" JACKSON (1895–?) was a blues artist with a unique twist: He imitated women's voices and made his career outside of Kansas City with the bands of King Oliver, Freddie Keppard, and Tampa Red.★

The female singer JULIA LEE (1902–1958) had an important local role. She welcomed and advised young musicians and played the gratifying role of "grandma." Her recorded work was prolific but uneven. Her best recordings shone with catchy rhythms, good humor, and playfulness (on *Julia Lee and Her Boyfriends:* Pausa).

Piano player JAY McSHANN (b. 1909) is representative of a Kansas City style, which he helped to create. Although he does not consider himself a great singer, he has a flawless sense of rhythm, an exceptional virtuosity, and a warm voice. He knew fame in the forties when he directed the big band that included at times Charlie Parker, Walter Brown,* and Jimmy Witherspoon.* Although most of his records correspond more to jazz than to blues, we recommend *The Early Bird Charlie Parker* (MCA) that included McShann's best moments of the forties, as well as the CD *Roll 'em* (Black & Blue), on which Jay McShann and T-Bone Walker* were brilliant.

Likewise, some albums of Count Basie and Andy Kirk are remarkable introductions to this Kansas City jazz-blues. This style certainly played an important part in the birth of a strong rhythm and blues on the West Coast and in New Orleans after the war.

The present blues scene in Kansas City is far from dead but no one has really explored it. Remembering an Alex King playing the blues in a small black club makes one think that there is here as well as in other areas a vein of blues and rhythm and blues still to be tapped.

JO-ANN KELLY

See White Blues

AL KING

See California

ALBERT KING

(Albert Nelson / b. 1924 / vocals, guitar)

Albert King is certainly one of the most important bluesmen of the sixties and seventies. At almost any given time he has succeeded in maintaining a blues presence in the black charts.

His shows are remarkable: Imperial and powerful, Albert dominates his musicians whose talent is mobilized to stress their leader's presence. The latter takes possession of the stage and the audience with total mastery to offer a ninety minute festival of guitar playing. His commercial success at a time when popularity for the blues seemed to disappear among the blacks explained the influence he had upon a number of musicians who drew their inspiration from his repertoire, his musical arrangements, and his guitar style: Larry Davis,* Andrew Brown,* Bernard Daniels, Artie White, L. C. Roby, McKinley Mitchell, Drink Small, and James DeShay. His influence today is heard in the music of Robert Cray,* Joe Louis Walker,* and Donald Kinsey.*

For a long time he was mistaken for B. B. King,* but Albert differentiated himself from B. B. He is very close to his rural roots, and he is much less sophisticated, even when his pieces are over-arranged. Albert's vocal style owes a lot to blues shouters like Joe Turner* and Jimmy Witherspoon.* His guitar style is definitely unique: The note takes off, keeps on vibrating for a long time, then disappears in a sudden glissando. This is Albert's "hallmark," borrowed by numerous musicians such as Son Seals* and Eric Clapton. One can find among the specialists of the bottleneck, Robert Nighthawk* and Elmore James,* the essential sources of his instrumental inspiration.

The road to fame was long for Albert King: From Mississippi to Memphis, from Chicago to St. Louis then again in Memphis, Albert has had varied degrees of success, and he has had several jobs (he drove tractors and worked in a factory). Around 1950 he was in Gary, Indiana, where he played the drums for John Brim on his beautiful "Tough Times" recorded for Chess. Albert made his first recordings for this label, singing and playing the guitar in a style inspired by the Chicago blues of the time.

Albert moved to St. Louis a few years later. He became a central blues figure there and recorded an excellent series of records for the Bobbin label without much commercial success. However, in 1962, the King label that had bought Bobbin managed to place "Don't Throw Your Love on Me So Strong" in the charts.

This small success enabled Albert to sign a contract with

■ Albert King. *(Photograph © by Larry Miller. Courtesy of Larry Miller and Archives and Special Collections, John Davis Williams Library, University of Mississippi)*

the rising Stax label of Memphis. This time he was advised by drummer Al Jackson, and he was surrounded by the best studio musicians in Memphis (Booker T. Jones, Steve Cropper, and The Bar-Keys) who knew the deep blues as well as soul. Albert King accumulated such hits as "Laundromat Blues," "Crosscut Saw," "Overall Junction," "As Years Go Passing By," "Born under a Bad Sign," and "The Hunter." Once he became valuable to Stax, Albert King signed album after album. There is almost no waste in his work of the time: *King Does the King's Thing* (Stax) is a strange idea that works perfectly (Albert King plays Elvis Presley!); *Jammed Together* (Stax) shows him with Cropper and Roebuck "Pops" Staples in a breathtaking tour de force of guitars; *The Lost Session* (Stax) is a very relaxed "forgotten" session in which Albert King was accompanied by John Mayall. In any case, three albums are outstanding: *Blues Power* (Stax); *I'll Play the Blues for You* (Stax), one of the great moments of postwar blues; and *I Wanna Get Funky* (Stax). All these albums were edited, reedited, mixed, and re-mixed, and they exist in different formats today.

After the unexpected bankruptcy of Stax in 1974, Albert King signed with Utopia/Tomato and did not really gain much from the move: mechanical arrangements, accompanists who did not always suit Albert, and a great amount of brass and strings. In spite of everything, Albert and his guitar named Lucy, both imperturbable, ended up winners through these trials: *Live!* and *New Orleans Heat* (Charly) are worth finding.

Despite two interesting albums for the Fantasy label at the beginning of the eighties, Albert King's career seems to have slowed down for the last ten years, although he still appears as convincing as ever in his live performances.

B. B. KING

(Riley Ben King / b. 1925 / vocals, guitar)

B. B. King has been the only true "superstar" of the blues for a long time. He is as popular among whites as he is among blacks. He is often present on television, radio, and in the soul and rock charts.

Born in Mississippi, this cousin of Bukka White★ (who gave him his first guitar when he was nine) sang in church and became a disc jockey in Greenville before moving to Memphis after the war. There he made his debut as a professional musician. Contrary to the other Delta artists who continued the traditional blues of that area by electrifying it, the young Riley Ben King turned to the chromatic styles of T-Bone Walker,★ and especially of Lonnie Johnson,★ whose music he listened to very carefully. He was also attracted to the swing bands, in particular that of Benny Goodman to which the pioneer of the electric guitar, Charlie Christian, belonged.

He harmonized all these influences to create and produce the most elaborate style in Memphis, where the primitive music of Howlin' Wolf★ and Joe Hill Louis★ triumphed. His vocals remind us of Walter Brown★; his electric guitar follows the melody and prolongs the notes in the middle of a cascade of shrill notes similar to Lonnie Johnson's. He is, like T-Bone

■ B. B. King. *(Photograph © by Paul Harris; used with permission)*

Walker, accompanied by a big band in which the brass dominates. He has a strong taste for sentimental ballads in the
manner of Lonnie Johnson, who was brilliant before the war.

At the radio station WDIA in Memphis he became "Blues
Boy" B. B. King and won the hearts of girls for whom he was
the image of success: Gold lamé costumes, bright cars, plas-
tered hair, city-like mannerisms, an extreme sophistication of
his music . . . the image of the "Negro" working in the cotton
fields and living in a shack was far away. He was a respected
black man, living in a city and successful.

B. B. King was one of the first bluesmen in Memphis to
record in 1949 for the Bihari brothers, before he moved to Los
Angeles. His success was then constant, and he was almost
always at the top of the charts with "Everyday," "Sweet Little
Angel," "Sweet Sixteen," "Three O'clock Blues," and "Ten
Long Years." This success made him incredibly influential
with other musicians: Almost all the guitarists who performed
after 1950 are indebted to him, when they don't copy him
exactly. Even in Chicago, where the influence of the Delta
blues was dominant until the end of the fifties, the success of
Otis Rush★ and Buddy Guy★ around 1958, who were original

guitarists but openly acknowledged his influence, demonstrates the domination of B. B. King's style.

This domination is overwhelming: Today, nine blues guitarists out of ten play like B. B. King, not to mention the scores of singers who imitate him.

As for B. B., he was able to lead his career in an exemplary manner. His only slack period was around 1966–68 when his musical formula was stalled: The black public was hungry for Otis Redding and the white public had turned toward the traditional blues of the Delta and Chicago. Within a few years he managed to gain or regain the favors of these two audiences; "The Thrill Is Gone" was a commercial hit in 1969 and opened the way for several blues ballads in the same vein. Rock fans then recognized him as one of the original masters of the electric guitar, much appreciated in this genre. All these commercial successes speak for themselves concerning his tenacity, his abilities to adapt, and his talent.

With quite a successful career, from the Memphis clubs to concerts with the group U2, B. B. King, unlike many black artists, remained faithful to his roots: He worked hard for the official recognition of the blues in the heart of the Deep South; he contributed financial and moral support to the creation of the Delta Blues Museum in Clarksdale; he supported the Center for Southern Studies at the University of Mississippi; and he assumed the role, from Carnegie Hall to Moscow, of "Ambassador of the Blues," in which he found personal satisfaction.

A great number of albums exist in every format. His first work (until about 1967) is, on the whole, first rate. Part of what he recorded in the seventies and eighties is rather mediocre because it sacrificed to the successive fashions of the times, and it did not age well.

We recommend unconditionally *The Best of B. B. King, Vols. 1 & 2* (Ace), *Let's Do the Boogie* (Ace), *Live at the Regal* (Ace), *Completely Live and Well* (Charly), *Live at the Regal* (MCA), and *Great Moments with B. B. King* (MCA).

EARL KING

See New Orleans

EDDIE KING

See Magic Slim

FREDDIE KING

(1934–1976 / vocals, guitar)

Those who had the luck to have seen Freddie King on stage know that he was a mighty figure: 6'7" with an athlete's build and a powerful and dynamic electric guitar that dominated a group of rare homogeneity.

Born in Texas, he was influenced early on by fellow Texan T-Bone Walker* and by B. B. King.* But his long stay in Chicago where he played in the taverns of the black districts with the bands of Little Sonny Cooper and Hound Dog Taylor* marked his music with a harshness that was absent in B. B. King. After 1960, under the skillful direction of producer and piano player Sonny Thompson, he recorded for the Cincinnati label Federal/King a series of blues vocals ("Have You Ever Loved a Woman?," "I Love the Woman," and "I'm Tore Down") and instrumentals ("Hideaway," influenced by Hound Dog Taylor; "Sensa-Shun"; "The Stumble"; and "San-Ho-Zay") which were big hits. These hits enabled him to pursue a national career, recording and touring regularly.

By 1964 he had recorded over one hundred songs for Federal/King. On the whole they are excellent, and his sure technique is supported by a flawless rhythm (*Takin' Care of Business:* Charly; *Gives You a Bonanza of Instrumentals:* Crosscut; and *Hideaway:* Gusto).

After the end of his contract with Federal/King he had a slack period; he recorded two mediocre albums for Atlantic, which were produced, however, by King Curtis. Only in 1970 after his association with rock singer Leon Russell did Freddie King rediscover his dynamism. Although he flirted with the rock public, he, nevertheless, retained the essence of his

■ Freddie King. *(Photograph © by Anton J. Mikofsky; used with permission)*

music: The three albums he recorded for the Shelter label constitute his best work. Works such as "Goin' Down," "Woman across the River," or his versions of "Big Leg Woman" and "Me and My Guitar" are subtle and powerful. He then recorded with British producer Mike Vernon a series of albums that were not as good, often accompanied by a disappointing Eric Clapton.

Freddie King was a musician in the prime of life, mastering his talent; moreover, he had a innate sense of the public. He would have become an important name in blues-rock if he had not been stricken by a heart attack during a concert in December 1976. His work remains significant.

LESTER "BIG DADDY" KINSEY

(b. 1927 / vocals, guitar, harmonica)

Big Daddy Kinsey had to wait until he was sixty to make himself known. At last he was appreciated by the general public thanks to an outstanding album *Bad Situation* (Rooster Blues), a successful tour in Europe, and a brilliant presence in the documentary of guitar player Jacques Lacava "Sweet Home Chicago." A second album in 1989, *Can't Let Go* (Blind Pig), confirms his presence.

This veteran who followed the usual itinerary of the bluesman—born in the Delta, moved to the North during the war—settled in Gary, Indiana, entertaining the local blues scene with John Brim, Albert King,* Jimmy Reed,* and Johnny Littlejohn.* Since Gary was not Chicago, Big Daddy, who worked as a crane operator to feed his family, traveled little and did not record and remained unknown until the tireless Jim O'Neal discovered him in the early eighties.

A master of the slide guitar, an excellent composer of contemporary blues, and influenced by Muddy Waters* and Albert King, Big Daddy created on these foundations the KINSEY REPORT, a half-family band with his sons Donald, Ralph, and Kenneth.

DONALD KINSEY (b. 1953), educated very young in such good hands, is indeed already a professional musician with a distinguished career. He belonged to Albert King's band with

■ Eddie Kirkland. *(Photograph © by Paul Harris; used with permission)*

which he played all around the world; he created the rock group White Lightning; he was hired by reggae kings Bob Marley then Peter Tosh with whom he recorded a lot. Back in Gary, Donald Kinsey devoted himself to his true roots: the blues he had learned from his father. The Kinsey Report without Big Daddy recorded two albums: *Edge of the City* (Alligator) and *Midnight Drive* (Alligator), which had a "progressive" sound and which certainly was at the border of rock and funk. However, some pieces—the superb "Answering Machine" with a beautiful slide guitar—showed that the lessons from "Big Daddy" were well learned.

Obviously, Donald Kinsey has a great future.

EDDIE KIRKLAND

(b. 1928 / vocals, guitar, harmonica)

In spite of his great talent Eddie Kirkland is relatively unknown. Born in Jamaica and raised in Alabama, Kirkland moved to Detroit after the war to make cars. He participated in the blues scene of that city and joined John Lee Hooker★ on several recordings. His superb voice which was deeply influenced by gospel enabled him to record under his own name in a few rare sessions.

After a few years filled with some tough experiences as a ghetto musician, he resurfaced in New York in 1961 long enough to record an excellent album (*It's the Blues Man:* True Sound) accompanied by saxophone player King Curtis.

More and more attracted to soul music, Kirkland settled in Macon, Georgia, after 1962 and became the guitar player for Otis Redding, whom he accompanied on several records. In return, Redding recorded him as the featured artist for his Volt label, and a 45, *The Hawg*, had some success.

Since then Kirkland has been living in Macon where he tirelessly continues to practice with his band the rough mixture of soul and blues that is his hallmark. He recorded a few albums, all excellent, for a few small labels (Trix, JSP, and Pulsar), although he is still largely unknown by the general public.

■
L

DENISE LaSALLE

See Soul

BENNY LATIMORE

See Soul

LAZY LESTER

See J. D. Miller

LEADBELLY

(Walter Boyd, also called Huddie Leadbetter / 1885–1949 / vocals, guitar, piano)

At age sixteen, Leadbelly played the piano in the brothels of Shreveport. It was the beginning of an eventful musical career that took him on the roads of Texas where he may have been a guide to Blind Lemon Jefferson* to the clubs of Greenwich Village and the music halls of Europe. Huge and powerful, Leadbelly was an inveterate womanizer and agressively quarrelsome, using his big Colt in his belt to settle his arguments. In 1917 he killed a rival over a girl and was sentenced to thirty years in Angola Penitentiary.

Paradoxically, his musical talents were useful to him there. A powerful guitarist, Leadbelly expressively used the twelve-string guitar, alternating bass notes in a style similar to Maybelle Carter and inspired by the flamenco which was widespread in this region close to the Mexican border. Like Mance Lipscomb* and Henry Thomas,* Leadbelly was not a bluesman but rather a songster whose immense repertoire stretched from lullabies to cowboy songs to blues.

When he interpreted the blues with his special technique, he created an original variation of the Texas blues, which, since it did not find an echo among the blacks, is almost an anomaly in blues history.

Leadbelly's talents were largely used to entertain the inmates and the wardens. When the ethnomusicologists John and Alan Lomax went to that area for the Library of Congress, in search of folk musicians, they were quickly led to Leadbelly. Lomax, who was looking for traditional songs, was obviously impressed by the variety and the range of Leadbelly's repertoire. After several attempts, Lomax managed to get Leadbelly released from prison.

Leadbelly then became the Lomax's chauffeur. In 1934 he was the first southern black to sing for a white northern audience in New York. Thanks to his eclectic repertoire and to Lomax, Leadbelly unexpectedly found himself amid the urban folk trend of the thirties around Greenwich Village. Along with Woody Guthrie, Cisco Houston, and Pete Seeger, Leadbelly conquered the white public, but he was diluting his Texas roots to the point that they could not be identified. Furthermore, his attempt in 1936 to record some blues for a black public was a commercial flop. After that time, Leadbelly's repertoire included folk songs gleaned more from Pete Seeger than from black folk themes.

After the war, Leadbelly went on tours in France, and his introduction of the blues to Europe certainly opened the way for other bluesmen to tour Europe. In 1949 the folk group the Weavers had success with the ballad "Goodnight, Irene," composed by Leadbelly. Unfortunately, he died before harvesting the fruit of this success.

Leadbelly's fame is based as much on his eventful life as on his music, a fame that increased in folk circles until he became a mythic figure. A recent movie based on his legend proves the current force of this myth.

Looking back, one can judge more rightly Leadbelly's place in the history of black popular music. Through his activities in New York and in Europe he boosted international recognition of the blues. He was the first to open the doors which were until then closed to blacks, and many artists rushed in. The extraordinary range of his repertoire and the fact that he recorded prolifically have preserved some themes that without him would have been forgotten. The musical talents of Leadbelly are less important than his legendary aura and the fascination he had upon several generations. An expressive singer but a very limited guitar player (he usually used a simple strumming, rare for the blues), his recordings belong much more to the "folk" genre than to the blues themselves. According to all the testimonies, Leadbelly was extraordinary on stage. This charismatic presence was not caught on record. The best of his recorded work comes from the period 1935–40, before Greenwich Village watered down his style and his repertoire. *Leadbelly* (Columbia), *Leadbelly* (Capitol) and *Early Leadbelly* (Biograph) are good albums including numerous blues that were interpreted vehemently and convincingly.

CALVIN LEAVY

(b. 1941 / vocals, guitar)

Little known outside his "bases," Calvin Leavy, born in Stuttgart, Arkansas, is nevertheless a significant bluesman, extremely appreciated by the blacks of the Deep South to whom he addresses himself almost exclusively.

His records are in jukeboxes in Arkansas, Tennessee, and Mississippi, and he has been playing regularly in clubs of the area for fifteen years. Since he was never noticed by the blues-revival public, he never went on international tours, nor did he record an album. This strange ignorance was probably due to the fact that Leavy is above all a southern artist; he never played in Chicago or in California. Also, he expresses himself in a modern style that is largely soul.

A big fan of Otis Redding, Leavy imitated Redding's mannerisms and his vocal style. Leavy's deep, warm voice can be attributed to his participation in the church choir when he was a child.

Half of his repertoire can be considered southern soul—still very popular in that area—the other half is modern blues with insistent bass notes that retain the influence of the Delta tradition. But he modernized it by opening it to more contemporary black music. Sent to Cummins Penitentiary for a minor crime, he told of his terrible experience in the extraordinary "Cummins Prison Farm," which he recorded in 1969 for the small Soul Beat label. This title was somewhat successful around Little Rock and Memphis. Taken up by the big Nashville producer Shelby Singleton, "Cummins Prison Farm" rocketed to the top of the hit charts in the South. It established Leavy as one of the rare successful bluesmen of the seventies. Already rhythmical and funky, Calvin Leavy's music is made especially brilliant by his very personal compositions. Besides numerous follow-ups to "Cummins Prison Farm," we must mention "Goin' to the Dogs," "Born Unlucky," "What Kind of Love," and especially "Thieves and Robbers," which enabled Leavy to be successful in the South in 1982.

Unfortunately, outside the usual road of the blues, Calvin Leavy has not yet recorded a single album.

The harmonica player WILLIE COBBS (b. 1940) is also a bluesman born in Arkansas and also too much ignored. His composition "You Don't Love Me," recorded in 1961, became a blues classic that was covered by several hundred musicians. But Cobbs enjoyed that only briefly, confining himself to a limited southern territory, although he did record several 45s for the local market. A versatile musician and intelligent composer ("Inflation Blues" and "Eating Dry Onions"), Cobbs certainly has the ability to make a name for himself if only a smart producer would give him a chance.

BONNIE LEE

See Zora Young

JULIA LEE

See Kansas City

J. B. LENOIR

(1929–1967 / vocals, guitar)

Dressed in a long black-striped coat, improvising on furious boogies, his voice dominating a band led by two saxophones, J. B. Lenoir was an extremely popular bluesman in Chicago from 1950 to 1960.

He mixed the Chicago blues of Muddy Waters* and Howlin' Wolf* with the deep sounds of swing bands. He dealt openly in his blues with social and political claims ("Eisenhower Blues"); Lenoir's music was a strange concoction of Jimmy Reed* revised and corrected by Lionel Hampton.

Pieces like "Mama Talk to Your Daughter" and "If I Give My Love to You" have an irresistible rhythm and spontaneity, and the gloomy "Korea Blues" still today retains its freshness; they enabled saxophone players Ernest Cotton and Alex Atkins to be brilliant, especially over the walking bass notes of Lenoir. The whole of his work recorded at that time for JOB, Chess, and a few other small labels is extremely consistent. It can be found on several Chess albums and on the CD *J. B. Lenoir* (Flyright).

Once he exhausted his formula, tiring the black audiences of Chicago, Lenoir, who had trained with Big Bill Broonzy* and Elmore James,* had no difficulty converting himself again to a false country bluesman for the blues revival. Advised by

Willie Dixon,* he thus appeared in 1965 on the European tour of the American Folk Blues Festival alone with his acoustic guitar as a poor black farmer of the South who played a few old blues after a hard day's work.

This incredible stage performance enabled J. B. Lenoir to attract the favor of the European public who had always been romantically looking for the "last blues singer." It also could have been disastrous for his career. In fact, the absence of a saxophone and of an electric guitar did not really change Lenoir's blues. More introspective, with more biting lyrics, both albums recorded for this new public with the brilliant drummer Fred Below* may be superior to his "electric" recordings, and they are essential additions to modern blues (*Alabama Blues:* L+R and *Down in Mississippi:* L+R).

After the Europeans, the white American public was just discovering Lenoir when he died in a car accident in 1967.

FURRY LEWIS

(Walter Lewis / 1893–1981 / vocals, guitar)

From the street concerts in Memphis at the beginning of the century to his association with rock superstars Don Nix and Leon Russell in the seventies, the road was long for Furry Lewis.

He moved from Mississippi to Memphis when he was very young and quickly became one of the most popular figures of taverns, dances, and country diners. His sense of the show, his funny stories, and his powerful bottleneck style gained him the favor of blacks and whites. After a railroad accident that cost him a leg, Furry was forced to survive by becoming a professional musician. He played endlessly, solo or with string bands, and went on tours with the medicine shows. He became an integral part of the musical scene of Memphis that included Will Shade and his Memphis Jug Band,* Memphis Minnie,* Gus Cannon,* Frank Stokes,* and Jim Jackson. As with many of these artists, Lewis's repertoire predates the blues. Because he played a great deal for a white public, he introduced in his performances a number of folk and popular songs of the time.

In 1927 Jim Jackson took Furry Lewis to Chicago to record. Between 1927 and 1929 he went to three sessions and recorded a total of twenty-three superb titles on which Lewis synthesized different styles that dominated the Memphis blues: He played bass notes like Frank Stokes; he used the bottleneck like Robert Wilkins;* and he used the phrases and repertoire of the popular Jim Jackson.

Then a thirty-year lapse in his recording career followed. Furry, settled nicely in Memphis, divided his time between his antique shop, a modest job as a city employee, and his guitar, with which he continued to entertain his neighbors and friends.

In 1959 the ethnomusicologist Sam Charters, looking in Memphis for black musicians from before the war, had no difficulty finding Furry again and recording him (*Furry Lewis: Folkways*). Unlike with other bluesmen, the years did not show on Lewis: His guitar style and his talents as an untiring storyteller were the same as in the beginning. Without any difficulty he undertook a new career. Through his regular performances at the annual Memphis Country Blues Festival and at many other concerts and festivals, he became one of the blues-revival figures and a member of the folk circles of Memphis. His picturesque character enabled him to appear in *Playboy* magazine and on several TV shows, and even to land a rather significant role in the film *W. W. Dixie and the Dancekings* with Burt Reynolds and Jerry Reed.

Hurled so suddenly to the forefront, Furry recorded excessively. Although he never really made any bad albums, he sang "John Henry" and "Casey Jones" so many times that it became routine.

Furry Lewis in His Prime (Yazoo) gathers some of his recordings of the twenties and is an essential collection. *Back on My Feet Again* (Prestige) and *Shake 'em on Down* (Fantasy) are undeniably Furry's best recordings after he was rediscovered.

MEADE "LUX" LEWIS

See Boogie-Woogie

SMILEY LEWIS

See New Orleans

LIBRARY OF CONGRESS

In 1928 four rich Americans—Andrew Mellon, John Barton Payne, a Mrs. Miller, and a Mrs. Parker—gave substantial amounts of money to the Library of Congress in order to create a department devoted to American popular music.

This remarkable service became increasingly important: Besides the preservation of records, radio programs, tapes, books, and posters, the Folklife Center of the Library of Congress edits numerous bibliographies, discographies, reference works, and records. Teams of researchers travel throughout the U.S. to record folk music and oral traditions. This considerable work of dynamic preservation has no equivalent in the world.

In 1933 department head John A. Lomax began a research program for southern folk with a great number of black musicians of blues, spirituals, hollers, work songs, et cetera. Between 1933 and 1942, mobile teams—two cars and one studio-truck—often lead by John Lomax, John Work, or the young Alan Lomax, made several trips to the South. With a fine-tooth comb they went through the plantations, the penitentiaries, the rehabilitation farms, the town markets, and more. During that period, they recorded over four thousand titles by at least 850 black interpreters. The list of artists discovered or rediscovered by Lomax is impressive: Son House,* Bukka White* (then at Parchman Penitentiary), Honeyboy Edwards,* the young McKinley Morganfield (who was not yet famous under the name of Muddy Waters),* Calvin Frazier, Blind Willie McTell,* Gabriel Brown, Oscar Woods,* and, of course, Leadbelly,* then serving a sentence in the Angola Penitentiary and for whom Lomax succeeded in securing a pardon.

Moreover, the Lomax team were smart producers: The quality performances they usually got from the artists, interspersed with interviews, are unique testimonies about the bluesmen themselves, their environment, and the blues in general.

Although recorded pieces by artists like Son House, Muddy Waters, and Leadbelly are available on several albums, many recordings were never distributed commercially. Currently, a specialized service of the Folklife Center transfers the fragile 78s to magnetic tape.

JOE LIGGINS

See California

LIGHTNIN' SLIM

(Otis Hicks / 1913–1973 / vocals, guitar)

Lightnin' Slim is the father of the swamp blues, a postwar music from the Louisiana country around Baton Rouge developed by producer Jay Miller.* The first black artist who recorded for Miller, Lightnin' Slim "introduced" many bluesmen who were thus able to cut some records thanks to him (Lazy Lester,* Silas Hogan,* and Whispering Smith*). Relatively speaking, he influenced the black music of that region in much the same way as Muddy Waters* influenced the Chicago blues.

Lightnin' Slim began a late musical career; it was only after he was thirty that he learned to play the guitar. It was the success of his Texas neighbor Lightnin' Hopkins that inspired him to perform in the taverns of Baton Rouge with his amplified guitar accented by a drummer and/or a harmonica player. Although he borrowed a few musical phrases from Hopkins, the comparison between the two artists does not go any further; Slim had neither the instrumental mastery nor the poetic sense of Lightnin' Hopkins. On the contrary, his slow and harsh voice with long insistent tones, the frequent use of percussion, and the support of powerful and evocative harmonica players were the original mark of Lightnin' Slim. No work deserves to be called swamp blues more than his does. With eyes closed, you can almost hear the lapping of the swamp and the call of the bullfrog. Moreover, Lightnin' Slim could turn the most traditional themes into original interpretations: A word in an aside accented by his guitar was sometimes enough to completely change the apparent meaning of a song. Thus, some classics, such as "Hoodoo Man Blues" and "Rock Me Mama," were so personalized that they nearly belonged entirely to Lightnin' Slim. The list of his original compositions from the gloomy "Bad Luck," his first success in 1954, to the raging "Rooster Blues" was quite long. Finally, Lightnin' Hopkins covered two of Slim's compositions, "My Starter Won't Work" and "It's Mighty Crazy," which marked the originality of his talent. His blues, dominated by an excessive self-pity, concealed a subtle humor that was irresistible.

Contrary to the fortune of his friend Slim Harpo, Lightnin' Slim did not see any national success, but he was one of the constant favorites of the black public of the Southwest. His commercial work (about eighty titles) recorded between 1954 and 1966 was of very high quality although his last sides, very rhythmical, did not have the profound feeling of his first recordings. The albums *Rooster Blues* (Excello), *Bell Ringer* (Excello), *The Early Years* (Flyright), *Trip to Chicago* (Flyright), and *The Feature Sides* (Flyright), plus the CD *Rollin' Stone* (Flyright), gather almost all of his work.

After 1966 Lightnin' Slim, who had an accident with a truck belonging to Miller, dared not show himself in front of his boss any longer, and he left for Detroit. In 1972 he started a short-lived career again, leaving Louisiana for Europe and the Montreux Festival.

Before his death, Lightnin' Slim recorded two good albums. Nevertheless, they remained far from the quality of the sides produced by J. D. Miller: *High and Low Down* (Excello) and *London Gumbo* (Excello).

LIL' ED

See Chicago

MANCE LIPSCOMB

(1895–1976 / vocals, guitar)

There is not much to say about Mance Lipscomb except that he was a singer and an exceptional guitar player and that he

■ Mance Lipscomb. *(Photograph © by Anton J. Mikofsky; used with permission)*

had developed throughout his quiet existence a philosophy filled with wisdom and fraternal love, which permeated all his music.

Born near the small town of Navasota, Texas, Mance Lipscomb was a sharecropper and then a small farmer. His guitar playing made him *the* musician of that community; he entertained Saturday nights and Sunday afternoons. He began playing the guitar around 1905, and he expressed himself in a style that clearly announced the blues. He was not, strictly speaking, a bluesman, but rather an interpreter of different popular themes, black and white. His fingerpicking style was closer to that of Mississippi John Hurt* or the East Coast guitar players than to that of Texas guitar players like Blind Lemon Jefferson.* Mance Lipscomb's music was soft, light, and pleasant.

In 1959 he accidentally met the ethnomusicologists Mack McCormick and Paul Oliver, who were struck by the abilities of that amateur musician who was then over sixty. Lipscomb then became—without giving up his farm life—one of the great discoveries of the blues revival. Until his death he performed in numerous concerts and festivals in which the depth of his human warmth as well as his extraordinary ease at the guitar earned him great admiration.

He recorded eight high-quality albums, among which was his first LP, *Trouble in Mind* (Reprise), which included a superb version of "Motherless Children," and *Mance Lipscomb, Vols. 1 & 2* (Arhoolie).

LITTLE MILTON

(James Milton Campbell / b. 1934 / vocals, guitar)

As with country music, the real stars of blues-soul music in the South retain their public for a long time. Little Milton is a good example of that longevity. After a career of almost forty years, he is still an important figure of black music, and his records still sell well in the Deep South.

Little Milton left the Mississippi Delta at a young age to go to Memphis where he learned the blues from Sonny Boy Williamson (Rice Miller)* and piano player Willie Love; with the latter he recorded several songs that were produced on the Sun and Meteor labels. He was full of energy, but he limited himself to imitations of B. B. King,* who was then a national success.

In 1958 he moved to St. Louis. With Oliver Sain he created the Bobbin label that signed Albert King* and Clifford Gibson. He then had his first hit with the excellent "Lonely Man."

But it was with the Chess label that he became a big name in black music. "We're Gonna Make It," "Blind Man," and "Who's Cheatin' Who?" are ballads that increased his public considerably. His beautiful, warm, and slightly husky voice, somewhere between Bobby Bland* and B. B. King, gained him the favor of the black public, females in particular. Strangely enough, Milton's career with Chess was not prolific in pure blues, except for the superb *Little Milton Sings Big Blues* (Chess) and the album *Grits Ain't Groceries* (Chess). On many titles Milton did not even play guitar, which was a shame since he was an excellent follower of B. B. King's style, smooth and enthralling.

In 1971 when he signed with Stax, the big Memphis label, Little Milton got close to the blues again, although his biggest success then, "Behind Closed Doors," was a country music hit, a genre Milton particularly liked. In 1974 Little Milton managed to have a hit with Sandy Jones' powerful composition, "Walking the Back Streets and Crying."

After Stax' bankruptcy, Little Milton went through a few difficult years until he was successful again thanks to the Malaco label for which he recorded many albums, the best of which is *Annie Mae's Café* (Malaco).

As with all the prolific bluesmen, the sides recorded by Little Milton have been reissued so many times with so many changes that it is difficult to know what is what. We recommend *Walking the Back Streets* (Stax), *Little Milton* (Chess), and *Blues 'n' Soul* (Stax). His Sun titles are featured on *Little Milton: The Sun Masters* (Rounder).

LITTLE RICHARD

(Richard Penniman / b. 1935 / vocals, piano)

This rock-and-roll pioneer draws his inspiration from the blues and gospel. His music is distinguished by a frantic and almost wild gusto and dynamism, an impression strengthened by his stage performances which often end with Little Richard jumping half-naked on his piano.

Born in Macon, Georgia, Little Richard began his career much more quietly: He was a choir boy at age twelve, a piano player for harmonica player Buster Brown,* and then in 1951 he won a radio talent contest and the opportunity to record a few songs for RCA, mainly blues ("Taxi Blues").

After several tours, a few records, and little success,

■ Little Richard. *(Photograph © by Paul Harris; used with permission)*

Richard sent a trial record to Art Rupe, director of the Specialty label. Rupe had become prosperous with the success of California rhythm-and-blues bands like that of Roy Milton★ and Joe Liggins.★ Right away Rupe was thrilled by Richard, and he recorded him in 1955 with the best musicians of New Orleans. The tempo is deliberately increased for the superb "Tutti Frutti," which was a hit among blacks and whites. That hit enabled Little Richard to get on the rock-and-roll train that was just starting to move. There was a succession of hits: "Long Tall Sally," "Slippin' and Slidin'," "Rip It Up," "Lucille," "Keep-a-Knockin'," and "Good Golly Miss Molly," which all became rock classics. In spite of the formidable competition in that field, Little Richard managed to stay at the top of the charts until 1957.

Very mystical, Richard interpreted the launching of the first Sputnik as a sign from above, and, following the advice of the band leader Joe Lutcher, he gave up the blues and rock-and-roll in order to become a preacher. When he suddenly changed his mind in 1963 to come back to rock, he found out that the music scene had changed a great deal; he was only a nostalgic memory for his subdued fans. He failed to renew either his popular success or the quality of his first recordings.

Despite the presence of Jimi Hendrix and the fiddle player Sugarcane Harris, his Vee-Jay sides recorded between 1964 and 1966 lacked conviction. He then tried to adapt to other musical trends without much success; he lives today virtually retired from the musical scene.

A must is the collection *Little Richard: The Specialty Sessions* (Ace), a testimony of the high quality of his music.

LITTLE SONNY

See Detroit

LITTLE WALTER

(Marion Walter Jacobs / 1931–1968 / vocals, harmonica)

In order to grasp the importance of Little Walter in blues history, it is important to place him in several situations: As a member of both Muddy Water's★ and Jimmy Roger's★ bands between 1947 and 1952, he built with them the postwar Chicago blues; as a gifted composer, he created many themes, several of which became blues classics; as a singer, with his direct, warm, and slightly husky voice, he gained success among American blacks between 1952 and 1958. Finally and especially, he revolutionized the approach to the harmonica: He drew his inspiration from prestigious older musicians, such as the two Sonny Boy Williamsons★ and Big Walter Horton,★ and he was successful in assimilating parts of their styles while creating his own personal style. Little Walter played large chords interspersed with many fast notes; he built solos and surprised the listener with his invention and originality in each phrase. He was the first to maximize the resources of amplification to make the harmonica sound like a saxophone (some critics justly compared him to Charlie Parker). This special sound that Walter created was much appreciated, and the list of his followers—from Louis Myers★ to Paul Butterfield★ and Charlie Musselwhite★—is so long that it is impossible to mention in its entirety. Little Walter's influence upon the development of the harmonica was very similar to that of B. B. King★ on the development of the guitar.

He moved from Louisiana to Chicago during the war, and there he soon became a beggar, playing the guitar or the harmonica in the flea markets on Maxwell Street. There he met Snooky Pryor,* who showed him a few tricks with the harmonica. He created a small band with Jimmy Rogers and Leroy Foster; Muddy Waters joined soon after. Around 1947, their dynamic country blues, both exuberant and amplified, gained the favor of the black migrants of Chicago, and these blues became the attraction of the Chicago clubs. Strangely enough, after 1948 Muddy Waters successfully recorded solo for Chess, but Little Walter limited himself to a few songs for several small labels.

The Blues World of Little Walter (Delmark) includes some of his best recordings; the rapid maturation of his harmonica style is clear, as it went from a very rural acoustic approach to an extremely complex and amplified style within a few months. After 1950 Walter appeared on Muddy's records. His contributions helped to turn Muddy's titles into masterpieces. It's almost pure chance that Len Chess* recorded Little Walter as the featured musician on a brilliant instrumental piece, "Juke," which was a big hit; it even reached number one on the rhythm-and-blues charts. After that Little Walter left Muddy Waters and created his own band with Louis and Dave Myers and drummer Fred Below,* who were then in the band of Little Walter's young rival, Junior Wells* (who, in return, replaced Little Walter in Muddy's band).

A long list of masterpieces followed after that, among which were several commercial hits: "Mean Old World," "Sad Hours," "Off the Wall," "Blues with a Feeling," and "Too Late." Walter was then a very demanding leader; he worked for weeks on a piece with his accompanists before recording. This gave his records a perfection and cohesiveness that were seldom equaled.

Walter was always a hard person to live with: violent, haughty, quarrelsome to the hilt, and always trying to deceive others. The huge success he enjoyed did not improve his character, and he had trouble keeping his musicians. After 1954 the hotheaded Myers brothers left their positions open for the taciturn and outstanding guitar player Robert Jr. Lockwood* and the quiet Willie Dixon.* Walter recorded a few beautiful records with them: "Last Night," "Mellow Down Easy," and "I Hate to See You Go." He reached number one again on the charts with "My Babe," an intelligent adaptation by Willie Dixon of the famous Negro spiritual "This Train."

However, the exhausting and endless tours throughout the U.S., the abuse of alcohol, and a conceit on the verge of megalomania began to show on Little Walter's music. In 1958 Lockwood left him, and the first signs of young black fans' dissatisfaction with the blues appeared. Little Walter's popularity kept on decreasing. He was affected by that a great deal, and he became increasingly difficult and demanding. After 1960 Walter seemed unable to regain the creativity of his earlier efforts. In the business sense, he was finished. Chess recorded him only rarely. In 1967 he went to Europe long enough to get in a knife fight with Sonny Boy Williamson (Rice Miller)* before flabbergasted admirers. The following year he was beaten to death during a fight in a Chicago alley.

He left an exemplary work that is largely available on Chess albums around the world. We recommend *The Best of Little Walter, Vols. 1 & 2* (Chess).

LITTLE WILLIE LITTLEFIELD

See California

JOHN LITTLEJOHN

(John Littlejohn Finchess / b. 1931 / vocals, guitar)

John Littlejohn, almost unknown beyond a limited circle of fans, is one of the best representatives of slide-guitar playing.

Born in Mississippi, he moved to Chicago where he spent years learning the trade in the black clubs of the South and West Sides. He polished a style that was inspired by Elmore James* as well as by the purest Delta tradition. In 1968 producer Chris Strachwitz, one of the best in that profession, discovered him and recorded him. *John Littlejohn and His Chicago Blues Stars* (Arhoolie) is outstanding; it includes a version of "Catfish" and several pieces on slide guitar. It attracted attention, and the following years he went to the Chicago studios and made several records for Chess and Bluesway (the excellent album *Funky from Chicago*). He then went on tour in Europe and in Japan and there recorded several albums.

But, tired of the exhausting life in Chicago, John Littlejohn went back to Jackson, Mississippi, in the eighties. He played in the local clubs, and he recorded for Ace and Rooster Blues, often accompanied by harmonica player Sammy Myers.* *So-Called Friends* (Rooster) was his latest album, on which he is somewhat drowned out by the brass section. He can do better.

LIVING BLUES

Even if historically speaking *Living Blues* was not the first blues magazine in English (*Blues Unlimited* came before by a good ten years), it was the first blues magazine that was printed in and distributed from the United States.

Created in Chicago by Jim O'Neal and Amy Van Singel, *Living Blues* quickly made a name for itself as the main blues magazine. Indeed, the writers had a big advantage over their European counterparts: They were where the action was, where the music really "lived." The interview of a bluesman in his home in Chicago that went on for days, even weeks, could not compare with a quick interview in Europe with a musician caught in his dressing room or between planes.

The first fifty numbers of *Living Blues* collected some great interviews. They are an incredible reference tool, even if the record column was the weak part of the magazine.

It is certain that *Living Blues* played an important role in the official recognition of this music in America. It gave the artists a mirror of their activities, and it gave the rest of the world a living image of the blues, whereas numerous European publications were more limited—by necessity—to historical studies of music. However, it is important to underline that *Living Blues* was for a long time—like the blues—able to develop itself thanks to the subscribers and readers from the other side of the Atlantic who constituted a large part of its readership.

After a slack period which almost doomed the magazine, and after the two founders withdrew, *Living Blues* moved to where the music it defended was born: Mississippi. Having become the rather official review of the remarkable Center for Study of Southern Culture of the University of Mississippi (whose director is the specialist Bill Ferris), *Living Blues* slacked off for a while. It was recently rejuvenated and became again the magazine that is a must to real blues fans.

However, this should not hamper the interest for European magazines that also have some excellent articles signed by the best blues specialists. Also worth reading are *Blues & Rhythm* and *Juke Blues* in Great Britain, *Block* in Holland, *Il Blues* in Italy, and *Jefferson* in Sweden. Let's also not forget *Soul Bag*, a great French review, whose only problem is that it is not in English.

ROBERT JR. LOCKWOOD

(b. 1915 / vocals, guitar)

If there is a bluesman who can claim he is really Robert Johnson's* heir, it is Robert Jr. Lockwood, whose mother lived with Johnson for several years; Robert Jr. learned his blues directly from Robert Johnson.

Strangely enough, Lockwood never wished to "perpetuate" the style of the artist who would become the most legendary bluesman in all blues history. This role that could have been fruitful seemed to be limiting to Lockwood, and instead of limiting himself, he preferred to evolve constantly. He went from the Delta blues to the Chicago blues with a strong predilection for a very jazzy style.

After 1941 Robert Jr. Lockwood recorded a series of records in the purest Johnson style. They were almost equal in quality to what his mentor had done (*Lonesome Road Blues:* Yazoo and *Windy City Blues:* Yazoo). But Lockwood hated to be reduced to that role. He even confessed he was tired of repeating impersonal themes all the time. A long stay in Memphis and in Arkansas and an association with Sonny Boy Williamson (Rice Miller)* for the radio program "King Biscuit Hour" led him to Chicago where he played guitar in many

■ Robert Jr. Lockwood. *(Photograph © by Anton J. Mikofsky; used with permission)*

recording sessions for Mercury and especially Chess. Little by little he gave up Johnson's style for a complex and inventive guitar style that was oriented toward jazz guitarists like Charlie Christian, Floyd Smith, and Django Reinhardt. He thus developed in Chicago an undeniable originality. This gave the records on which he participated a particular charm that was central to their success. These include many records of Sonny Boy, Otis Spann,* and Little Walter.* It is probably with the latter that he is the closest, for Walter was successful with his jazzy approach to the blues and their long association produced remarkable results.

Especially known as an accompanist, Robert Jr. Lockwood recorded few titles under his own name in the golden age of the Chicago blues: quite beautiful albums on Mercury, Decca, and JOB that are together on the album *Robert Lockwood & Johnny Shines* (Flyright) and some pieces accompanied by piano player Otis Spann on a Candid album.

Lockwood started late in his career to record albums under his own name: *Steady Rolling Man* (Delmark) was conceived as an homage to Robert Johnson; it revealed Lockwood as the leader of a Chicago group consisting of Louis Myers* and Fred Below.* Finally, with *Contrasts* (Trix) and *Does Twelve* (Trix) Lockwood shows a mixture of Delta tradition and jazz innovation.

Of particular appeal is the album that Lockwood recorded with Johnny Shines* in 1980, *Hangin' On* (Rounder), that gave these two followers of Robert Johnson the opportunity to combine their talents again.

CRIPPLE CLARENCE LOFTON

See Boogie-Woogie

LONESOME SUNDOWN

See J. D. Miller

JOE HILL LOUIS

(1920–1957 / vocals, guitar, harmonica, drums)

Along with Doctor Ross,* Joe Hill Louis was the most accomplished among the many one-man bands in Memphis. He was a seasoned guitar player whose insistent phrases revealed a strong influence of Delta blues. His clear and precise harmonica style was outstanding considering that he usually played the guitar, the drums, and the harmonica all at the same time. Although his drum effects were limited, they lent his music a primitive touch. The whole thing was amplified to the point of saturation; it gave a heavy and powerful sound that was extremely effective and original.

Not much is known about Joe Hill's life. He may have come to Memphis from Mississippi after the war. He performed in the streets and clubs by attracting attention with his talents as a one-man band. He was one of the first bluesmen to be recorded by producer Sam Phillips.* Between 1949 and 1957 he recorded over fifty titles for many labels, big and small, under several stage names, alternating slow blues with fast boogies.

Despite the relatively high number of records, he never managed to get out of the Memphis ghetto. In 1957 he died of tetanus because he did not have money to pay for the vaccine.

It is unfortunate that his work is difficult to find, except on the anthologies *Lowdown Memphis Harmonica Jam* (Nighthawk), *Downhome Delta Blues* (Nighthawk), and *Sun: The Blues Years* (Sun Box).

LOUISIANA

Louisiana is historically, geographically, and culturally at the crossroads between the Southeast and the Southwest. No other American state has as much originality. That mosaic is reflected in the blues of the state: The acoustic blues of Robert Pete Williams* is rooted in the tradition of neighboring Texas; the swamp blues of producer J. D. Miller* joins Baton Rouge's Lightnin' Hopkins'* influence with that of Jimmy Reed*; the Acadian region watched the Cajun blues or zydeco develop, represented primarily by Clifton Chenier.* Finally, New Orleans created a postwar rhythm-and-blues style that incorporated the wind instruments of Dixieland with the old piano tradition of the city and the beat and depth of rural blues.

All these particular styles represent important trends in blues history; Louisiana has hosted or been home to them all.

LOUISIANA RED

(Iverson Minter / b. 1936 / vocals, guitar, harmonica)

Was it the tragic life of Louisiana Red (his mother died when he was a year old and his father was lynched by the Ku Klux Klan) that gave such a genuine touch to his performances? Whatever the inspiration, his long career turned him progressively into one of the last representatives of the Delta blues style, which in the beginning he strove to imitate.

He recorded very early under several names (e.g., Guitar Red and Playboy Fuller) for Chess and other labels by imitating Muddy Waters* and Lightnin' Hopkins* (in *Forest City Joe/Louisiana Red:* Chess).

In 1962 Red was taken in hand by producer Henry Glover, and he achieved a certain success with "Red's Dream," a blues with devastating humor that described Red battling with Khrushchev and Fidel Castro.

This title and some other remarkable ones appeared on the album *The Back Porch Blues* (Roulette/Vogue). Red's talent as an original and expressive composer remained his strong point. On the other hand, he assimilated the musical styles of Jimmy Reed,* Muddy Waters, and Elmore James.* He is adept at slide guitar. After that excellent album, Red had a slack period for ten years. Discovered again by Herb Abramson, he recorded a mammoth session for Atlantic that produced two very good albums: *Louisiana Red Sings the Blues* (Atlantic) and *The Devil's Blues* (Red Lightning).

He became a favorite in concerts and clubs in Europe. Red then recorded a great number of albums that often were slapdash and repetitive. An excellent session on the Blue Labor New York label was recently reissued on CD: *Midnight Rambler* (Tomato). On it, Red played with striking realism the role of the Delta bluesman alone with his acoustic guitar.

Louisiana Red is able to produce remarkable things, but he needs to be well managed and surrounded by good musicians.

WILLIE MABON

(1925–1985 / vocals, piano, harmonica)

In spite of Willie Mabon's commercial hits in the fifties—
"Poison Ivy," "I'm Mad," "The Seventh Son," and especially
"I Don't Know," inspired by Cripple Clarence Lofton,★ he
died somewhat forgotten, and his name is seldom mentioned
among important blues musicians.

Mabon may have been too atypical. Born in Tennessee but
working in Chicago in a style much closer to that of Charles
Brown★ or Little Willie Littlefield★ than to that of Otis
Spann,★ this piano player recorded for Chess with his own
back-up band and not with the regulars of the great blues
label.

Mabon's music reflected his relaxed lifestyle: His suave
voice suggested chromatic blues in which the sophistication of
the lyrics was combined with an often biting humor. He was
able to play the piano brilliantly, although he often contented
himself with a simple accompaniment, both elegant and
sober. He was at his best when he played slow blues with simple phrases on the harmonica which he played simultaneously.

After the mid-sixties, he had the usual slack period that
affected bluesmen of his time.

Two albums cover his great period in Chicago: *The Seventh
Son* (Crown Prince) and *I'm the Fixer* (Flyright). We hope to
see the excellent *Shake That Thing* (Black & Blue) reissued.

MAGIC SAM

(Samuel Maghett / 1937–1969 / vocals, guitar)

A nephew of Shakey Jake★ (who may have played an important role in the development of his style), Magic Sam was—
along with Otis Rush★ and Buddy Guy★—one of the major
renovators of the Chicago blues in the late fifties. He created

the West Side sound that adapted the guitar style of B. B. King* to the oppressive environment of Chicago, and added numerous musical features of gospel, especially the profuse use of the minor scales. This style, which in a way announced soul music, did not have a real influence on black musicians beyond Chicago, although it was popular there.

Thanks to his wonderful singing, both tight and sensual, dramatic and smooth, and to the originality of his compositions, Magic Sam gained the attention of the young black public right after his recording debut for Cobra (*All Your Love*), which he made at age twenty. Unfortunately, when he came back from his brief military service, he failed to rekindle his first success. From 1960 to 1968 Sam played in some miserable clubs for ridiculous amounts of money. But his sincerity, his artistic sense, and his persistence finally earned him the notice of producer Bob Koester for whom he recorded two outstanding albums: *West Side Soul* (Delmark) and *Black Magic* (Delmark), which brought him unanimous praise from the critics. Today, they are considered classics of the Chicago blues. *Magic Sam's Legacy* (Delmark) includes some unedited records from these sessions.

The year 1969 looked promising for Sam: a tour in Europe, an outstanding performance in Ann Arbor, contracts, an album project on a major label . . . Unfortunately, a heart attack took him away in November 1969.

His Cobra records constitute the best of the Chicago blues, the quintessence of the West Side sound; they are now on CD: *Magic Sam* (Flyright). Some wonderful titles by Sam can be found on the album *The Late, Great Magic Sam* (L+R) and on several anthologies: *Sweet Home Chicago* (Delmark) and *Out of Bad Luck* (Flyright). It should be noted that several albums produced in the eighties in the U.S. under the name of Magic Sam were imitations, on which Sam did not appear at all. This is a strange sign of the fame of a great musician who had a great deal left to do.

MAGIC SLIM

(Morris Holt / b. 1937 / vocals, guitar)

An unquestionable revelation of the Chicago blues in the late seventies, Magic Slim was pulled from anonymity and plunged into international fame. He went from Florence's, a small and cramped club where he was a regular, to the big stages of the festivals.

A gloomy but constant mainstay of the West Side clubs of Chicago in the mid-seventies, Magic Slim nevertheless remained a country boy from Mississippi; he only transplanted his Delta blues seed to Chicago. This put him a lot closer to the postwar bluesmen than to the scathing guitar players of the West Side sound.

In fact, this timid giant moved to Chicago only in 1965, which may explain the constant Delta influences on his style.

Magic Sam* was his childhood friend, and Slim got his nickname from him. He learned his trade in the bands of Slim Willis and Shakey Jake* before he created his own band, the Teardrops, which gradually became one of the prototypes of the juke box bands that were able to play anything upon request and that are still found in many places in the black ghettos and in juke-joints in the South. Although his repertoire was eclectic, Magic Slim managed to personalize every song he played: With a heavy but smooth rhythm—a walking bass line with funky riffs—and a powerful gravelly voice, he created a unique atmosphere almost immediately. He was brilliant in slow blues. His guitar style may seem rather limited, but it is incredibly expressive and smooth, effectively using a vibrato reminiscent of musicians from the Delta blues tradition like Eddie Taylor* or John Lee Hooker.*

Despite his excellent first 45, "Love My Baby," a dark and introspective piece, Magic Slim had to wait until 1975 when French producer Marcelle Morgantini came to Chicago, to sign at last his first album, *Born on a Bad Sign* (MCM), a great success that drew attention to that generous personality and that strong and authentic music.

Following that opportunity, Magic Slim came out of the

slump that then surrounded the Chicago bluesmen. He toured Europe and America and signed an increasing number of contracts for clubs and festivals throughout the country.

For a while Slim had health problems, but he seems to have asserted himself firmly as a significant bluesman, certainly not as a creator but as a steady representative of the Chicago blues.

He probably recorded too many records that were not well produced. His best albums are *Raw Magic* (Alligator) and *Highway Is My Home* (Black & Blue), both made in France. With more time and a band with more instruments, a piano and a tenor saxophone, for instance, Slim could have really recorded a magic album. The death of his old friend and accompanist, Alabama Junior Pettis, who was a real support in the band, unbalanced the solidity of his combo.

In a similar vein, two other Chicago musicians can be associated with Magic Slim. They also emerged in the eighties:

HIP LINKCHAIN (Willie Richard / 1936–1989) was certainly a limited singer-guitar player, but he was also deeply rooted in the Delta tradition via Chicago. His composer's talents put him much above the average bluesmen. After having scoured the clubs of the Windy City and having recorded a few 45s for several small labels, he seemed to obtain a certain success before his death.

EDDIE KING (Edward Milton / b. 1938), a singer and guitar player from Alabama, is also an old hand. He created his straightforward style after Freddie King★ and Little Milton★; he recorded with Detroit Junior★ and Little Mack Simmons. He had to wait until his fifties to record his first album, the excellent *The Blues Has Got Me* (Double Trouble), on which his sister, Mae Bee May, a great singer, was brilliant. Eddie King, who has become a guitar player of KoKo Taylor,★ is preparing an album for Alligator.

J. J. MALONE

(b. 1935 / vocals, piano, guitar)

Only in the early eighties did blues fans realize the musical richness of the San Francisco Bay area. J. J. Malone was a revelation there, even though he had already had a long career.

Born in Alabama, J. J. Malone had the usual childhood of a rural black bluesman: misery and music. He sang at the local church, learned guitar and harmonica before piano (his main instrument), and moved to California to find a paying job. It was only in the late sixties that he managed to live off his music, after long stints in several bands. He met producer Ray Shanklin, owner of the Galaxy label, for whom he recorded a series of 45s in a style somewhere between soul and rhythm and blues, with "Danger Zone," "One Step Away," and especially "It's a Shame," with which he was successful locally. Shanklin, who was impressed by Malone's talents as a composer and an arranger, gave him responsibilities in the expanding record company Galaxy/Fantasy. J. J. was then in an important position; he advised Little Johnny Taylor,* Big Mama Thornton,* and Sonny Rhodes.* He wrote—without signing them—a good many Creedence Clearwater Revival tunes (Sonny Rhodes said that the famous Creedence sound would not exist without Malone). He also met scores of musicians, including white singer-guitar player Troyce Key, who had been famous for a short while as a rockabilly artist. Troyce and J. J. teamed up and bought a club near Fresno, the Eli's Mile, which became a center of California blues.

Despite his strong local popularity, J. J. Malone had to wait until the late seventies to be able to record again, this time substantially. He appeared briefly but brilliantly on his friend Sonny Rhodes' record: *I Don't Want My Blues Colored Bright* (Advent); then he was featured, along with Troyce Key, on the excellent *I've Got a New Car* (Red Lightnin') and *Younger Than Yesterday* (Red Lightnin') on which their good humor and their joy in playing are irresistible. The sources from which the two friends drew their inspiration are varied: Lightnin' Hopkins,* Roy Milton,* and Don & Dewey. But on these two albums J. J. recorded several wonderful slow blues on which his voice, which seemed to emerge from behind a curtain of whiskey vapors and smoke, was remarkably effective. A sensitive piano player who favors trills after the fashion of Walter Roland,* Malone is above all an excellent composer who creates evocative metaphors. Later on he developed all these qualities on other albums, and particularly on *The Enemy Called Hate* (Cherrie), produced carefully by Schoolboy Cleve. Through more than ten wonderful pieces, both personal and lyrical, J. J. seems to be a master of combining all the influences he gathered throughout his long career.

It is certain that along with Sonny Rhodes, Phillip Walker,* and Robert Cray,* J. J. Malone is one of the most important names of the current West Coast blues.

MANDOLIN

Coming from Italy and linked closely to "serenades," this instrument had a spectacular development in the United States in white folk music, particularly in modern bluegrass. On the other hand, the mandolin was never important for the blues. However, it is present in most prewar rural string bands, for example, the Memphis Jug Band* and the Mississippi Sheiks.* Several musicians were real virtuosos with that otherwise limited instrument: Carl Martin* and Ted Bogan (both still playing in Chicago), Yank Rachell,* and Charlie McCoy.* It is important to note that these musicians are as skillful with the mandolin as with the guitar or the fiddle. In general, the mandolin was used to create atmosphere, and mandolin solos are rare in blues history.

The mandolin barely survived the electrification of the blues despite the existence of an electric mandolin, quite popular in country music.

Johnny Young,* besides being a good guitar player, was the only true follower of that instrument in the modern blues. But his technique, which favored a note-by-note style, made the mandolin much similar to the electric guitar, to the point that it was difficult for the unsophisticated listener to distinguish between the two.

CARL MARTIN

See East Coast Blues

PETE MAYES

See Joe Hughes

PERCY MAYFIELD

(1920–1984 / vocals)

Percy Mayfield is a good example of a major California blues artist whose importance was underestimated for a long time. He was not really one of the creators of that trend, but his direct and indirect influence—especially as a composer—was tremendous after 1950, and scores of bluesmen claiming to have been impressed by his talent have covered his blues faithfully and with consistency. "Please Send Me Someone to Love," "Strange Things Happening," "I Need Your Love So Bad," "It Serves You Right to Suffer (Memory Pain)," and "My Mind Is Trying to Leave Me" became classics through the interpretations of artists such as John Lee Hooker,★ Lowell Fulson,★ and Jimmy Dawkins.★ Mayfield was also the composer of several songs for Ray Charles★ between 1962 and 1964: for example, "Hit the Road, Jack," "Danger Zone," "But on the Other Hand," and "Tell Me How Do You Feel."

This function overshadowed Mayfield's own recordings. His career as a soloist might have been more important if he had not been injured in a terrible accident in 1952 that left him disfigured and substantially changed his voice. After that, Mayfield kept on recording under his own name and devoted himself to his talent for composing.

His own recordings were generally outstanding. He was a subtle baritone; he favored a curious lowering of the notes and frequently repeated the last line of the couplet, thus insinuating more than singing. He often created a melancholic atmosphere that surrounded the audience. He confessed to having been deeply influenced by church sermons. Indeed, his compositions in an unusual moralizing fashion stressed human weaknesses and the ravages of alcohol and unhappy love.

Three excellent compilations of his first records enable us to judge Percy Mayfield's work: *The Voice Within* (Route 66),

My Heart Is Always Singing Sad Songs (Ace), and *Poet of the Blues* (Specialty). He also recorded some albums for Tangerine and RCA that deserve to be reissued.

In 1983, shortly before he died, Percy recorded an album with Phillip Walker* entitled *Hit the Road Again* (Timeless).

JERRY McCAIN

(b. 1930 / vocals, harmonica)

His drawling and nasal voice, so southern, and his excellent harmonica style would have certainly allowed him to have a better career, but Jerry McCain never agreed to leave his "home." Born in Gasden, Alabama, McCain remained faithful to his native soil, and he ventured very little farther than Nashville, Tennessee, or Jackson, Mississippi.

He made his recording debut in Jackson in 1952 for the Trumpet label of Lillian McMurray, with the classics "Wine o' Wine" and "East of the Sun." Then with Excello in Nashville he had a few regional hits that furthered his reputation: "That's What They Want (Money)" covered by Little Johnny; the hilarious "My Next Door Neighbor"; and the southern saga of the unemployed: "Welfare Cadillac" and "Courtin' in the Cadillac." Through these songs, Jerry McCain revealed himself as a remarkable composer with a blatant and biting humor in the great tradition of rural blues.

A beautiful instrumental "Red Top," taken up by CBS and "728 Texas," a noticeable achievement with the chromatic harmonica for Jewel, enabled him to go on tours for a while with some of the great names of black music, Freddie King,* Rufus Thomas,* and Otis Redding.

Although very popular locally, he vegetated on small labels and clubs of the "chitlin' circuit." As is often the case, it was with a blues-rock group, this time the Fabulous Thunderbirds, who covered his "She's Tuff," that people outside the circuit realized his existence. In 1989, finally again on an important label, Jerry McCain recorded an excellent album *Blues 'n' Stuff* (Ichiban).

Jerry McCain has behind him a rather considerable discography scattered on countless labels. Except for *Midnight Beat*

(Charly) that gathers his titles for Jewel, there is no collection of his best work.

At age sixty, as young and inventive as ever, McCain seems almost to have a career *ahead* of him.

TOMMY McCLENNAN

(1908–1962 / vocals, guitar)

Tommy McClennan's reputation was such in the Mississippi Delta region that Bluebird record producer Lester Melrose★ decided to bring him to Chicago to record. With the help of Big Bill Broonzy,★ Melrose found McClennan near Yazoo City in 1939.

The small stature of McClennan contrasted with the spirit of his singing and the almost ferocious rage of his guitar style, although he compensated for his lack of subtlety with his surprising sense of rhythm. He was the last great Delta bluesman who expressed himself in the pure country blues style and who was a big hit among blacks. His verve in his compositions, often aggressive and even mean, was in perfect harmony with his music, and the forty-one records made between 1939 and 1942 made him very popular. His most famous composition, "Bottle Up and Go," had allusions about the whites' duplicity that was only slightly veiled, once getting him thrown out of a club where he was performing.

Generally speaking, his pieces were blues with a quick tempo, very energetic and interspersed with savory interjections directed to his guitar or his bass player.

His success was such that Melrose recorded McClennan's best friend, Robert Petway. Petway also was a brilliant Delta bluesman who expressed himself in a style similar to McClennan. He was the first bluesman to record "Catfish Blues" that was to become famous a few years later after Muddy Waters'★ version of it under the name of "Rolling Stone."

After the war, neither McClennan nor Petway managed to record again. They totally disappeared from the active scene of the blues, although they were among the first to have prepared the way for transplanting the Delta blues to Chicago.

Although no trace of Petway is known, McClennan remained in Chicago where he was seen occasionally with Elmore James* and Little Walter.* He died of alcoholism in 1962.

Except for *Cotton Patch Blues* (Travelin' Man), there are no recordings of McClennan and Petway at this time.

CHARLIE AND JOE McCOY

See Memphis Minnie

ROBERT LEE McCOY

See Robert Nighthawk

JIMMY McCRACKLIN

(b. 1931? / vocals, piano, harmonica)

A rather atypical artist of the San Francisco Bay area, Jimmy McCracklin remained unrecognized for a long time. He has denigrated his first records that have been deemed obscure compared to his later successes in the soul field; on the other hand, these successes were judged too "commercial" by blues fans.

But, in light of the studies made by Tom Mazzolini, Per Notini, and Jonas Bernholm, McCracklin's work was reevaluated; it now appears to be an essential part of the San Francisco blues.

Although McCracklin himself said he was born in 1931 in Helena, Arkansas, this date seems unlikely: He recorded as early as 1945 in Los Angeles after having been in the navy. He spent his childhood largely in St. Louis listening to Walter Davis,* who influenced the first records he made solo and with pianist J. D. Nicholson.

As did many musicians around the San Francisco Bay area, McCracklin worked with producer Bob Geddins. McCracklin recorded for Geddins, and he also wrote several blues for other artists like Lowell Fulson,* with whom Jimmy was obviously close. His style during a good part of his first career, which was prolific and successful—until about 1957—was close to Fulson's style: a slightly husky voice with some wonderful interlacings of the piano and the guitar. The guitar was often played by the excellent Robert Kelton, then more and more by Lafayette Thomas,* one of the main figures of the Texas-California guitar style.

Working for Chess in 1957, McCracklin had a big hit with "The Walk," which became a rock-and-roll classic. That success made him a national star. McCracklin then recorded a series of strong records on which there was a flawless brass section. After 1962 he renewed his relationship with Bob Geddins and had several big artistic and commercial hits on the Art-Tone label: "Just Got to Know," "Shame Shame Shame," "Every Night Every Day," and especially "Think." These titles make McCracklin one of the great composers in blues history, with his depth of feeling, his sense of phrasing, and his conciseness and efficiency.

In the seventies and eighties, Jimmy McCracklin was more and more recognized by the regular blues public, both national and international. Nevertheless, he still retained the favors of a middle-aged black public, who always identified itself—despite the wall of silence of some media—with the best stylists of rhythm and blues. Several albums for Minit, Stax, and Evejim show that McCracklin was able to adapt his career to the essential qualities of the California blues, for whom he is finally an important figure.

Rockin' Man (Route 66), *I'm Gonna Have My Fun* (Route 66), and *You Deceived, Man* (Crown Prince) are indispensable collections of his first career. *Jimmy McCracklin* (Chess) gathers all the records cut for this label. *High on the Blues* (Stax) and *Same Lovin'* (Evejim), more recent, are also important.

FRED McDOWELL

(1905–1972 / vocals, guitar)

Only in 1940 when he settled on a small piece of land near Como, Mississippi, did Fred McDowell finally have enough money to buy his first guitar. He played all the time for his neighbors and friends and for Saturday night dances.

However, his main activity was farming. As a guitar player, he became a follower of the bottleneck style, quickly mastering this style. He was an intense and brilliant guitar player, able to make a thousand nuances of his instrument with his bottleneck, while creating an irresistible rhythm with his style of alternating bass notes. Moreover, he was a singer with an enthralling melancholic voice that was entirely absorbed in his music. In fact, although he did not record before the war, McDowell was one of the major Delta bluesmen. His style and the intensity of his performances were similar to that of Son House.* Like Son House he was not a great composer, but he took traditional themes and personalized them so much that he made them his, for example, "Kokomo Blues," "Highway 61," and "Red Cross Store."

Not very ambitious, never having planned a real musical career, Fred McDowell would not have left us his music if, one day in May 1959, the tireless ethnomusicologist Alan Lomax had not crossed his path. Lomax realized immediately the importance of his discovery, and he recorded Fred. His records are now gathered on *Mississippi Fred McDowell* (Heritage).

However, McDowell did not become known to white blues-revival fans until 1962. He then performed at the Newport Festival in 1964. He also performed at the American Folk Blues Festival in 1965 in Europe. Along with Robert Pete Williams* he was one of the major discoveries of this blues revival. In the sixties and seventies he performed in numerous concerts and festivals around the world. When the Rolling Stones covered his version of the spiritual classic "You Got to Move," McDowell was given substantial copyright benefits. He also signed a contract with Capitol, which resulted in a superb album *I Do Not Play No Rock and Roll* (Capitol), on which Fred played the electric guitar with his usual mastery. He used that formula again on the excellent *Fred McDowell and His Blues Boys* (Arhoolie) and *Somebody Keeps Calling Me* (Antilles).

Among the best of his many albums are *Delta Blues* (Arhoolie), *Fred McDowell, Vol. 2* (Arhoolie), and *Fred McDowell and Johnny Woods* (Rounder).

Fred managed to buy a gas station on Highway 61 near Como, Mississippi, shortly before he died. He is still a much-revered figure of the local bluesmen in that town (Jessie Mae Hemphill,* R. L. Burnside,* Napoleon Strickland, Ranie Burnette . . .).

BROWNIE McGHEE
AND SONNY TERRY

(Walter McGhee / b. 1915 / vocals, guitar) and (Saunders Teddell / 1911–1986 / vocals, harmonica)

Brownie and Sonny had the most fruitful and longest association in blues history—thirty years. However, far before Sonny's death, the duo had split on bad terms; their life "together" was unbearable.

Both born on the East Coast, they represent the typical blues of that area. Sonny Terry was a great virtuoso with the harmonica. He used it in quite a different way from that of the influential Chicago bluesmen: not amplified, but trying to imitate noises in nature or those of human activities (e.g., trains and hunting dogs). He actually had a very primitive style—a gruff and cocky vocal style—reflecting the rural tradition of the Appalachian mountains, whether black or white. Strictly speaking, he was more a folk musician than a bluesman. In fact, he belonged for a long time to the folk circles of New York (with Woody Guthrie, Pete Seeger, and Leadbelly*).

Brownie McGhee is a singer-guitar player who drew his inspiration directly from Blind Boy Fuller,* whose name he used (Blind Boy Fuller #2) in his first recordings in 1940. A musician devoid of genius, but capable of good moments, he is an excellent blues composer, whose often bitter lyrics contrasted with the happy exuberance of Sonny Terry's harmonica. However, his exaggerated mannerisms and sense of self-satisfaction spoiled many of his recordings.

Brownie McGhee and Sonny Terry were both discovered in Carolina by promoter J. B. Long, who was Blind Boy Fuller's manager. After a short-lived solo career, Sonny Terry appeared

■ Brownie McGhee. *(Photograph © by Anton J. Mikofsky; used with permission)*

in the famous concert organized by John Hammond, "Spirituals to Swing," in 1938. McGhee and Terry's association began in 1940. In New York they managed to take part in all the musical trends of the city (blues, rhythm and blues, the

■ Sonny Terry. *(Photograph © by Anton J. Mikofsky; used with permission)*

"folk boom," blues revival, etc.), they even appeared on poster bills of several Broadway plays and sang for many films.

They recorded prolifically, and their best recordings are side by side with the worst. Their best work was done in the period 1946 to 1958 when it was directed primarily to the black public of Harlem. Alone or with other outstanding musicians (Mickey Baker,* Bob Gaddy, Champion Jack Dupree,* and Big Chief Ellis), they made an excellent series of recordings, among which are *Old Town Blues, Vol. 1* (Ace), *Whoopin' the Blues* (Charly), and *Climbin' Up* (Savoy).

They recorded after 1960 either as a duo or each on his own many albums that often were not good. *Midnight Special* (Fantasy) and *Blues Is Truth* (Tomato) are competent. Later in life, the two artists at times seemed to be completely indifferent to their undertakings. But blues history will reserve a place for Brownie McGhee, an excellent lyric writer, who continued the blues of Blind Boy Fuller and Gary Davis; and for Sonny Terry, who was too quickly labeled "folk," despite numerous recordings and despite his last performances (especially in the film *The Color Purple*), which show that he was a great instrumentalist.

STICKS McGHEE

See New York

JAY McSHANN

See Kansas City

BLIND WILLIE McTELL

(1901–1959 / vocals, guitar)

Although his roots are in the East Coast tradition, Blind Willie McTell escapes classification. He was a remarkable blues singer, but he was also comfortable with ragtime, rural dances, gospel, and popular prewar tunes as well as with themes of white rural music. Moreover, his high and clear voice, often in falsetto, was similar to that of country singer Jimmie Rodgers,* whose repertoire McTell partly adapted.

As a street singer, McTell developed a great vocal power and, above all, a brilliant guitar style, which today makes him highly respected by folk guitar players. He expressed himself with the difficult twelve-string guitar and showed unequaled eclecticism and virtuosity. His fingerpicking style was perfect, both in ragtimes modeled after Blind Blake* and on bottleneck. Contrary to most East Coast guitar players, he played an irregular fingerpicking: Each musical phrase was a whole, dealt with separately according to his mood and to the inflections of his singing.

Although his records do not seem to have been successful commercially, Blind Willie McTell recorded prolifically for several companies from 1927 until 1956. It seems that his fame in Atlanta, where he earned a living by playing in the streets, at the markets, or in parking lots upon the request of passersby, was tremendous. He thus attracted all the big record companies that were scouring the East Coast hoping to find new talents. Furthermore, unlike many other artists, he was easy to find, and his eclectic repertoire was another plus for him. He appeared under several record names (e.g., Blind Sammie, Georgia Bill, and Pig'n' Whistle Red) at Vocalion, Victor/Bluebird, Decca, Columbia, either by himself or with guitar player Curley Weaver or with Fred McMullen or Ruth Willis or Kate McTell. In 1940, Alan Lomax interviewed him and recorded him for the Library of Congress. After the war, he recorded several titles for Atlantic, Regal/Savoy, and Prestige (which, in fact, got possession of the recorded bands for its private use) before disappearing mysteriously. He left behind him an aura of legend that fascinates many experts. Only the stubbornness of the ethnomusicologist David Evans—who was able to find and to interview Kate McTell—helped us know more about Willie's life and personality, as well as the exact date of his death.

One can admire the extraordinary talent of McTell on *Blind Willie McTell* (MCA), *The Early Years* (Yazoo), and *1927–35* (Yazoo). *Love Changing Blues* (Biograph) and *Trying to Get Home* (Biograph) were made after the war, and although inferior, these records are still good quality.

LESTER MELROSE

See Chicago

MEMPHIS

In the nineteenth century Memphis became the cotton capital and exchange center at the crossroads for the southern states: Tennessee, Mississippi, Missouri, Arkansas, Alabama, and Louisiana. Memphis was the main entertainment center for farmers, landowners, and sharecroppers, white and black, along the banks of the Mississippi River.

Hence at the beginning of the twentieth century, the black district between Beale and Fourth street, later occupied by Handy Park (as homage to W. C. Handy*), was reserved for gambling, drinking, prostitution, fights, and, of course, music. All day long, street bands walked along Beale Street, bands composed primarily of string instruments in contrast with New Orleans Dixieland bands or jug bands. Around 1925 there reigned the Beale Street Sheiks, formed by guitar players Dan Sane and Frank Stokes,* creator of the Memphis blues; bottleneck specialist Furry Lewis,* who sold his medicines between songs; and the new Memphis queen, the breathtaking Memphis Minnie.* A great number of musicians, drinkers, gamblers, swindlers, and prostitutes met in the clubs on Beale Street until late into the night. The most famous club on Beale Street, PeeWee's, had a sign with the following biting humor: We do not close before the first murder.

Very close to Frank Stokes, guitar player JIM JACKSON (1880–1937) was one of the big entertainers in Memphis. A dancer, singer, guitar player, storyteller, and seller of magic potions, he was so popular that he finally drew the attention of the big companies Victor and Vocalion. His four versions of "Kansas City Blues" recorded in 1927 sold more than one million copies, phenomenal for that time. Much of his repertoire was composed of songs that often predated the blues ("Old Dog Blue"), with sustained bass notes in a style characteristic of Memphis. In 1930, at the peak of his fame, Stokes disappeared without a trace.

Maybe even more popular than Jackson and Stokes, the MEMPHIS JUG BAND was formed by and around Will Shade (Son Brimmer / 1894–1966). These musicians created jug bands, modeled after washboard bands of early jazz, in particular, the Clifford Hayes' Jug Blowers. Formed around a stable structure composed of Will Shade (harmonica, guitar, jug), Robert Burse (guitar), Milton Robey (fiddle), Ben Ramey (kazoo), and Charlie Burse (guitar and banjo), the Memphis Jug Band also welcomed piano player Jab Jones, fiddle player Charlie Pierce, and singer-guitarists Laura Dukes and Memphis Minnie★ as well as Bo Carter★ and Casey Bill Weldon.★ Between 1927 and 1934, they cut about eighty records: waltzes, traditional themes of black or white rural music, vaudeville tunes, pop music of the time (like the old "I'll See You in the Spring When the Birds Begin to Sing"), and of course the blues. Extremely popular among whites and blacks, they performed as far away as Colorado. The best of their recorded work is on the double album *The Memphis Jug Band* (Yazoo).

Following the way traced by Will Shade, many jug bands were formed in Memphis between 1928 and 1932:

For years, JACK KELLY'S SOUTH MEMPHIS JUG BAND, created by guitar player Jack Kelly and fiddler Will Batts, has been the daily entertainment of the big Peabody Hotel. Their show is unique, composed of numerous comedy skits and songs. They have recorded about thirty titles.

While harmonica player Jed Davenport and his jug band are particularly famous for their furious "Beale Street Breakdown," GUS CANNON'S JUG STOMPERS is considered by connoisseurs as the best of all jug bands. The banjo player GUS CANNON (1883–1979) was already well known in Tennessee under the stage name of Banjo Joe, for renditions of traditional themes like "Salty Dog" and "Old Hen Cackle." His introduction to guitar player Ashley Thompson and harmonica player Noah Lewis inspired him to create his own jug band in 1928. Noah Lewis was a remarkable musician. Many of his students are now more famous than he is, for example, Hammie Nixon, John Lee "Sonny Boy" Williamson,★ and Big Walter Horton.★ Noah Lewis's presence made Cannon's Jug Stompers more famous than their rivals. The whole of the recordings made by the Stompers between 1928 and 1930 is on the superb album *Cannon's Jug Stompers* (Herwin). In 1962 the folk group The Rooftop Singers took a composition of

Gus Cannon's, "Walk Right In," to number one on the charts. That earned Cannon substantial royalties as well as a short-lived comeback; he even recorded an album for Stax.

These few musicians are only the best known from Memphis. We can appreciate their talents on the anthologies *Lowdown Memphis Barrelhouse* (Mamlish), *Memphis Blues* (RCA/Bluebird), and *Memphis Jamboree* (Yazoo).

After 1945, the Memphis blues scene changed completely. The jug bands and string bands became rare on Beale Street. They were replaced with the electric blues then popular in the clubs of the black district. Memphis served many talented artists who came from neighboring states: one-man bands like Joe Hill Louis* and Doctor Ross*; the exuberant Rufus Thomas, Howlin' Wolf,* and Sonny Boy Williamson (Rice Miller)* and their students James Cotton* and Junior Parker*; guitar players with a heavy and dirty sound, Willie Johnson and Joe Willie Wilkins; Woodrow Adams; piano players Albert Williams, Roscoe Gordon, Billy "Red" Love, and especially the King of Beale Street, the disc jockey of the first black station, WDIA, Blues Boy King,* whose ultrasophisticated style opened the way to Bobby Bland* and Little Milton* before influencing blues history and a good part of contemporary music.

In 1948, the Bihari brothers came from Los Angeles to record the Memphis bluesmen for their labels Modern/RPM/Meteor. Indeed, despite the long musical tradition in Memphis, the cotton capital did not have a good recording studio.

Then SAM PHILLIPS intervened. Recognizing the problem, he decided to invest his capital in the creation of modern and well-equipped recording studios, MRS (Memphis Recording Service). He had always had a passion for the rural music, black or white, and he became the talent scout for the Bihari brothers and the Chess* brothers, for whom he recorded Walter Horton, Howlin' Wolf, and Sonny Boy Williamson (Rice Miller). In 1952, he created his own record label, Sun. He recorded a great many remarkable bluesmen (some of whom became famous, Little Milton and Junior Parker, in particular), without the commercial success he had hoped for: The market for black records was too limited for an ambitious small label like Sun. Phillips began looking for a white artist who would sing in the fiery and sensuous style of the blacks; in 1954 he found Elvis Presley. Presley recorded a mixture of hillbilly and blues, thus creating his extraordinary style. Following Presley, many new musicians came: Carl Perkins, Jerry Lee Lewis, Johnny Cash . . .

Sam Phillips continued his undertaking with the same flair until about 1968. He recorded many artists and all genres of southern music, but unfortunately with fewer and fewer bluesmen. Sam Phillips' talent, his label, and his artists were the object of a real cult, especially among rock-and-roll fans. The Sun catalog, which has been thoroughly studied, was largely reissued: *Sun Records: The Blues Years* (Sun Box), *The Blues Came Down from Memphis* (Charly), *Lowdown Memphis Harmonica Jam* (Nighthawk), *Sun Records Harmonica Classics* (Rounder), and the four compact discs *Sun: The Black Music Originals* (Sun) include the essentials of that remarkable production.

After the mid-sixties, there was a double phenomenon: The blues seemed to pick up among young blacks who were attracted en masse to the southern soul of Otis Redding, Aretha Franklin, and Booker T. and the MG's. Memphis was once more at the center of that new black music, and the context and tradition of the Memphis sound born then was rooted significantly and obviously in the blues. Two record companies in Memphis replaced Sun. First Stax, where Al Jackson, Jr., Steve Cropper—a remarkable southern white guitarist—and Booker T. Jones produced an excellent work with very bluesy records from Jimmie Hughes, Johnny Taylor,* Rufus Thomas and his daughter Carla, the Staples Singers— among whom the lead guitarist and singer Roebuck "Pops" Staples was deeply immersed in the Delta tradition, William Bell, Albert King,* Little Milton,* Isaac Tolbert, and more.

In Stax's shadow, producer and band leader Willie Mitchell managed the small Hi label, which also contributed to the creation of the Memphis sound: The less-polished sound, the talent of the house musicians (The brothers Leroy and Teenie Hodges, sons of Leroy Hodges, Sr., who played a central role, although unknown, in the Memphis blues of the sixties, and piano player Billy Always) gave an irresistible appeal to numerous Hi records. Also the superb Al Green, O. V. Wright,★ and Ann Peebles★ are soul singers with a large dose of blues in their music. Guitar player Big Lucky Carter and singer and harmonica player Amos Patton—a nephew of Charlie Patton★—are little-known bluesmen, but both are very talented, as can be heard on *Hi Records: The Blues Sessions* (Hi).

Furthermore, not only was Memphis the melting pot of a rapidly evolving black music, but it also became an important center of the blues revival and attracted many white fans and musicians, such as guitarists Backwards Sam Firk (Michael Stewart), Bill Barth, and John Fahey. They organized the annual River City Blues Festival, which enabled many traditional bluesmen to make themselves known to a young white public. Next to veterans like Furry Lewis, Bukka White,★ Robert Wilkins,★ Sleepy John Estes,★ Houston Stackhouse, and Joe Willie Wilkins, who resumed playing, this Memphis blues revival allowed new names to come to light: singer and guitar player Willie Morris, Earl Bell, Nathan Beauregard; harmonica player Memphis Sonny Boy; piano players Big Sam Clark, Memphis Piano Red Williams; and singer Ma Rainey. For these artists, listen to *Memphis Blues* (Echo), *More Memphis Blues* (Echo), *Kings of Country Blues, Vols. 1 & 2* (Arhoolie).

The decline of the black music scene in Memphis in the mid-seventies reported by most specialized magazines was in fact only true in appearance. Beale Street was then deserted and Handy Park looked like fallow land, but the blues and southern soul were still alive in the black clubs of Memphis and West Memphis. Specialists David Evans and Bill Ferris needed only to scratch the surface in order to reveal an underground but active blues scene. Thanks to their action and changing attitudes, the blues from then on was seen as an integral part of the cultural heritage of the city: Beale Street was classified as a "historical street"; an important documentation center, the Center for Southern Folklore, opened its doors to the blues; several music festivals featured blues and soul;

many chic clubs, such as the famous Blues Alley, opened their doors; and the official W. C. Handy Award began to be presented yearly to the best blues artists in the country.

All this made it possible for a limited but real rebirth of the Memphis blues, which is, above all, a presentation of many talents who were playing in the dark for limited audiences. The wonderful female singer and harmonica player Joyce Cobb; piano player Booker T. Laury; guitar players Fred Sanders and Clarence Nelson; and saxophone player Prince Gabe (Ed Kirby) were thus able to obtain regular engagements. The tireless David Evans discovered numerous talents in black clubs and recorded them for his High Water label: the Fieldstones,* the Hollywood All Stars, Little Applewhite, and the outstanding singer and guitar player Junior Kimbrough.

With the new attitude of many middle-aged blacks who admitted their taste for the southern soul/blues and the successes of southern labels like Malaco, La Jam, and Ichiban, Memphis looked more and more like a blues capital. The blues history of Memphis—almost a century long—does not seem to be about to disappear.

MEMPHIS JUG BAND

See Memphis

MEMPHIS MINNIE

(Lizzie Douglas / 1896–1973 / vocals, guitar)

For almost thirty years, Memphis Minnie was the great female star of the blues. This short, attractive woman was a mighty figure. Carving out a place for herself in a tough, antifeminist world, she dominated the Chicago blues scene between 1930 and 1950 along with Big Bill Broonzy and Tampa Red.* Moreover, she contributed a great deal to the blues style of that city. Her shrill and drawling voice and her rural blues style were totally different from that of the early female blues singers* (e.g., Bessie Smith,* Ma Rainey,* and Ida Cox*). Even at the peak of her fame, Minnie was still a country woman, and her blues was that of her childhood with, of course, the necessary modernization and electrification to keep the favor of a more and more urban public.

At a very young age, Memphis Minnie played the guitar in the streets of Memphis and married Casey Bill Weldon,* who was then part of the Memphis Jug Band. But her first records, cut in 1929, were with the singer-guitar player who had become her second husband, Kansas Joe McCoy.* In fact, Joe sang with his harsh voice, and Minnie complemented the pieces by playing the guitar remarkably, with precise and scathing notes in a flawless rhythm. Minnie was a superb but often underestimated guitar player. In 1930, she recorded "Bumble Bee," a great blues classic. The commercial success of that piece brought recognition to Minnie as the star of the duo she formed with Joe McCoy. They came to Chicago in the early thirties, and their career grew until they parted around 1935. Minnie was soon remarried to guitar player Ernest "Little Son Joe" Lawlar, with whom she created an incredible duo that was tremendously popular. "Nothing in Rambling," "In My Girlish Days," "Black Rat Swing," and "I'm So Glad" were big hits, for Minnie's singing and guitar blended perfectly with those of Little Son Joe, who seemed to have had a particularly positive role on his wife's career and music. Increasingly powerful, their blues took on a dramatic intensity characteristic of the postwar Chicago blues.

After the war, they played an important role in the emergence of the new Chicago blues; they also gave financial and moral support to Little Walter,* Muddy Waters, and Jimmy Rogers.* After 1950, the public favored these new stars more and more, but to the detriment of the old hands, and Minnie Johnson was now herself an old hand. She recorded a few more titles for JOB and Chess (with Little Walter), but she left both Chicago and music after her husband died in 1957.

Paralyzed, Minnie spent the last years of her life in a convalescent home, unjustly forgotten. Only at the very end of her life did journalists and her follower, British singer Jo-Ann Kelly,* come to see her several times and prove to her that her superb contribution to the blues history was not forgotten.

Her work—close to two hundred titles—was largely reissued. *I Ain't No Bad Gal* (Portrait), *Memphis Minnie, Vols. 1 & 2* (Blues Classic), and *Memphis Minnie: Hoodoo Lady* (CBS/Sony) are essential. *Love Changin' Blues* (Biograph) and *Gonna Take the Dirt Road Home* (OJL) include some of her later titles, and although they were not as brilliant as the first ones, we recommend these albums.

Although Minnie had met him in Memphis, her most famous husband JOE McCOY came with his brother CHARLIE McCOY (about 1900–51) from Jackson, Mississippi. They had recorded extensively there and played with the Mississippi Sheiks* and Tommy Johnson.* Although Joe McCoy was a good guitar player, Charlie, also a mandolin player, was far superior. But, besides a few excellent records under his own name, most of his titles were recorded with his brother Joe.

Before being separated from Minnie, Joe recorded numerous records under several stage names (e.g., Kansas Joe, Big Joe, Georgia Pine Boy, and Mississippi Mudder). Ambitious and extroverted, he soon became a central figure in the Chicago blues scene in the thirties, and Decca Records hired him as manager. He kept this job until 1942, after having discovered many talents.

After 1936 Joe and Charlie McCoy, along with Herb Morand, a trumpet player from New Orleans, formed the HARLEM HAMFATS, whose unrestrained jazz/blues was very popular in the chic clubs of Chicago. The public's passion for the Hamfats was extraordinary, especially when Joe, called "Hamfoot Ham," sang in-vogue jazz tunes with a flawless swing and daring words. This band became so famous at dance clubs that for a short time it was the favorite band of the Chicago mafia, playing for Al Capone on several occasions.

The war and El Petrillo's band marked the end of this type of music, and neither Charlie nor Joe McCoy recorded after 1942. In fact, they disappeared from the music scene. Both died in the early fifties.

Even though Joe and Charlie McCoy were significant artists in blues history and even though they recorded many titles for major labels, only one album, *The Harlem Hamfats* (Folklyric), is available. The rest is scattered on several anthologies, pirate albums, and some hasty compilations with poor sound quality.

■ Memphis Slim. *(Photograph © by Paul Harris; used with permission)*

MEMPHIS SLIM

(Peter Chatman / 1915–1988 / vocals, piano)

When he died, Memphis Slim was recognized in America as a sort of "prodigal son," especially in Memphis. But Peter Chatman, alias Memphis Slim, had to move to France in 1962 to pursue a profitable music career.

A powerful and subtle pianist, as comfortable with slow blues as with boogie-woogies, gifted with a vibrant and expressive voice, an inventive composer, Memphis Slim was a great bluesman who harmonized the influences of Roosevelt Sykes,★ Speckled Red, and Albert Ammons.★ However, he always liked very affected vocal effects, and this "flaw" increased with the years.

When Memphis Slim arrived in Chicago in 1939, he was already an accomplished musician, having mastered the style that he had created in the southern barrelhouses. He was taken, like many new immigrants, under Big Bill Broonzy's★ wing, and he soon started playing in the many clubs of the city and became Washboard Sam's★ piano player. Sam recorded him for Bluebird in 1940, with a series of titles on which Slim performed accompanied by a single bass player.

The funny "Beer Drinking Woman" and the shocking "Grinder Man Blues" were somewhat successful.

Especially after the war Memphis Slim was a favorite bluesman of Chicago blacks with pieces like "Having Fun," "Mother Earth," "Wish Me Well," and the classic "Everyday I Have the Blues." Following the example of Roosevelt Sykes, he had a good band, inspired by the Kansas City groups, in which there were remarkable musicians: bass player Big Crawford, saxophone players Alex Atkins and Ernest Cotton, and the outstanding guitar player M. T. Murphy. This was the most brilliant and creative period of Memphis Slim's career, as represented in his recordings for King, Mercury, Chess, United, and Vee-Jay.

In 1959, he was one of the first performers to get on the blues-revival train. He quickly learned the traditional folk themes and created a bass/piano duo with his friend Willie Dixon.★ Together they enjoyed success among the young white public in the clubs of Greenwich Village and at the Newport Festival, where they performed with Pete Seeger and Joan Baez. Encouraged by this success, they repeated the same numbers for the first tour of the American Folk Blues Festival in 1962. But the following year, Memphis Slim went back to Europe with his guitar player M. T. Murphy, and he gave a breathtaking recital of Chicago blues. Captivated by France, Slim decided to stay there. He performed regularly in that country, in the Parisian cabaret "Les Trois Maillets," and also at many concerts and festivals. Only at the very end of his life did a few Americans realize that they had ignored a great artist and a great blues and boogie-woogie piano player.

The first part of his career is available on the records *The Real Folk-Blues* (Chess), *Rockin' the Blues* (Charly), *Messin' around with the Blues* (Gusto), and *Memphis Slim USA* (Pearl). After his stay in Europe, Slim recorded too many albums not to fall into a routine, but the following albums are worthwhile: *All Kinds of Blues* (OBC/Carrere), *I'll Just Keep on Singing the Blues* (Must), *Raining the Blues* (Fantasy), and the remarkable *Southside Reunion* (Blue Star). His accompanists often were great guitarists, such as M. T. Murphy (who was a major player in the Blues Brothers band), Lafayette Thomas,* and Billy Butler.

MERCY DEE

(Mercy D. Walton / 1915–1962 / vocals, piano)

This Texas piano player with a solid touch, who was educated in the tough school of the barrelhouses, is today nearly forgotten. Nevertheless, Mercy Dee is the immortal author of the classic "One Room Country Shack," which was later covered by scores of blues and rock musicians. There was more to his recorded work than this incredible masterpiece; for example, pieces like "G.I. Fever" and "Dark Muddy Bottom" are also memorable.

He came to Oakland, California, from Texas in 1938. Mercy Dee quickly became popular in the clubs of that black suburb of San Francisco. His bitter wit and his lyrical sense were perfect for his monotone voice, which the Texas bluesmen like so much, and contrasted with his powerful way of playing the piano. He was noticed by producer Bob Geddins and recorded for many small labels before he signed with Specialty and Imperial. After the success of "One Room Country Shack," Mercy Dee unsuccessfully used other formulas close to rhythm and blues, like the furious "Come Back Maybellene," inspired by Chuck Berry.* Little by little people forgot him, but before his sudden death, he cut a good album: *Mercy Dee* (Arhoolie).

Some of his best songs are on the excellent compilation *G.I. Fever* (Crown Prince).

MIGHTY SAM

See Soul

AMOS MILBURN

(1926–1980 / vocals, piano)

A pioneer of rhythm and blues and black rock-and-roll, Amos Milburn was extremely successful in the years 1949–53. His warm voice, his devastating piano style, and the irresistible rhythm of his small band enabled him to influence the music scene for a long time.

Born on the border between Louisiana and Texas, Milburn learned very early to play the piano. He practiced it on Sundays in his church and on Saturday nights in the local barrelhouses, where he got that powerful touch of the right hand that made him a success. He enlisted in the Marines during the war and was stationed for a long time in California. In the black clubs of Los Angeles and San Francisco he encountered the sophisticated and urban blues, dominated by brass instruments, new in that region.

Influenced by the first hits of Charles Brown,* Nat King Cole, and Roy Milton, he created a band with several other musicians, following Milton's model and adding a very strong rhythm that gave his band an intense swing. During a tour in Texas, where he accompanied the singer-guitarist Smokey Hogg,* he was noticed by Mrs. Callum, a producer who recorded him at the end of 1945 in Los Angeles studios for Aladdin.

Only when he was managed by the saxophone player and producer Maxwell Davis did Milburn have some commercial success: "Chicken Shack Boogie"; "Hold Me Baby"; "In the Middle of the Night"; and his savoury alcohol trilogy in particular, "Bad, Bad Whiskey," "Let Me Go Home, Whiskey," and "One Scotch, One Bourbon, One Beer" are masterpieces for their eloquence and dynamism.

Milburn's music influenced the nascent rhythm and blues of New Orleans, where he was extremely popular. Fats Domino* and Little Richard* acknowledged Milburn's influence on them.

The straight rhythm, the harsh sounds of the tenor saxophones, and the musical flights at the piano announced the urban trend of rock-and-roll that the pale Bill Haley was to embody. In fact, Milburn was ahead of his time by about ten years, but, unlike Fats Domino and Joe Turner,* he did not manage to capitalize on this originality and become a rock-and-roll star.

After 1953, Amos Milburn was seldom successful despite a few wonderful hits and a few attempts to come back. It was too late (his health was then too shaky) when the international public recognized him as a great name of rhythm and blues.

His work was largely reissued on several labels. Today, *Amos Milburn and His Chicken Shackers* (Route 66), *Rock, Rock, Rock* (Route 66), and *Let's Rock a While* (Route 66) give a good idea of the excellence and the perennial youth of his music.

J. D. MILLER

In 1948, J. D. Miller, a modest businessman from Crowley, Louisiana, started a record company there, promoting and producing local musicians in several genres (country, rock-and-roll, cajun, and the blues). As for the blues, Miller realized that many popular black artists who played regularly around Baton Rouge had never been recorded. Miller solved that problem: He recorded two famous local artists, Slim

Harpo* and Lightnin' Slim,* and he let his friend, Ernie Young, edit and distribute them. Young was the creator and owner of Excello records in Nashville, Tennessee. Slim Harpo's "I'm a King Bee" and Lightnin' Slim's "Bad Luck" were commercial hits. For the next fifteen years, J. D. Miller continued to produce records that often were locally or nationally successful.

Because of the constant quality of his production, Miller was esteemed by blues fans throughout the world. With his artists he created what was improperly called the "Excello Sound" and sometimes more rightly "the swamp blues." Indeed, J. D. Miller was able to capture the rural blues of that swampy region and, behind the harsh voices of his artists, the wailing harmonicas, the electric guitars, and the numerous percussion effects. It is almost possible to feel the sticky heat of Louisiana and to hear the call of the bull frogs. This was the blues, gravelly, primitive, and poignant, and deeply influenced by Lightnin' Hopkins* and Jimmy Reed*; however, it had its own character, which made this swamp blues immediately recognizable.

Generally speaking, J. D. Miller was able to obtain the best from his artists, and although his production methods were often criticized by musicians, we can only be impressed by the exceptional results and the consistent quality. We do not minimize the considerable talent of the artists that Miller discovered when we say that without the skillful presence of this producer it is likely that we would not have known this Louisiana blues style, nor that it would have had the exact form that we know.

Except for the big "stars" of the swamp blues, Slim Harpo and Lightnin' Slim, one of the most interesting artists discovered by Miller was LONESOME SUNDOWN (Cornelius Green / b. 1928), a modern guitar player and follower of Guitar Slim.* After being in several local bands, including Clifton Chenier's,* Lonesome Sundown began a personal career under Miller's direction. He recorded a few regional hits, like the gloomy "Lonesome Lonely Blues" and the savory "My Home Is a Prison." But he gave up the blues for religion in 1965. We recommend *Lonesome Sundown* (Excello), *Bought*

Me a Ticket (Flyright), and *Lonesome Whistler* (Flyright). At the end of the seventies, Sundown agreed to play the blues again for a short time, time enough for the wonderful album recorded with Phillip Walker,* *Been Gone Too Long* (Alligator). Too bad he decided to be silent again. His voice and his guitar will be missed in the blues world.

The excellent harmonica player LAZY LESTER (Leslie Johnson / b. 1933) was the accompanist for most local artists. He also was in Lightnin' Slim's band before he finally recorded under his own name. A good technician, more influenced by Wayne Raney than by his Chicago peers, Lester often expressed himself in a style that was closer to rockabilly than to swamp blues. His greatest hit, "I'm a Lover Not a Fighter," was also a great hit for the British rock group the Kinks. *True Blues* (Excello) and the compact disc *Lazy Lester* (Flyright) gather the essence of his recorded work. After he had given up music in 1966, Lazy Lester made an amazing comeback in the blues scene in 1988, recording *Lazy Lester Rides Again* (King Snake) and then *Harp and Soul* (Alligator).

Another great harmonica player used by Miller was MOSES "WHISPERING" SMITH (1932–1984), who accompanied Lightnin' Slim and Silas Hogan and then recorded a few titles as the featured musician. A powerful singer, a straight and unsophisticated harmonica player, "Whispering" Smith made a quick comeback in the early seventies. He had time to record the good album *Over Easy* (Excello). His old titles are scattered on several anthologies.

The guitar player SILAS HOGAN (b. 1916) began a professional career only in 1962, following the advice of Slim Harpo, who introduced him to Miller. Although Hogan's style was very close to Lightnin' Slim's, it was also different due to his polished compositions ("Trouble at Home") and his strange suave voice. The albums *Trouble* (Excello) and *Free Hearted Man* (Flyright) included all his songs. Rediscovered in 1970, Silas remains more or less active around Baton Rouge where he embodies a disappearing tradition. *The Godfather* (BSW) is his last album.

The superb piano player from Texas, KATIE WEBSTER (b. 1939), who was nicknamed "200 pounds of joy" does not, strictly speaking, represent the swamp blues. She has interpreted soul and pop pieces ("Sea of Love"), but she sure knows what she sings when it's about the deep blues as shown, for example, on her records with guitar player Ashton Conroy. She was noticed by Miller for the precision of her right hand and the expressiveness of her playing. She enhanced numerous recordings of Miller's in all genres. While she was a studio musician, she led a personal career and directed a band of seven musicians. She eventually joined Otis Redding's band. *Katie Webster* (Flyright) is a compact disc that sums up the best of her first work. After a long time playing in cocktail lounges, she managed a comeback and recorded the excellent *You Know That's Right* (Arhoolie), *The Swamp Boogie Queen* (Alligator), and especially *Two-Fisted Mama* (Alligator), her more recent album.

The singer and guitar player CLARENCE GARLOW (1911–1986), born in Beaumont, Texas, also recorded for Miller. His abrupt and ornate style was the first and lasting source of influence for fellow Texan Johnny Winter.* Despite a few small local successes, Garlow's career was not financially fruitful. His music was excellent: *New Bon Ton Roola* (Flyright).

ERNEST "TABBY" THOMAS (b. 1929), singer, piano player, and guitar player, was born in Baton Rouge. He has behind him a long career; he has been recording since 1952, for the most part for Miller. His greatest success, "Hoodoo Party," recorded in 1961, is still a classic of the Louisiana blues. Tabby remains active in the blues scene in Baton Rouge with his son, guitar player Chris Thomas, whose sound is inspired by Jimi Hendrix (*Blues Train:* Maison de Soul).

Numerous other artists in Louisiana recorded for Miller: for example, harmonica players Jimmy Anderson, Sylvester Buckley, and Polka Dot Slim (aka Vince Monroe or Mr. Calhoun); guitar players Blue Charlie Morris, Johnny Johnson, Leroy Washington, and Boogie Jake (a cousin of Little Walter*); piano player Tal Miller; and saxophone player Lionel Torrence. They can be found on numerous anthologies such as *Louisiana Swamp Blues* (Flyright), *Baton Rouge Harmonica* (Flyright), *Baton Rouge Blues* (Flyright), *It's Your*

Voodoo Working (Flyright), and *The Real Blues* (Excello). The Flyright label produced over fifty compilations, often of a very high quality and almost solely produced by J. D. Miller.

This swamp-blues style was also represented by some artists who did not necessarily record for Miller, but for other producers such as Eddie Shuler of Lake Charles, Floyd Soileau, Huey Meaux, Roy Ames, and Harry Oster. Other names worth mentioning are Clarence Edwards, the excellent steel guitar player Hop Wilson, Cookie and the Cupcakes, Smoky Babe, Butch Cage, Guitar Junior (Lonnie Brooks),* Henry Gray, Guitar Kelley, and Raful Neal.* In the seventies, producers Chris Strachwitz and Mike Vernon tried to capture the swampy sound perfected by Miller. *Country Negro Jam Session* (Arhoolie), *Louisiana Blues* (Arhoolie), and several anthologies of the Goldband or Maison de Soul labels are worth listening to closely.

Not many musicians play the swamp blues today except for a few old bluesmen who often have turned to zydeco, the only down-home music that is popular today among Louisiana blacks.

ROY MILTON

(1916–1983 / vocals, drums)

Between 1945 and 1953 Roy Milton's band was extremely popular among the black public: "R. M. Blues," "Milton's Boogie," "Rainy Day," "Confession Blues," and "Them There Eyes" made it to the top of the national charts. "R. M. Blues" was even number one in California for almost all of 1946.

Born in Oklahoma to a rich family, Roy Milton was influenced by the big swing bands of Kansas City (Count Basie and Jay McShann*). When he settled in California in 1953, Roy decided to create his own swing band. An eloquent and witty composer, a dynamic singer and an irresistible entertainer, he also managed to have a brilliant band. It was dominated by female piano player Camille Howard, who was as beautiful as she was talented, and the powerful saxophone players Buddy Floyd and Benny Waters. This group quickly became the favorite band of Los Angeles nightclubs.

Combining the power of the Kansas City band, the eloquence of the jazz bands of Harlem, and the chromatic blues of Charles Brown,* Roy Milton was one of the great creators of postwar rhythm and blues, and he opened the way for rock-and-roll. Right after the war he was one of the biggest black stars in the United States; he went on many tours throughout the country. Although thanks to rock-and-roll Joe Turner* became popular again, Milton with a similar repertoire failed to keep his public after 1955. Despite a short-lived comeback with Red Light in 1961, his activities were more and more limited.

Roy Milton recorded prolifically for a great number of labels, several of which he owned.

Grandfather of R&B (Jukebox Lil), *Big Fat Mamas* (Jukebox Lil), and *Roy Milton and His Solid Senders* (Specialty) include his best songs.

MISSISSIPPI SHEIKS

The existence of string bands, with guitars, fiddles, bass, and mandolins or banjos, dates back to the nineteenth century. In rural America, they were the only source of dance music. These bands, both black and white, had a similar repertoire: waltz, polka, folk themes, blues, and popular tunes of the time. At the beginning of the century, one of the favorite string bands in Jackson, Mississippi, was that of Ezell Chatmon, who was for a while accompanied by his nephew, guitarist Charlie Patton.* Of the eleven sons of Ezell, all musicians, Lonnie, Bo, Sam, and their adopted brother, Walter Vincson, followed in their father's tracks and around 1926 created the "Mississippi Sheiks" (a name chosen because of the famous Rudolph Valentino film). They were able to play (without transition) ragtime pieces, blues, and the country tunes of Jimmie Rodgers. All multi-talented, exchanging fiddles and guitars in the middle of a piece, the Sheiks rapidly became extremely popular around Jackson. They were the heart of *Jackson Blues,* that also included the influential Tommy Johnson,* Ishman Bracey, and the McCoy* brothers. In 1930 they recorded one of their compositions, "Sitting on

Top of the World," that instantly became a national hit, selling millions of copies. This piece, today a part of the American folk repertoire, was covered by a great number of musicians, including Bob Wills, Bill Monroe, Ray Charles,* Howlin' Wolf,* Doc Watson, Harry Belafonte, Frank Sinatra, Cream, and the Grateful Dead.

Encouraged by this success and also that of the hot "Stop and Listen," the Sheiks were famous for a short while. That fame took them across the whole country and gave birth to many imitators. But, after 1933, the Mississippi Sheiks were unable to regain the fame of "Sitting on Top of the World," and after a last session for Bluebird in 1935, they stopped recording. Their work includes about a hundred songs, the best selection of which is on the album *Mississippi Sheiks* (Mamlish).

Apart from his appearance with the Mississippi Sheiks, the singer-guitar player Bo Chatmon was a popular bluesman under the stage name BO CARTER (1898–1965). His career began in 1928 and lasted until 1940. He produced nearly 130 titles solo or with a brother or two. His melancholic voice, his swinging guitar, and his risky compositions full of double-meaning, made him the most popular black musician in Mississippi. After the Sheiks disappeared, he continued to record and travel across the U.S. His work was not considered as serious as that of fellow Louisianan Charlie Patton or Skip James,* and it was ignored for a long time.

The three albums devoted to him, *Greatest Hits* (Yazoo), *Twist It Babe* (Yazoo), and *Banana in Your Fruit Basket* (Yazoo), confirm Bo Carter's talent and eclectism that gave him tremendous commercial success often beyond the black public.

The guitar player WALTER VINCSON (1901–1975) also recorded a few solo titles while playing with the Mississippi Sheiks. After 1935 he began a solo career in Chicago. He did record a few beautiful sides under his own name in 1940–41, and he accompanied several singers, among whom was Little Brother Montgomery.* After the war, he brought the Mississippi Sheiks together with Sam Chatmon on two occasions. Shortly before his death, thanks to the journalists of

Living Blues magazine, he got the royalties he deserved for his help in composing "Sitting on Top of the World."

The youngest of the Chatmon brothers, SAM CHATMON (1900–1983), was active in clubs in San Diego and in blues festivals. Although he had recorded a few duos with his brother, Lonnie, it was the blues revival that saved him from oblivion. In the many festivals and concerts in which he performed, Sam Chatmon revealed himself as a superb guitar player whose style, created in Jackson at the beginning of the century, changed because of long stays in Memphis and on the West Coast. Several excellent albums confirm his incredible enthusiasm, especially *The Mississippi Sheik* (Rounder) and *Sam Chatmon and His Bar-B-Q Boys* (Flying Fish).

McKINLEY MITCHELL

See Soul

LITTLE BROTHER MONTGOMERY

(Eurreal Montgomery / 1906–1985 / vocals, piano)

Little Brother was one of the last great prewar piano players who was still very active in the eighties. Born in the backwoods of Louisiana, he became a professional piano player right after his teens and settled in New Orleans. His particular talents enabled him to get out of the cheap taverns and brothels to play with several Dixieland bands. A pro in the techniques of classic jazz, he left for Jackson, Mississippi, around 1920. There, he mixed with Tommy Johnson,* the Chatmon brothers (soon to be the Mississippi Sheiks*), Skip James,* and Johnny Temple,* and they influenced one another for the better. When he came back to New Orleans in 1928, he had created a synthesis between the jazz piano derived from Jelly Roll Morton and the rough style of the barrelhouses of Mississippi: He was comfortable playing ragtime, jazz, boogie-woogie, and the blues. Moreover, he was able to improvise beautifully in a highly personal style: rolling bass notes of the boogie on a slow syncopated rhythm with staccato notes in the upper registers. In this style, he recorded in 1930 his superb

■ Little Brother Montgomery. *(Photograph © by Anton J. Mikofsky; used with permission)*

"Vicksburg Blues," which was to inspire Lee Green and then Roosevelt Sykes,* who recorded it as "Forty-Four," one of his most famous pieces.

Brother went to Chicago in 1931, and he quickly became a popular figure in the black taverns. He recorded a few titles for Bluebird before returning to the South. There, he created a great swing band and combined blues, popular songs, and dances and was locally very successful.

After the war he went back to Chicago and played the piano in many recording sessions for some jazz bands as well as for blues singers like Otis Rush* and Magic Sam.* Except for several albums he recorded as the featured player after 1959 for blues-revival fans, it is surprising that he recorded only a few records under his own name in Chicago, although he was known to have an important repertoire.

In fact, he did not really like to sing, his quavering and uncertain voice limited his possibilities a great deal.

There are very few available records that gather the best songs recorded before the war by this important blues artist.

JOHNNY AND OSCAR MOORE

See California

JOHNNY B. MOORE

See Chicago

BUDDY MOSS

(Eugene Moss / 1914–1984 / vocals, guitar, harmonica)
Buddy Moss represented the smooth style of the East Coast particularly well. While very young, he played in the streets in Atlanta with Blind Willie McTell,* Curley Weaver,* and Fred McMullen; all of them had already recorded many songs. Bewildered by the ease with which Moss played the harmonica and the guitar (he imitated perfectly the popular Scrapper Blackwell*), Weaver and McMullen took him to New York in 1932 to record him. It seems that Buddy Moss also impressed

the producers of New York, and between 1932 and 1933 he recorded a total of twenty-four songs. Moss and his accompanists interpreted the traditional repertoire of the Carolinas-Georgia-Virginia region with an enthusiasm that has seldom been equaled. These magnificent titles were reedited with extreme care on the collection *Atlanta Blues* (JEMF). Enjoying a wide popularity, Moss played all the time and grew as a guitar player. In his last recorded titles, he proved to be an astonishing virtuoso. His swing was exceptional for a guitarist; he played in the style of that region characterized by a stream of quick notes. That was also Josh White's* style; his manner of playing the guitar was sometimes hard to differentiate from that of Buddy Moss.

In 1934, following a fight that led to the death of his rivals, Buddy Moss was sent to prison. That tragic incident almost ended his career, for he recorded only a few titles in 1941 with Brownie McGhee.*

Thirty years later, Moss went to a concert in Atlanta to see his friend Josh White. Josh pushed him to resume a professional musical career, long enough to record the excellent *Rediscovery!* (Biograph). But, disenchanted by his former failures and mistrusting the sudden interest of young whites for his music, Moss performed only sporadically and locally and refused to go on tours or to record any longer.

His work has an intense quality and is available on *Georgia Blues* (Travelin' Man) and *Red River Blues* (Travelin' Man).

MUDDY WATERS

(McKinley Morganfield / 1915–1983 / vocals, guitar)

Muddy Waters was one of the main creators of postwar Chicago blues and a central figure in blues history. Because of his music as well as his personality, he influenced many musicians in both blues and rock.

Born in Mississippi, Muddy Waters was influenced himself by Son House,* whose bottleneck guitar style he admired. He was also impressed by the records of Big Bill Broonzy* and Robert Johnson.* Toward the end of the thirties, he drove a tractor on the Stovall plantation and played in a small local

■ Muddy Waters. *(Photograph © by Paul Harris; used with permission)*

string band. The folklorist Alan Lomax was at that time looking for Robert Johnson, who was already dead; he instead
found Muddy and recorded him for the Library of Congress.

These recordings were issued twenty years later, and they
revealed a young and shy Muddy Waters, with real musical
potential.

This sensitivity and this aptitude to leave his mark in all his
interpretations and his goal of always giving the best of himself
enabled Muddy Waters to have one of the most exemplary
careers in blues history. When he arrived in Chicago in 1943,
John Lee "Sonny Boy" Williamson* and Big Bill Broonzy*
helped him. People soon noticed his powerfully emotional
singing and the sounds, new at the time, that he got from his
electric guitar with his bottleneck when he played in the
Chicago taverns. From 1947 on, the Chess brothers recorded
him in this style, which was, in fact, the archetype of the
Chicago blues of that time: A style that was tough and uncompromising and that disturbed the existing values—Jazz
Gillum,* Big Bill Broonzy, Washboard Sam,* etc.—that were
deemed too polished by blacks who came from the Deep
South. Muddy Waters' success increased when he added to
his band guitarist Jimmy Rogers,* the extraordinary harmonica player Little Walter,* and drummer Elgin Evans. The
combination of these astonishing talents made an exemplary
Chicago blues band. "Rolling Stone," "Louisiana Blues,"
"Long Distance Call," "Honey Bee," "Baby, Please Don't
Go," and "I'm Ready" are testimonies of that privileged
moment; they are absolute masterpieces.

Muddy Waters' success among blacks did not diminish
until the early sixties, and the list of musicians who played in
his band is a list of "who's who" of the Chicago blues: harmonica players Junior Wells,* Big Walter Horton,* and James
Cotton*; guitar players Pat Hare, Buddy Guy,* Sammy
Lawhorn, and M. T. Murphy; bass player Willie Dixon*;
piano players Otis Spann* and Pinetop Perkins*; drummers
S. P. Leary, Francis Clay, and Fred Below*; etc.

From 1963 on, the increasing fame of the Rolling Stones
(who took their name from Muddy's 1950 hit) and that of other
British groups who openly recognized Muddy's influence,

drew the attention of a young white public to Muddy when his commercial success among blacks was decreasing. The whole of his recorded work was then directed toward this new public, from *Muddy Waters at Newport* (MCA) to the *Woodstock Album*. Even though nothing was really bad, there were a number of repetitions, excesses, and abuses. However, some albums rise above the others: *Folksinger* (MCA), a wonderful acoustic album, rich in dramatic intensity; *Fathers and Sons* (MCA), which showed him with the brilliant harmonica player Paul Butterfield* and guitar player Mike Bloomfield*; and *Can't Get No Grindin'* (MCA).

During the last years of his career, he was managed by Johnny Winter.* Muddy kept on performing in Europe and in America, more and more for a young white public. He was surrounded with young musicians and rightly called himself the "father of the blues." In spite of age and fatigue that left a mark on his music, he gave the best of himself and his personal charisma until his death. It was extremely rare when there was not at least several exceptional moments in his concerts. The four albums recorded with Johnny Winter demonstrate that fact and *Muddy "Mississippi" Waters* (CBS/Blue Sky) is still the best live recording of Muddy.

His main work, between 1948 and 1963 for Chess on 78s, then on 45s, is almost entirely reissued today in many countries in all formats. *The Best of Muddy Waters* (MCA), *Trouble No More* (MCA), *The Real Folk Blues* (MCA), *More Real Folk Blues* (MCA), and *The Chess Box: Muddy Waters* (MCA) are indispensable to all blues collections.

With Muddy Waters' sudden death in 1983, one of the last major representatives of the postwar Chicago blues was gone. He left his mark not only on blues history but, through his constant influences, on all popular music of the twentieth century.

CHARLIE MUSSELWHITE

(b. 1944 / vocals, harmonica, guitar)

Born in the heart of the Mississippi Delta, the son of a man who traveled all the time, living off several jobs, among which was street musician, Charlie Musselwhite was raised by an aunt who didn't want him. His childhood was eventful. At age twelve, he worked in a mill; he was the only white among mostly black female workers who made him their pet. Thanks to one of them, he met Will Shade, the creator of the Memphis Jug Band,* still active at the time. The young Charlie quickly learned to play the harmonica from the old bluesman. Musselwhite was then more and more connected with the circle of old hands of the Memphis blues, and in 1962 he met Big Walter Horton,* who had just come back from a visit in Chicago. It was a big moment for Charlie, who then decided to become a musician. The same year, he left Memphis for Chicago. He played the guitar in the streets of Chicago—he was an excellent follower of the bottleneck—and he played the harmonica, especially at the flea markets of Maxwell Street. He was one of the few whites to play the blues in the middle of the black ghetto. Recommended by Big Walter, he played with Robert Nighthawk,* Johnny Young,* and John Lee Granderson, and, despite his youth, he was admitted in the blues clubs of the South Side. He met there Little Walter,* whose records he admired, Sonny Boy Williamson (Rice Miller)* and Muddy Waters,* who took him under his wing. It seems that at that moment, preoccupied by the future of the blues that was forsaken by the young blacks, Muddy helped as much as possible the very few young whites who played in the Chicago clubs. Thanks to him the southern Musselwhite met with the young Yankees Mike Bloomfield,* Paul Butterfield,* Barry Goldberg, Pete Welding, and Norman Dayron, who recorded an incredible number of rare and precious tapes, some of which were edited almost twenty years later, and revealed that rich encounter between white and black bluesmen.

After the huge and unexpected success of Paul Butterfield's first album in 1965 on Elektra, Charlie Musselwhite was recorded by Vanguard as a rival of Butterfield. Musselwhite appears briefly on the anthology *Chicago/The Blues Today, Vol. 3* (Vanguard), where he played a duo with Big Walter Horton. The following year, at age nineteen, he recorded his first album, *Stand Back* (Vanguard).

Despite the presence of cumbersome accompanists that were imposed on him, such as the ridiculous guitar player Harvey Mendel, this album has a few good qualities: several original compositions, including many blues about being uprooted that always dominated Musselwhite's work; an excellent voice that did not try to imitate the black resonance, contrary to many other white singers of that time; but, especially, his mastery of his instrument. Precise, clear, and expressive, his harmonica style showed above all that he had learned the lessons of his masters perfectly.

After that time, Charlie Musselwhite never stopped progressing. *Stone Blues* (Vanguard) and *Tennessee Woman* (Vanguard) are uneven albums, whose flashiness is at times irritating, but there are some wonderful things too, in particular, a version of "Talkin' 'Bout My Friends" from A. C. Reed* and the extraordinary instrumental piece "Christo Redemptor."

Musselwhite left Chicago suddenly at the beginning of the seventies to settle in California. The albums he recorded then for Arhoolie (*Takin' My Time* and *Goin' Back Down South*) with Robben Ford's band were excellent. They are reissued on the CD *Memphis Charlie* (Arhoolie). He accompanied other bluesmen as well for this label, producing moving, high-quality blues. In particular, his accompaniment of Big Joe Williams,* whom Musselwhite had met in the South and then in Chicago, was impressive. Not since John Lee "Sonny Boy" Williamson* had Big Joe—undeniably one of the most difficult bluesmen to follow—played next to a harmonica player who had so much feeling and intelligence for his music (on *Thinkin' of What They Did to Me:* Arhoolie).

Under the California sky, Charles Musselwhite struggled constantly to be perfect, and he distanced himself more and more from the influence of the two Walters (Little and Big). *Leave the Blues to Us* (Capitol), in which he found a particularly eloquent Mike Bloomfield, revealed none of the inexperience and youthful excesses that hampered his first LPs; it is an excellent album. Increasingly involved in the California blues scene, Charlie became friends with the great guitar player

Johnny Heartsman,* who produced and embellished with his guitar the excellent *Times Gettin' Tougher Than Tough* (Crystal Clear). At the same time he created a harmonica class. The class became his primary occupation, and throughout the years Musselwhite educated many of the current harmonica players of the West Coast. He wrote an instruction book for beginners and recorded the excellent album teaching guide *The Harmonica According to Charlie Musselwhite* (Kicking Mule).

Following a lapse in the early eighties, Musselwhite reemerged after overcoming serious injuries from a car accident. On the West Coast as well as in Europe, Musselwhite promoted himself as one of the best harmonica players still active. His elegant, refined, concise, inventive, and innovative style became more and more polished as we can see on the remarkable *Tell Me Where Have All the Good Times Gone?* (Blue Rock It), recorded with Robben Ford. Overwhelmed by Muddy Waters' death, Charlie gave that his best work recorded to date. Since then he has been active worldwide and has recorded with a very tight band (*Ace of Harps; Signature*). Charlie is one of the very best bluesmen around.

LOUIS MYERS

(b. 1929 / vocals, guitar, harmonica)

Louis Myers, a veteran of the most beautiful moments of the Chicago blues, lives today—like Jimmy Rogers* and John Brim—slightly outside the local scene that the post-Magic Sam* guitar players dominate.

Already impregnated with the Delta blues, the young Louis came to Chicago in 1941 and soon after created his own band, the Aces, who, in 1950, included his brother Dave playing bass, Fred Below* playing drums, and Junior Wells* on harmonica. After Wells left the band, the Aces became the backup band for Little Walter,* whom Myers, himself an excellent harmonica player, often replaced on stage when Walter was busy elsewhere.

With or without the Aces, Louis Myers recorded a great

deal behind Otis Rush,* Junior Wells, Little Walter, Muddy Waters,* and Bo Diddley* and occasionally under his own name.

A warm baritone singer and a good guitarist, Louis Myers, who often used the slide, recorded some very beautiful titles ("Just Whalin'" and "Top of the Harp") and a really good California album (*I'm a Southern Man:* Advent).

Louis Myers is far from being old enough to retire. He is one of the last active musicians of the traditional Chicago blues. After fourteen years of silence, he returned to the studios for the Earwig label and recorded *Tell My Story Movin'*.

SAMMY MYERS

(b. 1936 / vocals, harmonica)

This nearly blind singer and guitar player, born in Laurel, Mississippi, remained stuck for a long time in the few blues clubs of Jackson. Sammy Myers' reputation was built on a handful of titles recorded in the fifties (the classics "Sleeping in the Ground" and "My Love Is Here to Stay") as well as his perfect harmonica style behind Elmore James.*

Three albums for the obscure TJ label might not have been enough to get him noticed if, one day in 1984, the Rockets, the group of the excellent Louisiana singer and guitar player Anson Funderburgh, had not performed in Jackson. Myers and Funderburgh enjoyed an immediate rapport, and Myers has been the band's singer and harmonica player ever since. He gave the band the experience, the depth, and the touch of authenticity of the real Delta blues.

The excellent *My Love Is Here to Stay* (Black Top), *Sins* (Black Top), and *Rack 'em Up* (Black Top) are outstanding works. They received good critiques and were awarded the W. C. Handy Awards. They combined harmoniously the irreplaceable experiences of a black bluesman and the technique of a good white musician. If this association can last, it should influence the blues of the nineties.

N

KENNY NEAL

See Raful Neal

RAFUL NEAL

(b. 1936 / vocals, harmonica)

For a long time, Raful Neal was known for having given the very young Buddy Guy★ a start in his band. Raful Neal deserves much more than this limited reputation. A powerful singer, a talented composer, and a good harmonica player—often more inventive than the other Louisiana musicians—he has been called the "Little Walter of Louisiana." Raful played all the Baton Rouge clubs and recorded for Peacock, Whit, and Fantastic, but, strangely enough, he did not record with J. D. Miller's★ company. His very percussive instrumental "Blues on the Moon" is still a classic of southern harmonica.

Thanks to the efforts of producer and bass player Bob Greelee, Raful Neal finally recorded his first album in 1987, the interesting *Louisiana Legend* (King Snake).

But from then on, the title that Raful Neal claims the most is that of father of KENNY NEAL (b. 1957); a singer, guitar player, and harmonica player, Kenny has proven to be one of the best bluesmen of his generation. He inherited the warm and smooth baritone voice of his father. Influenced by Buddy Guy but also by other guitar players from Louisiana, such as Rudolph Richard and Guitar Gable, he is a very complete instrumentalist. His compositions waver between the down-home style of his father, Albert King,★ and Robert Cray.★

Big News from Baton Rouge (Alligator), *Devil Child* (Alligator), and *Walking on Fire* (Alligator) give us reason to believe we can expect more good things from Kenny Neal.

JIMMY NELSON

See California

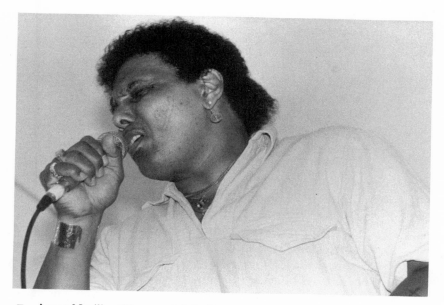

■ Aaron Neville. *(Photograph © by Paul Harris. Courtesy of Paul Harris and Archives and Special Collections, John Davis Williams Library, University of Mississippi)*

NEW ORLEANS

More than any other big American city, New Orleans has been a crossroad of cultures that all influenced, to different degrees, its music.

In this cosmopolitan city, this big heterogeneous harbor, the black community was relatively free from racial tension more than anywhere else in the South. It is thus not surprising that the music in New Orleans was a combination of influences: Anglo-Saxon, Spanish then Mexican, Caribbean, Franco-Acadian, Creole, and, of course, black. As early as the beginning of the century, the ragtime bands—soon the Dixieland—sprang up in the Storyville district, the center of gambling, drinking, prostitution, and constant fights, where the nightclubs were open till dawn.

As the cradle of jazz, New Orleans was overlooked in its importance to the blues, with this importance being denied even before 1950. Nevertheless, this crossroad city, situated between the big blues states of Texas and Mississippi attracted black farmers and sharecroppers en masse looking for adventure, entertainment, or work. What was original in New Orleans was that these blacks who had come from neighboring regions encountered a real local "aristocracy," composed of the descendants of the black overseers of the past slave markets, who did not feel like welcoming those they still considered coarse peasants. Their musical tradition (country blues) was thus confined to an underground, from which it was very difficult to leave.

Until 1945 another difficulty for local musicians was the lack of proper recording studios in New Orleans. The rare ones who recorded (e.g., Lonnie Johnson* or Little Brother Montgomery*) did so in Chicago or in New York, often times thanks to the impromptu trips of big record company producers who were then scouring the South for new talent.

However, after Jelly Roll Morton, the city was considered an endless reservoir of piano players and, before the war, Cousin Joe* and Champion Jack Dupree,* both piano players from New Orleans who had moved to the North, recorded successfully.

Only after the war did a different local blues develop. With the creation of recording studios (especially that of Cosimo Matassa), the arrival on the record market of ambitious and independent producers (Lew Chudd and his Imperial label; Art Rupe and Specialty; and even the interest shown by the Chess* brothers for the local blues) and with the decline of Dixieland jazz, there was room for a new black pop music. This music was represented with brio by Professor Longhair* and Fats Domino.* It was characterized by an extreme sophistication, the predominance of the piano, and a double bass line created by interspersed guitar and bass. This provided the opening of this blues to all forms close to pop music (rhumba, Cajun, and Dixieland), to which we need to add the strong influence of the Kansas City swing bands (Joe Turner* was in New Orleans in 1945) felt in the vocal power of the singers and the increased trumpet and saxophone solos. Everything was surrounded by an unrestrained good humor.

After the national success of Roy Brown* and Fats Domino

in 1949, New Orleans became one of the most creative centers. Its urban and sophisticated blues, easier than those of Chicago and Mississippi, contributed a great deal to the birth of the urban rock-and-roll.

After 1954 Joe Turner, Fats Domino, and Little Richard,* who made some clubs like the DEW DROP INN in New Orleans very famous, were the first black stars accepted by a young white public tired of the syrupy songs of Tin Pan Alley.

Without becoming a real national star as he had hoped, DAVE BARTHOLOMEW (b. 1920), trumpet player and band leader, had a big influence upon the local blues scene. The son of a Dixieland musician, he led his own band in 1946, which included drummer Earl Palmer and saxophone player Red Tyler. In 1949 he recorded "Country Boy," a success for the small DeLuxe label. But Bartholomew was going to establish himself as a producer-arranger and as a talent scout; he discovered Roy Brown and Fats Domino, who was then a piano player in his band. In the fifties, in association with the Imperial Company, he was at the center of all record production in New Orleans, co-writing a majority of the hits of the local artists. His great talent as a producer can be felt in many of the sessions he directed.

PAUL GAYTEN (b. 1920), another band leader and the nephew of the famous Little Montgomery, had some success with "True," a romantic ballad in the style of Nat King Cole. Then, he played for Chess the role that Bartholomew played for Imperial. He discovered and recorded a great number of artists of rhythm and blues and rock-and-roll, among whom were Clarence "Frogman" Henry, famous for his imitations of a frog, Bobby Charles, and the female singer Annie Laurie (on *Creole Gal:* Route 66).

Another discovery by Chess, piano player and singer JAMES "SUGAR BOY" CRAWFORD (1923–1960), directed Cane Cutters, one of the best rhythm-and-blues bands of New Orleans. That band's intense rhythm and contagious spirit made him extremely popular until about 1960, when Sugar Boy was lynched by the Ku Klux Klan.

A guitar player for Sugar Boy Crawford, SNOOKS EAGLIN (Ford or Fird Eaglin / b. 1936) was nearly a legendary figure thanks to his first songs and to his accompaniments of Professor Longhair. The ethnomusicologist Harry Oster discovered the blind musician playing in the New Orleans streets to survive. Snooks then began a strange recording career as a "rural bluesman." In fact, he was especially comfortable with a small band, playing the tunes of Fats Domino and Dave Bartholomew (*Down Yonder:* Sonet and *Out of Nowhere:* Black Top).

ARCHIBALD (Leon T. Gross / 1912–1973) was a singer and a piano player who deeply influenced Fats Domino. He had a series of small hits, such as "Stack O Lee" ("Stagolee") in 1950. His roots are in Dixieland.

When the singer LLOYD PRICE (1934–1988) covered "Stagolee" in 1959 and modernized it, he had an international success. It is especially the first part of his career that attracted the attention of the blues and rock-and-roll fans. In 1952 "Lawdy Miss Clawdy" made him a great precursor of Little Richard (*His Original Recordings:* Specialty).

A superb singer who started as a choir boy, guitar player GUITAR SLIM (Eddie Jones / 1926–1959) recorded for Specialty in 1954 the vibrant "Things I Used to Do," which is still a blues classic. A remarkable showman and a pioneer of electric experimentation on the guitar, Guitar Slim had a few hits ("Story of My Life" and "Done Got over You") before he died. He influenced Albert Collins,* Lonnie Brooks,* and Buddy Guy,* among others. (*The Things I Used to Do:* Ace.)

One of Guitar Slim's disciples, EARL KING (Silas Johnson / b. 1934) left his mark with the ballad "Those Lonely, Lonely Nights" in 1955. A popular figure of the New Orleans scene, Earl has continued to record in all genres (*Trick Bag:* EMI). Recently, he recorded a good album on the Black Top label: *Glazed.*

Finally, guitarist SMILEY LEWIS (Amos Overton Lemmon / 1920–1973) also had big hits with "I Hear You Knocking" and "The Bells Are Ringing." Although his guitar style was relatively scanty, he was a powerful blues shouter, and the titles he recorded under the direction of Dave Bartholomew are among the best of the New Orleans blues. (*I Hear You Knocking:* EMI).

The prolific blues and rock-and-roll scene of New Orleans

was first-rate. Many more names need to be mentioned too, but they do not always belong to the blues field: the Neville brothers (Aaron and Art), who emerged after thirty years of semi-obscurity, Big Boy Miles, James Wayne, Huey Smith, Jessie Hill, Larry Williams, Robert Parker, Allen Toussaint, The Meters, Dr. John, and others.

It is important to underline the positive role played, since the mid-eighties, by the Black Top label and pianist Ron Levy; they both undertook a real campaign to rediscover and to promote local old hands, along with discovering new talents.

Ace, Bandy, Chess, MCA, Flyright, and Krazy Kat have reissued scores of old titles, and on compact disc, Rounder. Let's mention *Crescent City Bounce* (Ace), *New New Orleans Music, Vols. 1, 2 & 3* (Rounder), *The Best of Ric and Ron* (Rounder), *Troubles Troubles* (Rounder), and *Loaded with the Blues* (Charly).

NEW YORK

Although New York (Harlem, in particular) was a great city for jazz after 1920, no regional blues style was actually developed there. Before the war, Decca studios recorded many blues, but the artists came from the southeastern states (Blind Boy Fuller,★ for instance). It was the blues-jazz of Harlem that produced male and female singers (Victoria Spivey,★ Blue Lu Barker, and Georgia White★) within the big swing orchestras that were fashionable then. Little by little, this swing trend would create the rhythm and blues of New York. The Apollo Theater was the favorite place to play, and the Atlantic label was the hot record company after the war.

As for the down-home blues, it was only after 1945 that a real New York current developed with the arrival in Harlem of numerous immigrants who came from the southeastern states, especially the Carolinas. It was natural for these immigrants to transplant the East Coast blues tradition; they were able to record for many small, rapidly evolving companies: Atlantic, Herald, Regal/Savoy owned by the producer Fred Mendelsohn, Old Town, and after 1954 the excellent Dire/ Fury label of Bobby Robinson.

■ Tarheel Slim. *(Photograph © by Anton J. Mikofsky; used with permission)*

However, the blues in New York never had the scope it had in Chicago or in San Francisco. It did not have a precise form, and it was not immediately recognizable. In fact, two categories of artists developed: The first, between 1955 and 1965, continued the acoustic tradition of the East Coast (Gary Davis,* Sonny Terry,* and Brownie McGhee*); the other, an electric blues, was borrowed from other regions (Chicago and New Orleans in particular). The East Coast blues was grounded in instrumental virtuosity and the use of jazz progressions, ragtime especially. It was essentially an acoustic art, hence not very applicable to noisy taverns. The delicate fingerpicking of Blind Boy Fuller (the most influential bluesman of the region) was not possible on the electric guitar, and whatever their origins were, the artists who had chosen to express themselves with an electric group in New York had to borrow from other styles that were then popular on radio and record.

An excellent example is guitar player TARHEEL SLIM (Alden Bunn / 1924–1977): He began his career under the influence of Gary Davis and Blind Boy Fuller. His first recordings in 1952 with piano player Big Chief Ellis were in that vein. In 1958, looking for a hit, he played a few pieces in the style of the Chicago blues (in particular, the splendid and furious "Number 9 Train"). He created a number of duets with his wife, Little Ann, in a style resembling Ray Charles,* and he managed to reach the charts with "It's Too Late." He played a lot in clubs and recording studios in which his superb guitar style was often imitated by other artists. Unable to repeat the success of "It's Too Late," he disappeared around 1965, but, shortly before his death, he was rediscovered by producer Pete Lowry, who recorded him on an excellent album in the style of his debut: *No Time at All* (Trix). His early work is available on *Lock Me in Your Heart* (Charly).

BUSTER BROWN (1924–1975) was an exuberant harmonica player. Not a great virtuoso, he was deeply set in the southeast tradition. In the forties he was more active in Carolina than in New York. He recorded a great deal for Bobby Robinson after his success in 1959, "Fannie Mae," which became a rock-and-roll classic. His best work is on *Good News* (Charly).

The one-man band WILBERT HARRISON (b. 1935) had a real triumph with his furious version of "Kansas City," the blues hit of Little Willie Littlefield,* also recorded in 1959 by Bobby Robinson. He made a short-lived comeback in 1970 after his "Let's Work Together" was covered by the Rolling Stones. The best compilation of his old titles is *Lovin' Operator* (Charly).

STICKS McGHEE (1917–1961), on the contrary, died destitute and unknown. This guitar player, the brother of Brownie McGhee, had, however, been successful in 1947 with "Drinkin' Wine Spo-dee-o-dee," a quick blues, later played by many jazz, blues, and rock artists. He produced other excellent titles for Atlantic and King without regaining any success (on *Sticks McGhee:* Crown Prince).

Guitar player CHARLES WALKER (1923–1975) did not have much commercial success, but he was constantly active in New York clubs until about 1965. He recorded with Buster Brown, with another harmonica player B. Brown, and with the fine piano player Lee Roy Little.

Singer-guitar player RALPH WILLIS (1910–1957) remained

faithful to the rural tradition of his native state, Alabama. Often accompanied by Brownie McGhee and Sonny Terry, after 1944 he recorded about fifty very inventive, rhythmic, and witty titles (*Ralph Willis:* Blues Classic).

ALEC SEWARD (1901–1974) expressed himself in the traditional acoustic style of the Southeast and added a certain dramatic touch that created a particularly moving atmosphere (e.g., "Late One Saturday Evening"). He recorded quite a lot with Louis Hayes, Woody Guthrie, and Sonny Terry. Today, he is almost completely forgotten. It would be good to reissue the excellent album he recorded for Elektra, and the other album, not as good, he recorded for Bluesville.

It is also important to mention pianist Harry Van Walls, guitarists Alonzo Scales and Leroy Dallas, and singer Billy Bland.

But New York was not limited to this blues scene and to these down-home artists. Rhythm and blues was extremely popular there for a while, and New York was the center of this trend, following the example of New Orleans and California. Numerous small bands included blues shouters, harsh saxophonists, and some very versatile guitarists playing in several genres.

MICKEY BAKER (b. 1925), born in Louisville, Kentucky, is certainly the archetype of the rhythm-and-blues musician. A formidable guitar player and at times a good singer, he was far less the bluesman he wanted to be than the arranger, producer, and guitar player of many sessions in New York. Under his own name he was successful with singer Sylvia Robinson in vocal duos between rock-and-roll and pop ("Mickey & Sylvia"). Settling in France after the mid-sixties, he worked there a great deal and recorded a few more nice things behind Memphis Slim,* Gatemouth Brown,* and Champion Jack Dupree.* Nothing he recorded under his own name is really good, except for a beautiful session for Black & Blue (*The Blues and Me:* Black & Blue). Today, he is no longer playing.

Like Baker, LARRY DALE (Ennis Lowery / b. 1923), an inventive and original guitarist, played for a great number of recording sessions in New York. He is particularly impressive on his work with Jack Dupree. Born in Texas, he is as comfortable playing blues as he is jazz (with Cootie Williams) or rock-and-roll. He recorded only a few titles under his own name, but he reappeared recently thanks to the efforts of the British critic John Broven.

WILD JIMMY SPRUILL (b. 1934) is still a major musician in New York recording studios. A great guitar player in blues, country, and rockabilly, he plays backup for many musicians, from Tarheel Slim to John Hammond, Jr.* The compilation *Wild Jimmy Spruill* (Krazy Kat) does not do him justice.

Piano player BOB GADDY (b. 1924) is an excellent singer influenced by the gospel songs of his childhood. He is the author of the dark and moving "Paper Lady" (on *Rip And Run:* ACE). He often proved that he had the makings of a great bluesman. He is currently working as a cook in a restaurant on Madison Avenue.

RUTH BROWN (Ruth Weston / b. 1928) is one of the great female pioneers of black rhythm and blues and of rock-and-roll. A subtle and suave singer, not far removed from a modern Lil Green,* Ruth reached the top of the charts in the fifties with "5-10-15 Hours," "Mama, He Treats Your Daughter Mean," and "Teardrops from My Eyes." Many of her first titles are wonderful blues enhanced by a flawless band (*Rockin' with Ruth:* Charly). She tried several times to make a comeback, but always met with difficulties.

TOMMY TUCKER (Robert Higgenbotham / 1933–1982) was a singer and guitar player of unequaled talent, closer to rock-and-roll but still a good bluesman. "Alimony" and "High-Heel Sneakers," two of his greatest hits, were in the vein of Jimmy Reed.* He was making a comeback when he died of food poisoning.

BIG MAYBELLE SMITH (1926–1972), another veteran of New York rhythm and blues, was a major figure of the famous Apollo Theatre in the fifties. An extraordinarily powerful singer, she recorded prolifically and was successful with pieces like "96 Tears" and "Don't Let the Sun Catch You Cryin'." The compact disc *Blues, Candy and Big Maybelle* (Savoy) includes some of her best blues.

Numerous anthologies reveal these New York blues: *New York Blues, Vols. 1 & 2* (Charly), *Old Town Blues, Vols. 1 & 2*

(Ace), *New York Notables* (Moonshine), and *Harlem Heavies* (Moonshine).

At present, a new blues scene is being reorganized, following the example of those that now exist throughout the U.S.: mainly white, with a few black veterans, directed to a public composed of students craving a "return to the roots" of American pop music. Harmonica players Bill Dicey, Paul Oscher (Brooklyn Slim), and Charlie Sayles, in the field for many years, may find at last their long-awaited breaks.

ROBERT NIGHTHAWK

(Robert McCollum or Robert Lee McCoy / 1919–1967 / vocals, guitar, harmonica)

Though not well known by the general public, Robert Nighthawk was one of the best Chicago blues artists. Influenced by Tommy Johnson★ and Tampa Red,★ Nighthawk developed an extremely clean style, in which his guitar was dominated by the smooth sound of his bottleneck, supported by a dark and expressive voice reflecting his introverted personality.

Nighthawk's career stretched from the thirties, when for a while he was a guitar player and harmonica player for Bluebird/Decca, until 1964. Although he was less well known than John Lee "Sonny Boy" Williamson★ or Muddy Waters,★ like them he helped to transplant the blues of the Deep South to Chicago.

After learning the guitar from Houston Stackhouse, a friend of Tommy Johnson's,★ Robert Lee McCoy—as he wanted to be called then, after his mother's name—began a career as an itinerant musician in Missouri, Arkansas, and Tennessee. He became friends with John Lee "Sonny Boy" Williamson, who took him to Chicago in 1937 to record for Bluebird. His first record was his only big hit: the classic "Prowling Nighthawk," from which he took his name. Between 1937 and 1941, he recorded several beautiful songs, including "Friar's Point Blues."

Immediately after the war Nighthawk was in Chicago, and he recorded a series of wonderful titles for Chess then

United/States: "Sweet Black Angel," which inspired B. B. King*; "Anna Lee"; and the magnificent "The Moon Is Rising." The subtle use of the electric guitar, whose strings he barely touched with his bottleneck, gave his music an exquisite and smooth sound that made his titles blues masterpieces. His technique influenced numerous guitarists: Muddy Waters,* Elmore James,* and especially Earl Hooker.*

Despite the quality of his recordings, Nighthawk failed to have the success he wanted. He had a small professional career in Chicago until 1953, then returned to the South and took an active part in the radio program "King Biscuit Hour." The vogue of the blues revival in the sixties enticed him to try a comeback in Chicago in 1964.

There he encountered a tough situation for traditional bluesmen. Except for a few concerts, the usual appearances in the South Side taverns, and the few titles recorded for Willie Dixon* and Chess, his comeback was disappointing. Before returning to the South, he recorded an interesting album for Pete Welding (*Robert Nighthawk/Houston Stackhouse:* Testament). He died in 1967 soon after having been paralyzed on one side. His recorded work is very important and is available in its entirety. *Robert Lee McCoy, Vols. 1 & 2* (Wolf) contain all the titles he made before the war; *Black Angel Blues* (Chess) is his superior production for Chess; *Bricks in My Pillow* (Pearl) carries his United/States titles. The amazing *Live on Maxwell Street* (Rounder) caught him live when playing in the famous flea market of Chicago where all the great bluesmen who had come from the Delta made their debuts.

O

JOHNNY OTIS

(b. 1921 / vocals, drums, piano, vibes)

Long before the northern states or Europe talked about "white blues," Johnny Otis, the son of Greek immigrants in

■ Johnny Otis. *(Photograph © by Norbert Hess. Courtesy of Norbert Hess and Archives and Special Collections, John Davis Williams Library, University of Mississippi)*

California, struggled to win the title of "Godfather of Rhythm and Blues."

As blacks settled into the poor districts of California cities and because his parents could not and did not want to move out, Otis became recognized by all as the "white Negro." Raised in the cult of the swing bands, Johnny quite naturally found himself playing the drums and then the keyboards in the bands of Harlan Leonard and Count Prince Matthews.

In the mid-forties Johnny led his own band and had a commercial hit in 1946 with "Harlem Nocturne." He opened his own club in Los Angeles (The Barrelhouse Club). He also created his own record company and then the "Johnny Otis Show," whose aim was to promote potential stars of rhythm and blues.

In the fifties he was active on all fronts: For the Texas labels Duke/Peacock he produced hits by Johnny Ace and Little Richard★; he discovered diverse talents, like Esther Phillips, Little Willie John (the creator of "Fever"), Mel Walker, Marylin Scott, Jackie Wilson, and Hank Ballard. Finally, he was at the top of the rock-and-roll wave (whose paternity he rightly claimed in part) by having two fantastic hits on Capitol: "Willie and the Hand Jive" and "Ma."

The decline of rhythm and blues in the sixties relegated Otis to obscurity. But this man's energy seems limitless. At the end of the sixties, he came back with his new show, introducing this time his own son, guitar player Shuggie Otis (who became linked to the rock of the seventies), and allowing some old California hands to resurface: PeeWee Crayton,★ Joe Liggins,★ Big Mama Thornton★ . . . .

Today semi-retired, the godfather of rhythm and blues sees his work clearly and proudly. From personal recordings to his tireless work to discover new talent, it won him a unique and significant place in the history of black popular music.

The Original Johnny Otis Show, Vols. 1 & 2 (Savoy) and *The New Johnny Otis* (Alligator) provide a good review of his career, which is highlighted in the work of his faithful biographer Norbert Hess.

P

JUNIOR PARKER

(Herman Parker / 1932–1971 / vocals, harmonica)

Like his long-time friend Bobby Bland,⋆ Junior Parker was
one of the most beautiful voices of the blues: deep and warm,
quite sophisticated, sometimes more similar to American
crooners than to bluesmen. This dualism can be found everywhere in Parker's music: Raised in Memphis with artists like
James Cotton,⋆ Pat Hare, and Sonny Boy Williamson (Rice
Miller),⋆ he was strongly influenced by them, and he was able
to create authentic blues. On the other hand, his admiration
for Nat King Cole and Johnny Ace led him to soften his style
considerably and to interpret more and more ballads.

Born in Memphis, Junior Parker learned to play the harmonica from Sonny Boy, and in 1947 he was very active in the
city clubs. His dynamism and his vocal talents made him
known locally, and he recorded in 1952 for the Bihari brothers
and later for Sam Phillips⋆ on the Sun label. He had two hits:
"Feelin' Good," an amazing adaptation of "Boogie Chillen"
from John Lee Hooker,⋆ and "Mystery Train," later covered
by Elvis Presley.

This brought him a contract with the Duke label of Texas,
for which he recorded blues, rock-and-roll, and ballads—the
latter genre dominated his work more and more—and
increased his commercial success with "Mother-in-Law
Blues," "Next Time You See Me," "Barefoot Rock," "Driving
Wheel," and "Annie Get Your Yoyo."

Unfortunately, few of his titles are available today. His Sun
titles are collected on *Mystery Train* (Rounder), and his best
Duke titles are on the album *I Wanna Ramble* (Ace).

After 1966, Junior Parker recorded several albums, often of
unequaled value, but that meant, along with his beautiful
warm voice and his Delta harmonica style, a real return to the
blues of his roots. Like many others, he died before he was

able to conquer the new white blues public. His compositions are regularly played and sung by numerous artists, including Sonny Rhodes* and Luther Johnson, Jr.*

SONNY PARKER

See Blues Shouters

CHARLIE PATTON

(ca. 1887–1934 / vocals, guitar)

Charlie Patton's place in blues history is considerable: He was one of the first Mississippi bluesmen to have recorded (in 1929), at which time he was probably over forty. That means that he had forged his style at the turn of the century, at a time when the blues, as we know it on record, was in gestation. His repertoire was amazingly diversified for a Delta bluesman: Along with blues, there were ragtimes, folk songs, themes borrowed from white rural music ("Running White"), and even some adaptations of popular tunes of the time.

His constantly brilliant and inventive guitar style was characterized by an extraordinary sense of rhythm, accentuated by hitting the bass notes, which created an incessant tension and movement. He particularly liked the use of the bottleneck, which he often played Hawaiian style, with the guitar flat on his knees. His singing was similar to his guitar style: He broke up his sentences and punctuated them by tapping on his guitar or by talking to it in many asides. All that seems to correspond to the personality of his legend: People in Mississippi still remember him as a violent and quarrelsome individual, a womanizer, an illiterate, raised on a large plantation where, in the years still close to slavery, he played the role of the "bad nigger."

Nevertheless, his popularity was considerable around Jackson where he was associated for a while with the Chatmon brothers and fiddler Willie Brown. After being discovered by producer H. C. Spears, he recorded substantially for five years before he died; his records were regional hits and a great number became classics ("Pony Blues" and "High Water Everywhere"). It was Patton who introduced Son House* to Spears, thus enabling him to make his first recordings.

His influence was considerable upon several generations of musicians. The "fathers" of the Delta blues, Tommy Johnson,* Son House,* Big Joe Williams,* and Tommy McClennan,* all created styles more or less derived from Patton's; in Chicago, Howlin' Wolf,* Eddie Taylor,* Honeyboy Edwards,* Johnny Shines,* and Johnny Young* never hid their admiration for Patton, whose themes they often covered; the superb guitar player Roebuck "Pops" Staples of the Staples Singers played in a manner directly inspired by Charlie Patton. Finally, the famous contemporary folk guitar player John Fahey learned to play the guitar with Patton's records. It was Fahey again who devoted a brilliant study to him (see Bibliography) and who took part in the production of a magnificent double album, including twenty-eight titles in chronological order of the recording with the full transcript of the lyrics, naturally called, *Founder of the Delta Blues* (Yazoo).

ANN PEEBLES

(b. 1947 / vocals)

Although she is before all else a soul singer, Ann Peebles has recorded too many blues to be ignored.

Her slightly cracked voice that has neither the depth nor the range of some of her colleagues is nevertheless direct and fascinating, in a register close to Tina Turner's.* Her extremely consistent work places her among the best female representatives of southern soul with a particular predilection for the very bluesy pieces, even the pure blues.

Born in St. Louis, Ann was involved in church choirs before she began singing the fashionable black repertoire. In the late seventies, performing in a Memphis club while on vacation, she was noticed by producer and band leader Willie Mitchell, who gave her a contract to record with Hi, the local company.

Her excellent album *Part Time Love* (Hi) in 1970 immediately put her in the black Top 40. Her touch of soul-blues that she sang with warmth and conviction was incredibly attractive. These qualities make her recorded work for Hi among the great black music of the seventies. She was particularly brilliant on pieces like "I Pity the Fool," borrowed from Bobby Bland*; the torrid "Keep Me Hanging On"; and the sensuous "I Can't Stand the Rain," a splendid ballad written with her husband, singer Don Bryant. The artistic success of that Hi recording was also due to the flawless production of Willie Mitchell that constantly emphasized the qualities of the singer, and to the talented guitar player Teenie Hodges, also responsible for some of the best hits of the Memphis sound.

The disco wave was rough on Ann Peebles, too involved in a bluesy southern soul to be popular among white blues fans or among young blacks who had turned entirely toward disco and funk.

However, the clear return to the genuine black tradition with labels such as Malaco, Ichiban, and La Jam is bringing Ann Peebles again to the forefront.

Her best titles are partly available on compact disc: *Greatest Hits* (MCA or Charly).

PEG LEG SAM

See East Coast Blues

PINETOP PERKINS

(Joe Willie Perkins / b. 1913 / vocals, piano)

After Otis Spann* died in 1970, Pinetop Perkins seemed to come out of nowhere and replace the great piano player in Muddy Waters'* band. Without ever trying to copy his late elder, Perkins handled the difficult and essential role of the pianist in Muddy Waters' band with talent and conscience. Spann—a student of Big Maceo*—had a much more modern approach to his instrument than Pinetop, who has always remained faithful to the same solid and straightforward style he learned in the Mississippi barrelhouses. In any case, being Muddy Waters'* piano player for ten years has attracted

■ Pinetop Perkins. *(Photograph © by Anton J. Mikofsky; used with permission)*

attention to Perkins, who has since recorded substantially under his own name.

Until then, Joe Willie Perkins had certainly not been inactive. Born in Belzoni, Mississippi, in the center of the Delta, he learned the piano very early. He was influenced by the records of boogie-woogie inventor Pinetop Smith,* whose nickname he borrowed, by Roosevelt Sykes,★ and by Leroy Carr,★ who remained his main source of inspiration. At the end of the thirties, Perkins was a well-known figure in the region, and he became friends with Robert Nighthawk★ and Sonny Boy Williamson (Rice Miller).★ Thanks to them, from 1943 to 1948 he became the regular piano player on the famous "King Biscuit Hour," broadcast daily from Helena, Arkansas. Nighthawk took him to Chicago, long enough to enlighten Nighthawk's first Chess recording session with his piano. But Pinetop did not like the North very much: He played for a short while in a big band, but he soon left for the South. In the early fifties he was playing around Memphis with Earl Hooker,★ Ike Turner,★ and Boyd Gilmore, and he recorded a title for Sam Phillips.★ Pinetop spent the next twenty years playing the juke joints in Mississippi and Arkansas. In the late sixties he went one more time to Chicago, just in time to take the place left by Otis Spann's death in Muddy Waters' band.

Thanks to that position, Pinetop—the elder in the band— became known as one of the last piano players to carry the southern rural tradition; he became a favorite musician of the American and European scenes.

Muddy Waters' death in 1983—unfortunately preceded by a sad separation of the two musicians—left Pinetop alone with his piano, dragging a heavy heritage.

Neither a great singer nor a piano master like Memphis Slim,★ he is, however, a fantastic representative of the barrel-house tradition.

He has recorded substantially these last ten years. He is at his best on the collections *Living Chicago Blues* (Alligator) and *Jacks and Kings* (Adelphi); the latter was recorded with the Nighthawks. Among his other recorded performances, *Pinetop Is Just Top* (Black & Blue) and *After Hours* (Blind Pig) are good ones. But he lacks the charisma of a leader, and that is evident on his albums.

SAM C. PHILLIPS

See Memphis

PIANO

The premiere instrument of clubs and public houses at the beginning of the century, the piano also accompanied many blues before the amplification of other instruments cast it to a secondary position.

Blues and jazz musicians quickly changed this "noble" and not really flexible instrument in many ways, the most famous of which consists of wrapping the hammers with rags so as to get a note muted enough to sound like the blue notes essential to the blues.

Several simultaneous movements developed among black piano players: ragtime, boogie-woogie, and the barrelhouse style, which was, in fact, the basis for boogie-woogie and which constituted the piano blues style par excellence. Rolling bass notes, the powerful touch of the right hand, and the constant use of counterpoints in the upper registers are characteristic of this style.

The most important blues piano players were Walter Roland,* Roosevelt Sykes,* Leroy Carr,* Charles Brown,* Memphis Slim,* Professor Longhair,* and Big Maceo,* who managed to make a brilliant synthesis of all the blues piano styles that came before. Since 1945, his influence has been considerable upon many blues pianists, the talented and sensitive Otis Spann* in particular.

Currently, a handful of piano players show a flair and a real liking for the blues: Katie Webster,* Henry Gray, Ron Levy, and Pinetop Perkins.* The piano is often replaced by other instruments with amplified keyboards, sometimes by electronic machines, which are unable to be as sensitive and evocative as their glorious ancestors.

The British Magpie label produced a remarkable piano series: *The Piano Blues, Vols. 1 to 21* (Magpie). Other great anthologies are *Piano in Style* (MCA) and *Atlantic Blues: The Piano* (Atlantic).

BOBBY PRICE

See Zydeco

■ Professor Longhair. *(Photograph © by Paul Harris; used with permission)*

LLOYD PRICE

See New Orleans

PROFESSOR LONGHAIR

(Henry Roland "Roy" Byrd / 1918–1980 / vocals, piano, guitar, drums)

Professor Longhair was the real creator of modern New Orleans blues. Indeed, he was the first to achieve a synthesis of the different musical trends of that city: blues, jazz, Dixieland, Cajun, Tex-Mex, and rhumba.

It is actually this last influence that dominated the brilliant piano style of the Professor, consisting of a rhythm with eight beats on which he superimposed very quick triplets with the right hand. This style has influenced all the piano players of postwar New Orleans: Allen Toussaint, James Booker, Fats Domino,★ Huey Smith, and Doctor John. Even his childhood friend, Champion Jack Dupree,★ borrowed substantially from Longhair. Generally, the whole rock-and-roll of that city, made famous by Fats Domino and Smiley Lewis,★ owes a lot to the style created by Longhair.

Roy Byrd, born in Bogalusa, moved to New Orleans at a young age. He tried several jobs, including boxing. His dynamism, his humor, and his talent as a piano player, a guitar player, a singer, and a drummer enabled him to perform in the numerous taverns of the city. In 1949, he recorded his first records for several labels; the same year he had his first commercial hit with "Mardi Gras in New Orleans," a piece with a furious rhythm, whose combination of French, Mexican, and Caribbean influences produced a unique piece at the time. Professor Longhair had several other minor hits: "Tipitina," "Go to the Mardi Gras," and the ballad "Cry, Pretty Baby." In spite of the superb artistic quality of these records, Professor Longhair was never able to top the national charts. He was especially famous among the other musicians of New Orleans.

Tired of a musical career that was not financially profitable, Longhair gave up the piano around 1964. He left behind over forty titles, all high-quality and impressive. Fortunately, they are on the albums *New Orleans Piano* (Atlantic) and *Mardi Gras in New Orleans* (Nighthawk).

In the early seventies, the passion for music seized the Professor again, and he easily resumed his activities in the circuit of clubs and festivals. He became one of the most popular figures of the famous annual New Orleans Festival and Heritage Fair. He recorded *Rock 'n' Roll Gumbo* (Dancing Cat), made with the great guitar player Gatemouth Brown★; *Crawfish Fiesta* (Alligator); and *The Last Mardi Gras* (Atlantic).

A great presenter of the secrets and rites of the superb Crescent City, Professor Longhair is now justly honored by his city: His "Mardi Gras in New Orleans" is its unofficial anthem.

SNOOKY PRYOR

(James Pryor / b. 1921 / vocals, harmonica)

Snooky Pryor's story is in itself a summary of the Chicago blues: Born in Mississippi, he learned to play the harmonica when he was about fourteen, and he moved to Chicago to work in a factory in 1940. There, he went to the clubs in the black ghetto, and he met John Lee "Sonny Boy" Williamson,★

who became his mentor. In 1946 he created a street band with Floyd Jones,* Eddie Taylor,* and Moody Jones. He is the first postwar bluesman to cut a record in a rural and electrified style, a style that became identified with the modern blues of Chicago ("Telephone Blues").

By 1963 he had recorded fourteen titles for several labels, without any commercial success. His records revealed a powerful singer and a harmonica player who electrified to the hilt a style influenced by John Lee "Sonny Boy" Williamson. Most of his titles are considered minor classics of the Chicago blues.

In 1963, tired of the dangerous, exhausting, and not very profitable life of a club musician, he gave it all up for the more comfortable life of a carpenter. His friend Homesick James* and the American magazine *Living Blues* convinced him to make a comeback in 1971, this time for the new blues public, essentially white. He went on several tours in Europe and in America with Homesick James, in which his powerful and direct style gained him numerous admirers.

A good composer of original blues based on traditional melodies, he recorded many albums. The best one, *Homesick James & Snooky Pryor* (Carline), is unfortunately no longer available.

After playing for a very short while in Willie Dixon's* band, Snooky retired more or less. Once in a while, he dips into the music world again, such as when he recorded an album with guitarist Steve Freund in 1988: *Snooky* (Blind Pig); in 1991, he recorded the good album *Too Cool to Move* (Antone's), demonstrating that to be a great harmonica player you need not only technique, but also the ability to blow with feeling.

Real Fine Boogie (Flyright) gathers the essence of his first work.

Q

QUEEN IDA

See Zydeco

R

YANK RACHELL

(James Rachell or Rachel / b. 1908 / vocals, mandolin, guitar)

Yank Rachell is in many respects a unique case in the blues world. He is one of the rare mandolin players of the genre. He developed a basic technique, which was successful in catching the difficult blue notes and the blues atmosphere. His known association with Sleepy John Estes★ ranks him among his equals. Before the war he recorded a few guitar pieces very close to the blues of Scrapper Blackwell.★ And although he was especially known by fans as a follower of country blues, he led with dynamism a small modern band, in which he was the electric guitarist.

If his sessions as the accompanist for Sleepy John Estes and John Lee "Sonny Boy" Williamson★ are famous, he also left on Bluebird a remarkable work that revealed his talent as a composer and as a forerunner of the postwar Chicago blues: "Hobo Blues," later covered by John Lee Hooker★; "Army Man Blues" covered by Big Joe Williams★; "Biscuit Baking Mama" by Eddie Burns★; "Lou Della" by Jimmy Rogers★; and "Up North Blues," on which Yank's guitar mingled harmoniously with Sonny Boy's harmonica. *James "Yank" Rachel, Vols. 1 & 2* (Wolf) are interesting, as are all of his titles.

His career after the war was not particularly rewarding despite a few concerts and festivals in Europe. More or less confined to Indianapolis by an exhausting job that was necessary to support his family, Yank worked in the studios only sporadically. His most beautiful piece is the outstanding *Yank Rachell* (Blue Goose), an entirely acoustic piece. His talents as a more modern bluesman were captured on *Blues Mandolin Man* (Blind Pig) and *Yank Rachell Chicago Style* (Delmark) too late to really be convincing.

But Rachell is still an important figure of the pivotal 1935–41 period, and as such he cannot be ignored.

MA RAINEY

(Gertrude Pridgett / 1886–1939 / vocals)

If Bessie Smith★ was the "empress of the blues," Ma Rainey was undeniably its "mother" and the first big commercial star of this rapidly blooming genre.

Born in Georgia, Gertrude Pridgett had a vocation for the theater very early on. She was on stage in 1900 and was hired in a traveling vaudeville show in which she sang, danced, and acted. In 1904 she married the dancer William "Pa" Rainey, and despite her young age she adopted the nickname of "Ma" Rainey.

She put on her show with the Tolliver circus and the Rabbit Foot Minstrels, where she gave some advice to the young Bessie Smith. The multi-talented "Ma" sang the blues of her childhood for this simple public composed of southern blacks. The emotion she put into her renditions gradually made her the outright star of these shows. A stout woman with a mouthful of gold teeth, ring-loaded fingers, and diamonds around her neck, she was a real music-hall star, and she acted as such toward her public and her musicians. As piano player Jack Dupree★ said (he had often seen her as a child): "She was really a dreadful woman. But when she opened her mouth, she was fascinating, and she made you forget everything. What a character! She was such a great singer."

Until about 1930, Ma Rainey was the true "queen of the South." When she realized she could not regain the popularity to which she was accustomed, Ma gave up the music hall to devote herself to the management of the two theaters that she had bought in her native town of Columbus, Georgia. During her short recording career (1923–1928), she recorded essentially the blues. Her sincere interpretations, her deep voice, and the seriousness she gave to their most trivial themes helped many of her recordings survive time despite their poor technical quality and some band effects that are today obsolete.

Like Bessie Smith, Ma Rainey was able to surround herself with the best jazz and blues musicians of the time: Louis

Armstrong, Tommy Ladnier, Papa Charlie Jackson,* Jimmy O'Bryant, and others. Her best titles were recorded in 1928: She was alone with only Georgia Tom Dorsey on piano and the superb Tampa Red* on guitar.

A good part of her work is available on Biograph and Milestone (*Ma Rainey:* Milestone). The VJM label reissued all her recorded work on *Ma Rainey, Complete Recordings in Chronological Order* (VJM). *Ma Rainey's Black Bottom* (Yazoo) is the best selection, with a superb sound.

A. C. REED

(Aaron Corthen / b. 1926 / vocals, t-saxophone)

A. C. Reed, saxophone player, a veteran of Chicago clubs and recording studios, began his career with Willie Mabon* and Earl Hooker.* During that time he was awarded a "golden saxophone" and the title of "king of the Chicago blues, saxophone version."

During the sixties, he recorded a great number of 45s for a horde of small labels, staying as close as possible to the vocal style of his presumed cousin, the famous Jimmy Reed.*

But if the lazy "This Little Voice" too closely resembled Jimmy Reed, "I Stay Mad" and the excellent "My Buddy Buddy Friends" were pieces full of the disenchanted and caustic humor that was A. C.'s mark.

Between 1970 and 1983, Reed was the regular sideman of Buddy Guy,* Junior Wells,* Son Seals,* and Albert Collins,* whose live performances and records were enhanced by Reed's rough and straight tone. This simple but essential style of Chicago blues led scores of rock musicians such as the Rolling Stones and Eric Clapton to use Reed's talents on some of their recordings. That encouraged A. C. to start a solo career at an age when others retire. "I Am Fed up with This Music," produced in 1983 in two versions, one X-rated, the other for more sensitive ears, is irresistibly funny: It enabled Aaron to win a W. C. Handy* Award (on the album *Take These Blues and Shove 'Em:* Ice Cube).

I'm in the Wrong Business (Alligator), on which A. C. expressed his regrets at not having been a boxer like Rocky or

Mr. T., is in the same vein, and with the support of Stevie Ray Vaughan and Bonnie Raitt, it was a commercial hit.

Let's hope that the oldest and nicest saxophone player in Chicago has a few more tricks in his bag for the pleasure of his admirers all over the world.

JIMMY REED

(1925–1976 / vocals, guitar, harmonica)

A simple set of walking bass notes, a few harmonica high notes, and a drawling accent that mumbled the words—that was Jimmy Reed. A lazy and languid music with lyrics similar to the ballads of much more sophisticated singers combined with the perfect rhythmic support of Eddie Taylor* and the subtle drummer Earl Phillips, all contributed to the huge popular success of Jimmy Reed. As far as his commercial success was concerned, Jimmy Reed—with twenty-two places in the American charts—from 1953 to 1966—was more successful than Muddy Waters,* Howlin' Wolf,* and all the other Chicago bluesmen.

In fact, his career can be compared more to rock-and-roll artists, although his music was one of the most direct and simple in blues history, and it was extremely close to his rural roots.

Born in Mississippi, Jimmy Reed went to Chicago in 1943 with his friend Eddie Taylor; then he settled in the neighboring town, Gary. He worked in a factory in the daytime; in the evenings he played the harmonica in the black clubs of that town with Taylor, John Brim, his wife, Grace, and Albert King,* who was then a drummer. Around 1952, Reed often played guitar and harmonica with Eddie Taylor. His sensitive and original repertoire, for the most part due to the imagination of his wife, "Mama" Reed, gained him local success. In 1953, Reed managed to record for Vee-Jay in the first stage of its development. "You Don't Have to Go," a simple request that Mama Reed had written to Jimmy, became an international hit. The Jimmy Reed "sound," with its heavy boogie-woogie bass line and its short harmonica phrases, became famous overnight. Reed and Taylor quit their jobs in the factory and in the small Chicago clubs for the profitable tours in the U.S. and the big concert halls. In 1957, Reed was one of the few bluesmen to be in the Billboard hit parade with "Honest I Do." The following years, it was hit after hit for Reed: "Baby, What You Want Me to Do," "Hush, Hush," "Big Boss Man," "Bright Lights, Big City," and "Shame, Shame, Shame" became classics that many artists later covered. The current repertoire of bluesmen in Chicago taverns is proof of the huge influence his music had on the blues of that city. But it may even be more pronounced in the South. Indeed, after 1957, the electric blues, from Texas to Mississippi, was copied mainly from that of Jimmy Reed: Slim Harpo,★ Frank Frost,★ Juke Boy Bonner,★ Lazy Lester,★ and a host of others, lesser known, successfully copied Jimmy Reed's musical formula. He was a favorite among English rock groups of the sixties: the Animals, the Rolling Stones, the Moody Blues, the Yardbirds, and the Spencer Davis Group. Even in the U.S. singers as different as Billy Lee Riley, Bobby Gentry, and Elvis Presley covered his songs. At the top of American popular music, it seemed that Jimmy Reed would be able to make a future for himself with no problem.

However, he proved unable to handle his success. In 1962, Jimmy Reed, continually drunk and forgetting more and more to show up for his engagements, alienated friends and fans alike. Eddie Taylor, the major promoter of his musical success, tired of having to always fight to keep his friend sober for a few hours. Taylor left Reed, as did all of his successors. In 1964, the unexpected bankruptcy of Vee-Jay left Reed with no record company. Increasingly frequent epileptic fits and a difficult separation from his wife accelerated his solitude and precipitated his fall. Although he did have some success ("Knockin' at Your Door" in 1966) and although he later recorded some albums for Al Smith's Bluesway label, Jimmy Reed was a shadow of his former self. He missed the commercial opportunity that the blues revival offered. During his performance on the European tour of the American Folk Blues Festival in 1968, he gave his most fervent fans the image of a man eaten away by sickness and the frantic abuse of alcohol, unable to stand on stage for more than ten minutes.

His successive comebacks were all cut short. He had just undergone treatment for alcoholism and had even planned a new comeback, when he died suddenly in 1976. The musical press, radio, and television paid homage to him, but the black ghettos, from Chicago to Houston, grieved in a more discreet, moving, and sincere way, revealing the extent of his popularity among his fellow men.

Jimmy Reed's work includes a series of superb hits between 1953 and 1959, then a few good moments alternating with a few total flops (until 1966), followed by a series of rather mediocre albums for Bluesway and disastrous albums for several small labels.

A good selection of his Vee-Jay titles are on two generous compact discs: *Big Boss Blues* (Charly) and *Rockin' with Reed* (Charly) and on *The Best of Jimmy Reed* (GNP) and *Ride 'em on Down* (Charly).

SONNY RHODES

(Clarence Smith / b. 1941 / vocals, guitar, fiddle)

From Texas to San Francisco, Sonny Rhodes followed the classic itinerary of West Coast bluesmen. Rooted in that regional tradition, he is a superb singer with sensuous tones that are reminiscent of Junior Parker.* He is also a very good composer strongly influenced by Percy Mayfield* and an interesting instrumentalist who drew his inspiration from Gatemouth Brown* as well as from Albert Collins* and his friend L. C. Robinson.* Through Robinson, he came to know the western-swing musicians of the forties, steel-guitar player Leon McAuliffe in particular.

Born near Austin, Sonny Rhodes developed an early interest in music singing in the church choir. As an ardent admirer of Junior Parker, he soon persuaded Parker to take him on as a valet, then as a chauffeur. The years with Parker were musically fruitful for Rhodes, who benefited from the good advice of his employer as well as from band members, especially guitar players Roy Gaines and Clarence Holliman. He recorded an obscure 45 in Texas, then he settled in the San Francisco Bay area, where he began his difficult integration into the clubs of Richmond, Fresno, and Oakland. His persistence finally paid off in the sixties when he became a popular figure locally. It was then he became friends with L. C. Robinson, who taught him to play the steel guitar and the fiddle, and also with piano player J. J. Malone,* who was then an arranger-producer of the Galaxy/Fantasy label. Thanks to Malone, Sonny Rhodes recorded a series of wonderful titles for Galaxy, either under his real name (Clarence Smith) or under a stage name.

But despite the quality of these records, Rhodes was unable to live off his music. His participation in the San Francisco Blues Festival of Tom Mazzolini and a long interview in *Living Blues* gave him the opportunity to perform in concerts, numerous clubs, and international tours.

Among the albums he recorded, the best ones are *I Don't Want My Blues Colored Bright* (Advent), made with his friend J. J. Malone, and *Just Blues* (Rhodesway), which included the poignant "Cigarette Blues."

In any case, Sonny Rhodes, who prolongs with warmth the purest blues tradition of the West Coast, is a first-rate artist. In 1991 he recorded the excellent *Disciple of the Blues* (Ichiban), proving he is still at his best.

FENTON ROBINSON

(b. 1935 / vocals, harmonica)

At a time when the blues is supposed to be making a comeback, it is shocking to see an artist such as Fenton Robinson neglected by the media and by record companies.

"A guitarist among guitarists," Robinson rightly deserves this title that was given to him in the past by a musical review.

A native of Mississippi and having, like so many others, gone to Memphis then to Chicago via Texas, Robinson is nevertheless influenced more by the Texas sounds of T-Bone Walker* and Gatemouth Brown* than by Muddy Waters.* A complete musician, a good jazzman, an extraordinary composer, and a singer with poignant phrases influenced by gospel, Fenton should be in the foreground of the blues. In fact, though, he is still largely unknown outside a limited circle of fans.

In 1957, Robinson, who was already a master of the guitar, recorded "Tennessee Woman" with B. B. King's* band. This title was a local hit that gave him the opportunity to sign a contract with the Texas Duke label. He recorded a handful of titles, among which was "As the Years Go Passing By," which became a hit for Albert King* and which was later covered by a number of blues and rock singers. In Houston, Fenton Robinson also accompanied his friend Larry Davis,* the simple singer-bass player, on the anthology *Angels in Houston:* (Rounder).

He then left for Chicago where he became acquainted with the creators of the West Side sound. With Magic Sam,* Otis Rush,* and Buddy Guy,* Robinson played an obscure but major role in the development of this style that is today identified with modern Chicago blues. Robinson himself was satisfied with a few local hits recorded for tiny labels. The admirable "Somebody Loan Me a Dime" is one of his compositions that the singer Boz Scaggs took to the top of the charts. Somewhat disenchanted, Fenton returned to the South, long enough to record a rather absurd album, *Mellow Fellow,* in Nashville.

It was the tireless and wise Bruce Iglauer who put Robinson back in the foreground with two extraordinary albums for the Alligator label: *Somebody Loan Me a Dime*—one of the best albums in blues history—and *I Hear Some Blues Downstairs*.

Unfortunately, Robinson's difficult character, a series of personal misfortunes, and bad luck caused him to sink back into oblivion in America. Europe and Japan knew his records and thanks to the stubbornness of the Dutch, he managed to record two more records (one every five years). He now lives in Little Rock, where he performs almost entirely for a local audience. *Blues in Progress* (Black Magic or Alligator) did not equal the two previous albums in spite of Junior Wells'* presence, but *Special Road* (Black Magic), a compact recorded in 1989, took up the splendor of "Somebody Loan Me a Dime." Currently, very few bluesmen exhibit such a breathtaking festival of invention, virtuosity, and instrumental mastery, along with obvious vocal and composing qualities, as does Fenton Robinson.

L. C. "GOOD ROCKIN'" ROBINSON

(Louis Charles Robinson / 1915–1976 / vocals, guitar, fiddle)

This Texan, L. C. "Good Rockin'" Robinson, first learned the bottleneck technique from his distant cousin, the street singer Blind Willie Johnson.* But later he was influenced by the western-swing bands, in particular, that of Bob Wills and his Texas Playboys, who, in the thirties and forties, made the state of Texas dance. He was familiar with Bob Wills'* guitar player, Leon McAuliffe, who seems to have taught him the Hawaiian guitar. At the same time Robinson was rapidly mastering the fiddle after the style of Wills, himself a great fiddle player.

In 1940, he moved to Oakland, California, where he created a small band with his brother, the harmonica player A. C. Robinson. In spite of his success when he performed on stage, he recorded only about ten titles between 1945 and 1954 for the producer Bob Geddins. His multiple talents on three instruments, the variety of his repertoire, from the "deep" blues in the manner of Lightnin' Hopkins* to the instrumentals of western swing, and his energetic sense for performing enabled him to get regular contracts in the California clubs, where he became one of the most picturesque and popular figures.

After 1969, he finally got the opportunity to record substantially for World Pacific (produced by Jimmy McCracklin*), Bluesway, and Arhoolie. *Ups and Down* (Arhoolie) is an excellent album on which L. C. Robinson is accompanied by the blues band of Muddy Waters* and the extraordinary piano player Dave Alexander.*

L. C. Robinson had a definite impact on the renewal of California blues in the seventies, influencing bluesmen such as Dave Alexander, Freddie Roulette, J. J. Malone,* and Sonny Rhodes.*

ROCKIN' DOPSIE

See Zydeco

ROCKIN' SIDNEY

(b. 1938 / vocals, accordion, guitar, harmonica, bass, drums)

An eminent member of the rich zydeco scene, Rockin' Sidney was propelled suddenly to the foreground with "My Toot Toot" right at the time when Clifton Chenier's crown, the "Zydeco King," was free. In the land of bayous and alligators, the fight was tough between the accordions of Sidney, Fernest Arceneaux,★ Rockin' Dopsie★ . . . .

If at the level of the instrumental virtuosity or the intensity of the singing Sidney is distanced by his rivals, he is undeniably a brilliant composer, an inventive arranger, and his music, incredibly danceable. These qualities can be seen on *Boogie, Blues 'n' Zydeco* (Maison de Soul/Krazy Kat); *My Zydeco Shoes Got the Zydeco Blues* (Maison de Soul), including the famous "Toot, Toot"; *Live with the Blues* (JSP); *Hot Steppin'* (ZBC); and *Squeeze That Thang* (ZBC). Some of his first titles are on *They Call Me Rockin'* (Flyright).

RODGERS, JIMMIE

See White Blues

JIMMY ROGERS

(James A. Lane / b. 1924 / vocals, guitar, harmonica)

Like many others, Jimmy Rogers went from Georgia to Chicago via Memphis after the war. He created his guitar style listening to records, especially those of Memphis Minnie★ and John Lee "Sonny Boy" Williamson.★ Since he wanted to reproduce by himself the sound of a small band, he developed a rhythm guitar style that was not particularly spectacular but was very effective.

In Chicago, he became friends with Muddy Waters,★ and accompanied by Little Walter★ and drummer Elgar Edmonds (or Elgin Evans), they created Muddy's regular band. Walter was then playing the guitar and Rogers the harmonica, until they both realized that they were playing the instrument that was least fitted to each of them. They changed their roles, and

■ Jimmy Rogers. *(Photograph © by Paul Harris; used with permission)*

Muddy found himself leading the most fantastic combination of musicians in the history of contemporary blues.

In 1950, at the end of a session reserved for Muddy Waters, Jimmy Rogers recorded the wonderful blues "That's All Right." It became an instant hit in Chicago, and Len Chess* understood that this guitar player was also a singer with a clear and flexible voice as well as a remarkable composer. From 1950 to 1959, Jimmy Rogers recorded about thirty songs, among which were an impressive number of masterpieces: "The World Is in a Tangle"; "I Used to Have a Woman," with the powerful piano player Eddie Ware (this was the first time a saxophone was used in the postwar Chicago blues); the oppressive "Money, Marbles and Chalk"; and the bitter "Back Door Friend." As for the lighter theme of "Walkin' by Myself," it gave Big Walter Horton* the occasion to play one of his most beautiful harmonica solos.

Although he was very much appreciated by the Chicago public, Jimmy Rogers was above all Muddy Waters' guitar player, and when tastes changed to the advantage of more brilliant instrumentalists, like Pat Hare and Buddy Guy,* Rogers gave up music and had several other jobs.

But in 1970, pressed by piano player Bob Riedy, he did come back. He played regularly in Chicago clubs, American festivals, and several tours in Europe. In spite of that, this great name of the Chicago blues is not very busy today.

Left Me with a Broken Heart (Vogue) and *That's All Right* (Chess) are largely available, and they represent the best Chicago blues of the fifties. The album recorded with Bob Riedy, the Aces, and Freddie King* in 1973, *Gold-Tailed Bird* (Shelter), has been reissued with many previously unreleased tracks on *Sings the Blues* (Shelter DCC). *Ludella* (Antone's), a recent session, finds Jimmy in the company of Kim Wilson and is also recommended.

WALTER ROLAND

(ca. 1900–1950 / vocals, piano, guitar)

Although he recorded about fifty titles under his own name between 1933 and 1935 and as many titles when he accompanied Josh White,* Sonny Scott, and Lucille Bogan, Walter Roland is still a mysterious figure in blues history. Indeed, we know little about his life, except that he was born in Alabama and that he was very popular around Birmingham when he was contacted by the ARC company to record. He went to New York three times—in 1933, 1934, and 1935, recording about twenty titles each time. Despite a few hits, he stopped recording and disappeared for good.

In any case, he was a great piano player as shown by his short but brilliant career: As comfortable in boogie-woogies as in slow blues, Roland—with his manner of playing and his singing—was direct and rural, without any trace of the sophistication found in the piano masters of Chicago (such as Jimmy Yancey* and Meade Lux Lewis*).

The superb piano style must not overshadow his guitar style, sometimes reminiscent of the fluid style of East Coast musicians such as Josh White,* who was present in the same studios in March 1935 and who recorded several titles with Roland at that time.

His fellow Alabaman LUCILLE BOGAN began her career in 1923; she had a big hit with "Sweet Petunia" in 1927. Until 1930 she was a superb rural singer with a powerful and unaffected voice, contrary to her more famous contemporaries, who came from vaudeville. Strangely enough, after a long break between 1930 and 1933, she changed her name to Bessie Jackson, as well as completely changing the timbre of her voice, so as to be, it seems, closer to her more famous rivals. From 1933 to 1935, she was brilliantly accompanied by Walter Roland, which meant a regular collaboration of these two artists from Alabama. During her entire career, Lucille Bogan showed a predilection for crude stories about prostitution. She disappeared at the same time as Roland after 1935.

These two excellent artists are together on *Piano Blues, Vol. 6* (Magpie) and *Bessie Jackson & Walter Roland* (Yazoo). Lucille/Bessie is the featured musician on *Women Won't Need No Men* (Agram).

DOCTOR ROSS

(Isaiah Ross / b. 1925 / vocals, guitar, harmonica, drums)

This amazing one-man band enlightened the Memphis blues scene after the war. He played his own style of Delta blues in the streets and in the clubs of Beale Street and in W. C. Handy* Park. An excellent harmonica player, the Doctor (thus called because of his particular abilities to cure people) is not as at ease as a one-man band as are Joe Hill Louis or Jesse Fuller.* John Lee "Sonny Boy" Williamson* provides the main source of his music, and numerous themes of the Doctor, his tense singing, mumbling the end of the phrases, and the essential harmonica style came from Williamson. He recorded a series of wonderful titles for Sun gathered on *His First Recordings* (Arhoolie) and *Sun Records: The Blues Years* (Sun Box).

Somewhat isolated when he went to Michigan, Doctor Ross reappeared once in a while to deliver his prescriptions, essentially to the European public, and he recorded several albums for Testament and Storyville. *One Man Band* (Takoma) captures one of his good live performances.

BOBBY RUSH

See Soul

OTIS RUSH

(b. 1934 / vocals, guitar)

Otis Rush's career can be divided into three phases: an extraordinary debut in 1956, where he appeared as a brilliant and original creator of the West Side sound of Chicago; a long slack period during which he recorded very little, but because of the success of his first titles, he was recognized as a legendary genius; and, after 1974, an active but disappointing comeback to the blues scene that forces us to think further about Otis Rush's real place in blues history.

He was born in Mississippi, then moved to Chicago at an early age. After years of practice in that city and of listening to a great number of records, Rush began to develop a unique

■ Otis Rush. *(Photograph © by Paul Harris; used with permission)*

musical approach that combined the guitar phrases of B. B. King★ and the tense and oppressive singing of the Chicago blues. His singing was dramatic and theatrical; his frequent use of minor keys expressed one of the most universal characteristics in contemporary blues: that of an artist, who is taciturn, introverted, pessimistic, and gloomy to the point of despair.

With a great local hit, "I Can't Quit You Baby," in 1965 for the small Cobra label directed by Eli Toscano, Otis Rush, with Buddy Guy★ and Magic Sam,★ created the West Side sound and opened a new era of Chicago blues, that of the young generation raised in the ghettos. Within a few years Otis Rush recorded about twenty titles for Cobra, most of which are big hits ("All Your Love," "My Love Will Never Die," and "Groaning the Blues"). Unfortunately, the commercial success of "I Can't Quit You" was not repeated.

All of the Cobra titles were reissued on compact disc: *His Cobra Recordings* (Flyright) is a fundamental collection. After the murder of Toscano, Otis Rush was never able to regain success, although his later recordings are generally first-rate: a few titles for Chess (*Door to Door:* Chess/Vogue); a few others for Duke in 1962, among which was *Homework;* and a session for Sam Charters in 1965 (on *The Blues Today, Vol. 2:* Vanguard).

After 1966 and his participation in the European tour of the American Folk Blues Festival, Otis Rush went through a tough time: few performances, a sterile contract with Capitol records, and an album that was excessively arranged (*Mourning in the Morning:* Atlantic). Nevertheless, he continued to perfect his style, adding the influences of Kenny Burrell, Jimmy Smith, and Albert King⋆ and inspiring enthusiasm in the few fans who managed to listen to him in the most poorly paid Chicago clubs. Appreciated by critics and by musicians like Duane Allman, Eric Clapton, and Mick Taylor, Otis Rush announced a comeback that finally happened after 1974. He toured in Europe and in Japan and recorded several albums. Despite some brilliant moments, his live performances did not usually correspond to his legend. Unstable and impulsive, his performances were often botched—even to the point of his quitting suddenly while on tour. With unexciting albums and mediocre performances, it seems obvious that Rush's success is behind him. This impression is further reinforced by the fact that Otis seems unable to compose the least notable new piece: He repeats endlessly and excessively his old hits or he interprets the Chicago blues classics, usually without conviction.

Two albums emerged, however, out of that slump: *Right Place, Wrong Time* (Hightone), carefully recorded and produced, and *So Many Roads* (Delmark), which captured a successful concert given by Rush in Japan in 1975. Despite everything, these are crumbs compared to the Cobra feast. Since then, there has been a long silence with a few irregular passages in concerts, festivals, a few totally unexpected tours, and a poor "live" album: *Tops* (Blind Pig). It seems that many producers, like Jim O'Neal, tried in vain to give Rush the opportunity to find his way back to the studios under favorable conditions.

In fact, fans might wonder how an artist who had apparently revolutionized his music could suddenly stop being creative. Otis Rush's deep personality needs to be stressed, of course; moreover, it is important to notice that many creators, in all areas, often were brilliant for short periods of time. We also would like to underline an often unnoticed fact: Behind the Otis Rush of the Cobra period was Willie Dixon,★ arranger, producer, and adviser of the young bluesman. Almost all of Otis Rush's big hits were due to Dixon's talent, which, also present at the sides of other artists (Buddy Guy, Charles Clark, Harold Burrage, and Magic Sam, on the Cobra label), seems to have played a major role in the creation of the West Side sound.

Otis Rush's exceptional temperament and his talents as a singer and a guitar player were, of course, necessary to produce equally splendid records, but without Willie Dixon, it is most likely that Otis Rush would not have reached that level, nor would he have adopted such an innovative style.

JIMMY RUSHING

(1903–1972 / vocals)

Jimmy Rushing, with a clear, strong voice, sang in the Kansas City style popularized by Joe Turner,★ but he preferred jazz to blues. A great figure of black American music, Jimmy Rushing was not really in favor with blues fans. Nevertheless, since its birth the blues evolved differently according to the regions or the schools. Rushing essentially represented the Midwest blues-jazz sound: He was able to lead a big band and to give it, by his mere presence, strength and movement.

Influenced by church songs, he began a career as a blues singer in 1923, the time of the urban and sophisticated "classic blues" played by jazz musicians like Tommy Ladnier, Love Austin, and King Oliver around female vaudeville singers. He remained faithful to that blues style and, probably because of that, he never was in favor with the white public.

In 1927, he became the regular singer in Walter Page's band before becoming the regular singer in Count Basie's wonderful band from 1936 to 1949. After he left Basie's band, he recorded under his own name, usually with big jazz bands, for numerous record companies: King, Parrot, Vanguard, CBS, RCA . . . Most of his records show his remarkable qualities as a singer: powerful, flexible, and emotional.

His record production is abundant and first-rate. Currently, we can listen to the powerful blues shouter on compact disc: *Jimmy Rushing* (RCA/Bluebird), *The Bluesway Sessions* (Charly), and *Good Morning Blues* (Affinity), which put together his best titles recorded with Count Basie. Rushing also recorded some brilliant titles for Vanguard with the excellent guitar player Roy Gaines.★

ST. LOUIS

At the intersection of the Mississippi and Missouri rivers, St. Louis is the end of the line for boats coming from New Orleans. Located at the natural border between the North and the South, St. Louis became an industrial center, attracting black immigrants who had left Memphis but who had not yet reached Chicago or Detroit. In 1917, the arrival en masse of black workers to the suburbs east of St. Louis gave rise to tragic racial confrontations that left a scar on the city.

In 1925, in the black district of Third, Lawton, and Jefferson avenues, many clubs and small bars became favored places for the blues. Except for Chicago and Memphis, St. Louis was probably the richest city, musically speaking, in the thirties. It was the melting pot in which the primitive blues of southern rural states became an urban and sophisticated blues, based on the delicate interaction of piano and guitar, which clearly announced the modern blues that would take place in Chicago ten years later: The piano provided bass notes, allowing the guitar to improvise freely, and the musician gave up playing chords for a melodic note-by-note progression.

The main representatives of this style are, of course, guitar players Lonnie Johnson★ and Henry Townsend★ and piano players Roosevelt Sykes,★ Walter Davis,★ Peetie Wheatstraw,★ and his presumed half-brother, Jimmie Gordon; all of them recorded prolifically in the thirties.

The backbone of the St. Louis blues was Jesse Johnson, a

record store owner and show organizer. Johnson deserves credit for having discovered most of the above talents and also many lesser-known talents, like the Sparks brothers (Aaron and Milton); guitarists Hi Henry Brown, Charley Jordan, and Henry Spaulding, the creator of the classic "Cairo Blues"; J. D. Short, a powerful singer but also a piano player with a simple technique; piano player Henry Brown, still a little active today; and singer Blind Blues Darby, who influenced Johnny Shines.* Let's also not forget the interesting female singers Alice Moore and Mary Johnson, Lonnie's wife.

All of these artists created a great brotherhood, which is obvious in the excellent anthologies *Good Time Blues* (Mamlish), *Hard Time Blues* (Mamlish), *The Blues in St. Louis* (OJL), *St. Louis Blues* (Yazoo), and *St. Louis Town* (Yazoo).

However, two strong personalities, very different from each other, stand out among the St. Louis artists. The singer ST. LOUIS JIMMY (1905–1978), a close friend of Roosevelt Sykes, had an uncertain career in the city clubs until the recording of his composition "Goin' Down Slow," which had a tremendous success and was played by dozens of artists. St. Louis Jimmy went to Chicago with Sykes and recorded for several labels before he co-founded the JOB label. His career as a singer was not spectacular (especially after a serious car accident); however, he did compose many blues that became hits for Howlin' Wolf,* Muddy Waters,* and Little Walter.*

CLIFFORD GIBSON (1901–1963) was a street singer famous in St. Louis for his complex guitar style (prolonged high notes, interspersed with doubled bass notes) and for his performing dog who accompanied him in his numbers. After being discovered by Jesse Johnson, he recorded about forty songs between 1929 and 1935, some of which are on the album *Beat You Doing It* (Yazoo). Although he played until the end of his life and although he recorded for the small local Bobbin label in 1960, Gibson died totally destitute, and his wife sold his body to a medical school to save burial fees.

After the war, the same Bobbin label recorded Little Milton* and Albert King.* But in the fifties the St. Louis blues scene was dominated by Ike Turner* and his numerous sidemen, recording many titles for small local labels.

Nowadays, the blues in St. Louis is kept relatively alive by a few personalities such as Johnnie Johnson, Chuck Berry's ex-piano player; producer-arranger Oliver Sain; Larry Davis*; James DeShay, a guitar player in the style of Albert King; singer David Lee; Robert Westmoreland; and collector Leroy Pierson and his Nighthawk label.

On the other hand, it is a moribund tradition that the acoustic bluesmen represent on the otherwise excellent anthology *Things Have Changed* (Echo Blues).

ST. LOUIS JIMMY

See St. Louis

SAXOPHONE

The saxophone was already in use at the dawn of the blues when the "classic" female singers recorded the first blues with jazz bands. But with the blooming of the rural blues between 1927 and 1938, the saxophone no longer seemed to belong to the blues world. However, around 1953 in Chicago, even artists as rooted in the tradition as J. B. Lenoir* and Jimmy Rogers* used saxophones for their recordings.

Few saxophone players were "pure" bluesmen. They were generally versatile musicians, as comfortable in blues as in rock-and-roll or jazz, performers such as Eddie Chamblee, Plas Johnson, Silas Austin, Julian Dash, Buddy Tate, Sam "The Man" Raylor, Noble Watts, Paul Williams, Arnett Cobb, Candy Johnson, and King Curtis. Talented artists such as J. T. Brown (the regular saxophone player for Elmore James),* A. C. Reed,* Eddie Shaw,* and Abb Locke, all strongly linked to the blues, are complete musicians, able to move with ease from one musical genre to the next.

The best anthology of the blues saxophone is *Atlantic Honkers: An R&B Saxophone Anthology* (Atlantic); also of interest are *Rootin' and Tootin'* (Charly), *Battin' the Boogie* (Charly), and *Honkers and Screamers* (Savoy).

SON SEALS

(Frank Seals / b. 1940 / vocals, guitar, drums)

At the lowest ebb of the blues in the seventies, Son Seals appeared on the scene as the exceptional discovery of a new black Chicago bluesman.

Son Seals has been immersed in the blues since his early years: His father played the trombone and also owned a small club in Arkansas. At age thirteen he was a drummer for Robert Nighthawk* and later for Earl Hooker.* Then he traveled throughout the U.S. with Albert King,* an old family friend, and his band. King's influence was very important on all of Son Seals' music. But Seals also drew inspiration from the established West Side sound of Magic Sam* and from the subtleties of Fenton Robinson.*

After the flourishing decade of the seventies, during which Son Seals recorded prolifically for the Alligator label and performed on the stages of America and Europe, he appeared as a new symbol of the modern blues. But recently Son Seals has been having a terrible slack period. A serious train accident in Scandinavia that decimated his band and shocked him has relegated Seals to the veteran category. But Son Seals is a powerful singer and a skilled and prolific composer. He also has what it takes to captivate a large public with his abilities as an arranger and guitarist.

The Son Seals Blues Band (Alligator); *Live and Burning* (Alligator), with A. C. Reed* in superb form; and *Bad Axe* (Alligator), his most recent effort, are among the best albums recorded by Son Seals.

ALEC SEWARD

See New York

SHAKEY JAKE

(Jimmie D. Harris / 1921–1990 / vocals, harmonica)

The enormous success of John Lee "Sonny Boy" Williamson,* in Chicago and in the South, convinced Shakey Jake to undertake a singing career around 1945. Although he was certainly not a great musician, his harmonica style, especially in slow blues, matched perfectly the warm and veiled timbre of his voice.

In fact, this rambler from Arkansas was a dabbler: A mechanic, a professional gambler (his nickname comes from "Shake 'em"), a record producer, and a show entrepreneur, he only took his musical career seriously between 1958 and 1964. At that time he performed regularly in Chicago clubs with his nephew, the great Magic Sam,* with whom he recorded a handful of titles. But it seemed that he played an important role as an advisor to Sam, and his impact on the emergence of the West Side sound should not be underestimated. After a few unconvincing tours in America and in Europe (in 1962 he was part of the American Folk Blues Festival), Shakey Jake settled in California, where he played a relatively important role with numerous white blues-rock groups, notably those of Rod Piazza and Hollywood Fats.

Among the albums he recorded, the following are worth remembering: *Mouth Harp Blues* (Bluesville/Ave); *Further on up the Road* (World Pacific), on which a very young Luther Allison* shone; *Make It Good to You* (Good Time); and *The Devil's Harmonica* (Polydor), accompanied by John Mayall and the superb guitar player Freddie Robinson.

EDDIE SHAW

(b. 1937 / vocals, tenor saxophone)

Eddie Shaw did not assert himself as a soloist until 1975 when Howlin' Wolf* died. Shaw had instead maintained the role of manager for Howlin' Wolf during the last years of Wolf's career.

In fact, he is an "old-timer," having knocked about Chicago's West Side for more than twenty years. Eclectic, he leads a band, owns a club, and plays the saxophone with several groups. He made a name for himself as a saxophone player. Born near Greenville, Mississippi, he learned to play the saxophone in his school years. He played in the Delta with Little Milton,* Oliver Sain, Charlie Booker, and Ike Turner.* It was Muddy Waters* who urged him to come to Chicago in

1957. An excellent musician able to produce the straight and harsh sounds of rhythm and blues, as well as long "jazzy" improvisations, Eddie Shaw had no trouble gaining recognition on the Chicago blues scene, especially among the young guitar players of the West Side, Otis Rush* and Magic Sam.* With Magic Sam he recorded his first solos, two excellent instrumentals, one of which was the fascinating "Blues for the West Side." Howlin' Wolf was already seriously ill when Shaw joined his band in 1972. But Shaw, enterprising and experienced, finally played a major role, organizing the tours and managing the life of the band. When Wolf died, Eddie Shaw took over his band—Hubert Sumlin,* piano player Detroit Junior,* bass player Shorty Gilbert, and drummer Chico Chism—and named it the Wolf Gang. He got numerous engagements all across the U.S. In 1977 Lillie Burnett, Howlin' Wolf's widow, financed Shaw's first album, the excellent but impossible to find *Have Blues Will Travel*. Shaw revealed himself to be an excellent composer and a powerful blues shouter. However, it was his performance on the anthology *Living Chicago Blues, Vol. 1* (Alligator) that made him famous. Touring America and Europe regularly in the eighties, Eddie Shaw gained recognition as an important blues artist. Strangely enough, despite his talents as a composer (e.g., "That's My Town"), Eddie Shaw recorded very little under his own name. *Movin' and Groovin'* (Isabel) is a worthy example of Shaw's talents, despite a few untimely interventions by guitar player Melvin Taylor.

For the past few years, Shaw—like other Chicago blues veterans—has appeared to stand aside, giving way to the flow of white bands playing blues-rock. However, much of today's blues-rock music lacks the authenticity of this Delta saxophone player, who, via Magic Sam and Howlin' Wolf, has already acquired his place in blues history.

THOMAS SHAW

(1908–1977 / vocals, guitar)

In spite of his late discovery—by Lou Curtiss, the owner of a record store in San Diego, California—in 1971, Thomas Shaw was a Texas bluesman of the first generation. Very active around Dallas-Fort Worth, he was associated with Blind Lemon Jefferson,* Ramblin' Thomas, Mance Lipscomb,* and, in particular, Funny Papa Smith,* the creator of the famous Texas blues "Howlin' Wolf." Smith and Shaw formed an extremely popular duo until 1934 when Shaw decided to leave for California.

After he was discovered by Curtiss, Shaw went on tours in the U.S. and in Germany, showing not only his ability to play the guitar but also his talents as a composer in the great Texas tradition that has always favored social or political comment. But in the fifties Shaw turned to religion and gave up the blues. Cautioned by his congregation against the "Devil's music," then dismissed by his church, it seems that he spent his last years in remorse, and in a certain way, in fear. His best album is still *Born in Texas* (Advent).

Around Shaw, Lou Curtiss tracked down other bluesmen of San Diego, showing one more time that the traditional blues is alive just below the surface, even in places where it was hard to imagine it active. Louis Major, Tom Courtney, Bob Jefferey, and Bonnie Jefferson are some of those artists with talent that nobody wanted to promote (on *San Diego Blues Jam:* Advent).

JOHNNY SHINES

(b. 1915–1992 / vocals, guitar)

Recognized by all as one of the greatest bluesmen, Johnny Shines never had the success of Muddy Waters,* which he could have claimed.

Johnny Shines was raised near Memphis, where he met many musicians with many different styles. But it was the deep Delta blues that influenced him. He made his debut in the thirties by imitating Howlin' Wolf,* who was then performing solo on the acoustic guitar. A few years later, he met Robert Johnson,* with whom he traveled for several months. The enigmatic Johnson left a deep mark on Johnny Shines' repertoire as well as on his guitar style, particularly the bottleneck. However, his vocal style (with a declamatory and almost

■ Johnny Shines. *(Photograph © by Anton J. Mikofsky; used with permission)*

shrill voice) was directly inspired by his long contact with a St. Louis singer, Blind Blues Darby, a talented but little-known figure.

In any case, when Johnny Shines arrived in Chicago during the war, he was an accomplished musician in full possession of a personal style based on the fusion of several influences. Extremely intelligent and sensitive, gifted with a certain poetic sense and a personal vision of the world, Johnny Shines managed to compose original blues full of powerful metaphors worthy of a great writer. When Lester Melrose* recorded him in 1946 for Columbia, it seemed he had a promising career. But, inexplicably, Columbia lost interest in that recording session (which could have also included the first commercial efforts of Muddy Waters), and these titles only became available in 1971 thanks to the efforts of critic Pete Welding.

A few years later, he recorded "Joliet Blues" and "So Glad I Found You" for Chess with Little Walter.* These masterpieces have a poetic density that is rarely achieved. But because Shines's style was in the same vein as Muddy Waters' style, Len Chess* chose not to create competition for his own star, thus leaving these titles un-released until 1970.

In 1952 Shines recorded a few pieces for the small JOB label, and at last he had the satisfaction of seeing his records sold. The breathtaking "Ramblin'," a quick blues on the bottleneck directly inspired by Robert Johnson, and the sarcastic "Brutal-Hearted Woman," on which the harmonica player Walter Horton* shone, are superb and can be found on the compact disc *Johnny Shines/Robert Jr. Lockwood* (Flyright).

But by 1959 Shines was without a contract, exhausted from performing in the clubs, disgusted by music, and thinking of giving it all up to be a mason.

However, Johnny Shines found, because of his records, a place in the heart of European fans. Thanks to the English review *Blues Unlimited* Shines was rediscovered and encouraged to play again and to record in 1965 for the anthology of Sam Charters, *Chicago/The Blues Today, Vol. 3* (Vanguard). From then on Johnny Shines had a commercial musical career: numerous concerts, festivals, and tours in America and in

Europe. He established himself as one of the most authentic and sincere Delta blues singers.

In the late seventies he joined with another close disciple of Robert Johnson, Robert Jr. Lockwood.* Soon afterward, Lockwood became paralyzed on one side. Shines' and Lockwood's combined talents can be heard on the 1980 album *Hangin' On* (Rounder).

Johnny Shines recorded many albums and showed that he was a great composer in the Delta tradition. A few albums are particularly interesting: *Johnny Shines* (Advent), with accompaniment by Phillip Walker's* band; *Standing at the Crossroads* (Testament); *Sitting on Top of the World* (Biograph); *Last Night's Dream* (Blue Horizon); *Nobody's Fault but Mine* (Black & Blue); and *Too Wet to Plow* (Tomato), with Louisiana Red* and Sugar Blue in top form.

FRANKIE LEE SIMS

(1917–1970 / vocals, guitar)

Frankie Lee Sims is, with Lightnin' Hopkins* and Lil' Son Jackson,* one of the great names of postwar Texas country blues. His influence on musicians around Dallas was considerable.

Although a nephew of the great Texas Alexander,* Sims did not accompany his uncle in his peregrinations. Instead he learned to play the guitar from Little Hat Jones, an important Texas bluesman whose music was dominated by a flamenco influence. Through Alexander, he met Smokey Hogg* and T-Bone Walker,* with whom he exchanged many musical ideas. On several occasions T-Bone Walker admitted to modernizing his style under the influence of Sims, who was fascinated by the electric guitar heard in jazz bands in the late thirties. Thus it was not surprising to find Sims, at the end of the war, leading a trio playing electric guitars. This gave him a great reputation around Dallas, and it enabled him to record substantially in the forties and fifties for several labels, especially the tiny Blue Bonnet, Specialty, and Ace. The powerful "Lucy Mae Blues," a masterpiece of rhythm and good humor, was a local success that Frankie repeated several years later with "Misery Blues." Staying at home, sharing his time between his music and his farm, he seldom left Texas, although for a few years he went on tours with one of his protégés, saxophone player King Curtis, with whom he recorded the famous "Soul Twist." The tireless Chris Strachwitz found him in 1969 with the intent to record him for his Arhoolie label, but Sims died of pneumonia a few months later.

Frankie Lee Sims, a laconic singer with a strange nasal phrasing, played his guitar style with the intensive repetition of a rhythmical pattern that he varied slightly at each movement, thus giving his music an irresistible dance beat. Also, he interspersed his solos with scattered, precise, snapping notes, rural in their approach but very modern in their sounds. Hence Frankie Lee Sims's importance in the Texas blues must not be underestimated. Lightnin' Hopkins—with whom he recorded on several occasions—also took some ideas from Sims. Above all, generous and affable, Frankie Lee Sims directed the debuts of a great number of musicians from Dallas: notably, King Curtis and one of his nephews, Johnny "Guitar" Watson,★ whose elegant and flowing style owes a lot to Sims.

Finally, Albert Collins★ also made his debut under the guidance of Frankie Lee Sims with the band of his relative, Little Frankie Lee, a major figure of today's California blues.

Lucy Mae Blues (Specialty) and *Walkin' with Frankie* (Krazy Kat) collect many of the titles recorded by Sims; other titles appear on diverse anthologies. But this important figure of Texas blues remains much too unknown.

SLIM HARPO

(James Moore / 1924–1970 / vocals, harmonica, guitar)

The Louisiana swamp blues that producer J. D. Miller★ has largely perfected would probably not be what it is without the decisive input of Slim Harpo, the Baton Rouge bluesman who had the most commercial success.

A drawling nasal voice, an extremely sober accompaniment (a guitar playing only a few riffs, a bass, and drums) and a few harmonica phrases: this is Slim Harpo's music. But beyond that simplicity, there was that unbridled humor of Harpo's compositions, that intense swing, and that undefinable atmosphere that is the essence of the Louisiana swamp blues.

Born near Baton Rouge, Harpo's decision to become a professional musician came after listening to the records of Jimmy Reed,★ who was then extremely popular in the South. In 1957 producer J. D. Miller,★ who owned recording studios in the small town of Crowley, recorded Harpo's "I'm a King Bee," a regional hit. It placed in the national charts, and a few years later it was one of the first hits for the Rolling Stones.

Slim Harpo distanced himself little by little from Jimmy Reed's influence that was so strong in his debut, and he created a style of his own. He also recorded rhythmic pieces, suitable for dancing, country music tunes ("Midnight Blues"), and even delicious ballads full of simplicity and freshness. One of them, "Rainin' in My Heart," recorded in 1961, reached high on the charts, and it gave Slim Harpo engagements throughout the country, even to the Apollo Theater of New York. "Scratch My Back," sung later by Otis Redding, "Tip On In," "The Hippie Song," and "Folsom Prison Blues" were also big hits. Slim Harpo, held in high esteem by British blues fans, was preparing for his first European tour when he died of a heart attack at age forty-six.

The overall level of his production was remarkably high. His sparkling, relaxed, light, and dancing blues are marked by a purity of execution. *I'm a King Bee* (Flyright) gathers on compact disc twenty of his best songs. *The Best of Slim Harpo* (Rhino), *Blues Hangover* (Flyright), *Got Love if You Want It* (Flyright), and *Shake Your Hips* (Flyright) are also interesting.

BESSIE SMITH

(1898–1937 / vocals)

Bessie Smith is still today the most famous female blues singer, and her memory is very much alive among numerous jazz and blues musicians, as well as among the fans for whom she is still the "Empress of the blues."

Her "rediscovery" by Janis Joplin, her tragic fate, and her tumultuous life are certainly a big part of her fame. Though her recordings are excellent, they are little different from those recorded by the other female blues singers who are today unjustly forgotten.

While very young, Bessie Smith took up a career as a comedienne and singer in the vaudeville tours so much appreciated by blacks between 1900 and 1930. In 1913 she was hired by the wandering troupe of the Rabbit Foot Minstrels, whose star was Ma Rainey.* It seems that the latter had a strong influence upon young Bessie's singing and the composition of her repertoire. The blues themselves were a bigger part of her repertoire than of any other female singer of the time.

In 1923 Bessie recorded her first 78 (*Downhearted Blues/ Gulf Coast Blues*), and all the qualities that were going to make her famous were already there: sincerity of emotion, absence of vocal effects so appreciated at that time but that are dated today, aggressive interpretation, and perfect sense of tempo. During the next few years, Bessie achieved a brilliant synthesis with vaudeville songs, country blues, and the jazz of the twenties. Her talents for composing were considerable: "Hot Springs Blues," "Backwater Blues," "Empty Bed Blues," and "Nobody Knows You When You're Down and Out" are great blues classics, covered by dozens, even hundreds of artists. She also surrounded herself with the best jazz musicians at the time (from Louis Armstrong to Benny Goodman).

Whereas the majority of female blues singers who came from vaudeville disappeared with the Depression, Bessie Smith managed, with difficulty, to survive. In 1933 she was back in the recording studios under the direction of producer John Hammond. Her second career looked promising when she died in a traffic accident in Mississippi.

Strangely enough, the circumstances of her death gained her the affection of the white public: According to the legend, Bessie Smith died in an ambulance while trying to be admitted in a hospital limited to whites. In fact, the tireless journalist Derrick Stewart-Baker did justice to that version: Bessie was horribly mutilated in that accident; she lost some of her limbs; and apparently she died before the ambulance had time to get there.

Whatever the true circumstances regarding her death, Bessie Smith's legend has continued to grow and her rich contralto voice has one way or another influenced most great female blues and jazz singers: Billie Holiday, Big Mama Thornton,* Janis Joplin . . .

The totality of her recorded work is available on Columbia/CBS. On compact disc, *Great Original Performances* (BBC) and *The Collection* (CBS) are an impressive technical tour de force with a higher sound quality than that of the original recordings.

BIG MAYBELLE SMITH

See New York

BYTHER SMITH

See Chicago

CLARA SMITH

See Female Blues Singers

CLARENCE "PINETOP" SMITH

See Boogie-Woogie

GEORGE "HARMONICA" SMITH

(1924–1983 / vocals, harmonica)

George Smith, today somewhat forgotten, was in fact one of the "greats" of the blues harmonica. Particularly gifted with the difficult chromatic harmonica, he explored sounds beyond what Little Walter* had done, and his influence on many white California harmonica players (Rod Piazza and Mark Hummell, in particular) should not be underestimated.

First a street musician in Helena, Arkansas, George Smith was one of the early users of electric amplification. In California, where he had moved to around 1955, he recorded several wonderful pieces ("Blues in the Dark" and "Telephone Blues") under several names (Little Walter, Jr.; Harmonica King; George Allen) without much commercial success.

■ George "Harmonica" Smith. *(Photograph © by Jon Sievert. Courtesy of Archives and Special Collections, John Davis Williams Library, University of Mississippi)*

Dividing his time between the West Coast and Chicago, he played for a while in Muddy Waters'★ band, which gave him the opportunity to appear substantially on the recordings of Muddy, Otis Spann,★ Sunnyland Slim,★ and Eddie Taylor.★

The blues boom of the sixties in Great Britain linked him to the Bacon Fat of Rod Piazza. Then he settled for good in Los Angeles and belonged to several bands with Big Joe Turner,★ guitar player Bee Houston, Big Mama Thornton,★ and, at the end of his life, with William Clarke, another student of his.

Harmonica Ace (Ace) compiles his best songs. He recorded a handful of albums in the sixties and seventies, but few of them, unfortunately, do justice to his great talent as a harmonica player. *Off the Blues* (Bluesway) is the best one.

J. T. "FUNNY PAPA" SMITH

See Texas

MAMIE SMITH

See Female Blues Singers

MOSES "WHISPERING" SMITH

See J. D. Miller

SOUL

Soul music is a specific genre of black music, often closer to the blues than people usually imagine. In the late fifties, the blues took different forms like rhythm and blues, the most "ethnic" of black popular music, but no longer attracted black youth nor the biggest part of the African-American community. They preferred, en masse, the musical integration of the Middle of the Road (M.O.R.), that is, American pop.

Between 1960 and 1964, the rhythm-and-blues hit parades were particularly eloquent in that respect. Almost all the bluesmen had disappeared, as well as black rockers like Little Richard,★ Larry Williams, and Bo Diddley.★ It seems that black music had turned to songs by Brook Benton, Billy Eckstine, Johnny Mathis, and Sammy Davis, Jr. In 1964 Billboard dropped all specific classification of black music for a generalized Top 40!

Then soul took over the blues; it was an ethnic answer to the integration and watering down of black music.

Whereas rhythm and blues—Fats Domino,★ Amos Milburn,★ Charles Brown,★ and also a few vocal groups—had incorporated in the blues some tendencies of forties pop, and rock-and-roll had married the blues to country, soul had united the dominant sounds of gospel with contemporary lyrics. The socio-political content was often very strong, the "message" was always present even if many pieces were above all invitations to numerous new dances with particularly risqué movements.

The black church struggling successfully against segregation was the model for this music. The musicians and their audience called one another "Brother" and "Sister" just like in the congregations, and they had "soul." The root of this music was once more the Deep South where the blues-colored soul remained the favorite music of blacks, especially among the poor. Its favorite place was the "chitlin' circuit," a great number of small clubs in the center of the black districts or along the southern roads.

In the fifties singer SAM COOKE (1931–1964) announced this great mutation of black music. From a religious background, Cooke chose to combine bluesy ballads and lay sermons with arrangements borrowed from gospel (e.g., "Chain Gang," "Laughing and Clowning," "Bring It on Home to Me," and "Red Rooster"). His stupid and tragic death (he was shot dead in a motel room) undeniably stopped him from being the black superstar of the sixties.

James Brown and Otis Redding, both much more deeply rooted in blues than it first seemed, are thought to be the founding fathers of soul music.

As usual, the development of this new music was due to the enterprising and curious spirit of independent producers. Berry Gordy in Detroit, who founded the Motown label; Jerry Wexler in New York, who redirected his Atlantic label (it already included a beautiful catalog of black blues and rock-and-roll); Stax, linked to Atlantic, whose Memphis studios would produce a substantial portion of the most bluesy soul of that period; and Hi, also in Memphis. Other centers also need to be mentioned: New Orleans with Marshall Sehorn and Allen Toussaint, Miami with Henry Stone, Los Angeles and its labels Capitol and Minit. At the end of the sixties, even the companies most oriented toward the blues (Chess, Vee-Jay, Imperial) recorded soul for the black public. True bluesmen such as Muddy Waters* and Howlin' Wolf* were dismissed or were directed toward the white blues-revival public or toward rock fans.

But at the beginning of the seventies soul itself became progressively deflated. It divided itself into many different genres: disco, break, funk, etc. Out of the mainstream, down-home soul, for the most part southern, directed to a black public with a low purchasing power, was vegetating on many small independent labels, and it looked like it was heading for the same suffocation as the blues. It found refuge in the same "chitlin' circuit." As Sebastian Danchin showed through several remarkable studies in *Soul Bag,* this southern soul—associated with the blues—has been enjoying a limited renewal from Memphis to Nashville, from Atlanta to Baton Rouge. New specific labels were created, such as Ichiban, La Jam, and Malaco in Jackson, Mississippi, in an attempt to fill the place left empty by Stax' bankruptcy. This ethnic renewal of the soul-blues parallels a reaffirmation of southern identity. Smokey Robinson, Marvin Gaye, Stevie Wonder, Junior Walker, Donny Hathaway, Wilson Pickett, Carla Thomas, Sam and Dave, Eddie Floyd, Aretha Franklin, Clarence Carter, and Booker T. and the MG's have been great soul stars, and they should be described in detail in other works that are more specific to that music, although many of them did interpret, here and there, some "good old blues."

The amazing BOBBY RUSH (b. 1940), a singer and a harmonica player, created, from Chicago to Jackson, a very faithful audience thanks to a kind of bluesy "folk-funk" with long monologues describing the life of blacks in the South. With a raw and acid humor and strong chauvinistic accents, *Gotta Have Money* (La Jam), *Wearing It Out* (La Jam), and *Sue* (La Jam) are particularly good.

DENISE LASALLE (Denise Craig / b. 1941) vegetated for a long time in crummy clubs before she became successful in the seventies with "Married but Not to Each Other," "Workin' Overtime," and "My Toot Toot" by Rockin' Sidney.* A star singer of the Malaco label, she displays the determination to find the roots of black music (*It's Lying Time Again:* Malaco and *Holding Down with the Blues:* Malaco).

BENNY LATIMORE (b. 1939) is an expressive and moving singer. His best hit is "Let's Straighten It Out" from 1974. He went through a long period of self-doubt before he reemerged at Malaco, but he has not yet matched the high quality of his first titles (*Slow Down:* Malaco).

The singer-guitarist ROEBUCK "POPS" STAPLES (b. 1915) began a career as a bluesman in his native Missouri. Having embraced religion, he became the leader of a fantastic family gospel group, the Staples Singers. *Respect Yourself*

(Stax) includes the best of his soul production and *Jammed Together* (Stax), which linked him to Albert King and Steve Cropper, shows the depth of his blues roots, especially in the enlightening version of "Tupelo," John Lee Hooker's★ piece.

RUFUS THOMAS (b. 1917) is also a veteran of Memphis and of the Stax label. He began his career as a disc jockey on station WDIA, recording for Sun and Sam Phillips★ the savory "Bear Cat" and "Tiger Man." A specialist of the "rubbing" dances inspired by animal positions ("Walking the Dog," "Do the Funky Chicken," and "Do the Funky Penguin"), he is still a sly fox of the blues ("Blues in the Basement"). But his most bluesy album, *That Woman Is Poison* (Alligator), does not have the inventive and quick wit of his zoological performances.

O. V. WRIGHT (1939–1980) was a great soul singer from Memphis, whose music had large doses of blues. Although talented, he had to deal with secondary labels. If talent alone were enough, he should have been more successful. For instance, "8 Men and 4 Women" is a real masterpiece, covered by Little Milton.★ *Gone for Good* (Charly) and *Here's Another Thing* (Charly) are also worth mentioning.

MARGIE EVANS (b. 1940), a native Louisianan, is also a singer with an unlucky career. She now lives in Los Angeles, but she is known in Chicago, where she recorded some blues for Willie Dixon★ ("29 Ways"), and in Memphis, where she consecrated the "Good Time Queen" and the Johnny Otis★ Show. It would seem that she deserves better than the handful of indistinguished albums she has recorded or the absurd reputation as "the new Bessie Smith" that people attached to her.

McKINLEY MITCHELL (1935–1986), a little-known pioneer of soul, left a beautiful musical heritage recorded in Chicago and Jackson ("The Town I Live In," "Trouble Blues," and "Road of Love").

Similarly, in Chicago and in Memphis OTIS CLAY recorded some beautiful blues on which guitar player Teenie Hodges shines. A tour in Japan and his sensational participation on the album *Roy Buchanan: When a Guitar Plays the Blues* (Alligator) gained him public recognition.

MIGHTY SAM (Sam McLain / b. 1943) is a remarkable blues, gospel, and soul singer who, too, was not very successful commercially. His performance on *Hubert Sumlin's Blues Party* (Black Top) gives hope for the excellent contemporary blues album that Mighty Sam is capable of.

Many other soul-bluesmen also deserve mention: Albert Washington, Nolan Struck, Bernard Daniels, Little Oscar, Howard Tate, Al Green, and Jimmy Hughes.

OTIS SPANN

(1931–1970 / vocals, piano)

The last student of Big Maceo,* Otis Spann also captured the title of the last great Chicago blues pianist. "He really had two hands!" as his leader and mythic "brother" Muddy Waters* said about him. But his extremely warm and muted voice, his flawless left-hand technique, his ability to create a dramatic tension in two chords, and his predilection for slow blues, as well as his great composing talent, should not be overshadowed by the fact that he was Muddy's piano player during most of his career.

Otis Spann had an unusual blues career: From Clarksdale, Mississippi, to Chicago; from the southern barrelhouses to the South Side taverns where, still very young, he met Muddy. Spann was primarily the backbone of Muddy Waters' band for decades. His presence gave a power to that band, that even Pinetop Perkins* could not duplicate.

Modest and unassuming, Spann was lucky to record as lead a piece called "Goodbye Newport Blues" on the album *Muddy Waters at Newport* (Chess) in 1960; he revealed himself to be a superb singer on this moving blues. The success of this album among the whites of the blues revival (it included the famous "Got My Mojo Working") enabled Spann to start a personal career, marked by a series of albums: *Otis Spann Is the Blues* (Candid); *Walking the Blues* (Candid), with Robert Jr. Lockwood*; *Half Ain't Been Told* (Black Cat), with Muddy Waters; the great *The Blues Never Die* (Prestige/Ace); and *Nobody Knows Chicago Like I Do* (Charly/Bluesway). With the British rock group Fleetwood Mac in 1970 Spann had his only commercial hit, "Hungry Country Girl," which was about the somewhat voracious appetite of his new wife, Lucille, herself a good blues artist. Unfortunately, Spann died of a heart attack a few months before the distribution of the 45.

VICTORIA SPIVEY

(1906–1976 / vocals, piano, ukulele)

Unlike almost all the other female blues artists of the twenties, this Texas singer and piano player was musically active until her death.

She began singing and acting as a comedienne when she was still a child. She traveled throughout Texas with several traveling shows before she finally settled in St. Louis. Her acid voice, her sarcastic blues, and her physical qualities gained the favors of the black public of the city. When she was noticed by a local producer, she signed a recording contract with Okeh in 1926. Her first record, a superb blues, *Black Snake Blues,* was a hit, and it became a classic, later recorded by dozens of artists.

Although Victoria began recording later than the other female singers who came from vaudeville, she also outlasted them. While most of these singers recorded their last commercial titles in 1928 and 1929, Victoria Spivey was still recording during the Depression, without a break until 1937. This exceptional success came from Victoria's extraordinary ability to adapt: While she retained the vaudeville influence, mixed with those of the traditional Texas blues (Blind Lemon Jefferson* remained one of her constant sources of inspiration), after 1929 she developed an aggressive and modern style that gained her the favors of the black public in New York and Chicago, where she had settled successively.

All together, her work is first-rate, and when Victoria's humor—full of imagery—had the fortune to be accompanied by great musicians, such as Lonnie Johnson,* Louis Armstrong, and Tampa Red,* it created masterpieces like the hot "Dope Head Blues," "Murder in the First Degree," and the great blues classic "T.B. Blues."

Around 1960, when the first impacts of the blues revival began to be felt, Victoria was living in New York. She had never really stopped acting or singing. With the same energy

■ Victoria Spivey with Muddy Waters. *(Photograph © by Anton J. Mikofsky; used with permission)*

that characterized her first career, she came back on stage and created her own recording company, Spivey. Her links with the folk milieux of Greenwich Village enabled her to perform on many albums of the Prestige/Bluesville company. Also, she pulled out of oblivion several female singers who had made their debuts at the beginning of the blues, singers like Alberta Hunter, Lucille Hegamin,* and Hannah Sylvester. With her friend Lonnie Johnson, Victoria was part of the European tour of the American Folk Blues Festival in 1963. Finally, she discovered and recorded numerous new talents on her label: Luther Johnson,* Lucille Spann, Olive Brown, Sugar Blue, and Bob Dylan, who was then playing the harmonica in the streets of New York with Big Joe Williams.* Dylan made his very first recordings for Victoria Spivey.

Although her voice and her timbre became a little softer along the years, Victoria Spivey never lost her talents to compose. The superb "Big Black Limousine," "Mr. Cab," and "Grant Spivey," from the sixties, demonstrate her great talents.

Strangely enough, Victoria Spivey never had luck with recording companies, to which she brought a lot of money when she was young. There are few or no reissues of her first and often excellent work, except for *Recorded Legacy of the Blues* (Spivey).

WILD JIMMY SPRUILL

See New York

STEEL GUITAR

When the guitar became an important instrument of popular music around the beginning of the century, it was obvious that the musician would have to, in some circumstances (e.g., concerts, noisy taverns, etc.), compensate for the instrument's lack of volume. Thus several types of guitars with acoustic amplification were created, in particular a guitar with a metallic resonator placed in the sound hole: The amplified sound is emitted by two "ears" around the hole. The steel guitar comes in several models, the most famous being the Dobro (invented by the DOpera BROthers) and the National, the one that bluesmen use the most.

The sound of that steel guitar is particularly superb when it is produced by the bottleneck, either the guitar is held in a normal way or flat on the lap as Hawaiian guitarists do.

In the blues, most bottleneck specialists use a steel guitar;

but strangely enough, few of them practiced the Hawaiian style, although it was good for hitting the blue notes and made it possible to easily reach the top of the neck. Kokomo Arnold,★ Casey Bill Weldon,★ Black Ace,★ and Oscar Woods★ are the main blues representatives of the Hawaiian guitar before the war. After 1945, the dominant influence of the western swing (a white rural music from Texas, very popular during the war), in which the electric steel guitar played a significant role, marked that instrument. This influence can be found in the style of the rare bluesmen (often from Texas) who play the steel guitar: L. C. Robinson,★ Hop Wilson, Fred Roulette, and Sonny Rhodes.★

FRANK STOKES

(1887–1955 / vocals, guitar)

Frank Stokes, who was tremendously popular in Memphis at the beginning of the century, is generally considered to be one of the founding fathers of the Memphis blues. He was the first to record in the delicate Memphis style, a placid and regular rhythm, far from the dramatic urgency of the Delta blues. In fact, like Jim Jackson,★ Stokes created his style before the blues was defined as we know it, and his repertoire was composed of popular songs, folk standards, and numerous blues themselves (that he interpreted in his own style). A prolific composer (it is said that he created several hundred pieces!) and a powerful singer, he was also an extroverted guitar player who practiced a perfect fingerpicking. That talent enabled him to play very inventive solos, at a time when instrumental virtuosity was not a must for a bluesman.

Born in Memphis, he performed at the beginning of the century in city streets and in Handy Park. His popularity gave him the opportunity to leave his job as a blacksmith and devote all his time to music. He joined several bands, but in 1920 his association with guitar player Dan Sane made him famous. They formed the Beale Street Sheiks, with two other fantastic guitar players: One played complex and regular alternated bass notes, while the other wove incessant arpeggios. These wonderful duets (about thirty), recorded from 1927 to 1929, are generally considered as the archetypes of the Memphis blues. "Mr. Crump Don't Like It," "Stomp That Thing," "It's a Good Thing," and their version of Bessie Smith's* "Nobody's Business If I Do" are great classics played today by numerous blues, country, bluegrass, and other musicians.

Although he no longer recorded after 1929, Frank Stokes continued performing in Memphis until the end of the forties. His influence was considerable; at the end of the sixties, the Memphis Country Blues Festival (that later became the River City Blues Festival) was in fact a "Frank Stokes festival": Furry Lewis,* Nathan Beauregard, Robert Wilkins,* and Joe Calicott played their Stokes's repertoire and imitated his style.

Also, he has influenced numerous white guitar players of the acoustic blues revival, in particular Stefan Grossman and Jo-Ann Kelly.*

The excellent album *Creator of the Memphis Blues* (Yazoo) includes his best titles.

BIG TIME SARAH STREETER

See Zora Young

SUGAR BLUE

(James Whiting / b. 1955 / vocals, harmonica)

After some unnoticed debuts in the U.S. when he was playing for tips in New York, and his sensational debut in France, where he has largely contributed to popularizing the harmonica blues, Sugar Blue has since then been a full-time American and a lovable figure of the contemporary blues.

He came from a musical family of New York and was deeply impressed by the records of Little Walter,* Big Walter Horton,* and Sonny Boy Williamson (Rice Miller),* thanks to whom he became familiar with the harmonica. He soon felt competent enough to play in the streets of New York. He met the excellent white harmonica players Bill Dicey and Paul Oscher (Brooklyn Slim), and he soon became actively involved in the small blues scene of New York. He accompanied Washboard Bill, guitar player Charles Walker,* and Louisiana Red.* He also recorded a few titles for Victoria Spivey.*

He is especially convincing on the albums of Johnny Shines,* *Too Wet to Plow* (Tomato), and of Brownie McGhee,* *Blues Is Truth* (Tomato). Because of the depth of the sound, the brusque and unexpected variations of the tonality, the expressive and complex phrases, Sugar Blue appeared as a great innovator of the harmonica blues, contrary to a great number of his peers, who were only imitating the great names of the past.

But it was hard to earn a living in New York playing the blues. He was persuaded by a French friend to try his luck in Europe. So he left New York to pace the streets and blow his harmonica in London and Paris. His crumpled beret on, his howling amplified harmonica, in the subway, on the sidewalks, Sugar Blue was everywhere, and he became a figure of the French capital. Interviewed or checked by the French police, he managed to be in the newspapers, cultivating the image of an "authentic bluesman looking in France for the fame he deserved and that was denied him in the United States." His harmonica in his hand, he jumped on the stage of all the Parisian concerts. Luther Allison,* Carey Bell,* Memphis Slim,* Archie Shepp, and also numerous rock groups were astounded, but they let this unexpected guest express himself at length. This technique finally paid off: Sugar Blue managed to appear briefly on an album by the Rolling Stones. He then performed in all the French festivals and showed both his instrumental virtuosity and his total lack of maturity. Usually, he began his number very well, but he did not know when to stop: Endless solos, a thin and reedy voice, pieces dragging along; whimsical and capricious, without presence nor warmth, Sugar Blue often became cumbersome.

Instead of making do with a comfortable but sterile French career, Sugar Blue came back to the United States in 1984, and he established himself as one of the best sidemen from Chicago to San Francisco. He appears to his advantage on Willie Dixon's* album *Hidden Charms* (Capitol).

Although his French recordings have little interest, we think that Sugar Blue is capable of producing something significant.

HUBERT SUMLIN

(b. 1931 / vocals, guitar)

Hubert Sumlin was the irreplaceable guitar player for Howlin' Wolf,* his mentor, his master, and his adoptive father! From 1955 until Wolf's death in 1976, Sumlin asserted himself in the band, first as a rhythm guitarist, then later as the band soloist. Invention and good taste dominate all his interventions which had a rare originality in a blues scene that was somewhat crushed by B. B. King's* influence. His way of making his guitar crackle and his glissando effects recall in fact the purest Delta blues. His style on "Spoonful," "Goin' Down Slow," "300 Pounds of Heavenly Joy," "Hidden Charms," and "Built for Comfort" reaches peaks that have seldom been equaled in the history of blues guitar.

Wolf's death was a personal tragedy for Sumlin. It was also the beginning of a long musical period of drifting. He recorded a few albums, more and more mediocre, and he attempted an abominable career as a singer. He was himself again when he was with saxophone player Eddie Shaw,* another veteran of Howlin' Wolf's band.

For a while, it seems that he resurfaced. His album *Hubert Sumlin's Blues Party* (Black Top), well produced by Ronnie Earl and Ron Levy, show him in a good spell *behind* the outstanding singer Mighty Sam.* *Heart and Soul* (Blind Pig), recorded with James Cotton,* is pretty much a musical success; but he is still pushed to sing, and he is better off not singing. *Healing Feeling* (Black Top) is more a Ronnie Earl-Darrell Nulisch set than Sumlin's. Let's hope that the man who was one of the best guitar players in Chicago will be well directed and managed so that he can regain his verve and invention.

SUNNYLAND SLIM

(Albert Luandrew / b. 1907 / vocals, piano)

This eternally young and enthusiastic veteran is one of the few still active piano players of the Chicago blues. His extremely limited style is interesting because it carries the mark of his

■ Sunnyland Slim (*left*) and Howlin' Wolf. *(Photograph © by Anton J. Mikofsky; used with permission)*

formative years when he played the piano in brothels and in movie theaters at the time of silent movies. He has been shouting the same blues for sixty years.

Influenced in the thirties by the famous Doctor Clayton, he recorded for RCA/Victor in 1947 under the nickname of "Doctor Clayton's Buddy," imitating totally and successfully the style of his idol, who had just died. Blues history will remember his capital role in the creation of the postwar Chicago blues: Along with a great number of personal recordings for many record companies, often short-lived, he introduced into the studios numerous bluesmen who were to become the pioneers of this new style. On the many recordings he has played on, the following names appear: Muddy Waters,★ Little Walter,★ Robert Jr. Lockwood,★ Leroy Foster, Snooky Pryor,★ Big Walter Horton,★ and Eddie Taylor.★

He never stopped playing in Chicago clubs with either his own band or with other bands (e.g., Howlin' Wolf★ and Willie Dixon★), and he created his own record production, Airway, which marked career beginnings of female singers like Big Time Sarah.★

Two albums include some of his first best titles: *Sunnyland Slim* (Flyright) and *Devil Is a Busy Man* (Official).

After 1960, he recorded many albums that often were mediocre. Nevertheless, *Sad and Lonesome* (Jewel) and *Slim's Got a Thing Going On* (World Pacific) with Luther Allison★ and Canned Heat★ are significant achievements worth looking for.

ROOSEVELT SYKES

(Theodore Roosevelt Sykes / 1906–1983 / vocals, piano)

Somewhat forgotten today, Roosevelt Sykes was an important performer in blues history; he was constantly present in studios and on stage from 1924, the beginning of his professional career, until his death. His influence upon blues piano players must not be underestimated.

Born in Arkansas, he identified himself especially with the St. Louis blues, the city in which he settled after having been an itinerant musician for a while with piano player Lee Green. In fact, it was Green who shaped Sykes's style, which summarized the piano blues of the thirties, known as *barrelhouse* because it was created in those taverns and dives where the player replaced the juke box of today. It was necessary to mark the beat strongly in order to be heard and to make the people dance. Sykes managed that perfectly: His powerful voice and his contagious good mood were enhanced by a vigorous style, which has influenced, directly or indirectly, most of the piano players to come, from Big Maceo★ to Memphis Slim.★

In fact, Sykes left Lee Green to his wandering life around 1928, and he rapidly became very popular in St. Louis. He was noticed by local promoter Jesse Johnson, for whom he recorded in 1929 the famous "44 Blues," a theme with rolling bass notes created by Little Brother Montgomery★ and later covered by Lee Green. This record was a commercial hit, and in 1929 Sykes started to visit the studios of Chicago and New York a great deal, recording about two hundred songs before the war for several companies and under different names ("Dirty Mother Fuyer," "Night Time Is the Right Time," and the savory "Honeydripper," which became his nickname). The public and the producers liked him so much that he

■ Roosevelt Sykes. *(Photograph © by Paul Harris; used with permission)*

became the house piano player for the big Decca label, where he accompanied nearly all the artists, from St. Louis Jimmy★ and Walter Davis★ to Lonnie Johnson.★

Whereas the socio-economic changes caused by the war and a modification of the tastes of the black public resulted in the disappearance of most of the musicians of the thirties, Sykes continued his career with as much success. Feeling that the fashion was changing, he was the first piano player to surround himself with a big band ("The Honeydrippers"), and in 1945 he was in Chicago to record prolifically for big (Bluebird) and small (Bullet) labels.

In 1952 he went to New Orleans, which remained his permanent residence until his death. There also, he had some influence upon the nascent rhythm and blues, and he recorded substantially for the local Imperial label. Again, he was one of the first artists to get on the blues-revival train and did not stop performing alone or on tours in the United States or in Europe, where he recorded many LPs.

From among all that production of, obviously, uneven value, he recorded his most inventive and brilliant ones between 1929 and 1950: *The Country Blues Piano Ace* (Yazoo) and *The Honeydripper* (Queen Disc). A great number of compilations could be made with his work for Decca, Bluebird, and Imperial. Among his later productions *Feel Like Blowing My Horn* (Delmark), with Robert Jr. Lockwood,★ rises above the rest.

T

TAJ MAHAL

(b. 1942 / vocals, guitar, harmonica, banjo)
Taj Mahal was famous for a while at the time of the American blues revival. Strangely enough, among Paul Butterfield,★ Mike Bloomfield,★ and Charlie Musselwhite,★ he appeared to be *the* young black who was playing blues-rock.

Born in Massachusetts, Taj Mahal was introduced to the

blues only through records, and it was only progressively that he finally identified himself with the bluesmen he was imitating (e.g., Blind Willie McTell* and Sleepy John Estes*).

At the musical level, Taj—who has listened a lot and retained a lot—is a superb singer with a husky voice, an interesting harmonica player, and an honorable acoustic guitar player in the folk tradition.

He could have certainly—like many other young people of his generation—started a career in rock, which would have been much more fruitful commercially. Slender and solitary, he preferred to travel around the world, in search of his black musical roots, from Africa and the Caribbean to Europe. Salsa and reggae as well as the blues became integral parts of his repertoire.

The Best of Taj Mahal, Vols. 1 & 2 (Columbia) and *Giant Step* (Columbia) are on compact disc; they include his titles that are closest to the blues.

TAMPA RED

(Hudson Woodbridge or Whittaker / 1903–1981 / vocals, guitar, kazoo, piano)

Tampa Red is one of the most striking musicians in blues history. The length of his commercial career (1928–60) and his eclecticism have paradoxically made him one of the least-recognized artists in blues history. Indeed, Tampa Red did not take part in the sixties blues revival, even though he expressed himself in all the styles likely to please black fans (acoustic solos, jazz, vaudeville, pop, etc.), building, instead, among blues fans the unjust reputation of a "dated" musician. Urban and sophisticated, he was truly an artist in the line of Lonnie Johnson.*

In fact, when one listens again to his best recordings of 1928, their modernism is striking, especially his guitar style. Tampa Red was indeed one of the first black musicians inspired by the Hawaiian guitarists of the beginning of the century, and he managed to adapt their sound to the blues. Tampa Red's nickname ("the guitar wizard") was an appropriate designation. In his first recordings in 1928 he was able to create a clear and pure sound with his bottleneck. Rarely equaled, this sound influenced most of the guitarists in blues and in rock using this glissando style, either directly or through his emulators (e.g., Robert Nighthawk* and Earl Hooker*).

After the huge 1928 success of his second record, *It's Tight Like That,* Tampa Red recorded 335 songs on 78s, a record in blues history! He was one of the few artists to survive the disappearance of Bluebird (a branch of RCA) during the war; he continued to record for RCA until 1953. Through his successive associations with piano players Georgia Tom Dorsey, Big Maceo,* and Little Johnny Jones,* Tampa Red created a style that has unquestionably influenced all modern blues. A great composer, he created an important number of standards that, covered by B. B. King,* Robert Nighthawk, Elmore James,* and even Fats Domino,* became blues and rock classics: "Susie Q," "It Hurts Me Too," "Sweet Little Angel," "Anna Lee," "Don't You Lie To Me," and more. Moreover, with his bottleneck he enriched numerous recordings of Big Maceo, John Lee "Sonny Boy" Williamson,* Memphis Minnie,* Ma Rainey,* Victoria Spivey,* and Charlie McCoy.*

After 1953, sick, prematurely old from alcohol abuse, and mourning the death of his wife to whom he was very much attached, Tampa Red left the musical scene only to reappear briefly in 1960 to record two mediocre albums for Bluesville and to perform in a few concerts on the West Coast.

It was only after 1975 and a series of articles in *Living Blues* and *Soul Bag* that there was a renewal of interest for this great creator. His first songs are among the best Chicago blues of the twenties and thirties, and after 1946 he was able to compete with Muddy Waters* (who imitated him on several titles) and Jimmy Rogers* on their own territory. His last titles recorded with Little Johnny Jones in the postwar Chicago blues style are pure gems and are on the same level as the hits of his rivals on Chess. Unfortunately, this recognition came late and Tampa Red could not enjoy it; he lived the remainder of his life in a psychiatric hospital until he died there, totally destitute.

Tampa Red's work has been largely reissued; the best

collection is *The Guitar Wizard* (Blues Classics). *Bottleneck Guitar* (Yazoo) includes some of his first titles, and *Tampa Red, 1944–52* (Krazy Kat) contains some of his last ones.

TARHEEL SLIM

See New York

ARTHUR "MONTANA" TAYLOR

See Boogie-Woogie

EDDIE TAYLOR

(1923–1985 / vocals, guitar)

The road followed by Eddie Taylor is representative of that of bluesmen in postwar Chicago. Born and raised in Mississippi, Eddie Taylor learned to play the guitar under the influence of Son House* and Charlie Patton*; he created a small band with his neighbor Jimmy Reed.* After the war he went to Memphis, then moved on to Chicago in 1949. There, his talents as a rhythm guitarist enabled him to accompany many artists, from Muddy Waters* to Elmore James.* He found his childhood friend Jimmy Reed there, and together they perfected the Jimmy Reed "sound" that, after 1953, would become the most popular musical format in blues history.

Despite the reputation that Taylor's flawless guitar style gained him among connoisseurs, he remained in the shadow of his partner. His serious and reserved temperament did not inspire the public with devoted enthusiasm. He did record a few superb titles under his own name from 1955 to 1957 for Vee-Jay but, except for a local success with "Big Town Playboy," he did not really have a solo career. Many of these Chicago blues classics can be found on the compact disc *Eddie Taylor/Jimmy Reed: Ride 'em on Down* (Charly).

After several disputes with Jimmy Reed, Taylor made a final break from him in 1965. He started his own band, playing regularly in Chicago clubs. He went on several tours in Europe where he was acclaimed as one of the best living blues guitar players. In fact, being certain of his personal talent and working frequently on his guitar, Taylor made tremendous progress after he broke up with Reed. His style became more modern, halfway between that of Albert King* and that of the traditional Chicago blues. He was an extremely expressive and fast guitar player, who was not justly recognized. He accompanied a great number of musicians for many labels and recording sessions, often playing a major role in the success of these records.

I Feel So Bad (Advent) is one of the few albums he recorded as the featured player. *My Heart Is Bleeding* (L+R) is interesting. *Still Not Ready for Eddie* (Antone's), recorded live in the famous club in Austin, Texas, makes one regret that there is not more interest for this excellent musician.

HOUND DOG TAYLOR

(Theodore Roosevelt Taylor / 1916–1975 / vocals, guitar)

"I like to make people happy with my music," Hound Dog Taylor said. The good humor, the perfect sense of rhythm, the absence of pretension of Hound Dog resulted in his music being able to effectively convey this passion for life and to make it contagious.

In fact, this disciple of Elmore James* who gradually came to master the bottleneck could have belonged to the mass of Chicago bluesmen who played in the disreputable clubs of the city for a few bucks each night if he had not been taken under the wing of producer Bruce Iglauer of the Alligator label. Until 1970, Hound Dog had only five titles that had been distributed (two 45s and a tune on the extremely rare album devoted to the American Blues Festival in 1967). Around 1966 he did record a session with Big Walter Horton* for Marshall Chess, the son of Len, but these originals were not issued until fifteen years later.

Nevertheless, his popularity in the black ghetto of Chicago was important up until his death, especially in his headquarters, the club Florence's. There, leading a trio of a great homogeneity—guitar player Brewer Philips and drummer Ted Harvey—he played successively the blues and the boogie-woogies for the great pleasure of the audience. Between 1970 and 1975, he was famous thanks to Bruce Iglauer, who made him record three albums on Alligator (*Hound Dog Taylor, Natural Boogie*, and *Beware of the Dog*). The saturated, heavy, and distorted sound that he produced attracted the public and the rock critics: Late recognition for this talented performer.

JOHNNY TAYLOR

See Little Johnny Taylor

KOKO TAYLOR

(Cora Walton / b. 1935 / vocals)

The singer who is recognized as the "queen of the Chicago blues" began early on a career as a singer of blues and rhythm and blues under the wing of Willie Dixon.* Born in Memphis but raised in the South Side of Chicago, she has sung with Junior Wells* and Buddy Guy.* She recorded a few titles for Victoria Spivey,* then for Dixon, who got her an excellent contract with Chess. For Chess, the superb ("What Kind of Man Is This?" and "I Got What It Takes") is alongside the worst ("Fire"). But, in general, the production is excellent thanks to sidemen such as Robert Nighthawk,* Johnny Shines,* and Buddy Guy. "Wang Dang Doodle," created by Howlin' Wolf,* was a big hit for her.

After her separation from Chess and Dixon, Koko began to realize her own success. Her powerful and somewhat monotone voice took on some pathos and joyful accents; her composing talents were freely expressed; and her sense of swing and her first-rate accompanists made her stage performances, as well as most of her albums, some of the great moments of traditional contemporary blues.

Southside Lady (Black & Blue) is interesting, but the albums recorded for Bruce Iglauer enabled her to rightly claim her crown of the blues queen. The breathtaking *I Got What It Takes* (Alligator) includes a number of outstanding titles, as do these albums for Alligator: *The Earthshaker, From the Heart of a Woman, Queen of the Blues, An Audience with the Queen,* and *Jump for Joy.*

Koko Taylor's success in Chicago, her charisma, and her kindness have encouraged a number of female singers to start a blues career: for example, Bonnie Lee,★ Valerie Wellington,★ and Zora Young.★

LITTLE JOHNNY TAYLOR

(b. 1943 / vocals)

Little Johnny Taylor is little known outside the black clubs of the South and of California. But in the chitlin' circuit, Little Johnny Taylor has been a star for nearly thirty years.

He moved from North Carolina to Los Angeles in 1950 in a rather strange way. He made his debut as a singer in church choirs, and he was part of several gospel bands, among which were the famous Mighty Clouds of Joy. When he was noticed by producer Ray Shanklin, he began a career as a soloist for the California Galaxy label. In 1963, his ironic 45, *Part-Time Love,* was a national hit; the tortured guitar of Arthur Wright matched Little Johnny's intense voice, his gospel tone, and final falsettos that punctuated this profane sermon.

Encouraged by "Part-Time Love," Little Johnny recorded some very good titles in the same vein, but he was never able to repeat his initial success.

When he signed with the Jewel label in the seventies, Taylor made a comeback thanks to another bitter composition based on a lover's triangle: "Everybody Knows about My Good Thing." The arrangements then became deliberately heavier, sometimes rather monolithic, and Little Johnny broke away, often sensibly, from the blues for a southern soul in which his vocal talents were great. Although he lives in California, Little Johnny Taylor is in fact an important name in the Deep South. His compositions are wonderful descriptions of the monotonous life in small towns and the sickening hypocrisy of the relationships between the sexes that characterize this culture. "Open House at My House," "It's My Fault Darling," and "I'm Not a One Woman's Man" are quite good, probably more because of the quality of the lyrics than of the music itself. But, because of the powerful imagery, they are directed above all to a large black public, and they put Little Johnny in the position of an authentic contemporary chronicler, the original role of the blues singer.

Associated for a while with Buster Benton,* Little Johnny Taylor had a slack period before his comeback with *Stuck in the Mud* (Ichiban) and the excellent *Ugly Man* (Ichiban). His first titles are in part available on *Greatest Hits* (Fantasy), and his Jewel titles can be heard on *Part-Time Love* (Charly).

It is important not to confuse Little Johnny Taylor with his two homonyms:

JOHNNY TAYLOR (b. 1938), a subtle singer with a sensuous voice, was for a long time at the top of the charts in soul and then disco ("Disco Lady" and "Reaganomics"). He has recorded some beautiful blues for Stax (*Raw Blues*). He made a comeback, like many of his peers, with Malaco (*In Control*).

TED TAYLOR (1937–1987) was another soul-blues singer with an extraordinarily ample and flexible voice. Quite comfortable in bluesy ballads, he never had the success he deserved (*Keep Walking On:* Charly).

TED TAYLOR

See Little Johnny Taylor

JOHNNY TEMPLE

(1906–1968 / vocals, guitar)

This blues singer from Mississippi is today totally forgotten. However, he was a big star among blacks of Chicago and New York between 1935 and 1941, during which time he recorded about seventy titles, some of which were hits. In general they are blues written by others, but he arranged them to fit his sophisticated and urban singing: "Evil Devil Blues" and "Cherry Ball" adapted from Skip James,* whom Temple knew well in Jackson, Mississippi; "Vicksburg Blues" from Little Brother Montgomery*; and especially "Louise, Louise," the blues of St. Louis singer Teddy Edwards, out of which Temple made a classic, later covered by numerous musicians, black and white.

In 1937–38, Johnny Temple was at times the singer for the

Harlem Hamfats,* a band led by the McCoy* brothers, playing regularly for the Mafia.

After the war, although he had recorded only four titles, Johnny Temple played an important role by welcoming the bluesmen who came from the South. His band, the Rolling Four, which played regularly in Chicago clubs until 1956, included at one time or another Homesick James,* Big Walter Horton,* Billy Boy Arnold,* and Elmore James.*

Later, sick and disenchanted, Temple returned South and gave up the blues to become a minister. His best titles are on *Johnny Temple* (B.O.B.).

SONNY TERRY

See Brownie McGhee

TEXAS

The "Texas domain" stretches west of New Orleans and includes the territory of Louisiana, Texas, Oklahoma, and New Mexico with, as a natural outlet along the Santa Fe Railroad, California.

This huge area was isolated for a long time from the rest of the United States and especially from the big northern industrial centers, which explains the development of particular cultural traditions. Toward the beginning of this century, the cotton boll weevil was ruining crops, and thousands of small farmers left for Dallas, Houston, and San Antonio, thus creating ghettos there.

Within that black community, old musical forms still existed. Also emerging was an original blues style with Spanish influence, especially through the introduction of flamenco phrasing in the melody. In the Texas blues, as demonstrated in the twenties by Blind Lemon Jefferson,* Little Hat Jones, and Rambling Thomas, is a singing which, contrary to that of the East Coast, is not always accompanied by guitar; the guitar responded more to the voice with arpeggio phrases over accented bass notes. Moreover, the Texas blues has imaginative and witty lyrics which tell a story, and they rarely fall into the trap of putting one traditional phrase after the other, common in Delta blues.

HENRY "RAGTIME" THOMAS (ca. 1874–1930) was one of the first American musicians to have recorded the blues. He was not at all a bluesman but a songster who played every instrument at the same time (guitar, harmonica, his curious pipes . . .) in an extraordinarily primitive style. Apparently, he played upon request along the Santa Fe Railroad. The twenty-four titles he recorded in 1927 are gathered on the album *Ragtime Texas* (Herwin), a fascinating document about the birth of the blues. Bob Dylan, inspired by the blues in his early albums, covered the song "Honey Just Allow Me One More Chance."

From Dallas to Shreveport to Texarkana, in market towns and camps of railroad workers, there were Leadbelly,★ Rambling Thomas, Texas Alexander★ and Lonnie Johnson,★ and Blind Lemon Jefferson★: the great creators of the Texas blues.

The influence of these men and the impact of their recorded work led to their style being standardized, and the second generation of Texas bluesmen drew their inspiration from them in a codified manner. In the thirties, the following musicians recorded: Willie Reed, Smokey Hogg,★ and Little Hat Jones; piano players Rob Cooper, Son Becky, Robert Shaw, Buster Pickens, and Alex Moore; and the interesting guitar player and singer: J. T. "FUNNY PAPA" SMITH (ca. 1885–1940). Smith, a musician with roots in the Texas tradition, was a brilliant composer; in particular, "Tell It to the Judge" and "Seven Sisters" are savory stories in two parts. He was also the author of "Howling Wolf," a theme that has since been used by almost all the bluesmen of the region.

The popularity of the white groups of western swing after 1930 also influenced the blues of that region: Black Ace,★ Oscar Woods,★ L. C. Robinson,★ and Hop Wilson owe a little to Blind Lemon Jefferson and a great deal to the white guitar player Leon McAuliffe, the right-hand man of Bob Wills, a great star of western swing. These artists created the basis for modern electric blues, sophisticated and with a lot of rhythm, that originated in Texas and developed in California.

Moreover, we find in the founders of this California-Texas blues (T-Bone Walker,★ Lowell Fulson,★ Gatemouth Brown★) the traditional characteristics of Texas blues with relaxed and urban features on the verge of affectation, totally absent in Chicago blues at the same time.

In the meantime, near Houston, expressing the simple style of the Texas country blues but innovative in electrifying it, Lightnin' Hopkins,★ Lil' Son Jackson,★ Smokey Hogg,★ and Frankie Lee Sims★ had, between 1946 and 1953, commercial hits as they recorded hundreds of records. They are testimonies to the last mutation of the traditional Texas blues, and they had a considerable influence, through mass media, upon bluesmen throughout the United States. But their presence in Houston should not diminish the muscular bands led by the tenor saxophone players who had a harsh sound, inspired by the groups of Kansas City and New Orleans, like those of Amos Milburn,★ King Curtis, and Arnett Cobb, who prepared the way for soul. Furthermore, considerable influence was asserted in that region by Chicago bluesman Jimmy Reed,★ and after 1965 black music in Texas became a mosaic of living local traditions, enriched and revivified by numerous external influences.

Neglected for a long time or limited to only down-home musicians (Lightnin' Hopkins and Smokey Hogg), Texas blues has had a renewal of interest for several years. The emergence of young musicians raised in that mold (Robert Cray★ and Joe Louis Walker★), the growing popularity of some veterans (Albert Collins★ and Johnny Copeland★), and the success of some white musicians around Austin (Stevie Ray Vaughan, Marcia Ball, Omar and The Howlers, and the Fabulous Thunderbirds) may explain this unexpected comeback of Texas blues. Nearly all the black ghettos in Houston disappeared due to Hispanic immigration; the clubs of Dowling Street and of the Third Ward, the former Hopkins' headquarters, have been transformed into cantinas.

This renewal of interest gave some obscure Texas names the opportunity to record and have some success on the "alternative" radio stations: Joe Hughes,★ ZuZu Bollin, Pete Mayes,★ and Cal Green.★ Lester Williams, Connie McBooker, the splendid piano player Elmore Nixon, Clarence Garlow,* and harmonica player Billy Bizor unfortunately are no longer around to enjoy this incredible salute to a past that Texas did not seem anxious to recognize or preserve.

Many anthologies are devoted to the different Texas blues.

For the prewar period: *Texarkana Louisiana Country* (Yazoo), *Blues from the Western States* (Yazoo), and *Piano Blues: Texas Santa Fe* (Magpie) provide an opportunity to hear the strange Texas piano tradition of Alex Moore and Texas Bill Day.

The Texas down-home blues is well documented on *Texas Blues, Vols. 1 & 2* (Arhoolie), *Texas Blues* (Blues Classics), *Down behind the Rise* (Nighthawk), *Water Coast Blues* (Krazy Kat), and *Texas Country Blues, 1948–53* (Krazy Kat).

The Texas blues-jazz, largely dominated by T-Bone Walker's influence, can be found on *Lyons Avenue Jive* (Ace), *Houston Jump* (Krazy Kat), *Down in the Groovy* (Krazy Kat), *Houston Shuffle* (Krazy Kat), *Fort Worth Shuffle* (Krazy Kat), *Guitar in My Hands, Vols. 1 & 2* (Moonshine), and *Angels in Houston* (Rounder).

ERNEST "TABBY" THOMAS

See J. D. Miller

HENRY THOMAS

See Texas

JAMES "SON FORD" THOMAS

See R. L. Burnside

JESSE THOMAS

(1910–? / vocals, guitar)

Jesse Thomas, a mysterious figure of Texas blues, was an important link between the rural blues of the beginning of the century and the electric blues of the San Francisco Bay area after the Second World War.

In 1929 Jesse Thomas recorded four titles in a style extravagant for the time which presaged the postwar country blues: staccato accented bass notes and scattered runs of high notes answering the singer who sings in a monotone, passionless voice, common among many traditional folk singers. After 1948 Jesse came back to the studios many times, continuing in the same style. He was often accompanied by some great bands in the fashion of the Texas-California rhythm and blues. Unfortunately, in 1960, after an astonishing soul 45, Jesse Thomas disappeared suddenly.

One can hear this strange interpreter on *Blues from the Western States* (Yazoo) and *Down behind the Rise* (Nighthawk). But Jesse Thomas deserves a whole album.

LAFAYETTE THOMAS

See California

RUFUS THOMAS

See Soul

BIG MAMA THORNTON

(Willie Mae Thornton / 1926–1984 / vocals, harmonica, drums)

One of a limited number of blueswomen in the fifties and sixties, Big Mama was a great Texas blues singer who, after a few small successes, was a sort of legendary interpreter, somewhat outside the raging show-business atmosphere of modern blues.

A church singer since she was a child, it was in her native Alabama that Big Mama was hired at age fourteen by a traveling show, the Hot Harlem Review, which used her powerful voice and her impressive build in order to try to make a new "Bessie Smith" out of her. However, it was with the "Johnny Otis★ Show" and in a furious rhythm-and-blues style that Big Mama managed to record her first hit, "Hound Dog" in 1952. Later sung by Elvis Presley, this theme became a rock-and-roll classic. All together, the thirty titles recorded by Big Mama

■ Willie Mae "Big Mama" Thornton. *(Photograph © by Jerry Hausler.*
Courtesy of Jerry Hausler and Archives and Special Collections, John Davis
Williams Library, University of Mississippi)

with Johnny Otis's band between 1951 and 1954 for the Peacock label are remarkable for the vocal presence and total cohesiveness.

After 1957 Big Mama went through a difficult slack period: No regular band, no recording contract, she got along playing small clubs on the West Coast, where she had settled. As with many black artists, the blues revival put her back on track. She performed in 1965 in the European tour of the American Folk Blues Festival and in 1966 in the Monterey Jazz Festival. The dynamism of her performances swept everybody along: She recorded two albums in a row for Arhoolie, and she got a regular contract with the California Sotoplay label. The success of the moving "Ball and Chain," covered by Janis Joplin, gained her the favor of the general public. She recorded several albums for Mercury and Vanguard; she performed in many tours and festivals; and she also worked regularly in California clubs with her excellent band, which included guitar player Bee Houston, harmonica player George Smith,* and piano player J. D. Nicholson. Then, drug and alcohol abuse ruined her health. Emaciated, unable to remain standing, "Big" Mama was still impressive with her swing during her last performances on stage. *Quit Snoopin' 'round My Door* (Ace) and *You Ol' Hound Dog* (Ace) gather her first essential titles; *Ball 'n' Chain* (Arhoolie) is a compact disc of her best titles recorded for Strachwitz; and *Stronger Than Dirt* (Charly) includes her two Mercury albums.

HENRY TOWNSEND

(b. 1910 / vocals, guitar, piano)

Townsend recorded a remarkable series of songs when he was just nineteen years old; almost all of them are classics of the prewar St. Louis blues (*St. Louis Blues:* Yazoo). He revealed both a talent to compose with feeling and an unmistakable instrumental ability, whether at the guitar (under the obvious influence of Lonnie Johnson*) or at the piano. This instrumental talent also enabled him to have a career as a studio musician, playing behind Robert Lee McCoy (Nighthawk*), John Lee "Sonny Boy" Williamson,* Walter Davis,* Roosevelt

Sykes,* Big Joe Williams,* and the Sparks brothers, on famous titles. He contributed to the creation of the St. Louis blues, which somewhat dominated the years 1935–40 and which combined guitar and piano with incredible charm.

He stayed in St. Louis instead of moving to Chicago where the record companies and recording studios were. Then, Townsend was on the fringe of the blues development. He would have certainly been a major figure of the postwar blues, but his evolving, sophisticated style took him toward modern blues rather than traditional country blues, a role to which the recordings he made after the blues revival have confined him. *Mule* (Nighthawk) and *Henry Townsend* (Springmaster) are interesting, but *Henry T. The Music Man* (Adelphi) is better.

WILLIE TRICE

See East Coast Blues

TOMMY TUCKER

See New York

IKE TURNER

(b. 1931 / vocals, guitar, piano)

Known as "Mr. Tina Turner," the former husband of the superb singer whom he developed deserves better than the stories written about him, usually for his troubles with the law.

Born in Clarksdale, Mississippi, the center of the blues, he quickly learned to play the piano and the guitar. In 1947 he became a disc jockey on a Clarksdale radio station, and he created a band, the Kings of Rhythm, influenced by Louis Jordan.* He recorded for the Chess* brothers, but the record was issued under the name of the group's singer, Jackie Brenston. This record, *Rocket 88,* was number one on the rhythm-and-blues charts in 1951.

In the fifties Ike Turner had an important role in discovering talent around Memphis. He also played on many recording sessions for Sun and Modern.

He left Chess to discover new talent for the Los Angeles producers, the Bihari brothers. He traveled everywhere in Mississippi, Tennessee, and Arkansas, and the list of bluesmen he recorded (he usually accompanied them on guitar or piano) is impressive: Bobby Bland,* B. B. King,* Driftin' Slim, Elmore James,* Howlin' Wolf,* and others. In 1953 he did the same fruitful job for Sam Phillips,* discovering Little Milton,* Rufus Thomas, and Joe Hill Louis.* He also recorded with his group—first in Mississippi and in Memphis, then in St. Louis—in a much more urban and sophisticated style than the artists he discovered. *Ike Turner and His Kings of Rhythm, Vols. 1 & 2* (Ace) consist of an excellent selection of his titles of that time.

Ike Turner realized his greatest commercial success when his second wife, Anna Mae Bullock, joined the band. Tina Turner, as she came to be called, was a powerful and statuesque singer whose qualities Ike knew how to bring out.

Ike and Tina were at last successful, going from crummy clubs in the Deep South to big concert halls all over the world. They opened for the Rolling Stones in their 1969 tour and aroused crowds of rock fans.

Nevertheless, the blues was never far away, as *Rockin' Blues* (Stateside) demonstrates. *Outta Season* (Liberty) and *The Hunter* (Blue Thumb), the latter with guitar player Albert Collins,* are the albums recorded by the couple that contain the most blues.

In the mid-seventies, the constant and increasingly violent fights between Ike and Tina brought about their separation. Tina managed the tour de force comeback with a commercial touch of pop-funk, but the unfortunate Ike is going through an agonizing period of drug and alcohol sickness, so common among today's bluesmen.

BIG JOE TURNER

(1911–1985 / vocals)

After having been at the top of the blues-jazz world, blues shouters today are seldom appreciated in a genre dominated by brilliant musicians. However, they have deeply influenced

■ Big Joe Turner. *(Photograph © by Anton J. Mikofsky; used with permission)*

blues history, and they have opened that music to a public that other more "ethnic" bluesmen could not reach. Above all, their music was excellent, and it has definitely withstood the test of time. Let's not forget Jimmy Witherspoon,* Jimmy Rushing,* and the great Big Joe Turner in particular, "The Boss of the Blues."

More than any other blues artist, he helped create the powerful vocal style of Kansas City by shouting his blues above a mesh of finely tuned brass led by a virtuoso pianist, such as Count Basie or Pete Johnson.* This Kansas City blues influenced the urban rock-and-roll popularized by Bill Haley.

Born in Kansas City, Turner sang in church before he worked as a barman in the same club where Pete Johnson,* the breathtaking piano player of boogie-woogie, performed. While making the drinks, Joe sang the blues and the boogies with his strong voice, accompanied by Johnson. The solo routine of Pete Johnson quickly became a vocal/piano duo of rare originality, attracting the blacks of the city en masse.

In 1938 Turner recorded his first hits, "Roll 'em Pete," "Piney Brown Blues," and "Rebecca." He was at Carnegie Hall in 1938 in what was the first big concert of black music directed toward the northern white public. Then he was everywhere: in Chicago with Elmore James,* at the Atlantic studios in New York, in California where he was a major figure in the Los Angeles clubs, and in New Orleans. In the fifties, thanks to the Atlantic label, he managed to be part of the rock-and-roll trend with "Teenage Letter" and "Shake, Rattle and Roll." By the end of his life, he made do too often repeating his old hits, but many of his records for the Pablo label showed him still in good shape and with prestigious blues and jazz names, from PeeWee Crayton* to Joe Pass and Count Basie. Even though his death in 1985 went relatively unnoticed, Big Joe Turner is still one of the bosses of the blues.

Early Big Joe (MCA), which includes his best songs from the thirties, is a must. *The Rhythm and Blues Years* (Atlantic), *Greatest Hits* (Atlantic), and *Big Joe Rides Again* (Atlantic) include many of his songs on that label. *Sings the Blues* (Kent) presents him with the great harmonica virtuoso George Smith* and guitar player Bee Houston. *The Best of Joe Turner* (Pablo) and *Big Joe Turner with a Roomful of Blues* (Muse) date from the end of his long career, and they still have a few wonderful moments.

T. V. SLIM

See California

■
V

DAVE VAN RONK

See White Blues

MAURICE JOHN VAUGHN

See Chicago

WALTER VINCSON

See Mississippi Sheiks

EDDIE VINSON

See Blues Shouters

■
W

CHARLES WALKER

See New York

JOE LOUIS WALKER

(b. 1949 / vocals, guitar)

Joe Louis Walker was born in San Francisco to migrant parents from Arkansas who had gone to California to pick fruit. He was raised with the sounds of his father's blues records, particularly those of Howlin' Wolf* and Amos Milburn.* He became a precocious guitar player and created several collegiate bands, influenced by the music of the Rolling Stones. Then, with his cousins, he started a rhythm-and-blues band in the style of saxophone player Junior Walker.

According to Joe Louis's own words, the "real blues" fascinated him. In folk clubs, he met Lightnin' Hopkins,* Fred McDowell,* Earl Hooker,* and Magic Sam* before he played with Mike Bloomfield.* With Bloomfield, he discovered the ever-blossoming scene of the black blues of San Francisco Bay in Oakland's black suburb.

Lowell Fulson,* Percy Mayfield,* PeeWee Crayton,* and Johnny Heartsman* led him gradually to the California style, but his blues style remained influenced by the Delta blues of McDowell, the records of Howlin' Wolf, and the gospel that he sang in his grandmother's congregation when he was very young. He made his first recordings with a religious band, the Corinthiens, in 1980.

After a few years of personal problems, a remarkable performance at the New Orleans Jazz and Heritage Festival brought him back exclusively to the blues. In 1987 he met producer Bruce Bromberg, who had just successfully promoted Robert Cray* and who was looking for other artists in the same vein.

Cold Is the Night (Hightone), *The Gift* (Hightone), and *Blue Soul* (Hightone) are three good albums of contemporary blues with a touch of soul and with ballads that have large doses of the California style that Joe Louis Walker prolonged by modernizing it. However, Walker is still most impressive on pieces influenced by the Delta blues, played with the bottleneck: "Moanin' News," "Quarter to Three," and "Alligator."

JOHNNY "BIG MOOSE" WALKER

(b. 1927 / vocals, piano, guitar, organ, harmonica)

Because he recorded under the names of Big Moose, Bushy Head, Moose John, and J. W. Walker in cities as far from one another as Chicago, New Orleans, and Los Angeles, Johnny "Big Moose" Walker was a mysterious figure for a long time. It was only at the end of the seventies that specialists managed to put the pieces of the puzzle together: Big Moose had already had a long career, when he was considered almost a newcomer in the Chicago blues.

Born in Clarksdale, Mississippi, to a black father and an Indian mother, Johnny Walker learned to play guitar, harmonica, and piano very early on; the latter was his favorite instrument. For a while he belonged to Ike Turner's* famous Kings of Rhythm; then he went to Helena, Arkansas, where he hosted the "King Biscuit Hour" radio program. He played with Delta bluesmen Robert Jr. Lockwood,* Sonny Boy Williamson (Rice Miller),* Joe Willie Wilkins, Pinetop Perkins,* Boyd Gilmore, and Elmore James.* Whimsical and hard to comprehend, Big Moose was everywhere at the same time but seldom where expected; moreover, he was never in the same place long enough to have a faithful audience. He recorded in Greenville, at the heart of the Delta, for Ike Turner; in Los Angeles for Johnny Otis* and with Lowell Fulson*; in New York with Curtis Jones* and Elmore James; and again with Elmore James in New Orleans. He was in Memphis, St. Louis, Kansas City, and Chicago where he recorded a few 45s (again under several different names), and where he was also the piano player for Ricky Allen, A. C. Reed,* Lilian Offitt, Muddy Waters,* and scores of other artists.

Finally, his long association in the sixties with Earl Hooker* did attract the fans' attention to this strong, efficient, and expressive piano and organ player. He is also a good singer with a somewhat shrill but very bluesy and often warm timbre. He appears under his real name on numerous albums for the Bluesway label. He recorded two titles as the featured player on Earl Hooker's album *Don't Have to Worry* (Bluesway) and at last recorded his first and brilliant album *Ramblin' Woman* (Bluesway).

In 1977 Johnny Walker gained due recognition for his superb performance in the excellent anthology *Living Chicago Blues, Vol. 2* (Alligator). A series of engagements and tours followed, as well as albums for Isabel and Red Beans.

Johnny "Big Moose" Walker, who knew bluesmen throughout the United States, successfully retained many different styles and adapted them to his own musical personality, deeply rooted in the barrelhouse tradition of the Deep South.

PHILLIP WALKER

(b. 1937 / vocals, guitar)

It took Phillip Walker a long time to emerge out of darkness, but since the mid-seventies he has been a major figure in the contemporary blues of the West Coast.

After a few long years of learning and practice with the bands of Long John Hunter and Clifton Chenier★ (with his friend Lonesome Sundown★), Phillip Walker went to El Paso, where he performed in several clubs. He went to California in the late fifties and created his own band, to which he added the vocal talents of his wife, Ina. In country, soul, and blues he was constantly active and recorded for several labels, either as the featured player or as accompanist to scores of artists, from Johnny Fuller★ to Driftin' Slim.

Rooted in the Texas tradition that goes back via T-Bone Walker★ and Lightnin' Hopkins★ to Blind Lemon Jefferson,★ Phillip Walker plays in the same style of blossoming staccato arpeggios. But Walker is also very modern and eclectic, open to all musical genres and evolutions, from the country sounds of the famous Bakersfield school (Buck Owens especially) to the more recent forms of black music (soul and then funk) via the obvious influence of California guitar players like Lafayette Thomas★ and Johnny Heartsman. An innovative perfectionist, Phillip Walker is also a brilliant technician whose instrumental virtuosity somewhat overshadows his talents as a singer with a very expressive voice.

Thanks to the legendary album *The Bottom of the Top*

(Playboy), Phillip Walker was revealed to a larger public. Other outstanding albums followed: *Someday You'll Have These Blues* (Alligator), *Tough as I Want to Be* (Rounder), and *Blues!* (Hightone).

T-BONE WALKER

(Aaron Walker / 1909–1975 / vocals, guitar, piano)

T-Bone Walker was one of the great innovators of the blues, and although his direct influence was less than that of B. B. King,* it is safe to say that he contributed significantly to the creation of modern blues.

Born in Texas, T-Bone met famous bluesmen such as Blind Lemon Jefferson* and Texas Alexander* at an early age. While very young he was a tap dancer in medicine shows. Then he performed in vaudeville shows, especially with singer Ida Cox.* In 1929 he recorded a 78 for Columbia: the recorded titles were two blues played on the acoustic guitar, in the Texas tradition.

Attracted more and more to the big swing bands, he associated with guitarist Charlie Christian and played the banjo in Cab Calloway's band. Around 1953 he was apparently one of the first musicians to adopt the electric guitar. He became tremendously popular because of that, and he got an engagement in California as a singer and guitar player in the band of Les Hite. In 1940 he recorded "T-Bone Blues," in 1942 "Mean Old World," and in 1947 his big hit "Call It Stormy Monday," often covered under the title "Stormy Monday Blues."

After 1947 T-Bone Walker led his own band, which included brass, piano, bass, and drums. This "small big band" created a music on which the suave voice of the singer seemed to float. Sophisticated, close to jazz and sentimental ballads, it is the blues of the West Coast; and T-Bone Walker, Charles Brown,* and Lowell Fulson* are its great creators.

T-Bone Walker's unique guitar style influenced scores of artists like Clarence "Gatemouth" Brown,* PeeWee Crayton,* and B. B. King. Rooted in Blind Lemon Jefferson's Texas tradition, T-Bone was also inspired by Lonnie Johnson* (the first guitar player to play note by note and not by chords). When T-Bone improvised a guitar solo, he seemed to unfold a string of notes in numerous arabesques. After 1947, no longer on the charts, T-Bone was still one of the most popular black stars in California and Chicago and in the South. He went on intense tours in these regions to the detriment of his health. He recorded prolifically for Capitol, Imperial, Atlantic, and Decca. In 1962 he was part of the first European tour of the American Folk Blues Festival, which enabled him to enjoy a great popularity among the European blues and jazz fans and to go back several times to Europe. From 1962 to 1975, he recorded many albums for this new public, but the quality was not always as high as that of his former titles.

Among the numerous compilations devoted to T-Bone, some are indispensable: *Low Down Blues* (Charly); *The Complete T-Bone Walker, 1940–54* (Mosaic); *The Complete Imperial Recordings* (EMI); and *T-Bone Blues* (Atlantic).

SIPPIE WALLACE

See Female Blues Singers

BABY BOY WARREN

See Detroit

WASHBOARD SAM

(Robert Brown / 1906–1966 / vocals, washboard)

Before the war Washboard Sam was one of the most popular artists in Chicago. Although he was one of the few musicians to play the washboard and to record for commercial purposes with this instrument, he was nevertheless a very urban artist. His blues style, extremely sophisticated, was often characterized by the creation of risky themes with humorous lyrics, which he sang with a deep but passionless voice, often in monotone, and surrounded by a jazzy accompaniment. The contrast between the eloquent use of his washboard and his accompanists was striking, with guitar players Big Bill

Broonzy* and Willie Lacey, piano players Memphis Slim* and Bob Call, bass player Ransom Knowlin, and several saxophone players, who were all regulars of the polished Bluebird Beat created by Lester Melrose.*

His friendship with Big Bill Broonzy enabled him to record about 180 songs between 1935 and 1949 for Melrose and the Bluebird label. His success among his contemporaries was considerable, and pieces like "I've Been Treated Wrong," "I'm Not the Lad," and "Digging My Potatoes" were in Chicago jukeboxes for years.

However, his career was very short. Washboard Sam and Jazz Gillum were influenced by the Bluebird Beat, and after 1945 Washboard Sam was unable to follow the evolution of what the black public wanted, the powerful and electric blues of Muddy Waters.*

After a last session with Big Bill for Chess in 1953, Washboard Sam stopped recording, and he did not even try to take advantage of the blues revival despite the fact that Memphis Slim and Willie Dixon* tried to persuade him to come back.

His work, although full of good moments, is often monotonous. *Washboard Sam* (Blues Classics) is the only available compilation of his work. It seems that with good judgment it would be possible to establish other collections that could document one of the most commercially successful prewar performers.

JOHN WATKINS

See Chicago

JOHNNY "GUITAR" WATSON

See California

KATIE WEBSTER

See J. D. Miller

CASEY BILL WELDON

(Williams Weldon / 1909–? / vocals, guitar)

Although he recorded nearly seventy songs between 1935 and 1938, Casey Bill Weldon is still an enigmatic figure in blues history. Apparently, he was born in Arkansas, although his nickname (Casey=K.C.) suggests an origin in Kansas City; he made his recording debut with Will Shade and the Memphis Jug Band* in 1927 in Memphis, but the two titles he recorded then were not out of the usual, and they contrasted with the rest of his career. He was said to be married for a short time to Memphis Minnie,* but unlike his successors, he never accompanied her on record. Finally, despite the commercial success of his 78s, he suddenly stopped recording in 1938; nothing more is known about his life, except that he might have been alive in Detroit around 1970. However, no one claims to have met him in person.

Weldon, even though he was quite an expressionless singer (like most bluesmen of the thirties), was a superb guitar player, using his steel guitar in the Hawaiian style, flat on his lap. Even though he expressed himself in the classic style of the Hawaiian guitarists who were then in fashion at the beginning of the century, he developed a unique approach to the blues and ragtime. Most of his titles are characterized by an exuberance, an enraged rhythm, and a brilliant technique that place him more in the line of the white Texas guitar players of western swing such as Leon McAuliffe and Strozer Quinn than in that of the black followers of the bottleneck.

Somewhat ignored today—although his brilliant style with the bottleneck would probably astonish those unfamiliar with him—Casey Bill was only parsimoniously reissued. *Bottleneck Guitar Trendsetters* (Yazoo) that he shared with Kokomo Arnold* is wonderful.

VALERIE WELLINGTON

See Zora Young

JUNIOR WELLS

(Amos Wells, Jr. / b. 1932 / vocals, harmonica)

Raised in Memphis and acquainted with Sonny Boy Williamson (Rice Miller*) when he was eight, it seemed natural that Wells chose the harmonica to express himself. In spite of laws forbidding minors in the taverns of Chicago, Junior Wells was playing in the bands of Tampa Red,* Little Johnny Jones, and Memphis Slim* before he created his own band, the Aces, with the Myers brothers and the great drummer Fred Below.* At that time, Wells was an inventive harmonica player who used the new resources of amplification, and he revealed himself in the early fifties to be the rival of Little Walter.*

Between 1953 and 1957 Junior Wells recorded some wonderful titles for the small States label, the best of which ("Hoodoo Man Blues" [with Elmore James*], "'Bout the Break of Day," and "Lawdy! Lawdy!") can be compared to Little Walter's titles. It is important to mention, however, that he composed very few original blues; he borrowed his blues from Sonny Boy's repertoire. Furthermore, whereas Walter could enjoy the production and distribution of the powerful Chess company, Junior Wells performed for very small labels, such as States, Profile, Chief, and USA. In 1962 he had his first commercial hit, a composition by producer Mel London, "Messin' with the Kid." This stage in Junior Wells's music is particularly well represented on the collections *Blues Hit Big Town* (Delmark) and *Messin' with the Kid* (Flyright).

After 1965 Junior Wells's career went in many directions. Associated with Buddy Guy,* he was still a regular of the Chicago clubs. Around 1966 he tried (with some commercial success) to imitate James Brown, and the artistic results, astonishing at the time, were substantial. Finally, discovered by producers Bob Koester and Sam Charters, he performed at concerts, colleges, and festivals, and he went on several tours in Europe (one of which was with the Rolling Stones). He then recorded several records for an almost exclusively young and white public, for whom he became a "living legend," thus

■ Junior Wells. *(Photograph © by Paul Harris; used with permission)*

being one of the rare active survivors of the "golden age of the blues."

Most of the albums recorded by Wells are first-rate, although some lack the verve and invention of his earliest work. If his vocal effects do not always correspond to his expectations, his harmonica style is a pale reflection of his talent of twenty-five years ago. The value of his records is generally due to the homogeneity of his accompanists, in particular the band of his friend Buddy Guy.

Chicago/The Blues Today, Vol. 1 (Vanguard), *It's My Life Baby* (Vanguard), *Coming at You* (Vanguard), and *Hoodoo Man Blues* (Vanguard) date from the sixties, and they are still of consequence. *Southside Blues Jam* (Delmark) and *On Tap* (Delmark), slightly inferior, are still, however, of a high level. Finally, *Pleading the Blues* (Isabel), an intimate session, is—in spite of its obvious qualities—still literally unknown.

For years, Junior Wells has been managing his past rather than his present. If he were well advised and well produced, it is possible that he could still give good recorded performances in a more contemporary register. His noteworthy participation in the hard-edged *Harp Attack* (Alligator) proves that Wells is still in fine form.

PEETIE WHEATSTRAW

(William Bunch / 1905–1941 / vocals, piano, guitar)

Today much forgotten, Peetie Wheatstraw was widely popular among blacks between 1930 and 1941. Originally from St. Louis, he lived for a long time in Louisville and in Indianapolis before going to Chicago in 1933. His style is characteristic of St. Louis: a subdued and lazy singing, with arrogant inflections that reflected his personality, and a simple piano style, accenting the bass notes, accompanied by brilliant guitarists, such as Charley Jordan, Kokomo Arnold,★ and Robert Lee McCoy (Robert Nighthawk★). There were few melodic variations in the themes, hence that impression of monotony. Peetie Wheatstraw's success was due in fact to the invention of the blues he composed. Indeed, he created a demonic character who loved erotic and violent themes composed of catchy and unabashed lines: "Suicide Blues," "Doin' the Best I Can," "Banana Man," and especially "Devil's Son-in-Law" and "The High Sheriff of Hell," evocative blues from which he took his nicknames.

He recorded about 150 titles for Decca, and he also participated in numerous recordings for other artists, such as Casey Bill Weldon,* Lonnie Johnson,* and Bumble Bee Slim.* In 1941 he was at the peak of his popularity when his car was hit by a train at a railroad crossing, killing him on the spot.

The rare collections that were devoted to him did not serve him well. A good selection of his best blues has yet to be made.

ARTIE WHITE

(b. 1937 / vocals)

There is nothing greatly original in the itinerary of Artie White. Born in Vicksburg, Mississippi, Artie "Blues Boy"—in homage to his idol B. B. King*—White began singing in church choirs, then he went to Chicago in 1956. The harmonica player Little Mack Simmons recorded him, and his "She's the One" had some success locally, confirmed by "Leanin' Tree." On it, Artie revealed himself as a powerful and sensitive emulator of Albert King* in his Stax period.

With a contract on southern labels, Ronn then Ichiban, from 1985 to 1987, this former trucker and bar manager then devoted himself entirely to music. In 1989, "Hattie Mae," an excellent contemporary soul-blues, was a hit in the South, thus establishing Artie White as the big Blues Boy who was on the road to fame.

It seems that White has a promising career ahead of him. All his albums are of a very good quality: *Blues Boy* (Ronn), *Nothing Takes the Place of You* (Ichiban), and *Where It's At* (Ichiban). *Thangs Got to Change* (Ichiban) may be the best one.

WHITE BLUES

White blues quite obviously creates a problem among blues fans. For some, blues is a "music without any skin color or nationality"; for others, the blues is a uniquely black American creation, and all whites who play blues are plagiarists. Moreover, some specialists thought that the rock groups of the sixties were the children of the blues, forsaken by blacks, whereas others saw in that phenomenon a fleeting influence among others, a fashion of the time. The relationships of the black blues with the white musical environment had five successive phases that have influenced the evolution of popular music.

1. The Origins: Blues and Country Music. The blues was born in the southern United States—probably at first in the Mississippi Delta region—within black rural communities in the late nineteenth century or the early twentieth century. Contrary to what people have thought for a long time, it was not slavery which created the blues but the tough segregation that reigned in the South from 1880 on. Blacks, humiliated, rejected, denigrated, had to turn to themselves and to draw from their own resources so as to create their culture, essentially musical and spiritual. The slavery years had probably already witnessed a large fusion between music of African and European origins. And black music that anticipated the blues was considerably influenced by whites. In fact, at that time there were very few differences between black and white popular music in the southern states. But segregation forced blacks to separate themselves from white culture, and they created a form of ballad essentially black, with its own code and rules, that was progressively called the blues. But segregation did not prevent all contacts. Indeed, the South became as never before the place of constant and fruitful musical exchanges. Black musicians used the Celtic ballad (the versification AAB of the blues comes directly from it); white musicians used the black blues. From its origins, country music appears to be influenced by the black mark of the blues, and it grew as a cousin, whose privileged status and the barriers that were erected to separate were unable to conceal a tight relationship. Black influence was abundant in early country music, but it was particularly strong upon musicians like Sam McGee, Dock Boggs, Riley Puckett, and especially Jimmie Rodgers,* who interpreted and created a majority of blues as such, instilling the blues genre into country music. And even if these white singers always defined themselves as country music artists ("hillbilly" then) that defined their skin color, they were in fact real white bluesmen. Country artists not only copied the black blues, but they also used it to create, vivify, and perfect their own music. Jimmie Rodgers' blues were in fact extremely original in style and in lyrics. His influence upon many black bluesmen was unquestionable and important. This great implicit solidarity of black and white music in the South is illustrated in many ways, one of which is the fact that the first star of the "Grand Ole Opry"—the first country music radio program aired from Nashville—was the black harmonica player De Ford Bailey, a bluesman! Also, the interdependence of blacks and whites is total when it concerns the themes used: for example, "Mystery Train," popularized by Elvis Presley, was borrowed from the black Junior Parker,* who had quite obviously heard it on the record of the white group, the Carter Family, who recorded it under the title "Cannonball Blues" in 1927. Country music borrowed incessantly from the blues, but certainly on a smaller scale the blues borrowed incessantly from country: Gene Autry, Bob Wills and all the western swing, Merle Travis, PeeWee King, Moon Mullican, Bill Monroe, and Hank Williams; then rockabilly— an original branch of country music—and now Doc Watson, Charlie McCoy,* Delbert McClinton, and many others. In fact, there is a southern culture and a southern music, whose black and white elements are at times differentiated, but for the most part they are so intertwined that it is often impossible to untie them. Where can we classify the likes of Steve Cropper, Duane Allman, Dr. John, and so many other southern musicians who had that intuitive comprehension of the blues that can only be acquired when one is raised in the very heart of a civilization where the blues is one of the pillars? Let's remember that all the recordings of the swamp blues, the down-home blues of J. D. Miller,* were made by southern musicians, mainly white, who probably would have never accepted being called "white bluesmen." However, beyond the prejudices and the conventions, the real and original white blues is there first: in the South, in the different variations of country music.

■ Bob Dylan, Phil Ochs, and Muddy Waters. *(Photograph © by Anton J. Mikofsky; used with permission)*

Often called the "father of country music," JIMMIE RODGERS was also the most influential of the early white blues composers and singers. Born James Charles Rodgers in Meridian, Mississippi, on September 8, 1897, he followed his father into work on the railroad, until after fourteen years—mostly as a flag man and breakman—he was forced by tuberculosis to find other work. He attempted without much success to establish a career as a popular singer until his discovery by Ralph Peer in 1927 set him off on a career recording blues and hillbilly music for Victor Records. He died on a recording date in New York City, at the Taft Hotel on May 26, 1933, short of his thirty-sixth birthday.

Among his best-known blues compositions are "Blue Yodel No. 1" ("T for Texas"), "Mule Skinner Blues," and "T. D. Blues." He is particularly well remembered for his recording of "Let Me Be Your Sidetrack," a raunchy blues song built on the variously attributed but probably communal title stanza.

A Jimmie Rodgers festival is held each summer in Meridian.

2. *The Northern Folk Boom.* The white singers of the North had not been indifferent to the blues, but they had, until the fifties, been in contact with it via jazz bands or bands influenced by jazz. Jazz was born long before the blues, from several influences whose black element was dominant but not unique, and it developed outside the blues. But the input of the blues was important in jazz; as a counterpart, the jazz input was important in the evolution of the blues in all stages of its development. There are more than just traces of blues among the white crooners in the North: Frank Sinatra, Doris Day, Bing Crosby, Julie London, et cetera. Peggy Lee, the vocalist of Benny Goodman's big band, had success with her versions of black blues: "Why Don't You Do It Right?," "I'm a Woman," and "Fever." But here again, she would not have wished—nor even have imagined—to be pictured as a "white blueswoman."

This desegregated notion was to develop in the fifties among the progressive intellectual circles of New York. In the thirties and forties, ethnomusicologists Alan Lomax and Charles Seeger had supported a musical movement that was anti-racist, anti-fascist, socialistic, and pro-union in New York; this music, collected in the South among whites and rural blacks, was labeled "folk." Little by little, led by the tireless Pete Seeger (Charles's son), the folk movement developed around southern musicians who had moved to Greenwich Village—for example, Woody Guthrie, Leadbelly,* Sonny Terry,* and Josh White.* In the late fifties, folk suddenly became the favorite music of northern college students who made it the idealogical symbol of their "revolt" against Yankee society. This folk trend brought about an original and unexpected interest for all old forms—that is, acoustic ones—of white and black southern music, with all the virtues. Thus many young Yankees started to collect blues records of the twenties and thirties, to idolize the artists and to revive the musical forms (*see* Blues Revival). Some of them went further, and, fascinated by the life and the social state of southern blacks, they played their repertoire, and they took the title of "white bluesmen." There was in this move a lot of sincerity but also a large dose of naivety: although they did not admit to it, these first "white bluesmen" found in the miserable condition of southern blacks a romantic image that never really existed. The young white bluesman, often a college graduate, distanced himself from Yankee society by singing and playing—with imitated accents and idioms—the repertoire of the poor southern blacks confined to ignorance and segregation. This appeared to many contemporary blacks as a new offense and another pernicious form of racism. The album *Blues Project* (Elektra) illustrates perfectly this acoustic, northern, and imitative white folk-blues. Mentioning these facts—necessary to the historical comprehension of the phenomenon—does in no way mean that this music is without any artistic value: from precursors like singer Barbara Dane or the subtle composer Eric Von Schmidt up to later artists like John Fahey, John Miller, and Mark Spoelstra, there often are excellent performances, but there are also many abominable moments when the album liner notes of the time are particularly irritating. If some representatives of this trend—Bob Dylan, Tom Rush, Jim Kweskin, Jorma Kaukonen—only rushed through the blues before they built their own musical niche, others remained somewhat faithful to their debut, thus becoming veterans on the present blues scene: Spider John Koerner, Dave Ray, Geoff Muldaur, Rory Block, Danny Kalb, and Tony Glover. Two exemplary names in particular are:

DAVE VAN RONK (b. 1936), the prototype of the bluesmen of the folk boom, a kind of relentless and uncompromising bard. A guitar virtuoso—he learned, like many, from Gary Davis*—an expressive singer with a cocky tone, he has recorded a few good albums for Folkway and Prestige.

JOHN HAMMOND, Jr., (b. 1942) loved Robert Johnson's* music very much. Hammond's father, a jazz and blues producer for Columbia, wanted to present Robert Johnson at Carnegie Hall in New York, and he instilled in his son this fascination. Hammond, Jr., thought he was some kind of white New York reincarnation of Johnson! After clumsy and excessive debuts that included the worst moments of the blues revival, John Hammond never stopped making progress and asserting his music. A singer without much talent and a poor guitar and harmonica player, Hammond managed to compensate for these limitations with excellent arrangements and the presence of first-rate accompanists. He has recorded many albums for Vanguard, Atlantic, and Rounder, especially the excellent *Big City Blues* (Vanguard), accompanied by the brilliant guitarists Billy Butler and Wild Jimmy Spruill; *Hot Tracks* (Vanguard); and *Frogs for Snakes* (Rounder).

3. The British Blues. After the war, the American presence in Europe and that of countless black GIs brought about an extraordinary interest for all types of American music, including the blues. Sharing the language and a common background, the British were the first ones to make this appreciation concrete by interpreting the music. If Lonnie Donegan, a renegade of jazz bands, popularized especially Leadbelly's blues, the guitar player Alexis Koerner and harmonica player Cyril Davies are the real precursors of the British blues. John Mayall founded after their model his Bluesbreakers, which included some of the best British stylists, guitarist Eric Clapton, in particular. But in London and in Liverpool, the motivations were not those of the young folk-boom Yankees; the chosen model here was the electric Chicago blues of Muddy Waters,★ Howlin' Wolf,★ Jimmy Reed,★ and Chuck Berry.★ These artists were admired and respected, without the slightest idea given to the complexity of the relationships between blacks and whites in American society. The young British imitated with unmethodical enthusiasm their idols and argued for their recognition. The blues bands of the sixties—the Yardbirds, the Moody Blues, the Animals, Them, the Who, and especially the Rolling Stones—initiated a movement that went far beyond the first objective, and they found themselves at the head of a movement that they had probably not wished for. Their huge international success and the fact that they named their sources openly and that they attempted obviously to contact the black electric blues considerably reoriented American music. The "British blues" itself had its ups and downs, the imitation of the beginning—that seems today puerile and unsystematic—gave way to a more mature approach that usually distanced itself noticeably from the blues. The best representatives of this British blues may have been Peter Green and Jeremy Spencer (from Fleetwood Mac), Tony McPhee, Stan Webb and Christine Perfect (from the Chicken Shack), Alvin Lee, Duster Bennett, and Irishmen Van Morrison and Rory Gallagher. But many others could be named, almost all the names of English rock made their debut in the blues.

Nevertheless, some British blues artists prevailed, such as the original guitarist STEFAN GROSSMAN, who became the faithful and demanding transcriber of country blues, and JO-ANN KELLY (1944–1991), probably the best British blues interpreter. Passionate and convincing, an excellent guitar player and a superb singer, with a neutral and strong tone in the pure Delta blues tradition, Jo-Ann always refused to take the easy way and be commercial; she devoted herself entirely to her style of blues that won over the most skeptical by her purity and her sincerity. Her best album is *Jo-Ann Kelly* (Blue Goose).

4. White American Electric Blues. The Rolling Stones' extraordinary success in the U.S. drew attention to the electric bluesmen of Chicago. Until then, very few whites had been interested in them. But it also enabled a few young Yankee musicians who for several years had been haunting the clubs in Chicago to surface. They quickly went from the acoustic folk-blues to the electric blues of the ghetto in which they saw a vital and irresistible beat that they tried to reproduce in their music. Leading frantic and sometimes dangerous lives in the black ghetto, Mike Bloomfield, Paul Butterfield, Elvin Bishop, Norman Dayron, Corky Siegel, Al Kooper, Barry Goldberg, Mark Naftalin, and David Bromberg wanted sincerely and above all to become bluesmen. They encountered the compassion of an always benevolent Muddy Waters, who witnessed sadly how young blacks became uninterested in his music. Muddy took under his wing his "spiritual sons" Paul Butterfield and Charlie Musselwhite,* and his example was largely followed among black bluesmen who gave—in this case—more than they ever got from white society. Little Walter,* Sonny Boy Williamson (Rice Miller),* James Cotton,* Big Joe Williams* (who taught Mike Bloomfield completely), and Smokey Smothers also played an important role in the development of these young northerners. The inevitable happened: Noticed outside the black ghettos, they became the white stars of the white blues, the American equivalent to British groups who played black music, inevitably whitened for a white public. The bitterness of some black musicians and writers regarding this phenomenon does not diminish the great exaltation of certain bluesmen—such as Muddy Waters—for the recognition it was bringing to their music, even if it was through their young students. The movement in the United States had begun, and the end of the sixties saw blues bands after the model of Butterfield's and Musselwhite's blooming everywhere.

PAUL BUTTERFIELD (1941–1988), the historic leader of this white electric blues, was born in Chicago. Fascinated by the use of the harmonica by such bluesmen as Little Walter and Big Walter Horton,* he managed in his turn to become a great virtuoso of this instrument. A mature singer, he had a huge success with his first album, *Born in Chicago* (Elektra), that seems today somewhat excessive. He experimented with all kinds of sounds that were sometimes far from the blues; he was even one of the great rock stars who electrified the crowds at Woodstock. He then disappeared, emerging sporadically long enough to record a poor and quickly forgotten album. In our opinion, his best performance was with Muddy Waters on the album *Fathers and Sons* (Chess).

Guitarist MIKE BLOOMFIELD (1944–1981) was an attractive individual. His autobiography, *Me and Big Joe*, revealed a fragile being looking for the mythical paternal image. He played guitar for Butterfield then for Bob Dylan and countless rock artists. He was a musician of uneven value, able to alternate between the excellent and the boring. *Between the Hard Place* (Takoma) seems to summarize his career well.

CANNED HEAT reached the American musical scene a few years later and created the basis of a white California blues drawing its inspiration from Chicago blues and Delta blues and also from the West Coast blues of Albert Collins* and even Cajun music. Although singer Bob Hite was a mighty figure, and guitar player Henry Vestine was much too talkative to be efficient, it was the rhythm section with its interesting

Hispanic inflections, and especially Al Wilson—a remarkable harmonica player—who gave the group its whole originality.

ROY BUCHANAN (1939–1988) also had a stormy life. Between country-rock and the blues, flirting with the hard sounds, it seemed that he was never as much at ease as in the real blues where his tortuous and expressive sounds found their natural outlet. Shortly before his death, he recorded a beautiful series of albums for the Alligator label, the best of which are, in our opinion, *When a Guitar Plays the Blues* and *Dancing on the Edge*.

Finally, we absolutely need to highlight JOHNNY WINTER (b. 1944), the strange albino from Texas who became a controversial rock superstar. Born in Beaumont, Texas, to a family of musicians, he played rockabilly as well as the blues of his black neighbors—Clarence Garlow* in particular. Discovered by producer Roy Ames, he performed in countless recording sessions under his own name and as an accompanist for many local bluesmen. Discovered by the rock press—an ultra-white who played black blues!—and thrown into the big stages in the North and in California, this unexpected success nearly made him sink for good, musically and physically. After years of crisis, he was calmer and hardened, and he devoted himself at the end of the seventies almost exclusively to the blues, producing Muddy Waters—one of his lifelong idols—and recording under his own name. He was a good singer, but he too often forced his voice; as a guitarist he played incredibly fast and with a furious attack, losing himself at times somewhere in his cascades of notes—these were moreover in the purest tradition of the Texas blues—and his work is of uneven value. In fact, and despite what was said about it, Johnny Winter belonged to this southern trend we talked about above: The time was right for him to be labeled a "white bluesman."

He recorded a lot, and his recorded work alternates the best with the worst. The best certainly is the series of recent albums recorded on the Alligator label (*Guitar Slim, Serious Business,* and *Third Degree*).

5. *White Blues Everywhere.* Far from slowing down or from declining, the movement of the white blues continued and even increased during the seventies in America, Europe,

Japan, and beyond, following the international recognition of this music. The blues is almost a necessary passage for every rock apprentice, and it is often limited in the press and rock literature to the singular role as the main source for rock, similar to the jazz press that gave blues the singular function of being the main source for jazz.

The confusion over white or black blues was amplified when blues giants like Muddy Waters and John Lee Hooker added numerous white musicians to their bands. In fact, the United States changed a lot: Segregation definitely exploded in the sixties; and the blues, *the music of segregation*, was then logically attributed and returned to the blacks.

Non-blacks—in the United States, Europe, and Japan—became the main commercial supporters of this music, and it was probably inevitable that the number of white bluesmen increased. It is important to acknowledge the tremendous success of blues-rock artists like the Nighthawks and George Thorogood on the campuses of Georgetown, Washington, or the Fabulous Thunderbirds near Austin's University of Texas to be convinced that the blues in the United States has itself become a music slightly underground for a young intellectual and largely white public. That does not mean that the black blues no longer exists—often quite close to there—but it does not have the support from the media, and its black audience is often made of poor and uneducated people who are not able to move successfully in the society. For a young black musician to have a blues career today it may be better to go through the universities or the underground because the paying public can be found there. Isn't that the approach of Johnny Copeland,★ Lonnie Brooks,★ Koko Taylor,★ Robert Cray,★ and Joe Louis Walker★? This does not mean at all that the circuit of the clubs of the black districts and ghettos does not exist. The resurrection of soul-blues in the South with labels like Malaco, Ichiban, and La Jam vie in showing the durability of this "chitlin' circuit." But financially it is much less profitable.

In any case, from looking at the rows in record stores, festival programs, and advertisements in specialized magazines, it becomes clear that year after year the blues whitens even more: John Nicholas, William Clarke, Jerry Portnoy, Paul

"Brooklyn Slim" Oscher, Lloyd Jones, Downchild, Curtis Salgado, Kim Wilson, Rod Piazza, Ron Levy, Duke Robillard, Angela Strehli, Marcia Ball, the late Stevie Ray Vaughan, and so many others are proof of that.

This evolution of the blues toward a whitening of the public as well as of the interpreters is a fact that *no* observer could have foreseen thirty years ago, but, nevertheless, it is undeniable. Of course, several questions need to be asked. Is it still the blues? Yes, in form, but what about in spirit, the roots, in the deep and emotional meaning? Where can this white blues go? Its twenty-five years in existence has already shown that it is in a shaky position: The further it goes, it naturally distances itself from its first inspirations, and it is accused of betrayal and usually becomes part of the great musical trend of rock; if it remains faithful to the blues of its beginnings, it inevitably stagnates and seems essentially imitative and repetitive.

This is a dilemma for the white bluesman who must really believe in his vocation in order to take this uncertain way, which shows brilliantly that the blues is still an ethnic music linked to the soul of the African-American people at a certain time of its history.

Beyond that, it is the blues—let it be white and black finally—in form but another blues as far as the meaning is concerned. To be convinced of that, one needs to note the tangible loss of substance in many contemporary blues recordings.

The black blues—because it asserted itself as a strong element with an overwhelming originality—was throughout this century the main root of western pop music. All the movements, all the trends, all the innovations drew at a certain time, directly or indirectly from that source.

Finally, when some excellent musicians like Rod Piazza, Honey Alexander, Ronnie Earl, Ron Levy, Duke Robillard, Steve Freund, Little Charly, and Rick Estrin introduce themselves less as "bluesmen" and more like the supporters of a return to a music close to American "roots music," the blues, hillbilly, rockabilly, rock-and-roll, et cetera, then they take on the role as performers of "alternative music" in the face of the mechanized fads of the Top 40 of all colors. They confirm with force that the blues light still guides the demanding musician and music full of feeling and emotion.

BUKKA WHITE

(Booker T. Washington White / 1909–1977 / vocals, guitar, piano)
Bukka White may be considered one of the masters of the Delta blues.

Born in Aberdeen, Mississippi, he was a sharecropper—and a musician when he felt like it. His guitar style was particularly original, somewhere amid Charlie Patton,⋆ the country music of 1900–1920, and the Hawaiian guitar (*Panama Limited*).

In the thirties, his local fame was important, and according to the legend, he gave his small cousin, the young Riley Ben King (the future B. B. King⋆), his first guitar.

He recorded only a score of songs before the war, but almost all of them became classics: "Aberdeen Mississippi Blues," "Parchman Farm," "Fixin to Die," "Sic 'em Dogs on Me," and "Panama Limited." They stood out because of his powerful voice, his particular guitar style, and the autobiographical lyrics, sometimes incredibly witty or with a reserved sensitivity. In our opinion, the best piece is "Parchman Farm," the description of the penitentiary in which Bukka stayed on several occasions, and where he met Alan Lomax especially, who had come to record the songs of the inmates for the Library of Congress. These superb titles from before the war have been partly reissued on *Aberdeen Mississippi Blues* (Travelin' Man).

If the artistic success of these 78s made the collectors look for these pieces, their absence of commercial success at the time (despite the presence of Washboard Sam⋆ on washboard, to sound more "modern") was total. Thus, after a few unsuccessful attempts to live off his music, Bukka White gave up his musical career to make more money as a secondhand furniture dealer.

When folk singers Bob Dylan and Buffy Sainte-Marie covered the classic "Fixin' to Die" in 1962, it gave the idea to two young guitar players in Memphis, Bill Barth and John Fahey, to write (based on the information in the autobiographical "Aberdeen Mississippi Blues") a letter to: Bukka White, blues singer, Aberdeen, Mississippi. They were surprised when they got a letter from him a few weeks later.

Another surprise came when they actually met Bukka: Instead of the moribund old man they expected, they found themselves before a fifty-three-year-old man who had never stopped playing for his pleasure and that of his neighbors.

It was for Bukka White the beginning of a new career that took him on tours all over the United States and Europe where his sense of the public and his talents as a musician and as a storyteller assured him a considerable reputation among country blues fans.

This second career enabled Bukka to record several uneven albums. His music had changed a lot (influenced by postwar sounds such as the Memphis blues because Bukka was then living in Memphis) and his voice was excessively harsh. The first album of his rediscovery, *Mississippi Blues* (Takoma or Sonet), is excellent, as well as his last one: *Big Daddy* (Biograph). He talked with sensitivity about his antique shop and about his granddaughter, with whom he discovered "the art of being a grandfather."

GEORGIA WHITE

(1903–1980 / vocals, piano)

Georgia White was one of the rare female blues singers of the postclassic era who could be compared to Memphis Minnie.* Although she did not belong to the world of vaudeville that had produced the first female blues singers (Bessie Smith* and Ma Rainey*), she managed to combine their influence with that of the southern barrelhouses. She was a powerful piano player in the tradition of these questionable places, where it was necessary above all to make oneself be heard. She used her instrument to enhance her amazing voice with a register that was rarely equaled.

She began as a jazz singer in Jimmy Noone's band in Chicago. She quickly became a star in the black clubs of the city, and in 1935 she began her career with Decca. Her repertoire with a biting irony, largely centered around stories of prostitutes and lesbians, enabled her to have a big commercial hit with such pieces as "Hot Nuts! Get 'em from the Peanut Man" and "I'll Keep Sittin' on It if I Can't Sell It," although sometimes she sang with brio a moving "Trouble in Mind."

Her jazz-blues style, contrary to that of most of her contemporaries, aged very little. It was based on the use of a strong rhythm section that announced the postwar Chicago blues and on the participation of excellent musicians like guitar players Big Bill Broonzy* and Ikey Robinson.

All together, the hundred or so titles that she recorded for Decca between 1935 and 1941 are first-rate. But the reissues are rare. We can only content ourselves with *Sings and Plays* (Rosetta), which, except for the fact that it includes the first version of the famous "Trouble in Mind," is satisfactory neither on the musical level nor on the level of sound quality.

JOSH WHITE

(1908–1969 / vocals, guitar)

This superb musician—one of the best guitar players in blues history and one of the great creators of the East Coast blues—has remained strangely unrecognized by blues fans.

Josh White was, between 1932 and 1936, a talented and prolific blues singer. After having briefly recorded with the preacher Blind Joe Taggart, he recorded seventy-five titles for ARC, either some blues under his own name or that of Pinewood Tom, or some spirituals under the name of The Singing Christian. Moreover, he accompanied several musicians, among whom were the pianists Leroy Carr* and Walter Roland.*

This East Coast musician was a very sophisticated singer and an eclectic and virtuoso guitarist, in the line of Blind Blake,* but also borrowing from other sources, especially those of Texans Blind Lemon Jefferson* and Lonnie Johnson.* In fact, his guitar style (a melodious line played note by note, interspersed with syncopated chords) was incredibly similar to that of the excellent Buddy Moss.*

Josh White came very early to New York, and he quickly

became integrated into the folk milieux of the metropolis. He recorded with Leadbelly,* Woody Guthrie, and Pete Seeger. After the Second World War he became a star of the clubs in Greenwich Village, and through his contact with this public and these musicians, who were strangers to the blues reality, his music became more and more polished to the point of being artificial. His instrumental virtuosity (that he displayed in all his recordings) can not make listeners forget dubious vocal effects and a sometimes disastrous accompaniment. This period, when he was often compared to Harry Belafonte, was in spite of all also the period when he made a series of very brilliant recordings in Chicago with a band led by Sonny Boy Williamson (Rice Miller*).

The general weakness of his last titles, their deceptively folksy side, was bad for his reputation. Nevertheless, he was a very important bluesman, historically and artistically, and all his work deserves a special reevaluation.

LYNN WHITE

(b. 1953 / vocals)

The Deep South apparently harbors endless musical riches, even in places such as Mobile, Alabama. It is from this place that Lynn White emerged, a superb singer influenced by the blues, soul, and funk of artists such as B. B. King* and Aretha Franklin.

A church singer at an early age, she progressively turned to profane music, and she displayed her talents in the clubs around Mobile. It was thanks to singer-composer-producer Ike Darby, whose record store she was managing, that she was able to record a series of 45s in 1977 collected on *Am I Too Much Woman for You?* (Darby). Wonderfully produced and properly and efficiently arranged with the help of very good local musicians, this record revealed an expressive singer with a suave and acid voice suggestive of a modern Lil Green.* Particularly effective in the slow blues like "Blues in My Bedroom," Lynn White had some local success with a more rhythmic piece, "I Didn't Make My Move Too Soon," a mischievous answer to a ferocious macho blues of B. B. King, which enabled her to go on tours with the latter.

Under the wing of producer Willie Mitchell, she became a star in the South, establishing herself as the soul-blueswoman "who is never at a loss for words." "I Wanna See Your Face Again," "Love and Happiness," and "Caught You with Your Love Down," this time in answer to Bobby Rush, were local hits. She still lacks national and international recognition. Her four albums for Mayo are first-rate, and for the most part they are available on two compact discs: "Yes! I'm Ready" (Waylo) and "Love and Happiness" (Waylo).

ROBERT WILKINS

(1896–1987 / vocals, guitar)

Not as well known as some other big names of the prewar Memphis blues, Robert Wilkins' talent, however, equaled Furry Lewis's.* Born in Mississippi, Wilkins came to live in Memphis when he was very young. He remained there until his death, a patriarch reigning over a sizeable family.

After having played with all the great artists of Memphis (Furry Lewis, Frank Stokes,* Jim Jackson,* Memphis Minnie*), Robert Wilkins was contacted in 1928 by Ralph Peer, who was seeking new talents for the Brunswick company. He then recorded several songs, one of them was "Rolling Stone," a blues in two parts. Its success in the South made its author the first black American to host a regular radio program. Robert Wilkins recorded a few more songs in 1935 without success. Then he devoted himself to several activities and became a Methodist minister in the forties. He kept on playing within the scope of his religious duties.

In 1964, a mere glance in the phone book by a fan resulted in his "rediscovery," and he performed at the Newport Festival the same year. If Reverend Robert Wilkins' voice took on the vehement inflections of sung sermons and if he devoted himself only to a religious repertoire, he was also a great musician in full possession of all his capabilities, whom the public of the Newport Festival acclaimed. His guitar style was even more brilliant than it had been thirty years before: a flawless fingerpicking style that enriched considerably the melodious progression. His bottleneck style, "Hawaiian style," was also impressive. His virtuosity was reminiscent of that other reverend, Gary Davis,* whom apparently he had never met.

Except for when the Rolling Stones covered his composition "The Prodigal Son," bringing him some substantial royalties, Robert Wilkins did not really take advantage of his rediscovery.

The Original Rolling Stone (Herwin) with his first recordings and *Memphis Gospel Singer* (OJL), made in 1964, are indispensible. There remain quite a few recordings made by Wilkins in the sixties and seventies that were never released.

BILL WILLIAMS

See East Coast Blues

BIG JOE WILLIAMS

(Joe Lee Williams / 1903–1982 / vocals, guitar)

Until the last moments of his life Big Joe Williams was still active as one of the last great bluesmen. A living legend, he performed in the most sordid ghetto clubs and at huge festivals with the same conviction for more than sixty years as a professional!

He was among the rare artists of his generation who never got flustered by the often extremely cold atmosphere of the European concert halls. It was an unforgettable experience to have seen him alone, vehemently singing the poignant themes he had collected or composed during his stays in the penitentiary of Angola, Louisiana, along the railroad construction sites, or with the itinerant musical groups who, around 1920, traveled all over the United States. He created an intense dramatic atmosphere through his fierce singing and his rhythmic style with a marked bass line interspersed with quick high notes that he reached on his old nine-string guitar.

Born in Crawford, Mississippi, he settled in St. Louis (after several tribulations) in 1925. There, he became friends with St. Louis singer Bessie Smith,* guitar player Henry Townsend,* and the popular pianist Walter Davis,* whom he often accompanied. Davis, a confirmed star of Bluebird records, took Big Joe Williams in 1935 to Chicago to record. Despite reservations of the producers about that primitive artist when fashion was in favor of sophisticated musicians, Big Joe recorded six songs. One of his compositions that became a blues classic, "Baby, Please Don't Go," was a big hit, and after that time Big Joe did not stop recording. Between 1938 and 1947, his association with harmonica player John Lee "Sonny Boy" Williamson* produced some blues masterpieces.

After the war, Big Joe was everywhere: in Chicago where he recorded for Vee-Jay, in Jackson where he recorded for Trumpet, in Shreveport for Specialty, and in St. Louis for Bullet. Everywhere and all the time, he lived off his music. He was "discovered" by the white public in 1957; he performed in tours, festivals, and concerts and became a talent scout for the Testament, Storyville, and Adelphi companies. He traveled to Europe many times, and he recorded several dozens of albums.

His recorded work is considerable. *Big Joe Williams* (Mamlish) and *Big Joe Williams and Sonny Boy Williamson* (RCA) include his titles recorded between 1935 and 1947. After the blues revival, *Tough Times* (Arhoolie); *Thinking of What They Did to Me* (Arhoolie), recorded with a brilliant Charlie Musselwhite*; and "Nine String Guitar Blues" (Delmark) may be his best albums.

ROBERT PETE WILLIAMS

(1914–1981 / vocals, guitar)

When the ethnomusicologist Harry Oster entered the Angola penitentiary in 1958 to record the inmates singing, he did not expect to find an artist as good as Robert Pete Williams. Williams had been there for two years while serving a life sentence, and he had never been a professional musician nor had he planned on being one.

However, he was one of the best representatives of the country blues that Oster had just discovered. Robert Pete Williams' music was so totally original and personal that only his singing, totally impassive though deeply moving, linked him to a blues tradition of the Southwest represented by Lil' Son Jackson.* Otherwise, the rest of his music is unique, and it is not possible to link it with any known trend. He played a progression in D minor, not common in the blues, and created a complex and insistent rhythmic pattern. Above all, Robert Pete Williams was a creator full of an extraordinary spontaneity: He never played any of his blues twice because they reflected musically and textually his mood at the time. For that, his lyrical improvisations reached poetic peaks, unequaled in the blues.

The extraordinary titles recorded by Williams in the Angola penitentiary are on *Angola's Prisoner's Blues* (Arhoolie) and *Those Prison Blues* (Arhoolie). One of the half-spoken titles by Williams, "Prisoner's Talking Blues," a true poem about despair, is a great blues masterpiece.

Robert Pete Williams was finally paroled largely thanks to Oster's intervention, similar to what Lomax had done for Leadbelly.* On probation in a forced residence at the home of a Louisiana farmer, he recorded the very beautiful *Free Again* (Prestige). He then performed in his first big concert at the Newport Festival in 1964. The general public was amazed to discover a singer with such rare dramatic intensity and force.

Williams then performed in numerous concerts, festivals, and European tours, living a quiet life between his music and his farm. He was amply recorded and, due to better living conditions, his tours exposed him to other blues styles, and his work became more eclectic and less dramatic, creating a place in history as one of the best rural postwar bluesmen.

JOHN LEE "SONNY BOY" WILLIAMSON

(1914–1948 / vocals, harmonica)

Although some of the first bluesmen had used the harmonica with impressive skill (especially Jaybird Coleman), it was John Lee Williamson who really made it an essential instrument of the blues. Using the harmonica as the main instrument meant a change for the other instruments: the guitar and the harmonica answer each other, the other instruments (second guitar, then successively the piano, the bass, and the drums) are used as a rhythm section. This formula set by Sonny Boy between 1937 and 1940 characterized the postwar Chicago blues, made famous through such bluesmen as Little Walter,★ Muddy Waters,★ and the Rolling Stones. So Sonny Boy Williamson's importance in blues history is significant, and in general it is recognized by all, critics and musicians.

Born in Tennessee, John Lee Williamson, nicknamed "Sonny Boy" because of his young age, learned to play the harmonica in Memphis, from Hammie Nixon and Noah Lewis in particular. He played with Sleepy John Estes★ (he imitated his vocal style), Yank Rachell,★ and his cousin, "Homesick" James Williamson.★ In 1935 he went to Chicago and was discovered by producer Lester Melrose, who, in 1937, recorded him for Bluebird with Robert Lee McCoy (Robert Nighthawk★) in a series of titles among which was his famous "Good Morning, Little Schoolgirl," later covered by dozens of blues and rock musicians. During that session, as well as those in 1938, the "sound" of Sonny Boy was still that of the rural blues, with emphasis on the harmonica and with the powerful Big Joe Williams★ as a rhythm guitarist.

After the incredible success of "Good Morning, Little Schoolgirl" Sonny Boy recorded dozens of records each year, almost nonstop. A friend of the prewar Chicago blues giant, Big Bill Broonzy,★ he played the role left vacant by the relative decline of the latter. He was at the turning point of the Chicago blues, welcoming and giving advice to new musicians like Muddy Waters, Forest City Joe, and Billy Boy Arnold.★ He was the master of the local scene, and as an artist he was deeply appreciated by his public. Sonny Boy's generosity and kindness permeated his blues, which generally were masterpieces of mischievous humor and poetry. "Dealing with the Devil," "Cold Chills," "Early in the Morning," "Bluebird Blues," "Checkin' Up on My Baby," and "Stop Breaking Down" became classics, but almost all his work was inspired and deserves to be listened to carefully. When he let himself play easier pieces ("Mellow Chick Swing" and "Polly, Put Your Kettle On"), he engaged in breathtaking harmonica feats. That, and his particular vocal style of mumbling the words unexpectedly, made his music irresistible. His music never stopped evolving; after 1945 the electrification of all instruments, including his harmonica, added a new dimension to it. It was a definitely urban blues but also aggressive, retaining and amplifying the force of the rural blues, far from the polished sounds of most "established" artists of the Chicago blues, whose popularity was certainly decreasing.

Although Sonny Boy was murdered at the peak of his fame, at age thirty-four, he left an unmistakable mark on blues history and a considerable influence on the artists (his themes have been, and still are, covered by many performers, in Chicago and elsewhere, and some harmonica players totally inspired by him like Billy Boy Arnold and Snooky Pryor★).

His essential work is today available: *Sonny Boy Williamson, Vols. 1, 2 & 3* (Blues Classics); *Throw a Boogie Woogie* (RCA), a compact disc he shared with Big Joe Williams; and *Rare Sonny Boy* (RCA/Bluebird). Williamson's recorded work is available in its entirety in chronological order on a five-CD set on the Document label.

SONNY BOY WILLIAMSON

(ca. 1910–1965 / Alex "Rice" Miller / vocals, harmonica)

Blues historians will have a hard time defining the real identity of this superb bluesman. Indeed, not only did Rice Miller take the name of the original John Lee "Sonny Boy" Williamson,★ but he also claimed that the other one was a hoax and not the real Sonny Boy Williamson! His numerous trips to Europe at the end of his life only added to the confusion: He would tell anybody anything, and only because of the tenacity of a few (in particular, Mike Leadbitter, the founder of the review *Blues Unlimited*) are we able to know his story.

Born in Mississippi, he led a life as an itinerant musician for nearly thirty years, gathering influences and perfecting one of the most brilliant and polished harmonica styles ever. In the thirties and forties, he knew and played with Robert Johnson,★ Howlin' Wolf,★ Robert Nighthawk,★ Robert Jr. Lockwood,★ and Houston Stackhouse. He traveled through Arkansas, Mississippi, and Missouri. After the war (and irregularly until his death), he hosted a daily radio program, "King Biscuit Time," broadcast from Helena, Arkansas.

Despite unquestionable popularity in the South, he recorded for the first time only after 1951, teaming with Elmore James★ to record the famous "Dust My Broom" and, under his own name, about twenty songs for the small Trumpet label of Jackson, Mississippi.

His first recordings (on *King Biscuit Hour:* Arhoolie, *Clowning with the World:* Trumpet) already have the qualities of Sonny Boy: an extraordinary instrumental virtuosity, an ability to create in an instant a romantic or dramatic climate, a sarcastic voice insinuating mischievously original, eloquent, and witty compositions. It was this devastating humor, an integral part of his style, that distinguished him from his peers. He was a great musician, but he was also a satirical poet.

The quality of his first recordings was heightened when Sonny Boy signed a contract with Chess in 1955 and recorded in Chicago with the best blues musicians of the city: Muddy Waters,★ Jimmy Rogers,★ Fred Below,★ pianists Lafayette Leake and Otis Spann,★ and his two favorite guitarists, Robert Jr. Lockwood★ and Luther Tucker. Pieces like "Don't Start Me to Talking," "The Key," "Nine Below Zero," "Checkin' Up on My Baby," "Bring It on Home," and "Help Me" are some of the most accomplished masterpieces of postwar blues, and they have become classics.

In 1963, Sonny Boy performed in the second tour of the American Folk Blues Festival, captivating fans with his stage presence and his flair for shows. He stayed in Europe for several months and performed in numerous concerts with American musicians and British groups, such as the Yardbirds and the Animals.

His role in the creation of the British blues-rock of the sixties is certainly not to be ignored. Despite his definite desire to "make London his home," Sonny Boy was back in Arkansas in 1965, long enough to host a few more shows of his "King Biscuit Hour" with his old friends drummer James "Peck" Curtis and guitarist Houston Stackhouse. He died in bed that same year.

Sonny Boy Williamson's work was incredible, and he

appears today as one of the great musicians in blues history. An uncommon personality, a musical genius, Sonny Boy Williamson was too individualistic to be a leader like his homonym or like Little Walter, although his influence was obvious upon harmonica players such as James Cotton* and Junior Parker.* His only flaw was not making a name for himself and thinking that he had to borrow that of John Lee Williamson to have his talent recognized.

The whole of his work is available on several collections. *The Chess Years* (Charly) includes all his songs in a boxed set. *Down and Out Blues* (Chess), *The Real Folk Blues* (Chess), and *More Real Folk Blues* (Chess) include only his classics.

The Blues of Sonny Boy Williamson (Storyville) contains half of a wonderful acoustic session made toward the end of his life. Finally, *Sonny Boy Williamson and the Yardbirds* (L+R), of uneven value musically speaking, is a historic recording: it was the first recording of a black bluesman with young British performers. One can listen to the first steps of a sober and efficient Eric Clapton.

RALPH WILLIS

See New York

EDITH WILSON

See Female Blues Singers

JIMMY WILSON

See California

JOHNNY WINTER

See White Blues

JIMMY WITHERSPOON

(b. 1923 / vocals)

This blues shouter, today somewhat forgotten, has displayed his talent in all contexts: jazz, rock, and even pop. But he is most comfortable in the blues.

Influenced at first by Big Joe Turner,* whose friendly rival he'll always be, Witherspoon began his professional career between 1941 and 1945. Stationed as a marine in Calcutta, he performed with the band Chic of Teddy Weatherford at the Winter Gardens Hotel.

When demobilized he decided to start to sing professionally. He moved to California, teamed up with band leader and piano player Jay McShann,* replacing singer Walter Brown.*

His beautiful, warm, and melodious voice quickly made him popular thanks to several pieces, among which was a wonderful adaptation of "Ain't Nobody's Business."

After 1952, when he broke up with McShann, Witherspoon started a many-sided and prolific career; he recorded in all genres, from the pop of Lou Rawls to rock (with Jessie Stone or Eric Burdon) to the spirituals (with the Trinity Baptist Choir). Usually recognized as a jazz singer, he recorded with Earl Hines, Ben Webster, Coleman Hawkins, Gerry Mulligan, and Buddy Tate for many labels.

He has been sick for several years and has been performing only sporadically. But at his peak, his voice was one of the "smoothest in America."

Many of his best and most bluesy sides have been reissued on CD: *Blowin' in from Kansas City* (Ace), *Jay's Blues* (Charly), and *Spoon So Easy* (Chess).

JOHNNY WOODS

See R. L. Burnside

OSCAR "BUDDY" WOODS

(ca. 1890–1950 / vocals, guitar)

Although the use of the Hawaiian guitar became common in rural white American music in the form of the Dobro, it seems that few bluesmen have used it. Oscar Woods was one of the main representatives of this style, and he may have been the most accomplished one. His recordings show a complete mastery of this difficult instrument with which he ventured many times beyond the blues into the difficult area of ragtime.

The only period of his life that we know well shows him as

a singer in the streets of Shreveport, Louisiana, where he demonstrated his guitar technique, played flat, to Black Ace* and Strozer Quinn. His reputation as a musician was considerable: The Decca and Vocalion companies recorded him three times from 1936 to 1938, either by himself or with a small group of musicians. All of these titles, about ten, are today considered classics, in particular, *Lone Wolf Blues* and *Don't Sell It, Don't Give It Away,* whose modernism is amazing.

Another proof of his fame: The famous country music singer Jimmie Davis, who was to become the governor of Louisiana, the author of "You Are My Sunshine," chose him as a lead guitarist on his first and superb recordings, inspired largely by the Texas blues.

In 1940 folklorists working for the Library of Congress discovered him; they recorded him substantially in the streets of Shreveport. Unfortunately, he disappeared after the war, and it seems that he died in the fifties. Between blues and country music—he anticipated western swing—Oscar Woods certainly deserves more attention from specialists and from the record companies which have his original recordings.

Rockin' Blues (Bear Family) and *Barnyard Stomp* (Bear Family) show Woods with Jimmie Davis. These very good sessions have a few pleasant surprises to those who do not know them.

The bluesman Woods—supposing we can qualify him as such—can be heard on: *Country Blues Bottleneck Guitar Classics* (Yazoo), *The Voice of the Blues* (Yazoo), *Blues from the Western States* (Yazoo), *Out Came the Blues* (MCA), and *The Slide Guitar* (CBS/Sony).

BIG JOHN WRENCHER

(1924–1977 / vocals, harmonica)

This excellent harmonica player—despite his limitation caused by his disability—made himself widely known only toward the end of his life. However, he played continually in the clubs of the Chicago Southside for nearly forty years.

Introduced to the blues by Robert Jr. Lockwood* and Sonny Boy Williamson (Rice Miller),* this gentle giant worked in a factory in Detroit (his most famous composition is "Goin' to Detroit"), but he played in the Southside, often at the flea market in Maxwell Street with Robert Nighthawk* and Johnny Young.* In 1958 he was injured in a car accident and his left arm was amputated; he became a professional musician out of necessity. A few titles recorded for several small labels and for producer Pete Welding helped to finally establish him among the white fans for whom he recorded two good albums: *Maxwell Street Alley* (Barrelhouse), with an incredible down home atmosphere, and *Big John's Boogie* (Bear), on which Eddie Taylor* was brilliant.

O. V. WRIGHT

See Soul

■
Y

JIMMY YANCEY

See Boogie-Woogie

MIGHTY JOE YOUNG

(b. 1927 / vocals, guitar)

"Mighty Joe," who is in no way similar to King Kong's rival, although he was given that nickname, was born in Shreveport, Louisiana. After a short stay in Milwaukee in the forties he moved to Chicago where he developed his guitar style combining the modernism of B. B. King* and the tradition of the Deep South bands of Howlin' Wolf,* Jimmy Rogers,* and Billy Boy Arnold.* He recorded a few obscure titles with Rogers and Billy Boy under his own name for Chess, Atomic-H, and Jiffy before he completely changed his guitar style, influenced by the Chicago West Side sound. He played a significant role in the creation of this style that is usually linked to Otis Rush* and Magic Sam.*

His expressive and generous style, his perfect coordination with the powerful band that surrounded him, enabled him to perform more as the featured player in numerous concerts and festivals in the United States and abroad. It also allowed him to record as the sideman with a great number of blues and soul artists (Magic Sam, Koko Taylor,* Lucille Spann, Detroit Junior,* Tyrone Davis, and Willie Mabon*). His own production is unfortunately low in quantity (five albums) but high in quality. *Blues with a Touch of Soul* (Delmark) anticipated the Chicago blues of the eighties; *Legacy of the Blues* (Sonet/GNP Crescendo), more traditional, is nevertheless an impressive success; and finally, *Chicken Heads* (Ovation) is one of the best soul-blues albums ever made, but unfortunately it is also hard to find.

Young today should be on a major label and enjoy the fruits of the music he helped to create at the same time as Jimmy Johnson* and Lonnie Brooks.* But, sick and having apparently left Chicago, he has not been recording for about ten years.

JOHNNY YOUNG

(1918–1974 / vocals, mandolin, guitar)

Johnny Young was one of the few mandolin players who was active on the postwar blues scene. His technique on that instrument distanced itself more and more from that of the string bands of the twenties and thirties. He developed a note by note melody line, which on his electric mandolin produced a sound similar to that of electric guitarists in the style of B. B. King.* Furthermore, Johnny Young was an excellent singer with a warm and expressive voice, whose inflections alone could give life to recordings.

Born in Mississippi and raised in Tennessee, Young was first influenced by the Mississippi Sheiks,* Memphis Minnie,* and the McCoy* brothers. Young brought this Tennessee atmosphere with him to Chicago in 1946. He was one of the first bluesmen to lead an electric band in Chicago and also one of the first southern immigrants to record several 78s in 1947–48 in the nascent style of the postwar Chicago blues.

Although he did not record from 1948 to 1963, Young performed regularly with his small band at the Maxwell Street flea market. There, he met producer Pete Welding, who recorded him and gave him new engagements. Within a few years Young became a popular figure in the festivals and concerts of the blues revival, during which his volubility, his dynamism, and his good-naturedness assured him constant success. From 1969 until he died, Young was a regular in the band of the young white piano player Bob Riedy with whom he appeared on the excellent *Lake Michigan Ain't No River* (Rounder).

Young recorded substantially after 1963. *Chicago Blues* (Arhoolie) is a great album on which Young and Big Walter Horton* are impressive. *Johnny Young and His Chicago Blues Band* (Arhoolie) teamed Young with the Muddy Waters blues band of that time (Otis Spann* and James Cotton* especially). *Johnny Young and His Friends* (Testament) is more introspective. It would be great to see a reissue of *Can't Keep from Jumping* (Bluesway), an album that showcases Young's mandolin style.

ZORA YOUNG

(b. 1948 / vocals)

One of the most refreshing developments in the blues toward the end of the seventies was the comeback of female voices: Joyce Cobb (also an excellent harmonica player), Vera Cobb, Lynn White,* and Jessie Mae Hemphill* in the South; the late Arelean Brown (a subtle singer and a remarkable composer), Jeanne Carroll, Sylvia Embry,* and Bonnie Lee in Chicago. Margie Evans in California seems to have added some femininity to a music which, with a few notable exceptions (Koko Taylor* and Big Mama Thornton*) had become almost exclusively masculine; the black female singers had essentially turned to soul, disco, and funk.

In fact, Zora Young came from this more modern and commercial music. Born in West Point, Mississippi, she sang in the church choirs before she came to Chicago in 1957. Influenced by Aretha Franklin and Gladys Knight, she decided to become a professional singer, and from 1970 on she performed in several Chicago clubs. There, she was discovered by Bobby King, an excellent singer and guitar player, who asked her to sing in his band. As with many bluesmen of that time, Bobby King had to divide his show into two parts in order to keep his public: He took care of the blues and instrumental parts, while Zora sang the recent Top 40 hits. She tried unsuccessfully to have a career like Donna Summer, but was drawn more and more to the blues. In the Chicago clubs, she met drummer Jump Jackson, Willie Dixon,* Junior Wells,* and Koko Taylor, who influenced her and urged her to devote herself more to the blues. She took part in a women's rally in Chicago and sang from then on at concerts, festivals, and nightclubs. In 1981 her performance in the very interesting French tour "Blues with the Girls" attracted the attention of fans. Her beautiful mezzo-soprano voice with sensuous inflections, as well as her stage presence and a certain mischievous nature, attracted recognition on the album *Blues with the Girls* (EPM). After an interesting 45 on Airway, Sunnyland Slim's* label, Zora recorded another good album: *Stumbling Blocks and Stepping Stones* (Blue Sting). Quite obviously, she has the ability to do even better and to assert herself as one of the important blues artists of the nineties.

VALERIE WELLINGTON (b. 1959), born in Chicago, sings in a vein similar to that of Zora Young. She has also taken the road that has become almost common now among the young blacks who are turning back to the blues. From dance music to soul to the blues, it was not until she met Ma Rainey* through a theater play that she came to know the music of her grandparents. *Million Dollar Secret* (Rooster Blues), recorded with John Littlejohn* and Magic Slim,* certainly suggests more good things to come.

BIG TIME SARAH STREETER (b. 1953), born in Coldwater, Mississippi, had the experiences of church choirs, soul, and Sunnyland Slim before she became a blueswoman noticed in Chicago and throughout Europe where she went on several tours. Her musical performance in the X-rated film with the buxom Seka enabled her to record a good album: *Undecided* (Blues R&B). She too should give us more.

BONNIE LEE (Bonnie Bevely / b. 1931) sang in Louisiana and in Texas before she came to settle in Chicago. She has recorded for several small labels (Ebony, Airway, and Black Beauty), but she is still waiting to make her first album. Her vocal register, close to Ruth Brown's* and Koko Taylor's, and her writing talents should also ensure her recognition very soon.

▪ Z

ZYDECO

Cajun music has known a renewal of popularity in North America as well as in France, where this rousing and dynamic music of the remote French-speaking cousins is thought of highly. Next to Cajun music itself, there is a black branch, zydeco, which at first was not differentiated from the white music. After the Second World War zydeco evolved considerably, getting closer to blues, rhythm and blues, and soul.

In fact, zydeco did not emerge until the late forties, and today it represents a small musical movement, practiced in Acadia, a parish near Lafayette, one of the main towns of Cajun country.

The Cajuns came from the "big disorder" of the mid-eighteenth century when the English, unable to curb the revolts of the Acadians (the former French colonists who had settled in the maritime province of Canada), decided to deport them en masse. Some of the Acadians were sent to England to rot in jail; others were sent back to France (where they would often secretly leave again for Canada); and still others were disembarked in small groups along the harbors of the Atlantic Coast of the English colonies in America. Most of them traveled to Louisiana, which was then still French. There they encountered colonists who had already settled and become middle-class; with no other place to settle, they were left to colonize the neighboring bayous, a big, deep, unhealthy swamp peopled by a handful of Indians. The Acadians—

■ Rockin' Sidney. *(Photograph © by Paul Harris; used with permission)*

Cajuns by corruption—needed manpower for their plans to populate the area, and they recruited some free blacks of New Orleans, who quickly adopted the French language, the Catholic religion, and the customs of the Acadians, to the point of looking and acting like real Cajuns! Because they had never owned slaves, the Acadians accepted these blacks as an integral part of their community, and they shared their cleared land with them. This is how, far in the bayous, completely isolated from the rest of the world, a real Cajun culture developed, which was mainly musical and gastronomic. Because few Cajuns knew how to read or write, they transformed their French into a particular dialect that was different from that which is spoken today in the maritime provinces where the Acadians come from.

The Civil War and the racial tensions in the South were insignificant in the Cajun country where blacks and whites lived the same way and side by side. At the musical level, Amédée (Amade) Ardoin was the first black Cajun to have recorded in New Orleans for Decca in the twenties, but his music is impossible to separate from that of white Cajuns such as Joe Falcon. It is a rural dance music that rests on the French-Canadian tradition with a few borrowings: Irish, German (the accordion was necessary, of course), Caribbean, Mexican, and African. In fact, Cajun music before the war had nothing to do with the blues.

After the war, the Cajun country opened to the outside world: economically, socially, and culturally. Segregation—which had never occurred as such in Acadia—influenced the way Cajuns and blacks evolved. The Cajuns, whose basic food consisted of beans (zarico), were more and more despised and called by that vegetable name, zydecos, that had already appeared in a Cajun song title, *Zydeco et pas salé* (The beans are not salted). There was also an important musical connection with country music (thanks to the radio show, "Louisiana Hayride," broadcast from Shreveport), an area in which many white Cajun artists made a name for themselves (e.g., Jimmy C. Newman, Al Terry, and Doug Kershaw) and added to it their own sound. In a similar movement, black Cajuns became more and more interested in the blues and in rhythm and blues. But since things are never simple in American music and in Acadia even less simple than anywhere else, it was a white man, Nathan Abshire, who recorded the first genuine Cajun blues ("Pine Grove Blues"). Zydeco, springing from this black differentiation, retains a considerable amount of traditional Cajun elements.

The relationship of zydeco with blues and rhythm and blues has been considered insignificant for a long time. But these connections were asserted by such artists as Phillip Walker* and Lonesome Sundown* and by Louisiana producers—J. D. Miller,* Floyd Soileau, Huey Meaux—hoping to have their records on the national market.

Clarence Garlow* with "New Bon Ton Roula," Boozoo Chavis with "Paper in My Shoe," and even Fats Domino* (proudly claimed locally) managed to pave the way for future Cajun performers such as Clifton Chenier,* who found in Chris Strachwitz the attentive and clever producer who would shepherd him to national and international recognition.

The interest shown to Chenier's zydeco in California, on the East Coast, and in Europe has enabled this small musical trend to develop. The disappearance of "King" Chenier brought about serious competition for his crown; zydeco records played all the time on the black stations of Louisiana. The extraordinary success of "My Toot Toot" by Rockin' Sidney* in 1985 brought even more listeners, artists, and records.

ROCKIN' DOPSIE (Alton Rubin / b. 1932) is the most serious candidate to succeed Chenier. A veteran of many local bands, this powerful accordion player and pleasant singer does not, however, have the charisma nor the creative power of his model. He has recorded many excellent albums: *Big Bad Zydeco* (GNP), *Rockin' Dopsie and the Twisters* (Rounder), and the compact disc *Saturday Night Zydeco* (Maison de Soul).

FERNEST ARCENEAUX (b. 1940), born in Lafayette to an old family of accordion players, is also a talented musician on that instrument and a convincing down-home singer. His modest status at the local level contrasts with the reputation he has in Europe thanks to Robert Sacre's efforts. We recommend strongly *Zydeco Stomp* (JSP) on compact disc.

BOBBY PRICE (b. 1943) has often sung in Fernest Arceneaux's band. Very close to the Louisiana blues roots of Lightnin' Slim, he is often considered to be the star of the band, and he has recorded the good album *Two Trains a Runnin'* (Blues Unlimited).

BUCKWHEAT (Stanley Dural / b. 1947), a singer, accordion player, piano player, and organ player, helped bring zydeco and soul closer together. Dynamic and very popular, he draws the crowds; his band "Ils sont partis" is hard to stop once it lets "le bon temps rouler." As comfortable in the old Cajun repertoire as in an irresistible funky zydeco, Buckwheat is still a powerful asset of zydeco today. The first-rate *100% Fortified Zydeco* (Black Top), *On a Night Like This* (Island), and *Buckwheat's Zydeco Party* (Rounder) must not make us forget his first albums for the *Blues Unlimited* label: "Ils sont partis" and "Take It Easy Baby."

C. J. CHENIER (b. 1957), King Clifton's son, is also a formidable candidate to succeed his father. A superb singer and a dynamic accordion player, he also has the advantage of leading his late father's band. *Let Me in Your Heart* (Arhoolie) is an impressive recording debut.

MAJOR HANDY (b. 1949), a wonderful singer with a sensuous voice and also a good accordion player, is the author of several beautiful compositions that combined zydeco tradition with the Chicago West Side sound ("I Won't Be Home for Christmas"). If his 45s for the J. J. Caillier label are impressive, his first album, *Wolf Couchon* (GNP), is far less. He must do better.

Let's not forget the veteran BOOZOO CHAVIS (Wilson Chavis / b. 1930) who opened the way for all the others. His music is more primitive and closer to white Cajun than that of his younger emulators, but it is hard to equal his dynamism and good humor. On a good day (sober, but not too sober), he is capable of a tour de force like *Paper in My Shoe* (Maison de Soul) and *Zydeco Homebrew* (Maison de Soul).

Finally, somewhat separate from the others and playing mostly in California, QUEEN IDA (Ida Guillory) combines zydeco, country, and rock-and-roll with unequal results. Very popular around Los Angeles where a rather significant Cajun community lives, Queen Ida has produced the excellent *Cookin' with Queen Ida* (GNP), *Zydeco* (GNP), and *On a Saturday Night* (GNP). The singer of the group, Al Rapone, is often clearly attuned to country music.

These artists as well as others like Morris Francis, Sampy, Wilfrid Chevis, Marcel Dugas, Willie Davis, Walter Polite, the Sam Brothers Five, Zydeco Incorporated (their incredible "Le bon graton" was a great hit in Acadia), and Harry Hippolyte also record regularly for a local market, geographically limited but blooming commercially. Veteran producers J. D. Miller and his son Mark, J. J. Caillier, Eddie Shuler, and Floyd Soileau have never been better.

■ Washboard Willie. *(Photograph © by Anton J. Mikofsky; used with permission) See* Detroit.

▪ BIBLIOGRAPHY

The blues was the object of more publications in the last decade than during the previous six. And some give a special place to recent research and new syntheses. In this bibliography we selected only the most important titles from the many in existence.

I. DISCOGRAPHIES

Down Home Music Blues & Gospel Catalog. El Cerrito, Ca.: Down Home Music, 1989.

Godrich, J., and R. M. W. Dixon. *Blues and Gospel Records 1902–43.* London: Storyville, 1983.

Leadbitter, Mike, and Neil Slaven. *Blues Records 1943–70, Vols. 1 & 2.* London: RIS, 1987–90.

Ruppli, Michael. *The Chess Labels, Vols. 1 & 2.* Westport, Conn.: Greenwood, 1983.

Scott, Frank. *Down Home Guide to the Blues.* El Cerrito, Ca: Acappella, 1991.

II. BOOKS ABOUT THE BLUES

Arnaudon, Jean-Claude. *Dictionnaire du blues.* Paris: Filipacchi, 1977.

Baker, Houston A., Jr. *Blues, Ideology and Afro-American Literature: A Vernacular Theory.* Chicago: The University of Chicago Press, 1984.

Bane, Michael. *White Boy Singin' the Blues.* London: Penguin, 1982.

Barlow, William. *Looking Up at Down: The Emergence of Blues Culture.* Philadelphia: Temple University Press, 1989.

Bas-Raberin, Phillippe. *Le Blues moderne, 1945–79.* Paris: Albin Michel, 1979.

Evans, David. *Big Road Blues.* Los Angeles: University of California, 1981.

Finn, Julio. *The Bluesman: The Musical Heritage of Black Men and Women in the Americas.* London: Quartet Books, 1986.

Grossman, Stefan, and Stefan Calt. *The Country Blues Songbook.* New York: Oak, 1973.

Harris, Sheldon. *Blues Who's Who?* New York: Arlington, 1979.

Herzhaft, Gérard. *Le Blues.* Paris: Presses Universitaires de France, Que Sais-je?, 1986.

Levet, Jean-Pierre. *Talkin' That Talk.* Paris: Soul Bag, 1986.

Oakley, Giles. *The Devil's Music.* London: B. B. C., 1976.

Oliver, Paul. *The Story of the Blues.* London: Penguin, 1972.

———. *Blues Fell This Morning: The Meaning of the Blues.* New York: Horizon Press, 1983.

———. *Conversations with the Blues.* New York: Horizon Press, 1983.

———. *Songsters and Saints.* London: Cambridge University Press, 1984.

———. *Blues off the Record.* Turnbridge Wells: Baton Press, 1985.

Palmer, Robert. *Deep Blues.* New York: Viking, 1981.

Pearson, Barry Lee. *Sounds So Good to Me.* Philadelphia: University of Pennsylvania Press, 1984.

Springer, Robert. *Le Blues authentique.* Paris: L Filipacchi, 1985.

Yourcenar, Marguerite. *Blues and Gospels.* Paris: Gallimard, 1984.

III. THE REGIONS OF THE BLUES

Ancelet, Barry Jean. *The Makers of Cajun Music. Musiciens Cadiens et Créoles.* Austin: University of Texas Press, 1984.

Bastin, Bruce. *Red River Blues: The Blues Tradition in the Southeast.* London: MacMillan, 1986.

Berry, Jason, Jonathan Foote, and Tad Jones. *Up from the Cradle of Jazz: New Orleans Music since World War II.* Athens, Ga.: The University of Georgia Press, 1986.

Broven, John. *Rhythm & Blues in New Orleans.* Gretna, La: Pelican, 1978.

———. *South to Louisiana.* Gretna, La.: Pelican, 1983.

Brunning, Bob. *Blues: The British Connection.* Poole, Great Britain: Blendford, 1986.

Escott, Colin, and Martin Hawkins. *Catalyst: The Sun Story.* New York: Music Sales, 1979.

Ferris, William. *Blues from the Delta.* New York: Doubleday, 1979.

Govenar, Alan. *Meeting the Blues: The Rise of the Texas Sound.* Dallas: Taylor, 1988.

Hannusch, Jeff. *I Hear You Knockin': The Sound of New Orleans.* Ville Platte, La.: Swallow, 1985.

Pearson, Nathan W. *Goin' to Kansas City.* Urbana, Ill.: University of Illinois Press, 1987.

Rowe, Mike. *Chicago Breakdown.* New York: Da Capo, 1981.

Sacre, Robert, Ed. *The Voice of the Delta.* Liège, France: Presses Universitaires de Liège, 1987.

Savoy, Ann Ellen. *Cajun Music: A Reflection of a People.* Eunice, La.: Bluebird Press, 1984.

IV. THE BLUESMEN

Berry, Chuck. *Chuck Berry: The Autobiography.* New York: Harmony, 1987.

Broonzy, Big Bill, and Yannick Bruynoghe. *Big Bill Blues.* Paris: Ludd, 1987.

Calt, Stefan, and Gayle Wardlow. *King of the Delta Blues: The Life and Music of Charlie Patton.* Newton, NJ: Rock Chapel Press, 1988.

Charters, Sam. *The Bluesmen.* New York: Oak, 1967.

Dance, Helen. *Stormy Monday: The T-Bone Walker Story.* Baton Rouge: Louisiana State University Press, 1987.

Evans, David. *Tommy Johnson.* London: Studio Vista, 1971.

Guralnick, Peter. *Feel Like Going Home.* New York: Outerbridge, 1984.

Harrisson, Daphne Duval. *Black Pearls: Blues Queens of the 1920s.* New Brunswick, NJ: Rutgers University Press, 1988.

Herzhaft, Gérard. *Un long blues en la mineur.* Paris: Ramsay, 1986. *Long Blues in A minor.* Translated by John DuVal. Fayetteville: University of Arkansas Press, 1988.

Joseph, Pleasant, and Harriet J. Ottenheimer. *Cousin Joe: Blues from New Orleans.* Chicago: University of Chicago Press, 1987.

Lubin, Jacques, and Danny Garçon. *Louis Jordan.* Paris: Soul Bag, 1989.

Sawyer, Charles. *The Arrival of B. B. King.* New York: Doubleday, 1980.

Shaw, Arnold. *Honkers and Shouters.* New York: MacMillan, 1978.

Turner, Tina, and Kurt Loder. *I, Tina, My Life Story.* New York: Wm. Morrow & Co., 1986.

White, Charles. *The Life and Times of Little Richard.* New York: Crown, 1984.

Wilson, August. *Ma Rainey's Black Bottom.* New York: New American Library, 1985.

V. BOOKS OUTSIDE THE BLUES

Carles, Philippe, André Clergeat, and J. L. Comolli. *Dictionnaire du Jazz.* Paris: Laffont, 1988.

George, Nelson. *The Death of Rhythm and Blues.* New York: Pantheon, 1988.

Gillett, Charlie. *The Sound of the City.* New York: Panthéon, 1984.

Heilbut, Tony. *The Gospel Sound.* New York: Simon and Schuster, 1971.

Herzhaft, Gérard. *La Country Music.* Paris: Presses Universitaires de France, Que Sais-je?, 1984.

Hirshey, Gerri. *Nowhere to Run: The Story of Soul Music.* New York: Times Books, 1984.

Hofstein, Francis. *Au miroir du Jazz.* Paris: La Pierre, 1985.

Illustrated (The) Encyclopedia of Black Music. New York: Harmony, 1982.

Malson, Lucien. *Le Jazz.* Paris: Presses Universitaires de France, Que Sais-je?, 1989.

Shaw, Arnold. *Black Popular Music in America.* New York: Schirmer Books, 1986.

Southern, Eileen. *The Music of Black Americans.* New York: W. W. Norton, 1983.

Vassal, Jacques. *Folksong.* Paris: Albin Michel, 1984.

Wilson, Charles Reagan, and William Ferris, eds. *Encyclopedia of Southern Culture.* Chapel Hill: The University of North Carolina Press, 1989.

VI. REVIEWS AND MAGAZINES

Living Blues. The University of Mississippi. Center for the Study of Southern Culture, University, MS 38677.

Soul Bag. 25, rue Trezel, 92300, Levallois Perret (France).

And also: In Great Britain: *Juke Blues, Blues & Rhythm;* In Italy: *Il Blues, Feelin' Good;* In Holland: *Block;* In Germany: *Blues Forum;* In Austria: *Blues Life;* In Spain: *Solo Blues;* In Canada: *Toronto Blues*

Society; and In the United States: a great number of blues societies such as Tucson Blues Society, Phoenix, Arizona.

Let's not forget: *Down Home Music Newsletter,* 10341 San Pablo Avenue, El Cerrito, CA 94530, which covers a great part of the phonographic edition; *Black Music Research Journal,* Center for Black Music Research, Columbia College, Chicago, 600 S. Michigan Ave., Chicago, IL 60605; *The Southern Register,* Center for the Study of Southern Culture, University, MS 38677; and *Cadence Magazine; downbeat; Guitar Player;* and *Guitar World.*

▪ SELECT DISCOGRAPHY

Each entry of the *Encyclopedia of the Blues* includes a selected discography. But, because of the current maze of original editions, reissues, cover changes, and compilations in three formats, we chose not to give a numbered discographic reference. The original titles of the compilations are with the 1990 label whenever possible.

However, with the increased use of the compact disc, it may be helpful to make a discographic selection of the major titles available in this format.

So here are two hundred references of important records available in 1992 on compact disc; they may be used as a basis for the creation of a blues record collection. But the market evolves so quickly that all this is given with extreme caution.

LUTHER ALLISON: *Here I Come* (Encore ENC 133C)
> One of the best recent recordings by Allison. But we'd like to see on compact disc the LPs that were taken out of the catalogs a long time ago.

FERNEST ARCENEAUX: *Zydeco Stomp* (JSP CD 220)
> A serious selection of songs by this accordion player and singer, with a few significant titles similar to the swamp blues interpreted with much feeling by the late bass player Victor Walker.

CHUCK BERRY: *The Chuck Berry Chess Box* (Chess CH6 80001)
> These three compact discs of Chuck Berry's best titles recount his career for Chess, accompanied by Johnnie Johnson, Otis Spann, Fred Below, and Willie Dixon.

BOBBY BLAND: *Two Steps from the Blues* (MCA MCAD 27036)
> A good compilation of Bland's titles recorded for the Texas Duke

label. There are still many blues and other good things in the Bland of that time.

MICHAEL BLOOMFIELD: *The Best of Michael Bloomfield* (Takoma 72815-2)
The best available compilation by that strange and engaging musician who, once a rock superstar, always remained faithful to the blues of his beginnings.

BLUES AT NEWPORT (Vanguard 92024)
The early sixties blues revival brought many great country bluesmen, who, until then, were living in obscurity, to large new audiences, chiefly via the Newport Festival. This CD is not only of historical interest but also features fine perfomances by country blues masters.

TINY BRADSHAW: *Breaking up the House* (Charly CD 43)
One of the best blues shouters, Tiny Bradshaw's powerful sax solos are enough to make one shudder.

LONNIE BROOKS: *Bayou Lightning* (Alligator CD 4714)
The first and best album recorded by Lonnie for the label of Bruce Iglauer. His Louisiana roots show and, adjusted by the West Side of Chicago, they are sometimes irresistible.

BIG BILL BROONZY: *Big Bill's Blues* (Portrait CD 44089)
An excellent selection of the Columbia titles of this great singer and guitar player. Some brilliant sidemen such as electric guitar player George Barnes and piano player Memphis Slim accompany Broonzy.

BIG BILL BROONZY: *Good Time Tonight* (CBS/Sony 4672472)
Easily the best Big Bill compilation available. This is not Broonzy the folk singer of later years, but the thirties king of Chicago's ghettos, with jazzy guitar licks, declamatory vocals, and salty lyrics. Top-notch musicians surround Big Bill throughout this essential set.

CHARLES BROWN: *All My Life* (Bullseye Blues CD 9501)
This recent effort by Brown is one of his best. Cool, moving, after-hours blues. Proof that blues is certainly not merely flashing guitar solos.

CLARENCE "GATEMOUTH" BROWN: *Texas Swing* (Rounder CD 11527)

An excellent and generous compilation of the albums recorded by Brown for Rounder. Gatemouth may not be exactly what he was in the fifties, but the sound of his Texas guitar is impossible to imitate.

NAPPY BROWN: *Something Gonna Jump Out of the Bushes* (Black Top CD 1039)

With excellent production and accompaniment, Nappy Brown resurfaces as a blues shouter.

ROY BUCHANAN: *When a Guitar Plays the Blues* (Alligator CD 4711)

The best album of white blues recorded by this rock guitarist who went back to the blues before he died.

BUCKWHEAT: *Buckwheat's Zydeco Party* (Rounder CD 11528)

This rich compilation includes the best titles recorded for Rounder by this candidate to the crown of the zydeco king, Clifton Chenier, but it is not as good as his albums published by *Blues Unlimited*, which are available on CD.

PAUL BUTTERFIELD: *The Paul Butterfield Blues Band* (Elektra 7294-2)

This first great album of white American blues has somewhat aged, and it sometimes seems disorganized. But it is a historic recording, as the first blues album to have reached one million copies in sales.

EDDIE C. CAMPBELL: *Mind Trouble* (Double Trouble DTCD 3014)

King of the Jungle, Campbell's first album, is superb, but it is not available on CD. This one is only slightly inferior, and it provides an opportunity to listen to one of the best Chicago bluesmen still active.

LEROY CARR: *Blues before Sunrise* (Portrait RJ 44122)

A classic of the thirties. Carr accompanied by Scrapper Blackwell and Josh White—two of the greatest guitarists in blues history—in synch.

RAY CHARLES: *The Great Ray Charles* (Atlantic 81731-2)
One of the best selections of this singer-pianist, one of the greats of blues and rhythm and blues.

CLIFTON CHENIER: *Bayou Blues* (Specialty SPCD 2119-2)
The first recordings by the Bayou King. Charming and dynamic.

CLIFTON CHENIER: *Bogalusa Boogie* (Arhoolie CD 347)
The entire "Bogalusa" session on CD, with many tracks never before released. This is Clifton at his best: hard-driving, steaming, relentless music. May be the best zydeco album.

CLIFTON CHENIER: *60 Minutes with the King of Zydeco* (Arhoolie CD-301)
Producer Chris Strachwitz obviously knew how to capture Chenier's energy and joy in playing on this outstanding collection from his Arhoolie recordings.

GARY "B. B." COLEMAN: *If You Can Beat Me Rockin'* (Ichiban CD 1018)
The best album yet from this strange southern bluesman. Sometimes lackluster but sometimes also very tasty.

ALBERT COLLINS: *Ice Pickin'* (Alligator CD 4713)
The association of Collins-Iglauer produced excellent results, among which was this superior collection. An impressive guitar.

ALBERT COLLINS / ROBERT CRAY / JOHNNY COPELAND: *Showdown* (Alligator CD 4743)
The collaboration of three great modern guitar players in the Texas-California style is obviously more than a simple trial session.

SAM COOKE: *The Two Sides of Sam Cooke* (Specialty SPCD 2119)
The best available CD by this soul pioneer who came from gospel and rhythm and blues.

JOHNNY COPELAND: *When the Rain Starts Falling* (Rounder CD 11515)
Copeland recorded this collection of his best work for Rounder on a

CD with a very generous playing time. Not everything is subtle but it is certainly efficient.

JAMES COTTON: *Cut You Loose!* (Vanguard VMD 79283)
An intimate session for this good singer and harmonica player who was one of the regulars in Muddy Waters' blues band. "Cut You Loose" is a very good version of this classic from Mel London's pen.

ROBERT CRAY: *Bad Influence* (Hightone HCD 8001)
The best Cray to date. Blues (the superb "Phone Booth"), soul, and ballads and Robert Cray's electrifying guitar.

ROBERT CRAY: *Who's Been Talkin'?* (Charly CD CLM 101)
Appearing first on Tomato but totally unnoticed, this album is the most bluesy of all those recorded by Cray. It includes the excellent "Who's Been Talkin'" (of Willie Dixon/Howlin' Wolf) and "Too Many Cooks," created by the obscure Jesse Fortune.

BO DIDDLEY: *Bo Diddley* (Chess/Vogue 600114)
A rich selection of the best Chess titles by this musician and singer, unique in the world of blues and rock-and-roll.

WILLIE DIXON: *The Willie Dixon Chess Box* (Chess CH316500)
More Willie Dixon the composer than Willie Dixon the singer is revealed in this set. Be careful with similar titles of other compilations!

FATS DOMINO: *The Best of Fats Domino* (Liberty CDP 7902942)
For incomprehensible reasons, Fats Domino did not enjoy the same recording favors as other black blues-rockers. One needs to be content with this CD while waiting for the necessary box set.

CHAMPION JACK DUPREE: *Sings the Blues* (King KCD 735)
A few good songs by this New Orleans piano player and singer from the fifties. But he did better, especially on the album *Blues from the Gutter* that we would like to see reissued on CD by Atlantic.

SNOOKS EAGLIN: *Out of Nowhere* (Black Top CD 1046)
The last CD recorded by Eaglin. Well surrounded and well produced, Snooks is convincing.

BLIND BOY FULLER: *East Coast Piedmont Style* (CBS/Sony 4679232)

An excellent selection of tracks by the forefather of Piedmont blues. Nimble guitar picking, double-entendre lyrics, relaxed and intricate music that had an enormous influence on many East Coast bluesmen and folk singers.

LOWELL FULSON: *Reconsider Baby* (Chess CD Red 14)

An ample selection of the Chess period from the fifties to the early sixties by this excellent and prolific creator of the California blues.

GRADY GAINES: *Full Gain* (Black Top CD 1041)

Little Richard's saxophone player, wonderfully accompanied by Roy Gaines, Clarence Holliman, and singer Teddy Reynolds. Superb Texas blues.

BUDDY GUY: *A Man and the Blues* (Vanguard VMD 79279)

The best of Buddy Guy's career, in the middle of a band very close to its leader. Otis Spann is brilliant on the piano. One of the best blues albums ever made.

BUDDY GUY: *On Chess, Vols. 1 & 2* (Chess/Vogue 600176 and 600213)

All of Guy's titles for Chess in two CDs. Of uneven value but a few excellent things and the evolution of a great musician of modern blues.

JOHN HAMMOND: *John Hammond* (Rounder CD 11532)

The albums recorded by Hammond for Rounder are substantially superior to those he recorded for Vanguard in the beginning. This compilation includes the best Rounder titles. Very convincing.

HARP ATTACK (Alligator 4790)

A successful super-session reuniting Cotton, Wells, and Carey Bell, three living legends of the blues harp, plus a younger but equally talented Billy Branch.

WYNONIE HARRIS / ROY BROWN: *Battle of the Blues, Vols. 1 & 2* (King KCD 607 and 627)

Two of the best blues shouters in action. No sentiment or frills. Rock-and-roll before it existed.

JOHNNY HEARTSMAN: *Sacramento* (Crosscut CD 1018)

The "godfather" of the Californian guitar and the producer of countless sessions stands behind the microphone for a rare appearance as the featured player. Outstanding.

Z. Z. HILL: *The Best of Z. Z. Hill* (Malaco MAL CD 342)

By himself Z. Z. Hill managed to bring soul-blues back to the southern Top 40. This compilation combines the excellent with the less brilliant.

JOHN LEE HOOKER: *40th Anniversary Album* (DCC CC DZS 042)

Some of the very first songs recorded by Hooker between 1948 and 1954, among which is "Boogie Chillen." All digitalized. Some great blues.

JOHN LEE HOOKER: *Boogie Chillen* (Charly CD 4)

A rich compilation of the titles recorded by Hooker for Vee-Jay (1955–65). A beautiful moment with the perfect bass of Eddie Taylor and a few appearances by Jimmy Reed on the harmonica.

JOHN LEE HOOKER: *House Rent Boogie* (Charly CD 62)

The necessary complement to the previous album. Same moments and same accompanists.

JOHN LEE HOOKER: *The Real Folk Blues* (Chess CHD 9271)

Some more "modern" titles recorded in the late sixties with Eddie Burns on guitar and with a good rhythm section.

LIGHTNIN' HOPKINS: *The Complete Prestige-Bluesville Recordings* (Prestige 7 PCD-4406-2)

Seven CDs covering all of Lightnin's Bluesville recordings of the early sixties. Not everything is worthwhile, but the tracks recorded in Houston with local friends are stunning.

LIGHTNIN' HOPKINS: *The Gold Star Sessions, Vols. 1 & 2* (Arhoolie CD 330/337)
Certainly some of the best sides ever waxed by the Big Boss of Texas country blues. Volume 1 is an absolute must. Volume 2, although less consistently dazzling, is its perfect companion.

LIGHTNIN' HOPKINS: *The Herald Recordings 1954* (Collectables CD 5121)
Blues and boogies recorded for the black public by the king of the Houston ghetto. Difficult to do better in this style.

LIGHTNIN' HOPKINS: *How Many More Years I Got* (Fantasy 98514)
One of the best sessions recorded by Hopkins in his long career. He is accompanied by his regular band from Houston with the brilliant harmonica player Billy Bizor. Blues dripping with feeling. Extraordinary.

SON HOUSE: *Death Letter* (Edsel ED-CD 167)
Son House, pioneer of the Delta blues and Robert Johnson's teacher, when rediscovered during the sixties blues revival. Passionate, devastating music, one of the best Delta blues albums ever waxed.

HOWLIN' WOLF: *The Howlin' Wolf Chess Box* (MCA/Chess CHD 3-9332)
Three-box set spanning Wolf's entire career. A fourth CD would have included almost all his complete work for Chess and is sorely missing. But with nearly four hours of fantastic music and a stunning booklet full of rare pictures, this Chess box is a must.

HOWLIN' WOLF: *The London Sessions* (Chess CH 9297)
Belated sessions of a sick Howlin' Wolf, but accompanied by some of the Rolling Stones, Eric Clapton, Steve Winwood, Ringo Starr, and the great guitarist Hubert Sumlin for a historic session.

HOWLIN' WOLF: *Memphis Days* (Bear Family BCD 15460)
The first titles recorded by Howlin' Wolf in Memphis for Sam Phillips demonstrate the rage to play.

HOWLIN' WOLF: *The Rockin' Chair Album* (Chess/Vogue 600111)
The best of the best moments of one of the greatest Chicago bluesmen in blues history.

HOWLIN' WOLF: *The Real Folk-Blues* (Chess CHD 9273)
Follows the previous album.

HOWLIN' WOLF: *More Real Folk-Blues* (Chess CHD 9279)
Same as the previous one.

JOE HUGHES: *Craftsman* (Double Trouble CD 3019)
The rediscovery of an obscure veteran of the Texas blues is an excellent surprise. Along the lines of T-Bone Walker.

ALBERTA HUNTER: *Young Alberta Hunter* (Jass CD 6)
The number of female blues singers on compact disc is too limited for us to reject the recording of this charming old lady, whom everybody applauded and who shows here what a character she was when she was young!

ELMORE JAMES: *Let's Cut It!* (Ace CDCH 192)
An exemplary selection of the first titles (Modern) of this great postwar bluesman.

ELMORE JAMES: *Shake Your Moneymaker* (Charly CD 34)
The king of the electric slide guitar renewed himself considerably by the end of his life, and he made his best recordings. Here they are.

ELMORE JAMES: *Come Go with Me* (Charly CD 180)
It follows the previous period. As good.

SKIP JAMES: *Today!* (Vanguard VMD 73120)
Rediscovered rather accidentally, this great creator of Delta blues seemed to be uncomfortable on the giant stages of the blues revival. However, this record is exemplary and one of the best country blues albums.

LONNIE JOHNSON: *Steppin' on the Blues* (CBS/Sony 467252-2)
The best compilation available on CD by this true originator on the guitar. The broad range of music created by Johnson encompasses blues, early jazz, ballads, and pop, all well represented here.

ROBERT JOHNSON: *The Complete Recordings* (CBS/Sony 4672462)
This boxed set with a wonderful booklet is an essential buy, long sought-after by blues fans all over the world. Its commercial success has opened many ears to the real blues feeling.

BLIND WILLIE JOHNSON: *Praise God I'm Satisfied* (Yazoo 1058)
Unbelievable country gospel by the supreme guitar evangelist. Raw vocals, incredible slide guitar playing, and magnificent music.

LOUIS JORDAN: *The Best of Louis Jordan* (MCA MCAD 4079)
Some of this saxophone player's best titles, a mix of jazz, rock-and-roll, and blues. Hilarious and exciting!

ALBERT KING: *I'll Play the Blues for You* (Stax 98711)
Probably the best album recorded by Albert King in the Memphis studios. Imperial and brilliant.

ALBERT KING: *Live Wire/Blues Power* (Stax SCD 4128-2)
Albert King's superb concert at the Fillmore in San Francisco. *Blues Power* is unmistakably a lesson in the blues.

ALBERT KING: *Live!* (Charly CDX 35)
This time in Montreux, Albert King unfolded his blues canvas around prestigious guests (Lowell Fulson, Rory Gallagher . . .) and a particularly receptive public.

B. B. KING: *Back in the Alley* (MCA MCAD 27010)
Before the superjump into the excessive commercialization that would progressively drown B. B. Some great titles of the sixties.

B. B. KING: *The Best of B. B. King, Vols. 1 & 2* (Ace CDCH 199 and 908)
Digitally re-mixed titles of the early sixties. A great period for B. B. King.

B. B. KING: *Do the Boogie!* (Ace CDCH 916)

The beginnings (well, almost) of the "Blues Boy" who was to become the international star we know today. Lucille, his guitar, could laugh or cry.

B. B. KING: *Live at the Regal* (MCA MCAD 31106)

For those who have recently seen the Blues Boy and who thought he was stuck in a rut: a vibrant and alive concert.

B. B. KING/BOBBY BLAND: *Together for the First Time . . . Live* (MCA MCAD 4160)

A generous concert by two great pros of American black music. Not everything is extraordinary, but everything is exemplary.

FREDDIE KING: *Texas Sensation* (Charly CD 242)

Although somewhat forgotten today, Freddie King was a fine singer and guitar player. This CD includes some of his best early recordings.

FREDDIE KING: *Takin' Care of Business* (Charly CD 30)

The first hits of this third King who was only prevented from serious competition with the other two by his unexpected death. "Hideaway," "San-O-Zay" . . . Indispensable classics.

FREDDIE KING: *Getting Ready* (Shelter SRZ 8003)

Between rock and blues, one of Freddie King's last albums, with a few former rock superstars. It really moves.

BIG DADDY KINSEY: *Can't Let Go* (Blind Pig CD 3489)

One of the late revelations in blues, accompanied here by all his sons. A good album.

LAZY LESTER (Flyright FLYCD 07)

A regular of the Louisiana swamp blues. He was called lazy, but he was only "laid back." Superb.

LEADBELLY: *Huddie Leadbetter's Best* (Capitol 92075-2)

This great singer and guitar player's recorded work has been much debated, and it is of unequal value. Here are his most bluesy titles.

J. B. LENOIR: *I Don't Know* (Chess/Vogue 670406)

Somewhat forgotten today, Lenoir made the good times in the South Side of Chicago. Some of his best titles for Chess.

J. B. LENOIR: *Alabama Blues!* (L+R CDLR 42001)

Still much superior to the previous one. Lenoir playing the acoustic guitar or with the great drummer Fred Below for one of the great records in blues history.

LIGHTNIN' SLIM: *Rollin' Stone* (Flyright FLYCD 08)

Irresistible. The songster of the bayou blues. A rich and delicious CD.

MANCE LIPSCOMB: *Texas Songster* (Arhoolie CD 306)

A great set by this wonderful Texas songster, one of the big blues revival discoveries of the late fifties. Gentle, low-key, spirited music.

LITTLE MILTON: *Little Milton Sings Big Blues* (Chess CHD 5906)

An album devoted to the blues by this regular of southern soul-blues. A superb singer and an expressive guitar player.

LITTLE MILTON: *Walkin' This Back Street* (Stax SCD 8514-2)

The perfect selection of Little Milton's best period with Stax. Blues and soul full of feeling.

LITTLE RICHARD: *The Specialty Sessions, Vols. 1, 2 & 3* (Ace ABOXCD 1-2-3-4-5-6)

All of the Specialty titles of this great rock-and-roll figure who is also a king of rhythm and blues. At full speed!

LITTLE WALTER: *The Best of Little Walter, Vols. 1 & 2* (Chess CHD 9192 and 9292)

The quintessence of the blues harmonica by one of the giants in blues history. Probably his best titles. We are waiting for a complete box set of his whole work.

LOUISIANA RED: *The Lowdown Back Porch Blues* (Vogue 600184)

The best album of this prolific singer-guitarist. With Muddy Waters,

Lightnin' Hopkins, and Elmore James. Plus the extravagant "Red's Dream."

TOMMY MCCLENNAN: *1939–42* (Travelin' Man TM CD 06)
An influential Delta blues singer and guitarist, McClennan made many very fine sides during his too-short recording career, the best of which are featured here.

JIMMY MCCRACKLIN: *On Chess* (Chess/Vogue 600165)
A great California bluesman that many will discover on this generous compilation of his Chess titles.

FRED MCDOWELL: *Mississippi Delta Blues* (Arhoolie CD 304)
McDowell was one of the major discoveries of the blues revival. A great Delta bluesman. This compilation includes his best titles.

BROWNIE MCGHEE: *The Folkway Years, 1945–59* (Smithsonian CD SF 40034)
Brownie without Sonny. McGhee recorded prolifically for the Folkway label, with mixed results. This faultless compilation selects his best work and proves how proficient a guitar player Brownie can be.

BLIND WILLIE MCTELL: *Early Years* (Yazoo 1005)
Wonderful selection of early tracks recorded by Blind Willie McTell, a true giant of prewar Atlanta blues. Essential.

MAGIC SAM: *West Side Guitar* (Flyright FLYCD 02)
Almost all the songs from the first part of his career by the one who revolutionized the Chicago blues. Excellent.

MAGIC SAM: *West Side Soul* (Delmark DD 615)
Chicago's West Side blues at its toughest by the main originator. One of the ultimate records of electric Chicago blues.

MEMPHIS MINNIE: *Hoodoo Lady* (CBS/Sony 467888-2)
Memphis Minnie, the blueswoman par excellence, made so many great records that it is a shame so few compilations of her work exist. This one is very good, with nice clean sound, although it is limited to her thirties sessions.

MEMPHIS MINNIE: *I Ain't No Bad Gal* (Portrait CD 44072)

Few bluesmen/women of the thirties and forties have found a place on compact disc. Minnie is breathtaking. The only regret is that there was so little playing time on a CD that could have easily included twice as many titles.

MEMPHIS SLIM: *All Kinds of Blues* (Prestige 98415)

Memphis Slim's best albums are not yet available on CD. We recommend this record that shows him by himself at the piano in a muted atmosphere.

MEMPHIS SLIM: *Rainin' the Blues* (Fantasy FCD 24702-2)

This is certainly not the best of Slim's recordings, but he is often accompanied by guitar player Lafayette Thomas, whose record adventures are far too rare for his talent. Worth listening to.

MERCY DEE: *Mercy's Troubles* (Arhoolie CD 369)

Stevie Ray and the Fabulous Thunderbirds spread the idea that Texas sound means loud and tough music. But the Texas blues was in fact (and still is in part) a slow-paced, low-key, mournful, and very moving music, epitomized by artists of stature like Mercy Dee, the creator of many classic blues ("One-Room Country Shack").

AMOS MILBURN: *Greatest Hits* (Official 86018)

The only available compact disc of this rock-and-roll pioneer. A great California bluesman. The selection is not great, but for lack of anything better and while waiting for other CDs, it will have to do.

MUDDY WATERS: *The Best of Muddy Waters* (Chess CHD 31268)

Really the "best" of one of the greatest bluesmen. A must.

MUDDY WATERS: *Fathers and Sons* (Chess CH 2-92522)

This album gathers Muddy and pianist Otis Spann with the white bluesmen of the sixties, Butterfield and Bloomfield; it does not lack punch or feeling.

MUDDY WATERS: *The Real Folk-Blues* (Chess CHD 9274)

MUDDY WATERS: *More Real Folk Blues* (Chess CHD 9278)

Two wonderful compilations including other titles among the best ones recorded by Muddy for Chess. An unforgettable experience for those who do not know him yet!

MUDDY WATERS: *The Muddy Waters Chess Box* (Chess CH 6-80002)

Three rich CDs in a beautiful box and a smart catalog. Many duplications of those songs in the previous albums but also a certain number of rare titles and a few unreleased ones.

MUDDY WATERS: *Trouble No More* (Chess CH 9291)

Some rarely reissued songs of this great Chicago bluesman in his middle period (1955–62). Less tough than the previous one but incredibly efficient. With the most beautiful version ever recorded of "Rock Me."

CHARLIE MUSSELWHITE: *Memphis Charlie* (Arhoolie CD 303)

One of the rare available CDs by this virtuoso harmonica player. This is probably not his best, but it is a rich selection and there are many good moments.

SAM MYERS / ANSON FUNDERBURGH: *Sins* (Black Top CD 1038)

SAM MYERS / ANSON FUNDERBURGH: *Rack 'em Up* (Black Top CD 1049)

Irresistible association between an old harmonica player and singer from Mississippi, formerly in Elmore James's band, and a young white Texas guitar player.

KENNY NEAL: *Devil Child* (Alligator CD 4774)

A rising star from Louisiana. The son of a renowned harmonica player (Raful Neal) who understood very well his father's lessons.

JUNIOR PARKER: *Mystery Train* (Rounder CD SS-38)

The entire Sun sessions by Parker, featuring the great original "Mystery Train." For good measure, tracks are added by a youthful James Cotton, without his harmonica, and glorious guitar player Pat Hare.

ANN PEEBLES: *Greatest Hits* (Hi CD 100)

The real "greatest" hits recorded by this remarkable southern soul-blueswoman. Hot and sensuous.

PROFESSOR LONGHAIR: *New Orleans Piano* (Atlantic 7225-2)

The pioneer of New Orleans rhythm and blues displaying his best works. Original and irresistible.

QUEEN IDA: *Cookin' with Queen Ida* (GNP/Crescendo GNPD 2197)

When Queen Ida is cooking, going into her kitchen is an adventure.

JIMMY REED: *Big Boss Blues* (Charly CD 3)

JIMMY REED: *Rockin' with Reed* (Charly CD 61)

Reed, the Chicago bluesman who had the most commercial hits among blacks, is probably not the most exciting to listen to. But his Vee-Jay titles on two generous compilations show that his simplicity was only on the surface and that his success came from a particular feeling to which many will be sensitive.

JIMMY REED / EDDIE TAYLOR: *Ride 'em on Down* (Charly CD 171)

Excellent titles of a young Jimmy Reed and almost all of what Eddie Taylor, the great guitarist behind Reed and John Lee Hooker, recorded as the featured player for Vee-Jay. Classic Chicago blues.

FENTON ROBINSON: *Somebody Loan Me a Dime* (Alligator 4705)

Fenton has brought more jazz into his blues without losing the raw edge of the music than anyone else in Chicago. The results are often brilliant. This album is one of the best produced in Chicago during the seventies.

FENTON ROBINSON: *Special Road* (Black Magic CD 9012)

A great unrecognized bluesman: a warm voice, superb arrangements, and what a guitar style! One of his best performances on record.

ROCKIN' DOPSIE: *Saturday Night Zydeco* (Maison de Soul MDS CD 104)

One of the great candidates for the crown of the Bayou King, the late Clifton Chenier. Good fun.

ROCKIN' SIDNEY: *Live with the Blues* (JSP CD 213)
The creator of the hit "My Toot Toot" in action. More blues than usual but very zydeco. Music to dance to.

JIMMY ROGERS: *That's All Right* (Chess CD Red 16)
A regular of postwar Chicago blues, Rogers played in all the bands of the city (with Muddy Waters, Little Walter . . .) but he recorded exemplary work under his own name.

JIMMY ROGERS: *Left Me with a Broken Heart* (Chess/Vogue 670409)
Despite some duplication of songs on the previous album and a few repetitions, this CD complements the other one pretty well.

OTIS RUSH: *His Cobra Recordings* (Flyright FLY CD 01)
One of the inventors of the West Side sound at the peak of his art. How could such a young man create such deep music? Outstanding.

OTIS RUSH: *Right Place, Wrong Time* (Hightone HCD 8007)
This album is an exception to the period when Otis Rush was adrift after his first titles for Cobra and Chess. Well balanced and well produced, this is an excellent moment of modern blues by one of its inventors.

SON SEALS: *Bad Axe* (Alligator CD 4738)
One of the few bluesmen who tried to live his blues in the seventies and eighties. Talent and energy. Memorable.

JOHNNY SHINES: (Hightone HCD 8028)
This excellent record, one of Shines' very best, is equally divided between acoustic tracks where Johnny is alone with his guitar and powerful titles backed by Phillip Walker's band.

JOHNNY SHINES/ROBERT JR. LOCKWOOD (Flyright FLYCD 10)
Two of Robert Johnson's students perpetuate his work while they build their own at the same time. Shines is wonderful in his presence and feeling; Lockwood, more technical, is far too unrecognized. A must.

SLIM HARPO: *The Best of Slim Harpo* (Rhino RI 70169)
> The great name of the swamp blues. This excellent compilation gathers his main hits.

SLIM HARPO: *I'm a King Bee* (Flyright FLY CD 05)
> More rare songs for a rich compilation that is as good as the previous one.

BESSIE SMITH: *1925–33* (Hermes 6003)
> Undeniably the "Queen" of female blues singers in action. A blues that does not age and which has almost become a necessary passage for every fan of black music.

BESSIE SMITH: *Great Original Performances* (BBC CD 602)
> A superior selection with incredible sound quality considering the time of the original recordings.

LITTLE GEORGE SMITH: *Harmonica Ace* (Ace CDCHD 337)
> Forget the "Little" tag. George Smith is a *big* name of the harmonica; his mastery on the chromatic has no equal. He has influenced almost all of today's West Coast harpists. Brilliant.

OTIS SPANN: *Otis Spann Is the Blues* (Candid CD 9001)
> Otis Spann, the best pianist of postwar blues, with Robert Jr. Lockwood, Robert Johnson's son. Fascinating.

OTIS SPANN: *Cryin' Time* (Vanguard VMD 6514)
> A good but later session. Spann is in great shape even if his accompanists are not all at the same level.

STAPLE SINGERS: *Respect Yourself* (Mobil Fidelity MFCD 832)
> "Rise high: respect yourself." Roebuck "Pops" Staples' advice whispered by his beautiful voice and enhanced by his strange guitar. Deeply bluesy soul in the best southern tradition.

HUBERT SUMLIN: *Hubert Sumlin's Blues Party* (Black Top CD 1036)
> Howlin' Wolf's great guitarist ruined a few records while trying to become a singer. Here, he had the good idea of staying behind the powerful "Mighty" Sam McClain.

EDDIE TAYLOR: (Hightone HCD 8027)

Eddie Taylor, one of the unsung heroes of postwar Chicago blues, has unfortunately made too few records on his own. This album cut in California in the company of Phillip Walker's band is his best. Simply wonderful.

HOUND DOG TAYLOR: . . . *and the Houserockers* (Alligator CD 4701)

A powerful album without any pretense except that of having a good time. The atmosphere of the bars in Chicago.

JOHNNIE TAYLOR: *Chronicle* (Stax FCD 60-006)

One of the great names of Memphis soul deeply influenced by the blues. What a rhythm.

LITTLE JOHNNY TAYLOR: *Ugly Woman* (Ichiban ICHCD 1042)

Much more rooted in the blues than his homonym, this little Johnny Taylor has a big and beautiful voice. A good album. Let's hope that his previous titles for Jewel are reissued on compact disc.

KOKO TAYLOR: *I Got What It Takes* (Chess/Vogue 600179)

A rich compilation of all the Chess titles recorded by Ms. Taylor at the dawn of her career. Not everything is good but what is excellent really is.

KOKO TAYLOR: *The Earthshaker* (Alligator CD 4711)

Far superior to her Chess titles, the Alligator albums of Ms. Taylor are much embellished, and they show her surrounded by a superb Chicago blues band led by the much unrecognized but excellent Sammy Lawhorn on the guitar.

BIG MAMA THORNTON: *Ball and Chain* (Arhoolie CD 305)

Another great lady of postwar blues. Mama Thornton is really big in this beautiful collection of songs from her three albums for Chris Strachwitz.

BIG JOE TURNER: *Greatest Hits* (Atlantic 81752-2)

Certainly the most rock-and-roll songs by this great blues shouter. Flawless.

BIG JOE TURNER: *Big Joe Rides Again* (Atlantic 90668-2)

The jazziest songs of this great bluesman. As good as his rock-and-roll titles. We are waiting for the rereleases of his first Decca titles.

MAURICE JOHN VAUGHN: *Generic Blues Album* (Alligator CD4763)

The promising debut of a new Chicago bluesman. To be followed.

EDDIE "CLEANHEAD" VINSON: *Back in Town* (Charly CD50)

This bald saxophone player and blues shouter, unrestrained in a festival hard to criticize. Eloquent and inventive.

JOE LOUIS WALKER: *Cold Is the Night* (Hightone HCD 8006)

Along with Robert Cray, he represents the new Californian generation. The ballads are sometimes stiff, but some blues influenced by great names such as Howlin' Wolf and McDowell are particularly effective.

JOE LOUIS WALKER: *The Gift* (Hightone HCD 8013)

T-BONE WALKER: *Low Down Blues* (Charly CD 007)

A selection of the first Capitol titles by this great bluesman. Not brilliant yet but on the way . . .

T-BONE WALKER: *T-Bone Blues* (Atlantic 8020-2)

This time, this is it: T-Bone is brilliant. Listen to "Evening" and you will be convinced. One of the ten greatest blues albums ever made. In a sumptuous presentation.

KATIE WEBSTER: *Two-Fisted Mama* (Alligator 4777)

From the Louisiana swamp blues to international recognition through Otis Redding's band, it was a long road for this sensational pianist. This recent album is also among her best ones.

JUNIOR WELLS: *Hoodoo Man Blues* (Delmark DD 612)

One of the very first Chicago blues albums. A young and energetic Junior Wells lights fire on every track, with the help of a tight combo led by Buddy Guy when he was a great blues guitar player. Very influential and a must.

JUNIOR WELLS: *It's My Life Baby* (Vanguard VMD 73120)
Probably one of the best albums of Junior Wells with a worked-up Buddy Guy. "Ouch!" is amazing.

JUNIOR WELLS: *Messin' with the Kid* (Flyright FLY CD 03)
There is plenty to digest in this rich compilation that includes titles from the sixties by Junior, who was looking for another way to commercial success. Some very good moments too.

ARTIE "BLUES BOY" WHITE: *Thangs Gotta Change* (Ichiban ICHCD 1044)
A revelation that came late, Artie is already mature, and his blues do not have a single wrinkle. Worth listening to.

BUKKA WHITE: *Legacy of the Blues* (Crescendo CD 10011 or Takoma 72701-2)
The great moments of Bukka White's rediscovery in the sixties captured on record.

LYNN WHITE: *Yes I'm Ready* (Waylo 269505-2)
The exquisite Lynn White showing that a real soul sister can also insinuate the blues. A vocal ginseng for the most tired.

ROBERT WILKINS: *The Original Rollin' Stone* (Yazoo 1077)
Before he became a singing reverend, Robert Wilkins was a fine bluesman, influential in the Memphis area. He is well represented in this worthwhile compilation.

BIG JOE WILLIAMS: *Shake Your Boogie* (Arhoolie CD 315)
(Almost) two of Big Joe's best albums recorded on one CD. The first session, recorded during the early sixties, catches Big Joe, just out of jail, in a bitter and moving mood. The other tracks, cut ten years later, showcase the bluesman at his toughest, with devastating slide guitar and fiery vocals, helped on some tracks by the incredible harp playing of Charlie Musselwhite. Magnificent music.

JOHN LEE "SONNY BOY" WILLIAMSON / BIG JOE WILLIAMS: *Throw a Boogie Woogie* (RCA 9599-2)
Two giants of the thirties and forties together on sumptuous RCA

titles. There is enough to make at least ten compact discs with what these two artists recorded. This is only an appetizer.

SONNY BOY WILLIAMSON (RICE MILLER) / WILLIE LOVE: *Clownin' with the World* (Trumpet 700)
A beautiful CD of previously unreleased titles by the second Sonny Boy on his recording debut. He was over fifty years old. Willie Love is an interesting pianist and singer from Mississippi.

SONNY BOY WILLIAMSON (RICE MILLER): *The Blues of Sonny Boy Williamson* (Storyville STCD 4062)
A great session of Sonny Boy in Europe. Often alone at the harmonica or with only M. T. Murphy's acoustic guitar, a blues lesson in a soft voice.

SONNY BOY WILLIAMSON (RICE MILLER): *The Chess Years* (Chess CD Red Box 1)
All the Chess sides recorded by Sonny Boy in chronological order on four CDs. An exemplary reissue.

SONNY BOY WILLIAMSON (RICE MILLER): *Down and Out Blues* (Chess CHD 31272)
Sonny Boy's classic titles for Chess. With the unshakable rhythm section of Below-Dixon, Muddy Waters, Robert Jr. Lockwood . . . .

SONNY BOY WILLIAMSON (RICE MILLER): *The Real Folk-Blues* (Chess CHD 9272) and *More Real Folk Blues* (CD 9277)
More extraordinary Chess titles: "Help Me," "Bring It on Home," and "Checkin' Up on My Baby." Those who do not know them are in for a treat. A must.

SONNY BOY WILLIAMSON (RICE MILLER) WITH THE YARDBIRDS (L+R CDLR 42020)
An average but historic album: the first encounter of a real black bluesman with an English Rock group in London in 1963. With a still-adolescent Eric Clapton.

JOHNNY WINTER: *Guitar Slinger* (Alligator CD 4735)

Probably the best album made by this strange Texas bluesman, capable of the appalling as well as the most interesting.

JIMMY WITHERSPOON: *Spoon so Easy* (MCA/Chess CHD 93003)

The bluesiest sessions waxed by Witherspoon in the Windy City find the velvet-voiced blues crooner in the company of top-notch Chicago musicians in the Chess studios.

MIGHTY JOE YOUNG: *Legacy of the Blues* (Sonet TCD 633)

A beautiful album of Chicago blues by a great singer-guitar player who has been too quickly forgotten.

JOHNNY YOUNG: *Chicago Blues* (Arhoolie CD 325)

Two tough Chicago blues albums by singer/guitar-player/mandolin-player Young on one CD. Johnny is in fine form throughout, helped by some of Chicago's best bluesmen (Muddy Waters, Cotton, Spann, Horton . . .)

▪ ANTHOLOGY

BARRELHOUSE BOOGIE (RCA/Bluebird 8334-1)
> The greatest pianists in the history of boogie-woogie (Meade "Lux" Lewis, Jimmy Yancey, Pete Johnson, Albert Ammons) in a breathtaking festival.

BLACK MUSIC ORIGINALS, Vols. 1, 2, 3 & 4 (Sun CD 1,4,7,10)
> Almost all the Sun records produced commercially in the fifties and sixties in chronological order of black blues and rhythm-and-blues artists.

THE BLUES, 1923–33 (BBC CD 683)
> The music is not always extraordinary, but it is an obvious and rare document of a historic period of the blues: that of the female blues singers.

THE BLUES CAME DOWN FROM MEMPHIS (Charly CD 67)
> A good selection of the best blues records published on the Sun label of Sam Phillips in Memphis. Notice the duplications with *Black Music Originals*.

BLUES IN THE BOTTLE (Big Beat CDWIK 71)
> Before Dylan, other young Yankees had discovered with a certain rage the blues of the twenties and thirties. Tom Rush, Dave Van Ronk, and Ramblin' Jack Elliott resist time very well.

BLUES WITH THE GIRLS (EPM FDC 5508)
> Zora Young, Bonnie Lee, and Big Time Sarah Streeter invite us to the blues. A good anthology with Hubert Sumlin on guitar.

BLUESVILLE, VOL. I: FOLK BLUES (Ace CDCH 247)
> Almost at the same time, a Bluesville label specialized in discovering

and recording the acoustic bluesmen of this good period. Old and new songs combine to create a very good selection of a label too much disparaged.

CHESS: ALBERT KING / OTIS RUSH / OTIS SPANN / B. B. KING (Chess/Vogue 600150)
Excellent titles, often unrecognized, recorded for Chess by these bluesmen.

CHESS: ELMORE JAMES / JOHN BRIM / FLOYD JONES (Chess/Vogue 600119)
Same as previous, but much better. Elmore James at the peak of his art. John Brim and Floyd James, two great Chicago bluesmen in the line of Muddy Waters, Jimmy Rogers . . . for an hour of great art.

CHICAGO BLUES HARMONICAS (Flyright FLYCD)
Titles on small labels (JOB, Artistic, Abco) of Chicago blues during a good period. Otis Rush, Homesick James, Johnny Shines, James Cotton, Junior Wells . . . ageless.

CHICAGO / THE BLUES TODAY, Vols. 1, 2 & 3 (Vanguard VMD 79216, 79217, 79218)
Recorded in 1965, these titles helped the blues-revival fans discover the "real" electric Chicago blues. Otis Rush, Homesick James, Johnny Shines, James Cotton, Junior Wells . . . This music still stands out.

LIVING CHICAGO BLUES, Vols. 1, 2, 3, 4, 5 & 6 (Sonet 30624, 30625, 30626, 30627, 30628, 30629)
Fifteen years later, a similar attempt with new musicians who came largely from the West Side, the toughest ghetto in Chicago. Many names succeeded (Jimmy Johnson, Lonnie Brooks) while others did not, but they are as excellent. A series as indispensable as the previous one.

LOUISIANA SWAMP BLUES (Flyright FLY CD 09)
The ideal anthology of Jay Miller's swamp blues, the creator of this blues style. Slim Harpo, Lightnin' Slim, Silas Hogan . . . When one listens carefully, one can hear the bullfrogs sing.

THE ORIGINAL AMERICAN FOLK BLUES FESTIVAL (Polydor 825-502-2)

1962: T-Bone Walker, John Lee Hooker, Memphis Slim, and Sonny Terry in Europe enabled a whole generation to discover the blues. A movement that has not stopped having an impact.

SAN FRANCISCO BLUES FESTIVAL (EPM FDC 5507)

Recorded in Europe, this San Francisco blues festival is first-rate, with its confirmations and its discoveries.

SUN RECORDS HARMONICA CLASSICS (Rounder CDSS 29)

Another anthology of Sun titles, devoted entirely this time to the harmonica players from Memphis and from the Delta in the fifties. Excellent.

THREE SHADES OF BLUES (Biograph BCD 107)

Three first-rate acoustic bluesmen (Bukka White, Skip James, and Blind Willie McTell) very poorly represented on compact disc.

ZYDECO FESTIVAL (Maison de Soul CD 101)

Many zydeco recordings exist on CD, probably a testimony to this style that exists today in Louisiana. This anthology gives the opportunity to hear some of the best representatives of this extravagant style of black music.

Note: This selection was made possible thanks to the following publications: *Down Home Music Newsletter and Blues Catalogue, The Official Catalogue of the Compact Disc,* and *Schwann Catalogue.*

▪ BLUES STANDARDS

In blues as well as in other ethnic and folk music, it is particularly difficult to know exactly who composed what, except for recent pieces which leave no doubt.

In the case of very old blues songs, there is the constant recourse to oral tradition that conveyed the tune and sometimes even the song itself while at the same time evolving for several decades. This was long before the first recording. The fact that such blues are attributed to Charlie Patton, Blind Lemon Jefferson, and Blind Blake often means that they were the first ones to record them.

For a long time, bluesmen (many of whom were illiterate) totally ignored the necessity (or even the existence) of copyright. Anyone could claim authorship of a piece. Producers-arrangers, in exchange for promoting the bluesman, or even the possibility for him to record, claimed part or all of the copyright. Thus the huge work of some blues "composers": Taub and Ling are in fact the Bihari brothers, who recorded B. B. King, Elmore James, and others, and they took over the rights of their compositions; Deadric Malone is Don Robey, the Houston producer and the owner of the Duke and Peacock labels; J. West is Jay Miller, et cetera.

The three hundred blues described here are among the most famous and most interpreted in blues history. This is an attempt, with varying degrees of success, to trace their origin and sometimes their evolution and to indicate the most original and striking interpretations.

AFTER HOURS

This instrumental, usually rendered on piano, is attributed to piano player Avery Parrish, who recorded it in 1940 with E. Hawkins' band.

AIN'T NOBODY'S BUSINESS IF I DO

A vaudeville piece, "composed" by Grainger and Robbins. Bessie Smith's brilliant version dates from 26 April 1923 (Columbia A 3898); the more rural and sensibly different version is by Frank Stokes, 30 August 1928 (Victor V 38500). Covered after the war by blues shouter Jimmy Witherspoon. It is this last version that has inspired countless singers.

ALABAMA BOUND

The origin of this folk piece dates back to the mid-nineteenth century. It was a piece for the banjo (and it remained as such in white southern music). The most famous rendition in the black tradition is Leadbelly's (Victor 27268) of 15 June 1940.

ALL BY MYSELF

A stroke of inspiration by Big Bill Broonzy, Washboard Sam, and Memphis Slim, who recorded it together on 17 June 1941 (OK 06427). Each one separately recorded this piece several times, before Fats Domino made it one of his biggest hits.

ALL YOUR LOVE

This title covers two very different blues by the great creators of Chicago's West Side sound. In 1957 Magic Sam wrote this piece (Cobra 5013) often attributed to the obscure but effective pen of Jimmie D. Harris (Shakey Jake). It has been covered by numerous bluesmen.

The other "All Your Love (Is Misloving)" was signed by producer Eli Toscano and Otis Rush for the first time in 1958 (Cobra 5032). John Mayall and his Bluebreakers popularized it.

ANGEL CHILD

Also "Poor Little Angel Child" or "What's the Matter with Your Poor Little Angel Child." Although it is usually attributed to Memphis Slim (1948 on Miracle M 145), "Angel Child" is most certainly an old piece of the Texas repertoire. Lipscomb, Hopkins, and Guitar Slim Green did the best versions.

AS THE YEARS GO PASSING BY

This modern composition was involved in numerous controversies. The copyright belongs to Don Robey (D. Malone), but the song was created by Peppermint Harris for Fenton Robinson (1958: Duke 312). Thanks to Albert King, Larry Davis, Mighty Joe Young, Eric Burdon, and George Thorogood, this piece has become a necessary passage of each bluesman or blues rocker.

AUTOMOBILE BLUES
See "Too Many Drivers"

BABY, PLEASE DON'T GO
One of the most played, arranged, and rearranged pieces in blues history. It is probably an ingenious adaptation by Big Joe Williams (31 October 1935 on Bluebird B 6200) of an old folk theme (Long John) dating back to the time of slavery. Joe often played what was to become his piece. The most exciting version is the one recorded with John Lee "Sonny Boy" Williamson ("Please Don't Go" on 1 December 1941, on Bluebird B 8969). "Turn Your Lamp Down Low," "Don't Go," and many other versions followed. In the years 1949–55, the piece was completely rearranged to make it a modern rhythm-and-blues piece (1951 by Billy Wright, 1954 by Rose Mitchell). In the sixties, Van Morrison and Them made a hit out of it. Big Joe, after several years of trials, finally obtained the copyright for this composition.

BABY, WHAT YOU WANT ME TO DO
A big hit for Jimmy Reed (7 August 1959 on Vee-Jay 333). Like almost all of Reed's pieces and whatever the official credits are, it is an original composition by his wife, Mama Reed.

BACK DOOR FRIEND
Is it a composition by Jimmy Rogers (James Lane), who recorded it on 11 February 1952 on Chess 1506? Or by Lightnin' Hopkins, who always claimed to be its author? Or is it simply a much older piece? The theme of "the friend who came in through the back door while the husband is leaving by the front" was one of the most frequently used in southern folklore.

BACK DOOR MAN
If the "back door man" is almost an emblematic figure in the South, this composition is an original by Willie Dixon. Recorded by Howlin' Wolf in 1966 (Chess 1777).

BACKWATER BLUES

Another recurring theme of the Deep South, the sudden and deadly risings of the Mississippi. Bessie Smith recorded her "Backwater" on 17 February 1927 (Columbia 14195). Big Bill Broonzy, John Lee Hooker, Muddy Waters ("Flood"), and many others covered it constantly until about the sixties.

BALL AND CHAIN

This big hit of singer Janis Joplin is an original composition by Big Mama Thornton.

BIG BOSS MAN

Another big hit of Jimmy Reed (Vee-Jay 380, 29 March 1960) due to the pen of the smart arranger-producer Al Smith. Mama Reed, who was humming behind her husband in the original version, must also have contributed to its success. It was covered many times, but nothing equals the obvious simplicity of the original.

BIG FAT MAMA

"Big fat mama with her meat shakin' on her bones / Everytime she shakes it the skinny woman loses her home." All the original qualities of the Deep South blues is in that great composition which was included in the repertoire of hundreds of musicians and singers. Tommy Johnson recorded this piece for the first time on 31 August 1928 on Victor 38535.

BIG LEG WOMAN

A variation on the previous song. Kokomo Arnold (who attributed it to John Russell) recorded a version on 11 September 1935 (Decca 7116). Johnny Temple made it a hit (17 October 1938 on Decca 7547) before Israel "Popper Stopper" Tolbert (1970) on Stax and Freddie King on Shelter.

BIG ROAD BLUES

Another outstanding blues classic, thanks again to Tommy Johnson's talent (3 February 1928 on Victor 21279). In the sixties, Big Joe Williams, K. C. Douglas, and Jim Brewer offered their versions of this incredible blues, very much inspired by the original.

BLACK CAT BLUES

The black cat (or female cat) and the black cat's bone are sexual metaphors dating from before the invention of the blues and belong to African-American folklore. Ma Rainey was the first one to record it in June 1928 on Paramount 12687.

BLACK GAL

Often attributed to Leadbelly, this theme may come from Texas folklore; it was recorded for the first time by Joe Pullum on 3 April 1934 (Bluebird B 5459). It is very likely an original composition of this much-unrecognized singer and piano player.

BLACK NIGHTS

This California composition of Jessie Mae Robinson was a big hit for Charles Brown (21 December 1950 on Aladdin 3076) and later for Lowell Fulson.

BLACK SNAKE BLUES

The Texas singer Victoria Spivey is undeniably the champion of the black snake that crawled up to her! (11 May 1926 on OK 8338). She had nearly ten versions. On 14 March 1927, her fellow Texan Blind Lemon Jefferson recorded an altered version "Black Snake Moan" (OK 8455) before "Black Snake Dream" (June 1927 on Paramount 12510).

BLUEBIRD

The most famous label of the thirties, Bluebird has inspired numerous artists who recorded for this company. John Lee "Sonny Boy" Williamson (5 May 1937 on Bluebird B 7098) called the bluebird and asked him to fly to Jackson, Tennessee, to give a letter to his wife, Miss Lacey Belle, who lived on Shannon Street! McClennan did the same thing on 20 February 1942 (Bluebird B 9037), followed by a crowd of emulators. John Lee Hooker and Howlin' Wolf dramatized this simple blues to the hilt.

BLUES HAD A BABY (The)

"The blues had a baby, and they called it rock-and-roll." This success of Muddy Waters accompanied by Johnny Winter (Blue Sky x 698 in 1977) resulted from Brownie McGhee's imagination.

BLUES BEFORE SUNRISE

An original composition by Leroy Carr/Scrapper Blackwell recorded by Carr on 21 February 1934 (Vocalion 02657) before it became a classic.

BLUES SHADOWS

Another California success that was covered beyond this regional area. "Blue Shadows" is a composition by pianist Lloyd Glenn recorded by Lowell Fulson (1950 on Swing Time 226).

BLUES WITH A FEELING

In May 1953 Little Walter created this unique composition (Checker 780) that became the necessary passage of every beginning harmonica player. The original has yet to be surpassed.

BON TON ROULET

The Cajun translation of "Let the good times roll," these good times that roll date back to the roots of Cajun folklore. Texas-Louisiana guitar player Clarence Garlow immortalized it on record (1949 on Macy's 5002).

BOOGIE CHILLEN

An original composition by John Lee Hooker (Modern 20-627 on 3 November 1948), "Boogie Chillen" is a quite free adaptation of the old folk piece "Mama don't allow me to stay out all night long" by the great Clarksdale/Detroit bluesman who, because of this big hit, would build his reputation as "King of the boogie." Hooker himself had nearly twenty versions of it (among which was a memorable one, with the blues-rock band Canned Heat). "Feel So Good" by James Cotton and "Feeling Good" (another commercial hit) by Junior Parker come, just slightly changed, from that insistent "Boogie Chillen."

BOTTLE IT UP AND GO

This is one of these salacious "nursery rhymes" appreciated by southern blacks in the thirties and forties. Generally attributed to Tommy McClennan (Bluebird B 8373 on 22 November 1939), it certainly is a much older and more traditional piece known in the South under the more frequently used (and more explicit) title "Shake It Up and Go." John Lee Hooker played several strangely dramatic versions.

BROKE AND HUNGRY

A blues classic, "Broke and Hungry" appeared for the first time by Blind Lemon Jefferson on Paramount 12443 in November 1926. Two forms, somewhat different, were done by Sleepy John Estes (26 September 1929 on Victor 38582) then by Walter Davis (12 July 1930 on Victor 23250) with, it seems, more commercial success. Usually it is Estes's version that serves as a model for the many bluesmen who have interpreted this theme.

BUMBLE BEE

Among the most interpreted titles, "Bumble Bee" is a composition by Memphis Minnie/Joe McCoy, and it was created on record on 18 June 1929 (Columbia 14542). Minnie went back often to her bumble bee, followed by dozens of bluesmen. John Lee Hooker (in 1971!) and Silas Hogan (in 1970) gave convincing renditions of this blues classic.

CALDONIA

"Caldonia, what makes you so stubborn?" An irresistible composition by Louis Jordan (AFRS-Jubilee 112 on 5 May 1944), still interpreted by many.

CANDY MAN

Quite obviously an Anglo-Irish folk piece imported to America. Usually associated with East Coast singers, "Candy Man" was recorded for the first time by Mississippi John Hurt on 28 December 1928 (on OK 8654).

CANNED HEAT

This canned heat is of course adulterated alcohol. A composition probably by Tommy Johnson (one of the great creators of the Delta blues) recorded on 31 August 1928 on Victor 38535. It may already have been a popular theme in that area. Countless versions of this "Canned Heat" followed (Nighthawk, Stackhouse) before the famous California blues-rock group of Al Wilson/Bob Hite made it their stage name.

CARELESS LOVE

Very likely inspired by an old Irish folk tune, "Careless Love" was played by country musicians as well as blues musicians. It seems that

Jimmie Tarlton performed the earliest version (1927). In black music, this piece is often associated with Lonnie Johnson. Homesick James revived (with the slide!) this old piece again in 1973.

CASEY JONES

Or "Talking Casey." This is an old folk tune, and it may not have originated in the black tradition. Casey Jones, the train conductor, appears in many traditional pieces ("Freight Train Boogie"). Furry Lewis recorded "Kassie Jones" on 28 August 1928 on Victor 21664. The piece has become obsolete in black tradition, but it remains common in country music (Johnny Cash, Doc Watson).

CATFISH

This catfish that the "beautiful women fished" is almost an anthem of the Delta blues. "Catfish" dates back to the twenties, but it was recorded for the first time on 28 March 1941 by Robert Petway (Bluebird B 8838) soon followed by his friend Tommy McClennan ("Deep Blue Sea Blues" on 15 September 1941 on Bluebird B 9005). Of course, Muddy Waters covered the theme in "Rolling Stone" in 1950, which gave its name to one of the most famous bands in rock history. We have counted about two hundred versions of "Catfish."

C. C. RIDER

See "See See Rider"

CHECKIN' UP ON MY BABY

John Lee "Sonny Boy" Williamson recorded this blues on Bluebird 34-0722 (14 December 1944), although it is generally attributed to the other Sonny Boy (Rice Miller). Junior Wells made it one of his key titles a long time ago. "Checkin' Up on My Baby" is often played by blues harmonica players.

CONFESSIN' THE BLUES

This piece created by Walter Brown/Jay McShann on 30 April 1941 on Decca 93734 was often incorrectly attributed to Little Walter, who recorded an extraordinary version (1958 on Checker 890).

COOL DRINK OF WATER BLUES

Another extraordinary composition by Tommy Johnson (3 February

1928 on Victor 21279). "I asked her for a glass of cool water, she gave me gasoline." This title was interpreted by many bluesmen under several titles, for example, "Cool Water Blues" or "I Asked for Water" (by Howlin' Wolf).

CORINNA, CORINNA

Blind Lemon Jefferson produced the first "Corinna Blues" in April 1926 (Paramount 12367), but this piece is attributed to Bo Carter, who recorded it on 18 December 1928 (Brunswick 7080). It became a musical standard of the thirties, and "Corinna" was covered by dozens of singers in all genres (western swing, pop, blues . . .) before becoming a sort of necessary rite for each apprentice folksinger of the sixties (Bob Dylan sang it). In 1971 Taj Mahal and Albert King brought "Corinna" back to its origins.

CRAWDAD

Another old piece of folklore probably from Louisiana. In rock-and-roll, the most famous version is by Jerry Lee Lewis; the bluesmen Smokey Hogg and Brother John Sellers also used it in their repertoires.

CRAWLIN' KING SNAKE

This king snake crawling toward the hole of his too unfaithful belle is very likely an old Delta blues from the twenties. Recorded for the first time by Big Joe Williams (Bluebird 8738) on 27 March 1941, it is the obscure Tony Hollins who obtained some success out of it in Chicago (on 3 June 1941 on OK 06351). John Lee Hooker made it one of his favorite titles, and there are many versions.

CROSSCUT SAW

Another fairly pornographic blues that must have belonged to the general repertoire of Delta blues. Tommy McClennan recorded the first version on 15 September 1941 (Bluebird B 8897), but it is Albert King (Stax 201 on 2 November 1966) who made it one of the necessary pieces of modern blues.

CROSSROADS

An original composition by Robert Johnson (ARC 7-05-81 on 27 November 1936), "Standing on the Crossroads" was covered by dozens of musicians. Adapted to the electric guitar, this theme was an important success for Elmore James (twice), Homesick James, and Eric Clapton, before it became an eccentric movie (from Walter Hill) about the musical heritage of Johnson.

DARK ROAD
See "On the Road Again"

DEATH LETTER BLUES
Son House's blues, which, according to testimonies, is directly responsible for the origin of Robert Johnson's famous "Walkin' Blues." House, whose influence was considerable in the Delta, recorded very little before the war, and it was not until 1964 that he recorded "Death Letter."

DECORATION DAY
This "decoration day" or "declaration day," depending on the version, is of course the Fourth of July, Independence Day. The theme might have been invented by Curtis Jones, but John Lee "Sonny Boy" Williamson was the first one to record it, on Bluebird B 7665 on 13 March 1938.

DIDDIE-WAH-DIDDIE
This light theme (maybe even pornographic) was recorded by Blind Blake on 17 August 1929 (Paramount 12888). Is it an original piece or the use again of a folk theme? In any case, many East Coast musicians, with few exceptions, had it in their repertoire.

DIGGIN' MY POTATOES
This was a big hit for Washboard Sam (Bluebird B 8211 on 15 May 1939) from the pens of Sam and Big Bill Broonzy, who later sang the piece. Billy Boy Arnold, James Cotton, and numerous others followed.

DIRTY DOZENS
These salacious "verses" are as old as mankind. Generally, the origin of this theme is attributed to piano player Speckled Red, who recorded it on 22 September 1929 on Brunswick 7116. The response was so great that he recorded it again on 8 April 1930 (Brunswick 7151). Roosevelt Sykes also gave a memorable version.

DOCTOR FEELGOOD

The "good medicine" to relax the patient dates back to the golden age of vaudeville. Walter Davis and Piano Red became specialists in this type of treatment.

DON'T START ME TO TALKIN'

Another necessary piece for all beginning harmonica players. Credit the sharp pen of Sonny Boy Williamson (Rice Miller) (in 1955 on Checker 824).

DON'T YOU LIE TO ME

Fats Domino and Chuck Berry had huge success with this composition by Tampa Red, who recorded it on 10 May 1940 on Bluebird B 8654. Many rock-and-roll classics originated in the blues of the thirties and forties.

DOWN SOUTH BLUES

This Sleepy John Estes blues (9 July 1935 on Decca 7325) may have been inspired by a piece with a similar theme by Alberta Hunter (May 1923 on Paramount 12036). But it is Estes's piece that became a blues classic.

DRIFTIN' BLUES

This is Charles Brown/Johnny Moore's first hit (Philo 112 on 14 September 1945). It established Brown as a star of black music, and it became a favorite theme of West Coast bluesmen. John Lee Hooker, who has always taken a lot from the repertoire of the California bluesmen, had one of the most dramatic versions.

DRIVIN' WHEEL

This is a composition by Roosevelt Sykes, who recorded it on 18 February 1936 on Decca 7252. After the war, Junior Parker made it a big hit, which explains why he is usually attributed with writing this classic. Luther Allison gave one of the best interpretations of this piece on Gordy.

DROP DOWN MAMA

"Drop down mama and let your daddy see . . ." Here again, the origin of this theme remains uncertain; it may be linked to the

Mississippi Sheiks and Bo Carter. Sleepy John Estes recorded the first version on 17 July 1935 (Decca 7289). The piece is still played by a great number of artists.

DUST MY BROOM

This is one of the most famous pieces in blues history. It might have been a traditional theme arranged by Robert Johnson, who recorded "I believe I'll dust my broom" on 23 November 1936 on ARC 7-04-81. Arthur "Big Boy" Crudup covered the theme in a different style on 10 March 1949 (Victor 40-0074), as did Robert Jr. Lockwood in November 1951 (Mercury 8260). It is of course Elmore James (August 1951 on Trumpet 146) who made it the classic as we know it. A necessary piece for every apprentice of the slide guitar. "Dust My Broom" has nearly as many versions as "Catfish."

DYNAFLOW BLUES

The "Dynaflow" was a car model very widespread in the United States in the fifties. This Johnny Shines' blues is in fact an updated version of "Terraplane Blues" by Robert Johnson.

EARLY IN THE MORNING

Three great blues have this title. The most famous is a composition by John Lee "Sonny Boy" Williamson, who recorded four versions of it; the first one was on 11 November 1937 (on Bluebird B 7302). This "Early . . ." is sometimes called "'Bout the Break of Day." Then there is the "Early in the Morning (On my way to school)," whose origin is uncertain and "Early in the Morning" more often known under the title "Mother-in-Law Blues," Junior Parker's composition.

EASY BABY

This piece of Magic Sam's repertoire (Cobra 5029) became a classic of the West Side sound; it comes in fact from the repertoire of rhythm-and-blues singer Ann Cole (Baton 224 on 28 January 1956). Magic Sam's rendition possesses a dramatic intensity far from the original. Luther Allison had one of the best versions (on Gordy).

EASY RIDER BLUES
See "See See Rider"

EMPTY BED BLUES

One of the most famous pieces by Bessie Smith, who recorded it on 19 March 1928 on Columbia 14312. For a long time, "Empty Bed Blues" was a necessary piece for every female singer proclaimed as the "new Bessie Smith." To all these imitations we prefer the beautiful version of Josh White on Elektra.

EVENING

This is a variety piece signed by Parish and White that T-Bone completely transformed and made a masterpiece (May 1945 on Rhumboogie 4002 and especially 27 December 1957 on Atlantic 8020). Jimmy Witherspoon also gave a memorable version of it on Prestige.

EVERYDAY I HAVE THE BLUES

This postwar blues was strangely credited to Memphis Slim (Peter Chatman). Apparently it is a composition of the Sparks brothers (Aaron and Milton), largely played in the taverns of St. Louis in the thirties. Aaron "Pinetop" Sparks recorded the first version of "Everyday I Have the Blues" on 28 July 1935 (on Bluebird B 6125). After the war it was a big hit for Lowell Fulson and Lloyd Glenn, who made it the classic we know today (Swing Time 196 on 18 July 1949).

EVERYTHING'S GONNA BE ALRIGHT

This is an original composition by Little Walter. "Ah'w Baby" (20 June 1957 on Checker 945) preceeds it by two years (21 July 1959 on Checker 930). Muddy Waters and numerous others made it a part of their repertoire. One of the most unforgettable versions is the exemplary one given by Junior Wells (Vanguard 9231).

EVIL

Another standard Chicago blues, "Evil," was written by Willie Dixon for Howlin' Wolf (25 May 1954 on Chess 1575). This was also an important hit for Muddy Waters (June 1977 on Chess 1680).

FEELING GOOD

This Junior Parker's success (1953 on Sun 187) is a skillful plagiarism of "Boogie Chillen" by John Lee Hooker.

FEVER

This composition by Davenport and Cooley was recorded by Little Willie John (1 April 1956 on King 4935), and it was covered by singer Peggy Lee, who placed it in the pop charts. Peggy's "white" version (with a special mention of Romeo and Juliet and Pocahontas) became a rock standard (Elvis Presley had a superb interpretation), whereas the substantially different original version is still part of the repertoire of many black musicians (Buddy Guy, Little Milton, and T-Bone Walker did their own versions of it).

FIRST TIME I MET THE BLUES

See "Good Morning, Mr. Blues"

FIVE LONG YEARS

The history of the metal worker who, for five years, worked hard in a factory and who gave his check every Friday night to his girlfriend, who nevertheless dumped him, is one of the few blues tunes to reach number one in the Top 40 charts. This deep blues of Chicago comes from Eddie Boyd's pen (19 June 1952, JOB 1007). A great number of versions followed, including the reserved version by Muddy Waters (2 May 1963, Chess 1862) and his new, fascinating interpretation at the American Folk Blues Festival 1963 (Fontana TL 5204).

FLIP, FLOP AND FLY

This rock-and-roll classic is the invention of Big Joe Turner, who initially recorded it for Atlantic on 28 January 1955.

FORTY-FOUR BLUES

"44 Blues" is a necessary piece for all followers of the "88" (piano). It is probably an original composition by Lee Green (16 August 1929 on Vocalion 1401), although this piece is often attributed to Roosevelt Sykes, a student of Green's, who recorded it on 14 June 1929 on OK 8702.

FRANKIE AND JOHNNIE

Or "Frankie and Albert." This early piece of Anglo-Irish folklore is arranged with the colors of the Far West for this bloody news item. Strangely enough, "Frankie and Johnnie" had as many versions in country music as in rock-and-roll and the blues. Mississippi John

Hurt's is one of its oldest recorded versions (14 February 1928 on OK 8560).

GOING DOWN SLOW

"Going Down Slow" is the lament of the high roller who is dying and calls his mother as he enumerates all the pleasures he has known in his life! Jimmie Oden (St. Louis Jimmy) is its father (11 November 1941 on Bluebird B 8889). An unforgettable version was recorded by Howlin' Wolf (with Willie Dixon as an off-stage voice) on Chess 1813 in December 1961.

GOING TO CHICAGO BLUES

This piece often interpreted by blues shouters was created by Jimmy Rushing with Count Basie's band in 1941.

GOOD MORNING, LITTLE SCHOOL GIRL

Many blues and rock artists sang this syncopated piece that came from John Lee "Sonny Boy" Williamson's imagination (Bluebird B 7059 on May 1937). He made it one of his standards.

GOOD MORNING, MR. BLUES

The origin of this famous blues probably dates back to Little Brother Montgomery ("First Time I Met You," 16 October 1936 on Bluebird B 6766). Jimmy Rushing, Big Joe Turner, and Buddy Guy (2 March 1960 on Chess 1753) had their own versions of it.

GOOD ROCKIN' TONIGHT

Elvis Presley's huge success is in fact Roy Brown's piece recorded in July 1947 on DeLuxe 1093. "Good Rockin' Tonight" has been interpreted by more white rockers than black ones.

GOT MY MOJO WORKING

One of Muddy Waters' big hits (1 December 1956 on Chess 1652), this furious piece was composed by Preston and Foster for singer Ann Cole (27 January 1957 on Baton 237). Ann and Muddy had gone on a tour together, during which she ended her set with "Mojo." Muddy then added his own lyrics and recorded it under his signature. Only with the threat of a lawsuit did Chess withdraw the 45 from stores until it was pressed with the right credit. But who today remembers the excellent rendition by Ann Cole?

GUITAR RAG

This instrumental tour de force credited to Sylvester Weaver (2 November 1923 on OK 8109) was largely overshadowed by the version given in September 1936 by Leon McAuliffe on steel guitar with Bob Wills' band. This "Steel Guitar Rag" remains a country classic.

HARD TIMES KILLING FLOOR BLUES

A sensational blues during the Depression, "Hard Times" was composed by Skip James and recorded in February 1931 on Paramount 13065. After his rediscovery in 1963, Skip recorded this wonderful piece several times. There are other great versions by Jack Owens and Jo-Ann Kelly.

HARLEM CAN'T BE HEAVEN

This composition is by the famous Doctor Clayton (who greatly influenced B. B. King, according to King himself) who recorded "Angels in Harlem" on 7 August 1946 on Victor 20-2153. Sunnyland Slim made it his favorite song for a long time. Other worthy Texas adaptations ("Houston Can't Be Heaven" and "Angels in Houston") are by Larry Davis, Smokey Hogg, and Peppermint Harris.

HELLO STRANGER

See "Miss Mattie Blues"

HELP ME

This necessary classic for every self-respecting harmonica player is due to the inspiration of Lafayette Leake and Sonny Boy Williamson (Rice Miller), who recorded it on 11 January 1963 on Checker 1036. In fact, this piece was a reprise of a hit by Booker T. and the MG's, "Green Onions," with particularly clever lyrics. Among the countless versions of "Help Me," let's remember those of Junior Wells ("Tribute to Sonny Boy Williamson"), Magic Slim, Luther Allison, Little Mack Simmons, and Fenton Robinson.

HESITATION BLUES

An old ragtime piece probably from New Orleans. It seems that Crying Sam Collins made the first recorded version (17 September 1927 on Gennett 6379), and Doc Watson recorded the most convincing version.

HIDEAWAY

This standard for every contemporary blues band is attributed to Freddie King (on 26 August 1960 Federal 12401). However, evidence shows that this instrumental was used as the opening number for Hound Dog Taylor for several years before it was recorded by Freddie.

HIGHWAY 49

Highway 49 starts at the Gulf of Mexico (Biloxi), winds through Mississippi and its capital, Jackson, then to Arkansas via Helena. It is especially famous for the blues that Big Joe Williams devoted to it (25 February 1935 on Bluebird B 5996). His best version is certainly that on 12 December 1941 (Bluebird B 9025) accompanied by John Lee "Sonny Boy" Williamson. Howlin' Wolf also had an unforgettable interpretation.

HIGHWAY 51

Highway 51 begins in New Orleans, becomes #55 in Mississippi, then is #51 again after Memphis on up to Chicago. The road of the big southern migration, "Highway 51" was sung by Curtis Jones (25 January 1938 on Vocalion 03990) with particularly strong lyrics: "I beg you, if I die before my time, don't bury my body along Highway 51." Memphis Slim and Bob Dylan interpreted this poignant blues with much feeling.

HIGHWAY 61

This is the blues road par excellence that links New Orleans to Memphis via Greensville and Clarksdale. Numerous clubs and taverns are scattered along this asphalt ribbon. Even though the singer-guitarist Willie Blackwell had called himself "61," it was Fred McDowell who immortalized this road in his many versions of "Highway 61" (Prestige 25010).

HOBO BLUES

Known as one of John Lee Hooker's favorite blues, "Hobo Blues" was in fact composed by Yank Rachell, who recorded Hooker on 3 April 1941 with John Lee "Sonny Boy" Williamson (on Bluebird B 8768).

HOLD THAT TRAIN, CONDUCTOR

Even though B. B. King made "Hold That Train" one of his biggest hits in 1960, it is a composition by Doctor Clayton recorded on 7 August 1946 on Victor 20-1995. Otis Rush and Buddy Guy ("Hold That Plane") did remarkable versions of it.

HONEST I DO

Another well-worn standard, Mama Reed's sentimental composition (Vee-Jay 253 on 3 April 1957) for her husband Jimmy Reed was in the black Top 40 for a long time. Tina Turner has interpreted it convincingly.

THE HONEYDRIPPER

There've been several "honeydrippers" in blues history. Roosevelt Sykes got his nickname after the success of his composition recorded 21 February 1936 on Decca 7164. Then, Joe Liggins, in another composition of the same title, quite different, for the Exclusive label in California in 1946. Both have been covered by other artists.

HONKY TONK

This instrumental, present in the repertoire of numerous bluesmen, is an original composition of Bill Doggett (on King in 1956).

HOOCHIE COOCHIE MAN

One of Muddy Waters' biggest hits, "Hoochie Coochie Man" was composed for him by Willie Dixon (Chess 1560 on 7 January 1954).

HOODOO MAN BLUES

Voodoo has a select place in the blues. But no other composition is as evocative as "Hoodoo Man Blues" created by John Lee "Sonny Boy" Williamson on 6 August 1946 on Victor 20-2184. The most powerful version (with a very different approach) is probably Lightnin' Slim's on Excello. Junior Wells on States then on Vanguard also gave an exciting interpretation.

HOUND DOG

This composition by the Leiber-Stroller team, may really be from Johnny Otis's pen and Big Mama Thornton (13 August 1952 on Peacock 1612). Elvis Presley's popular version is a rock-and-roll classic.

HOUSE OF THE RISING SUN

This old ballad, likely with a black origin from New Orleans, was substantially interpreted by blues artists Leadbelly and Josh White, among others.

HOW LONG BLUES

Often called "When the Evening Train's Been Gone." Recorded on 19 June 1928 by Leroy Carr on Vocalion 1911, "How Long" was the biggest hit of the Carr-Blackwell duo. It was also recorded by many musicians and singers in all genres. T-Bone Walker and Joe Turner had wonderful versions.

I ASKED FOR WATER

See "Cool Drink of Water Blues"

I CAN'T QUIT YOU BABY

This composition by Willie Dixon was the only real commercial success for Otis Rush (Cobra 5000 in 1956). The best version may be Little Milton's (December 1968 on Checker 1212).

I DONE GOT OVER IT

T-Bone Walker, James Cotton, and Junior Parker have given convincing interpretations of this beautiful autobiographical composition by Guitar Slim (Eddie Jones) recorded on 27 October 1953 on Specialty 482.

I DON'T KNOW

This famous blues was a hit for Willie Mabon in 1952 (Parrot 1050). The piece was composed by pianist Cripple Clarence Lofton (Solo Art 12009 in 1939).

IF I HAD POSSESSION OVER JUDGEMENT DAY

See "Rollin' and Tumblin'"

I'M A KING BEE

Coming from the blues of Memphis Minnie, Bo Carter, and Muddy Waters using a rhythm of Lil' Son Jackson, "I'm a King Bee" is nevertheless a piece signed by Slim Harpo and recorded in 1957 on Excello 2113. It was the Rolling Stones' first important hit.

I'M A MAN

Bo Diddley was inspired by the "Hoochie Coochie Man" of Willie Dixon/Muddy Waters for his "I'm a Man" (recorded 2 March 1955 on Chess 1602), which was a big success. Muddy, cut to the quick, responded immediately with "Mannish Boy" (24 May 1955 on Chess 1602). Over one hundred different versions exist of these two similar blues, proclaiming the sexual feats of their authors.

I'M GONNA DIG MYSELF A HOLE

The story of the draftee who digs a hole to wait out the war seems to have dragged along before it was recorded by Arthur Crudup on Victor 22/50-041 on 24 April 1951. A few months later, this blues was covered successfully by Jimmy Rogers, who called it "The World's in a Tangle."

I'M GONNA MOVE TO THE OUTSKIRTS OF TOWN

This famous blues was recorded by Casey Bill Weldon on 3 September 1936 (Vocalion 03373), but Jazz Gillum made it a hit (30 June 1942 on Bluebird B 9042). Many versions were recorded by Leadbelly, Big Bill Broonzy, Ray Charles . . . .

I'M IN THE MOOD

It was of course with glances cast toward Benny Goodman that John Lee Hooker recorded his "I'm in the Mood" (and with a nod at Roosevelt Sykes), one of his biggest hits on 7 August 1951 on Modern 835. Since then he has recorded at least a dozen versions of this title, most recently accompanied by Bonnie Raitt. Big Boy Crudup recorded a similar title but with a much different inspiration in 1945 (Bluebird 340746).

I'M READY

Willie Dixon's original composition for Muddy Waters in the style of "Hoochie Coochie Man" and recorded by Muddy on 1 September 1954 on Chess 1579.

I'M SO GLAD

This spiritual probably dates back to the beginning of the blues. Skip James had the most accomplished version, a real instrumental tour de force, on Paramount 13098 in February 1931. There exist many

recorded versions of this piece; the most unforgettable ones are Fred
McDowell's and Eric Clapton's.

IT HURTS ME TOO

One of the most interpreted blues, "It Hurts Me Too" dates back to
Tampa Red, who created it on 10 March 1941 on Bluebird B 8635.
Elmore James (Chief 7004 in 1957) and especially Junior Wells
(Chief 7035 in 1962) made it a small hit.

IT'S TIGHT LIKE THAT

The twenties and thirties knew a surge of risqué songs. "Tight Like
That" was a popular theme thanks to Tampa Red and pianist
Georgia Tom Dorsey, who later became an evangelist (24 October
1928 on Vocalion 1216).

IT SERVES YOU RIGHT TO SUFFER

The California singer and composer Percy Mayfield is the author of
this blues under the title "Memory Pain" (1950 on Specialty). John
Lee Hooker did several versions with the title "It Serves You Right to
Suffer," including an exceptional one in 1967. Jimmy Dawkins and
Jimmy Johnson were inspired by Hooker in their own interpretations
of this very deep piece.

JACK O' DIAMONDS

"Jack O' Diamonds" originated in Mexican folklore, then it went to
Texas where it was part of the repertoire of every local songster.
Apparently Blind Lemon Jefferson recorded it the first time on 20
May 1926 on Paramount 12373. Countless renditions have followed.

JOHN HENRY

It is even more difficult to trace the origin of this "John Henry," who
dug tunnels through all the mountains in the United States. Probably
a black song, it belongs to the American folk repertoire. Leadbelly,
Sonny Terry, Memphis Slim, Big Walter Horton, and Buster Brown
have sung his exploits.

JOHNNY B. GOODE

This rock-and-roll classic was composed by Chuck Berry and
recorded on Chess 1691 on 18 February 1958. Countless bluesmen

have interpreted this composition, often without much innovation when compared to the original, which is still brilliant.

JUKE

"Juke" was the opening instrumental number of the Aces' performances on stage. First Louis Myers then Junior Wells and finally Little Walter, the band's harmonica players, played it before the beginning of the concert. In May 1952, Chess used the end of a tape during a recording session of Muddy Waters and Jimmy Rogers to capture the "Juke" of Little Walter, sideman for the other two. It was number one in the rhythm-and-blues charts, and it established the career of Little Walter.

JUST A DREAM

The dream theme that enables the extrapolation of daily problems is a constant one in black folklore. Big Bill Broonzy used it with incredible brio in "Just a Dream," recorded for the first time on 5 February 1939 on Vocalion 04706. Muddy Waters, Champion Jack Dupree, and Louisiana Red ("Red's Dream") have covered the song brilliantly.

JUST A LITTLE BIT

This piece became one of the sensational standards of contemporary blues. At first it was an innovative piece by Roscoe Gordon (21 April 1959 on Vee-Jay 332). Among unforgettable versions are those of Little Milton, Magic Sam, and Robert Jr. Lockwood.

KANSAS CITY

This incredible success of Wilbert Harrison recorded on 25 February 1959 on Fury 1027 is in fact the interpretation of a piece by Little Willie Littlefield recorded on 15 August 1952 on Federal 12110. "Kansas City" is now a well-known rock-and-roll standard. The version by Wanda Jackson is particularly exciting.

One must not confuse this Kansas City with "Kansas City Blues," its remote cousin, created successfully by Jim Jackson on 10 October 1927 on Vocalion 1144.

KEEP YOUR HANDS OFF HER

Or ". . . Off Him" or ". . . Off My Woman." Big Bill Broonzy composed this famous blues and recorded it for the first time on 31

October 1935 on Bluebird B 6188. After many versions, "Hands Off"
was number one for singer Priscilla Bowman, accompanied by piano
player Jay McShann in 1955 on Vee-Jay 155. It is this version that is
usually copied today.

KEY TO THE HIGHWAY

It seems that "Key" is Big Bill Broonzy's composition recorded by
Jazz Gillum on 9 May 1940 on Bluebird B 8529. Big Bill, in his turn,
recorded this piece on 2 May 1941 (OK 06242). Little Walter, Sonny
Terry and Brownie McGhee, Chuck Berry ("I Got a Booking"), and
many bluesmen have sung this title successfully.

KILLING FLOOR

This "Killing Floor" is only remotely linked to "Hard Times Killing
Floor Blues" from Skip James, although Howlin' Wolf, a Delta bluesman, was certainly inspired by it. His "Killing Floor" (Chess 1923
recorded in August 1964) was covered brilliantly by Albert King and
Sonny Rhodes.

KIND-HEARTED WOMAN

This original composition by Robert Johnson was his first recorded
piece (23 November 1936 on ARC 7-03-56). Robert Jr. Lockwood,
Johnny Shines, Muddy Waters, and Louis Myers included it in their
repertoire with a similar feeling.

KOKOMO BLUES

Or "Old Original Kokomo Blues." Having borrowed it from the
Scrapper Blackwell songbook, Kokomo Arnold made it his trade-
mark and recorded it for the first time on 10 September 1934 on
Decca 7026. "Kokomo Blues" is the primitive version of "Sweet
Home Chicago" by Robert Johnson. It is important to mention that
Kokomo Arnold also used, it seems, for the first time on record, the
expression "dust my broom."

LAST NIGHT

The author of Little Walter's piece (Checker 805, 5 October 1954), a
necessary passage for every apprentice harmonica player, is Little Bill
Gaither, who was mourning the death of his idol Leroy Carr (15
December 1934). The same number with many similar phrases was
covered by Brownie McGhee about Blind Boy Fuller.

LET ME PLAY WITH YOUR POODLE

Or "Let Me Play with Your Yoyo." This semi-pornographic blues was tremendously popular in the thirties. Tampa Red (6 February 1942 on Bluebird 34-0700) preferred the poodle. Blind Willie McTell had preceded him with the yoyo, but the piece was judged too shocking and was released only in the seventies!

LET THE GOOD TIMES ROLL

It seems that every blues band, black or white, let the good times roll. Apparently Louis Jordan is at the origin of this phenomenon; his "Let the Good Times Roll" goes back to 1946. Koko Taylor shouted this piece quite convincingly.

LEVEE CAMP MOAN

Or often "Levee Camp Blues." This workers' camp on the levees created in order to contain the Mississippi and its affluents has often been celebrated since Texas Alexander recorded his wonderful "Levee Camp Moan" on 12 August 1927 on OK 8498. Big Joe Williams, Robert Pete Williams, and Lightnin' Hopkins gave beautiful interpretations of this very primitive blues.

LITTLE BY LITTLE

A superb composition of producer Mel London for Junior Wells, who recorded it in 1957 on Profile 4011. Other numerous good versions exist by Wells himself and by Charlie Musselwhite.

LONESOME BEDROOM BLUES

Sometimes "Lonesome in My Bedroom," this deep blues in the style of Leroy Carr/Scrapper Blackwell is an original composition of Curtis Jones recorded on 28 September 1937 on Vocalion 03756. There are countless reissues of this classic, including Muddy Waters' particularly good version.

LONESOME ROAD BLUES

Numerous blues have this title. The most famous and most interpreted comes from Big Bill Broonzy, who recorded it on 17 December 1940 on OK 06031.

LONG DISTANCE CALL

"Long Distance Call" was for a long time one of Muddy Waters' favorite pieces, which he recorded and rerecorded. The origin of this telephone blues is the simple "Long Distance Moan" of Blind Lemon Jefferson (Paramount 12852 on 24 September 1929), but Muddy's piece is far more famous (Chess 1452 on 23 January 1951).

LOOK OVER YONDER'S WALL

The position of the man who is somewhat disabled and has not been drafted and who takes advantage of that to entertain lonely married women has inspired many postwar blues. This one happens to be the most famous. From Jazz Gillum's imagination; he recorded it on 18 February 1946 on Victor 20-1974. The piece has been transposed from one war to the other until Vietnam. "Look . . ." remains a much-played blues in Chicago, and it is often incorrectly attributed to Elmore James, who recorded a superb version of it in 1961 on Fire 504.

LOSING HAND

There are numerous losing hands in the big blues game. That of Ray Charles—probably his best blues—recorded on 17 May 1953 on Atlantic 1037 and that of Eddie Boyd (less known but as good), with Buddy Guy on the guitar, recorded in August 1965 on Decca LP 4748 are above the game!

LOUISE

One of Johnnie Temple's most beautiful compositions, "Louise" was recorded for the first time on 12 November 1936 on Decca 7244; its tremendous success led to a second version by Temple on 14 May 1937 on Decca 7337. Big Bill Broonzy recorded it on 9 June 1936 on ARC 7-06-65. For almost forty years, countless bluesmen sang the exploits of sweet "Louise." Very dramatic versions were done by Robert Pete Williams, Howlin' Wolf, and John Lee Hooker.

LOVE HER WITH A FEELING

This smart advice was authored by Tampa Red, who recorded this blues on 16 June 1938 on Bluebird B 7822. Another version of this blues by Tampa is even more remarkable (7 March 1950 on Victor 22/50-0084), with Little Johnny Jones playing the piano. Junior Wells was particularly able to use the advice of Tampa Red.

LOVE IN VAIN

This beautiful composition by Robert Johnson was recorded on 20 June 1937 on Vocalion 04630. The Rolling Stones produced a well-known rendition with a vibrant slide guitar solo.

LOVE ME, MAMA

A variation of "Rock Me, Mama" inaugurated by Big Boy Crudup on 24 April 1951 on Victor 20/47-4367.

MAGGIE CAMPBELL

One of the loves of Tommy Johnson, who immortalized her on 4 February 1928 on Victor 21409. According to David Evans, Tommy Johnson was in love with Maggie, the wife of a black farmer. "Maggie Campbell" was sung by a great many emulators of Johnson: Robert Nighthawk, Houston Stackhouse, and even Muddy Waters in "Meanest Woman" (Chess 1765 in June 1960).

MAKE ME A PALLET ON THE FLOOR

A very old piece of black folklore that joined the southern "common ground," "Make Me a Pallet on the Floor" is usually associated with the street singers in Memphis. Mississippi John Hurt popularized it, while Jo-Ann Kelly and Doc Watson had the best versions.

MAMA DON'T ALLOW . . .

This too is an old dance piece that dates back to the beginning of the blues. It seems that Cow Cow Davenport recorded it for the first time on 22 June 1929 (Vocalion 1434). Under this name or similar ones, this piece continues to be among the repertoire of numerous country music, New Orleans jazz, and blues bands. "Boogie Chillen," John Lee Hooker's famous hit, used part of the lyrics of this ancestor of the boogie-woogie.

MAMA, TALK TO YOUR DAUGHTER

J. B. Lenoir had some success in Chicago with this boogie-blues (1954 on Parrot 809) still played by numerous bluesmen today. Lenoir was certainly inspired by Ruth Brown ("Mama, He Treats Your Daughter Mean," Atlantic 986 on 19 December 1952).

MANNISH BOY

See "I'm a Man"

MATCHBOX BLUES

This blues and rock-and-roll classic comes from Blind Lemon Jefferson, who created it on 14 March 1927 on OK 8455. Hundreds of versions followed. Carl Perkins transposed it to rock.

MEAN OLD FRISCO

A real blues monument, "Mean Old Frisco" was recorded by Arthur "Big Boy" Crudup on 15 April 1942 on Bluebird 34-0704. Crudup was certainly inspired by the many blues based on trains ("Panama Limited"). Anyway, this "Mean Old Frisco" was a big hit, and it gave rise to countless different versions, among which was Lightnin' Slim's and Muddy Waters'.

MEAN OLD WORLD

This famous blues probably came from Big Bill Broonzy, who recorded it on 31 January 1937 on ARC 7-07-64. T-Bone Walker—who made it one of his pieces—recorded his first version on 20 July 1942 on Capitol 10033 with Freddie Slack's band. Little Walter, to whom the title is often credited, recorded a unique version of "Mean Old World" in October 1952 on Checker 764.

MELLOW DOWN EASY

Little Walter's big hit was signed by Willie Dixon and recorded on 5 October 1954 on Checker 805. Paul Butterfield and ZZ Top made it known beyond the blues. Little Walter's version is still unequaled.

MELLOW PEACHES BLUES

This old piece of the Delta is often titled "Don't Your Peaches Look Mellow Hanging upon Your Tree." Sometimes the peaches are replaced by other fruit as mellow but of different sizes and shapes: "apples," "plums," . . . Yank Rachell with "Peach Tree Blues" (11 December 1941 on Bluebird B 9033) apparently inaugurated the series that Big Joe Williams annexed to his repertoire.

MERRY CHRISTMAS, BABY

One of the most famous blues of Charles Brown/Johnny Moore recorded in 1947. Its "definite" version was recorded on 4 September 1956 on Aladdin 3348.

MESSIN' WITH THE KID

This blues as a macho profession of faith was a great success for Junior Wells; it was signed by Mel London. Wells recorded it the first time in 1961 on Chief 7021, Muddy Waters responded immediately, proclaiming that he was still preeminent in the Chicago blues ("Messin' with the Man" in June 1961 on Chess 1796).

MIDNIGHT SPECIAL

Lomax put this piece from the beginning of the century back on the midnight train. Leadbelly, Josh White, and Sonny Terry and Brownie McGhee made it one of their favorite pieces.

MILK COW BLUES

Kokomo Arnold milks his cow the best and gave the best advice on how to do it on 10 September 1934 (Decca 7026), but it is undeniably Sleepy John Estes who created the piece on 13 May 1930 on Victor V 38614. The rockers heard the message: Elvis Presley, Eddie Cochran, and a crowd of their emulators sang the exploits of that "prodigal cow" by accelerating the tempo substantially. Arnold preferred to make the pleasure last.

MISS MATTIE BLUES

John Lee "Sonny Boy" Williamson praised Mattie's charms in "Mattie Mae Blues" on 4 April 1941 on Bluebird B 8797. Baby Boy Warren was entranced, and he recorded at least three different versions, followed by Louis Myers, Sonny Boy #2, and even Muddy Waters! Often titled "Hello Stranger."

MR. DOWNCHILD

"Mr. Downchild" is most certainly a Robert Johnson composition that he never recorded. It is Robert Jr. Lockwood who transposed this blues and taught it to Sonny Boy Williamson (Rice Miller), who finally recorded it on 4 December 1951 on Trumpet 168. Robert Jr. Lockwood had a brilliant version very close to the style of his mentor Robert Johnson on Trix 3307 (8 June 1973). It is interesting to note that in the live version recorded by Sonny Boy in 1963 with the Yardbirds, Eric Clapton recorded his very first solo.

MONEY

Berry Gordy's composition for the Miracles, "Money," was often played by bluesmen. There are beautiful versions by Buddy Guy and John Lee Hooker.

MY BABE

This title written by Willie Dixon for Little Walter and recorded on 25 January 1955 on Checker 811 brought Walter tremendous success. In fact, it was a profane plagiarism of an old Negro spiritual, "This Train."

MY BABY LEFT ME

Another composition by Arthur "Big Boy" Crudup recorded on 8 November 1950 on Victor 22/50-0109 and made famous by Elvis Presley, then Wanda Jackson.

MY BLACK NAME

This is a marvelous, poignant blues about the condition of the "nig-ger" offered by John Lee "Sonny Boy" Williamson on 11 December 1941 on Bluebird B 8892. John Lee Hooker, Big Joe Williams, and Lightnin' Hopkins delivered this somber message with incredibly dramatic force.

MY LITTLE MACHINE

"There is something that is not right in my little machine." This veiled complaint about the damaging effect of impotence was cred-ited to John Lee "Sonny Boy" Williamson; it was recorded on 17 May 1940 on Bluebird B 8892. Contagion seems to have been big: Jimmy Rogers, Eddie Taylor, and Driftin' Slim were contaminated whereas Lightnin' Slim and then Lightnin' Hopkins gave a more personalized variation ("My Starter Won't Start This Morning")!

MYSTERY TRAIN

Before being a hit for Elvis Presley and also a recent movie, "Mystery Train" was a small success for Junior Parker, who composed it in 1953 (Sun 192). He probably was inspired by an old Celtic ballad popularized by the Carter Family.

NIGHT TIME IS THE RIGHT TIME

Roosevelt Sykes seems to have drawn from the old vaudeville tradi-tion to create this beautiful piece he recorded on 29 April 1937

(Decca 7324). Other versions by Sykes followed as well as by a great number of bluesmen, among whom was John Lee Hooker who included it in his "I'm in the Mood."

NOBODY KNOWS YOU (WHEN YOU'RE DOWN AND OUT)

One of the most beautiful compositions by Bessie Smith, who recorded it on 15 May 1929 on Columbia 14451, forcing the crowds of her female imitators to try (in vain) to equal her through the following decades.

OFF THE WALL

This is Little Walter's famous instrumental recorded in January 1953 on Checker 770. Big Walter Horton always claimed to be the composer, and he recorded it in Memphis on 28 May 1953 for Sun. This is a necessary exercise for every harmonica player who wants to convince himself of his technical quality.

OH! RED

Joe McCoy's composition, recorded with the Harlem Hamfats on 18 April 1936 (Decca 7182), was a tremendous success. Nearly everybody had a rendition in the thirties and forties, even Howlin' Wolf.

ON THE ROAD AGAIN

A beautiful moving blues in the purest Delta tradition, "On the Road Again" was composed by Floyd Jones following the success of "Dark Road." Tommy Johnson's influence is omnipresent in these two great blues. Canned Heat was successful with this piece in the late sixties.

ONE BOURBON, ONE SCOTCH, ONE BEER

The specialist of the odes to alcoholism, Amos Milburn, is the author of this piece that clearly foreshadows rock-and-roll. Other variations are "Bad Bad Whiskey," "Vicious Vicious Vodka," and "Let Me Go Home, Whiskey."

ONE-ROOM COUNTRY SHACK

This poignant blues was penned by Texas piano player and singer Mercy Dee Walton, who recorded it in 1953 on Specialty 458. Several remarkable versions were turned in by Buddy Guy (probably his best piece on the Vanguard album 79272 of 18 September 1967), Fenton

Robinson, and John Lee Hooker. A great blues classic that is still being interpreted.

OUTSKIRTS OF TOWN
See "I'm Gonna Move to the Outskirts of Town"

PARCHMAN FARM
Bukka White's autobiographical piece about Parchman Penitentiary was recorded on 7 March 1940 on OK 05683. Mose Allison drew his inspiration from it in a rather remote way for his famous piece, as did John Mayall.

PART-TIME LOVE
Almost everybody has sung "Part-Time Love" since Little Johnny Taylor recorded it in July 1963 and made it number one for several months on the charts. It is a composition by Clay Hammond, a good soul singer.

PENITENTIARY BLUES
A superb Texas blues classic composed by Blind Lemon Jefferson and recorded in February 1928 on Paramount 12666. Smokey Hogg, Lightnin' Hopkins, Lil' Son Jackson, and almost all the Texas bluesmen did their own versions of it. Lowell Fulson's ("I'm Prison Bound") in 1948 may be the most poignant one.

PINETOP'S BOOGIE WOOGIE
The archetype of the boogie-woogie if not the first boogie recorded, "Pinetop's" is of course Pinetop Smith's boogie recorded on 29 December 1928 on Vocalion 1245. One volume would not be enough to list all those who have interpreted it since then.

PINK CHAMPAGNE
In the area of alcoholic sagas by Amos Milburn, this "Pink Champagne" has a place sparkling with humor and rhythm. It was composed by Joe Liggins and recorded in 1950 on Specialty.

PLEASE, SEND ME SOMEONE TO LOVE
Another durable California piece, "Please" was composed by Percy Mayfield, who recorded it in 1950 for the Specialty label. From

Junior Parker to B. B. King, who has not recorded a version of this beautiful ballad?

PONY BLUES

A great Delta blues, "Pony" was created by Charlie Patton on 14 June 1929 on Paramount 12792. Honeyboy Edwards, Big Joe Williams, and "modern" groups like the Fieldstones in Memphis have interpreted it.

POOR BLACK MATTIE

Another great theme of the Mississippi Delta, "Mattie" comes from the blues of Tommy Johnson and Charlie Patton. R. L. Burnside made it one of his favorite pieces, but we can also find Mattie in the repertoire of several Chicago bluesmen like Louis Myers.

POOR BOY

"Poor boy . . . a long way from home" is as much a part of black folklore as it is of white folklore, and its origin is quite questionable. It is probably an old English piece revised by Appalachian musicians. Strangely enough, "Poor Boy," after decades of being a standard refrain, especially in country music, resurfaced among postwar bluesmen: Big Joe Williams, John Jackson, Fred McDowell, and Howlin' Wolf, who gave a sensational rendering in December 1957 on Chess 1679.

PRISON BOUND BLUES

One of Leroy Carr's famous compositions, he recorded it for the first time on 20 December 1928 on Vocalion 1241. Countless versions followed, from Big Bill Broonzy to Muddy Waters.

PRODIGAL SON

This old spiritual, more or less "arranged," was a small hit for Robert Wilkins, who recorded it under the title "Rolling Stone" on 7 September 1928 on Victor 21741. Forty years later, the Rolling Stones took up the title "Prodigal Son" and gave a nice royalty check to Wilkins, who, in the meantime, had become a reverend. The final version of "Prodigal Son" recorded by Wilkins was on 16 February 1964 on Piedmont PLP 13162.

RAMBLIN' ON MY MIND

This alternative to "Dust My Broom" is also a composition by Robert Johnson in the same format, recorded on 23 November 1936 on ARC 7-05-81. Robert Jr. Lockwood's version is one of the best.

RECONSIDER BABY

Lowell Fulson's composition from 27 September 1954 (Checker 804), "Reconsider Baby," enabled hundreds of musicians to practice their persuasive talents as singers. "Reconsider" retains an incredible force when sung by Fulson, Tina Turner, and Elvis Presley (who had a sensational version on RCA).

RED CROSS STORE

This Red Cross store comes from black folklore of the First World War or from the Depression. Leadbelly was considered (maybe wrongly) as the inventor of this piece (1935 for the Library of Congress) that Fred McDowell helped to popularize after 1965.

RED RIVER BLUES

The Red River, especially Texan, was celebrated by the Georgia bluesman Buddy Moss on 16 January 1933 on ARC 8-03-61. The theme had some success before the war.

RED ROOSTER

Obviously inspired by Charlie Patton's "Banty Rooster" (14 June 1929 on Paramount 12792), this "Red Rooster" has the unmistakable signature of Willie Dixon, who composed it for Howlin' Wolf (recorded on Chess 1804 in 1961). The Rolling Stones covered the piece several years later and made it one of their first big hits.

RIVER'S INVITATION

This gloomy river invitation was created in Percy Mayfield's imagination (1950 on Specialty), and it was very successful. A great many singers have interpreted this superb ballad, from Junior Parker to James Cotton (April 1968 on Vanguard 9283).

ROCK ME, BABY

The origin of this classic blues is "Rockin' and Rollin'" composed by Lil' Son Jackson and recorded on 16 December 1950 on Imperial

5113. B. B. King made "Rock Me, Baby" one of his great hits, as did Muddy Waters, to whom this beautiful blues is attributed ("All Night Long" on 29 December 1951 on Chess 1509; "Rock Me" on 1 December 1956 on Chess 1652). It is difficult to make an inventory of the number of interesting variations of this "Rock Me." Big Joe Turner's "Rock Me" (13 June 1941 on Decca 8577) is a totally different piece.

ROCK ME, MAMA

Lil' Son Jackson was probably inspired by "Rock Me, Mama," a similar piece by Arthur "Big Boy" Crudup and recorded on 15 December 1944 on Bluebird 34-0725. But "Mama" had its own life, different from that of "Baby," giving rise to a number of convincing emulators.

ROCKY MOUNTAIN BLUES

A powerful blues about the risks of the traveler crossing the Rocky Mountains, "Rocky Mountain Blues" was composed by Little Bill Gaither and recorded on 27 August 1937 on Decca 7434. The success must have been significant, because Bill recorded on 29 June 1939 a "New Rocky Mountain Blues" (Decca 7760). This theme was covered and dramatized even more by Lightnin' Hopkins and J. B. Lenoir.

ROLL 'EM, PETE

A direct boogie-woogie, this "Roll 'em Pete" is by Pete Johnson, the great Kansas City piano player, and Joe Turner, who sang it (30 December 1938 on Vocalion 4607). Numerous versions of this classic helped to immortalize Pete Johnson's name even more.

ROLLIN' AND TUMBLIN'

This great Delta blues classic was recorded for the first time on 14 March 1929 on OK 8679 by Hambone Willie Newbern. Charlie Patton ("Down the Dirt Road Blues" on 4 June 1929 on Paramount 12854) created a similar piece. "Rollin' and Tumblin'" was interpreted by hundreds of artists of the Delta and of Chicago: Muddy Waters, Son House, R. L. Burnside, Sunnyland Slim . . .

ST. JAMES INFIRMARY

Associated with Louis Armstrong and interpreted by numerous bluesmen, this piece dates from the eighteenth century as proven by Doc

Watson's superb "St. James Hospital." "Infirmary," the blues version, was the object of attentive care by Rhythm Willie, Dave Van Ronk, Dave Alexander, and Josh White, who gave the most exciting version.

ST. LOUIS BLUES

Like many blues of the beginning of the century "St. Louis Blues" was appropriated by W. C. Handy. Bessie Smith's beautiful version in June 1929 in the film of the same name may be considered as the archetype of this blues which has been interpreted to excess, from the female blues singers to Chuck Berry.

SAME THING

Willie Dixon's powerful composition for Muddy Waters (9 April 1964 on Chess 1895) and for Koko Taylor ("I Got What It Takes" on 30 June 1964 on Checker 1092). Like many Chicago standards, the origin of this piece lies in Mississippi. Bo Carter on 15 December 1930 recorded "The Same Thing (The Cats Are Fightin' About)" on OK 8858.

SCRATCH MY BACK

This invitation is credited to the slightly acid pen of Slim Harpo (Excello 2273 in 1966). Since then, the success of this small southern classic never failed, and from Otis Redding to Gary Coleman, "Scratch My Back" became the necessary passage of every blues-rock group.

SEE SEE RIDER

Here again we have a real blues standard. Before being sensational, this delicious piece, very likely from vaudeville, was created by Ma Rainey on 16 October 1924 on Paramount 12252 with Louis Armstrong playing the cornet stop. Also often called "C. C. Rider" or "Easy Rider." The structure of the piece betrays an East Coast origin.

SEE THAT MY GRAVE IS KEPT CLEAN

One of Blind Lemon Jefferson's most famous compositions. He recorded it in October 1927 on Paramount 12585. "See . . ." is a wonderful half-blues, half-spiritual piece played in arpeggio. Bob Dylan, John Lee Hooker ("Two White Horses"), and Lightnin' Hopkins also had breathtaking versions.

SHAKE 'EM ON DOWN

This very old risqué nursery rhyme was fixed on record by the great masters of the Delta blues: Bukka White (2 September 1937 on Vocalion 03711), Big Joe Williams (12 December 1941 on Bluebird B 8969), Fred McDowell, Tommy McClennan (22 November 1939 on Bluebird B 8347), and R. L. Burnside.

SHAKE IT BABY / SHAKE THAT THING

In the blues there are countless invitations to "shake that thing," tempered by the advice ". . . but don't break it." Charlie Patton (14 June 1929 on Paramount 12869) gave this advice, covered by dozens of musicians. The Mississippi Sheiks and Bo Carter passed the tradition on to John Lee Hooker, who in 1962 had a big hit with an adaptation of this old "thing."

SHAKE YOUR MONEYMAKER

A variation on the previous songs. Elmore James gave a shattering version which made him almost the sole performer of this piece (Fire 504 in 1961).

SHORT-HAIRED WOMAN

A Lightnin' Hopkins' composition, and one his first hits, recorded on 15 August 1947 on Aladdin 3005. There are numerous renditions of this small Texas classic and women's reactions to Hopkins, who did not want a wife with "shorter hair than mine."

SINNER'S PRAYER

Lowell Fulson's beautiful composition recorded in 1950 on Swing Time 237. Ray Charles (on 17 May 1953 on Atlantic 1021) and Lightnin' Hopkins had remarkable interpretations.

SITTING ON TOP OF THE WORLD

Nearly all pop, blues, and country singers sang "Sitting on Top of the World," the favorite piece of Bonnie and Clyde. It was composed by Walter Vincson and A. Chatmon, who recorded it with their group, the Mississippi Sheiks, for the first time on 17 February 1930 on OK 8784.

SIXTEEN TONS

This folk song was due to Merle Travis's imagination. Big Bill Broonzy, B. B. King, and the Platters did wonderful versions of it.

SKY IS CRYING (The)

This is one of Elmore James's wonderful compositions, which he recorded in November 1959 on Fire 1016. It is possible that producer Bobby Robinson helped James compose the particularly poetical lyrics. From among the many versions, let's remember those of Freddie King, Albert King, Sonny Boy Williamson (Rice Miller), and, most recently, the late Stevie Ray Vaughan.

SLEEPING IN THE GROUND

This modernized version of "I'd Rather See You Dead," a traditional piece of the Delta blues, is by harmonica player Sammy Myers, who recorded it in 1957 on Ace 536. Robert Cray had an excellent version.

SLOPPY DRUNK

This piece was identified with Jimmy Rogers, who recorded it numerous times (the first time on 13 April 1954 on Chess 1574). In fact, it was composed by John Lee "Sonny Boy" Williamson and called "Bring Me Another Half a Pint" recorded on 12 November 1947 on Victor 22-0021.

SMOKESTACK LIGHTNIN'

A sensational piece by Howlin' Wolf—maybe his best one—from January 1956 on Chess 1618, "Smokestack Lightnin'" refers directly to Charlie Patton's "Moon Going Down" (14 June 1929 on Paramount 12854).

SOMEBODY LOAN ME A DIME

This superb modern blues is part of the repertoire of one out of every two blues artists. It was composed by Fenton Robinson in 1967, but it was covered by rock singer Boz Scaggs.

SOMEDAY, BABY

One of the most famous blues. Also known under the titles "Trouble No More" (Muddy Waters), "Things Have Changed" (Big Maceo), "I Ain't Gonna Be Worried No More" (B. B. King), et cetera. Sleepy John Estes, its composer, recorded it on 9 July 1935 on Decca 7325.

SPOONFUL

Popularized by Howlin' Wolf (then by Cream), "Spoonful" was composed by Willie Dixon and recorded in June 1960 on Chess 1762.

However, once again, it is important to go back to the origin: Charlie Patton on 14 June 1929 ("A Spoonful Blues" on Paramount 12869).

STAGOLEE

Or Stackolee or Stack-O-Lee . . . This old tune of Anglo-Irish folklore has been interpreted as country, rock-and-roll, and blues. "Stagolee" was celebrated with talent by Champion Jack Dupree, Mississippi John Hurt, Archibald . . .

STATESBORO BLUES

Composed by Blind Willie McTell and recorded on 17 October 1928 on Victor 38001, "Statesboro Blues" resurfaced with the blues revival. Taj Mahal gave a wonderful modernized version.

STEP IT UP AND GO

This is the East Coast version of the Delta standard "Bottle Up and Go." Blind Boy Fuller recorded what is considered to be the definitive version of this old piece on 5 March 1940 on Vocalion 05476. Doc Watson interpreted it remarkably.

STOOP DOWN BABY

The spirit of this quick blues dates back to Bo Carter, but it was recorded by Chick Willis in 1972 and has since then been very successful.

STOP BREAKING DOWN

Another composition by Robert Johnson which was covered many times. Recorded on 20 June 1937 on Vocalion 04002 by Johnson and popularized by John Lee "Sonny Boy" Williamson in his version of 19 October 1945 on Victor 20-3047, "Stop Breaking Down" was covered countless times: Louis Myers, Junior Wells, Johnny Young . . .

STORM IN TEXAS

A hit for the late Stevie Ray Vaughan comes in fact from Larry Davis ("Texas Flood" recorded in 1958 on Duke 192). Whispering Smith, Fenton Robinson, and Albert King produced beautiful versions.

STORMY MONDAY BLUES

Sometimes also called "Call It Stormy Monday," this was one of the famous blues composed by T-Bone Walker and recorded for the first time in 1947 on Black & White 637. What bluesman does not have his own version?

SUGAR MAMA BLUES

John Lee "Sonny Boy" Williamson's composition, "Sugar Mama Blues" was recorded on 5 May 1937 on Bluebird B 7059. Big Joe Williams, John Lee Hooker, and Howlin' Wolf had breathtaking renditions. Tampa Red had another "Sugar Mama Blues" (23 March 1934 on Vocalion 02720), and Williamson may have been slightly inspired by it.

SWEET HOME CHICAGO

Robert Johnson composed this piece from Kokomo Arnold's "Kokomo Blues," and he recorded it on 23 November 1936 on Vocalion 03601. "Sweet Home Chicago" became one of the most popular pieces of the Chicago blues and beyond, thanks to Magic Sam, Junior Parker, and the Blues Brothers.

SWEET LITTLE ANGEL

Tampa Red recorded "Black Angel Blues" on 23 March 1934 on Vocalion 02753, a beautiful sentimental blues that Robert Nighthawk covered in a wonderful version on 12 July 1949 (on Aristocrat 2301) and retitled a few months later so as to increase the sales: "Sweet Little Angel." (The "black" was judged too offensive for some ears!) Tampa Red recorded his title again on 7 November 1950 by calling it "Sweet Little Angel" (Victor 22-0107) and by using Nighthawk's slide-guitar part. Finally, B. B. King turned it into the hit we know today, covered by hundreds of musicians, from Buddy Guy to Otis Rush and many bluesmen apprentices, black and white.

SWEET SIXTEEN

Another big hit for B. B. King in 1960 on Kent 330, "Sweet Sixteen" is a modernization of the piece with the same title recorded by Walter Davis on 25 February 1935 with Big Joe Williams on Bluebird B 5931. The piece with nearly the same title created by Chuck Berry ("Sweet Little Sixteen") in 1958 on Chess 1683 is totally different. Through B. B. King, "Sweet Sixteen" remains an almost necessary standard for each blues band.

TAKE A LITTLE WALK WITH ME

Usually attributed to Robert Johnson, it was first recorded by Robert Jr. Lockwood on 30 July 1941 on Bluebird B 8820, followed shortly by John Lee "Sonny Boy" Williamson. Jimmy DeBerry and Little Johnny Jones came up with some superb versions after the war.

T. B. BLUES

This wonderful and poignant composition about the damages of tuberculosis is undeniably linked to Victoria Spivey, who recorded it on 27 April 1927 on OK 8494. Among the countless versions, John Lee Hooker's (in 1971 on Bluesway) is extremely good.

T-BONE SHUFFLE

T-Bone Walker is responsible for this blues instrumental. This swinging piece is somewhat forced as a necessary standard of Texas-California guitar. T-Bone recorded it a first time on 6 November 1947 on Comet T-53, but his most beautiful version is unquestionably the one of 21 April 1955 on Atlantic 1065. In 1985 the trio Johnny Copeland/Albert Collins/Robert Cray opened their album *Showdown* (Alligator 4743) with "T-Bone Shuffle."

TERRAPLANE BLUES

"Terraplane" was a popular car model in the thirties. Robert Johnson composed "Terraplane Blues" on the theme of the lover anxious to see his mistress (23 November 1936 on ARC 7-03-56) who begs the road workers not to block the way. This theme was revisited countless times, with more contemporary models than "Terraplane." Frank Edwards, Johnny Shines, and Howlin' Wolf had superb renditions of this wonderful blues.

THAT'S ALL RIGHT / THAT'S ALL RIGHT MAMA

"That's All Right Mama" was created by Arthur "Big Boy" Crudup on 6 September 1946 (Victor 20-2205), and the piece was a big hit in Memphis and Chicago. Of course, Elvis Presley—advised by Sam Phillips—covered this blues and rather accelerated the tempo, thus inventing rockabilly. In the blues, Clarence "Gatemouth" Brown and Albert King performed wonderful versions of this piece.

THINGS I USED TO DO

Another piece that was used over and over. However, "Things I Used to Do" remains a classic of the New Orleans blues, composed by Guitar Slim and recorded for the first time on 27 October 1953 on Specialty 482. "Things" was covered by PeeWee Crayton, Tina Turner, Lonnie Brooks, and Joe Turner.

THREE O'CLOCK IN THE MORNING

Lowell Fulson composed this beautiful piece recorded on 17 June 1948 on Down Town 2002. B. B. King gave us the standard version in 1952 on RPM 339.

THRILL IS GONE (The)

This beautiful ballad in a minor key was a big hit for B. B. King in June 1969 on Bluesway 61032. It was first done by Roy Hawkins on 25 April 1951 on Modern 826.

TIN PAN ALLEY

"Tin Pan Alley" became a little like the "national anthem" of the West Coast blues. As for its origin, there is a composition by Walter Davis, "Fifty Avenue Blues" (5 May 1937 on Bluebird B 7021), covered by Curtis Jones as "Bad Avenue Blues" on 11 October 1937 (Bluebird B 7387) and finally as "Tin Pan Alley" on 19 August 1941 on OK 06494. Guitar Slim Green adapted it to California, and Jimmy Wilson then Al King provide the definitive version with which the West Coast musicians identified themselves.

TOM MOORE'S FARM

One of the most famous compositions by Lightnin' Hopkins, "Tom Moore's Farm" (created in May 1948 on Gold Star 640) resulted in his being beaten up by white farmers implicated in this blues.

TOO MANY DRIVERS

This Texas blues standard (sometimes christened "Let Me Ride in Your Automobile," "Too Many Drivers at Your Wheel," or simply "Automobile Blues") is usually associated with Smokey Hogg, who recorded it in 1947 on Modern 20-532. Big Bill Broonzy recorded an early version on Vocalion 05096, May 11, 1939. Hopkins covered it on "Automobile Blues" (Gold Star 666 in 1949), and Lowell Fulson did too on Swing Time 325 in 1951, thus placing what was certainly an old piece of Texas Alexander's in the charts.

TROUBLE IN MIND

This ballad that has been recorded over and over again in jazz, blues, and pop is an original composition of pianist Richard M. Jones for singer Georgia White. Together, they recorded it on 12 May 1936 on Decca 7192. In the blues, Big Walter Horton created one of the most fascinating versions.

TROUBLE NO MORE

See "Someday Baby"

TRUCKIN' LITTLE WOMAN

The often celebrated exploits of this erotic little woman were very successful among blacks in the thirties and forties. Big Bill Broonzy (30 March 1938 on Vocalion 04205) and Blind Boy Fuller (29 October 1938 on Vocalion 04603 but covering an earlier piece "Truckin' My Blues Away") claimed authorship.

TUPELO

Since Charlie Patton's "High Water Everywhere" (October 1929 on Paramount 12909), the whims of the Mississippi River, which engulfed villages during its floods, have been sung by many bluesmen. "Tupelo," largely based on Patton's composition, is an incredible spoken composition of John Lee Hooker's of April 1959 (on Riverside 838). Albert King and Roebuck "Pops" Staples had an exciting version on Stax 0047.

T.V. MAMA

One of the most extraordinary compositions of Big Joe Turner, this "T.V. Mama" with her big screen was recorded for the first time with Elmore James on 7 October 1953 on Atlantic.

V-8 FORD BLUES

Or "Ride in Your Funeral." This minor classic of the East Coast blues is probably the work of Buddy Moss, who recorded it on 21 August 1935 on ARC 5-11-58.

VICKSBURG BLUES

This is a famous piano piece, the ancestor of "44 Blues" from Roosevelt Sykes/Lee Green. It is likely that it is the work of Little

Brother Montgomery, who recorded it in September 1930 on Paramount 13006.

WALKING BLUES

Probably built on the model of "Death Letter" of Son House, "Walking Blues" was recorded by Robert Johnson on 27 November 1936 on Vocalion 03601. A striking piece, both on the musical and the literary level, "Walking Blues" fascinated many bluesmen. Muddy Waters, Johnny Shines, Luther Johnson, and Johnny Winter had original and fascinating interpretations.

WANG DANG DOODLE

Willie Dixon's composition for Howlin' Wolf (June 1960 on Chess 1777) was a big hit by Koko Taylor in November 1965 on Checker 1135.

WEDNESDAY EVENING BLUES

John Lee Hooker had an ear in the direction of Charles Brown when he created this tense blues on 27 February 1950 on Modern 20-746.

WHAT'S THE MATTER WITH THE MILL?

The lament of this poor man unable to grind his grain any longer because of a mill not functioning well is an old pornographic piece by the duo Memphis Minnie/Joe McCoy recorded on 11 October 1930 on Vocalion 1550. This light type of song was very popular in the thirties and forties. "What's the Matter . . ." was covered many times, but it is undeniably Bob Wills who had the most brilliant version on 29 September 1936. Muddy Waters played this piece in 1972 on Chess 2143 under the title "Can't Get No Grindin'."

WHEN THE SAINTS GO MARCHING IN

This antediluvian Negro spiritual was "bluesified" by Papa Lightfoot in an extraordinary version on the harmonica in 1954 for Imperial. Fred McDowell and Frank Edwards also played beautiful renditions on the bottleneck.

WHEN THINGS GO WRONG

See "It Hurts Me Too"

WHISKY-HEADED WOMAN

This rather traditional piece of Delta blues is linked to Tommy McClennan, who recorded it on 22 November 1939 on Bluebird B 8373. Canned Heat made it one of their big hits.

WHO'S BEEN TALKING?

Composed by Howlin' Wolf, who recorded it on three occasions: in 1956 under the title "Going Back Home" (Chess 1648), on 24 June 1957 on Chess 1750, and finally on 3 May 1970 with Eric Clapton. Robert Cray covered it on his first album (Tomato 7041).

WHY DON'T YOU DO RIGHT?

"Why Don't You Do Right?" is a beautiful ballad in a minor key from the smart pen of Joe McCoy for the smooth Lil Green who recorded it on 23 April 1941 accompanied by Big Bill Broonzy on Bluebird B 8714. Lil Green's success inspired Peggy Lee who "whitened" the piece with Benny Goodman's band in 1945. Amos Milburn, Johnny Otis, and, recently, the buxom cartoon creature in "Roger Rabbit" have interpreted this piece that brings to mind the best crop of the forties.

WONDER WHY

This blues comes from the imagination of producer Mel London, who composed it under the title "Will My Man Be Home Tonight" for Lilian Offitt (1959 on Chief 7012). Jimmy Dawkins, Earl Hooker, Otis Rush, and dozens more made it a standard of contemporary Chicago blues.

YOU DON'T HAVE TO GO

A huge success for Jimmy Reed on 30 December 1953 on Vee-Jay 119, Mama Smith's composition started her husband's career and enabled many bluesmen to fill their albums.

YOU DON'T LOVE ME

The riff of "You Don't Love Me" has inspired quantities of bluesmen, from Magic Sam to Buddy Guy via Albert King. However, this is an original composition by the southern singer-harmonica player Willie Cobbs, who recorded it for the first time on the small Mojo label 2168 in 1961.

▪ BLUES ARTISTS
AND THEIR INSTRUMENTS

The major performers often conceal excellent musicians who recorded few or no titles under their own names.

Here, then, is a list of primary and secondary blues musicians who played the following instruments:

- ▪ fingerpicking guitar: Most often traditional or rural bluesmen practiced the technique played with two, three, or four fingers of the right hand, generally on the acoustic guitar. This style is widespread in country blues.

- ▪ lead guitar: with a pick or the thumb. This technique was quite common in the thirties and forties, widespread after the war and with the electrification of instruments.

- ▪ harmonica.
- ▪ piano.
- ▪ accordion.

For bass, drums, fiddle, and mandolin, we refer to the individual listings in the Encyclopedia.

We try to mention the recording that is most characteristic of each musician's style.

FINGERPICKING GUITAR
(+ SLIDE GUITAR)

Woodrow Adams, "The Train Is Coming," (+)
Pink Anderson, "Gonna Trip Out Tonight"
Kokomo Arnold, "The Twelves," (+)
Barbecue Bob, "Going Up the Country," (+)

John Henry Barbee, "Cotton Pickin' Blues," (+)

Nathan Beauregard, "Highway 61"

Black Ace, "I'm the Black Ace," (+)

Scrapper Blackwell, "Blues in E"

Willie "61" Blackwell, "Machine Gun Blues"

Blind Blake, "Southern Rag"

Son Bonds, "Weary Worried Blues"

Charlie Booker, "Charlie's Boogie Woogie"

Avery Brady, "Poor Kennedy"

Jimmy Brewer, "Big Road Blues"

John Brim, "Tough Times"

Big Bill Broonzy, "Guitar Rag"

Bumble Bee Slim, "Bleeding Heart Blues"

R. L. Burnside, "Poor Black Mattie," (+)

Joe Callicott, "You Don't Know My Mind"

Carolina Slim, "Your Picture Done Faded"

Bo Carter, "I'm an Old Bumble Bee"

Leonard Caston, "I'm Gonna Walk Your Dog"

John Cephas, "Reno Factory"

Sam Chatmon, "Ash Tray Taxi"

Cryin' Sam Collins, "My Road Is Rough and Rocky"

Elizabeth Cotten, "Freight Train"

Country Jim, "Dial 110 Blues"

Arthur "Big Boy" Crudup, "Death Valley Blues"

Reverend Gary Davis, "Samson and Delilah"

Maxwell Street Jimmy Davis, "Two Trains Running"

Jimmy De Berry, "Take a Little Chance"

Willie Dixon, "Weak Brain, Narrow Brain!"

K. C. Douglas, "Fanny Mae"

Snooks Eaglin, "Alberta"

Clarence Edwards, "Cooling Board"

Frank Edwards, "Gotta Get a Gettin'"

Honeyboy Edwards, "Sweet Home Chicago," (+)

J. D. Edwards, "Crying"

Sleepy John Estes, "Someday Baby"

Baby Face Leroy Foster, "Rollin' and Tumblin'"

Calvin Frazier, "Have Blues Will Travel," (+)

Blind Boy Fuller, "Rag, Mama, Rag"

Jesse Fuller, "San Francisco Bay Blues"

Lowell Fulson, "Stormin' and Rainin'"
Little Bill Gaither, "In the Wee Wee Hours"
Clifford Gibson, "She Rolls It Slow"
John Lee Granderson, "A Man for the Nation"
Guitar Slim Green, "Alla Blues"
L. C. Green, "Remember Way Back"
John Hammond, Jr., "Tallahassee Woman," (+)
Jessie Mae Hemphil, "She-Wolf"
King Solomon Hill, "Down on My Bended Knee," (+)
Silas Hogan, "Trouble at Home"
Smokey Hogg, "Penitentiary Blues"
John Lee Hooker, "Bus Station Blues"
Lightnin' Hopkins, "Jake Head Boogie"
Son House, "Preachin' Blues," (+)
Lawyer Houston, "Dallas Bebop Blues"
Howlin' Wolf, "The Red Rooster," (+)
Mississippi John Hurt, "Monday Morning Blues"
J. B. Hutto, "Pet Cream Man," (+)
Jim Jackson, "Old Dog Blues"
John Jackson, "Step It Up and Go," (+)
Lee Jackson, "Juanita"
Lil' Son Jackson, "Roberta Blues"
Elmore James, "Shake Your Moneymaker," (+)
Homesick James, "Homesick," (+)
Skip James, "Cherry Ball Blues"
Blind Lemon Jefferson, "Matchbox Blues"
Bobo Jenkins, "Democrat Blues"
Larry Johnson, "Don't Get Mad with Me"
Robert Johnson, "Walkin' Blues," (+)
Tommy Johnson, "Slidin' Delta"
Blind Willie Johnson, "Take Your Burden to the Lord," (+)
Elijah Jones, "Katy Fly"
Floyd Jones, "Dark Road"
Little Hat Jones, "Two String Blues"
Charley Jordan, "Gasoline Blues"
Luke Jordan, "Church Bell Blues"
Arthur "Guitar" Kelley, "Number 10 at the Station"
Jo-Ann Kelly, "Hard Times Killing Floor Blues," (+)
Spider John Koerner, "Southbound Train"

Willie Lane, "Black Cat Rag"

Leadbelly, "Bourgeois Blues"

J. B. Lenoir, "Alabama Blues"

Ernest Lewis, "West Coast Blues"

Furry Lewis, "Natural Born Eastman," (+)

Lightnin' Slim, "Bad Luck"

Charlie Lincoln, "Jealous-Hearted Blues," (+)

Hip Linkchain, "Cold Chills"

Mance Lipscomb, "Buck Dance," (+)

Little Son Joe, "Ethel Bea"

Robert Jr. Lockwood, "Little Boy Blue," (+)

Lonesome Sundown, "My Home Is a Prison"

Joe Hill Louis, "Western Union Man"

Louisiana Red, "Louisiana Blues," (+)

Robert Lowery, "Crossroads," (+)

Magic Sam, "Looking Good"

Carl Martin, "Trouble on Your Hands"

Tommy McClennan, "I'm a Guitar King"

Charlie McCoy, "Baltimore Blues," (+)

Ethel McCoy, "Bumble Bee"

Joe McCoy, "Please Baby"

Fred McDowell, "Keep Your Lamp Trimmed and Burning," (+)

Brownie McGhee, "Living with the Blues"

Sticks McGhee, "Money Fever"

Blind Willie McTell, "Searchin' the Desert for the Blues," (+)

Memphis Minnie, "In My Girlish Days"

Memphis Willie B., "61 Highway"

Luke "Long Gone" Miles, "Hello, Josephine"

Flora Molton, "The Titanic," (+)

Buddy Moss, "Chesterfield," (+)

Muddy Waters, "My Home Is on the Delta," (+)

Hambone Willie Newbern, "Way down in Arkansas," (+)

Robert Nighthawk, "Maggie Campbell," (+)

Jack Owens, "Hard Times Killing Floor Blues"

Charlie Patton, "High Water Everywhere" (+)

Robert Petway, "Catfish Blues"

Charlie Pickett, "Down the Highway," (+)

Dan Pickett, "Baby, How Long," (+)

Pinebluff Pete, "A Woman Acts Funny"

Pinetop Slim, "John Henry," (+)
Eugene Powell, "Poor Boy Blues," (+)
Doug Quattlebaum, "Good Woman Blues"
Yank Rachell, "Katy Lee Blues"
Bonnie Raitt, "Tribute to Fred McDowell," (+)
Dave "Snaker" Ray, "Fixin' to Die," (+)
Boyd Rivers, "You Got to Move"
William Robertson, "Love Blues," (+)
Lonesome Jimmy Lee Robinson, "Rosalie"
Jimmy Rogers, "Money, Marbles and Chalk"
Cool Papa Sadler, "Do Right Mind"
Alec Seward, "Late Saturday Evening"
Thomas Shaw, "Jack of Diamonds"
Johnny Shines, "Ramblin'," (+)
Frankie Lee Sims, "Walkin' with Frankie"
J. T. "Funny Papa" Smith, "Howling Wolf"
Smokey Smothers, "Black Cat Blues," (+)
Smoky Babe, "Regular Blues"
Arthur "Big Boy" Spires, "Murmur Low"
Mark Spoelstra, "France Blues"
Freddie Sprueill, "Tom Cat Blues"
Wild Jimmy Spruill, "Scratchin'"
Houston Stackhouse, "Canned Heat"
Frank Stokes, "It Won't Be Long Now"
Hubert Sumlin, "Taters and 'matos"
Taj Mahal, "Stagolee" (+)
Tampa Red, "Seminole Blues," (+)
Tarheel Slim, "No Time at All"
Eddie Taylor, "Stroll out West," (+)
Hound Dog Taylor, "Alley Music," (+)
Johnny Temple, "Louise Blues"
Henry Thomas, "Old Country Stomp"
James "Son" Thomas, "Shake 'em on Down," (+)
Jesse Thomas, "Blue Goose Blues"
Tommy Lee Thompson, "Highway 80 Blues"
Big Son Tillis, "Cold Blues"
John Tinsley, "Keep Your Hands off Her"
James Tisdom, "Model T. Boogie"
Henry Townsend, "Mistreated Blues"

Richard Trice, "Pack It Up and Go"
Willie Trice, "Good Time Boogie"
Baby Face Turner, "Blues Serenade," (+)
T. V. Slim, "Hold Me Close to Your Heart"
Dave Van Ronk, "St. James Infirmary"
Walter Vincson, "Rats on My Cheese"
Charles Walker, "Driving Home"
Wade Walton, "The Red Rooster"
Baby Boy Warren, "Hello, Stranger"
Curley Weaver, "Some Rainy Day," (+)
Boogie Bill Webb, "Boogie"
Casey Bill Weldon, "Arlena," (+)
Bukka White, "World Boogie," (+)
Josh White, "St. James Infirmary"
Robert Wilkins, "Rolling Stone," (+)
Big Joe Williams, "Razor Sharp Blues," (+)
Bill Williams, "Pocahontas"
Jimmy Lee Williams, "Shortening Bread," (+)
JoJo Williams, "All Pretty Women"
Robert Pete Williams, "Midnight Boogie," (+)
Ralph Willis, "Gonna Hop on down the Line"
Johnny Winter, "Mean Mistreater," (+)
Oscar Woods, "Lone Wolf Blues," (+)
David Wylie, "You're Gonna Weep and Moan"
Johnny Young, "Pony Blues"
John Lee Ziegler, "Poor Boy," (+)

LEAD GUITAR (FLATPICKING)

Luther Allison, "Drivin' Wheel," (+)
Mickey Baker, "Do What You Do," (+)
Lefty Bates, "Rock Alley"
Royal Earl Bell, "I Need You So Bad"
Bobby "Guitar" Bennett, "When Girls Do It"
Wayne Bennett, "Rockin'"
Buster Benton, "Money Is the Name of the Game"
Chuck Berry, "Johnny B. Goode"
Edgar Blanchard, "Mr. Bumps"

Mike Bloomfield, "Lovin' Cup"

Blue Charlie, "Don't Have No Friends"

Little Joe Blue, "Me and My Woman"

ZuZu Bollin, "Stavin' Chain"

Lonnie Brooks, "Mr. Hot Shot"

Andrew Brown, "I Got News for You"

Clarence "Gatemouth" Brown, "Okie Dokie Stomp"

Texas Johnny Brown, "The Blues Rock"

Mel Brown, "The Combination"

Roy Buchanan, "Roy's Bluz," (+)

Eddie Burns, "Don't Let Money Change You"

Eddie C. Campbell, "Santa's Messin' with the Kid"

Big Lucky Carter, "Goofer Dust"

Goree Carter, "I'm Your Boogie Man"

Joe Carter, "Take a Little Walk with Me," (+)

Eric Clapton, "Everybody Ought to Change"

Eddie Clearwater, "Hillbilly Blues"

Gary B. B. Coleman, "Scratch My Back"

Albert Collins, "Defrost"

Johnny Copeland, "Old Man Blues"

Robert Cray, "Phone Booth"

PeeWee Crayton, "Texas Hop"

G. L. Crockett, "Look Out, Mabel"

Larry Dale, "Let the Doorbell Ring"

Larry Davis, "Texas Flood"

Jimmy Dawkins, "Marcelle Morgantini's Cassoulet"

Bo Diddley, "I'm a Man"

Snooks Eaglin, "Down Yonder"

Johnny Embry, "Johnny's Bounce"

Johnny Fuller, "Train Train Blues"

Lowell Fulson, "Guitar Shuffle"

Anson Funderburgh, "Talk to You by Hand," (+)

Roy Gaines, "Gainesville"

Clarence Garlow, "Crawfishing"

Lacy Gibson, "Drown in My Own Tears"

Boyd Gilmore, "Ramblin' on My Mind," (+)

Cal Green, "White Pearl"

Clarence Green, "Crazy Strings"

Guitar Shorty, "Hard Life"

Guitar Slim, "Things I Used to Do"

Buddy Guy, "Moanin'"

Pat Hare, "Gonna Murder My Baby"

Hi-Tide Harris, "Charlie Stone"

Peppermint Harris, "Fat Girl Boogie"

Johnny Heartsman, "Frisco Blues"

Clarence Holliman, "Soul Twist"

Earl Hooker, "Apache War Dance," (+)

Bee Houston, "Things Gonna Get Better"

Joe Hughes, "Shoe Shy"

Long John Hunter, "Old Red"

Elmore James, "Knocking at Your Door," (+)

Jimmy Johnson, "Take Five"

Lonnie Johnson, "Four Hands Are Better Than Two"

Luther Johnson, "Impressions from France"

Luther Johnson, Jr., "Got to Have Money"

Syl Johnson, "Suicide Blues"

Willie Johnson, with Howlin' Wolf, "Mr. Highway Man"

Albert King, "Flat Tire"

B. B. King, "King's Special"

Bobby King, "My Babe"

Earl King, "Trick Bag"

Eddie King, "The Blues Has Got Me"

Freddie King, "San-Ho-Zay"

Saunders King, "S. K. Blues"

Big Daddy Kinsey, "Kinsey Special," (+)

Donald Kinsey, "Answering Machine," (+)

Eddie Kirkland, "Train Done Gone," (+)

Eddie Lang, "The Fooler"

Sammy Lawhorn, "After Hours," (+)

Calvin Leavy, "Cummins Prison Farm"

Smiley Lewis, "Slide Me Down"

Jimmy Liggins, "Drunk"

Lil' Ed, "Young Thing," (+)

Little Milton, "Walking the Back Streets and Cryin'"

Little Oscar, "Suicide Blues"

John Littlejohn, "Catfish," (+)

Magic Slim, "Teardrops"

Pete Mayes, "Lowdown Feeling"

L. C. McKinley, "Blue Evening"

Johnny Moore, with Charles Brown, "Driftin' Blues"

Oscar Moore, with Nat King Cole, "Route 66"

M. T. Murphy, "Matt's Guitar Boogie"

Louis Myers, "Money, Marbles and Chalk," (+)

Kenny Neal, "Devil Child"

Chuck Norris, "Messin' Up"

Jimmy Nolen, "Wipe Your Tears"

Morris Pejoe, "She Walked Right In"

R. S. Rankin, "Midnight Bells Are Ringing"

Sonny Rhodes, "Cigarette Blues," (+)

Fenton Robinson, "The Getaway"

Freddie Robinson, "The Creeper"

L. C. Robinson, "Jack Rabbit Boogie," (+)

Otis Rush, "Rock"

Buddy Scott, "Roadblock"

Isaac Scott, "Going Back to Oakland"

Ray Sharpe, "Linda Lu"

Byther Smith, "What Have I Done"

Arbee Stidham, "My Heart Belongs to You"

Hubert Sumlin, with Howlin' Wolf, "300 Pounds of Joy"

Eddie Taylor, "Crosscut Saw," (+)

Melvin Taylor, "Depression Blues"

Lafayette Thomas, "Lafayette's Coming"

Tabby Thomas, "Hoodoo Party"

Ron Thompson, "Blue Chariot," (+)

Luther Tucker, "Tuckerology"

Ike Turner, "Grumbling"

Floyd Valentine, "Off Time"

Maurice John Vaughn, "Computer Took My Job"

Joe Louis Walker, "Alligator," (+)

Phillip Walker, "The Bottom of the Top"

T-Bone Walker, "Strollin' with Bones"

Willie D. Warren, "Detroit Jump"

Josh White, "House of the Rising Sun"

Joe Willie Wilkins, "Mr. Downchild," (+)

Jody Williams, "Lucky Lou"

Lester Williams, "Lost Gal"

Hop Wilson, "Chicken Stuff," (+)

Smokey Wilson, "Go Go Train"
Johnny Winter, "Good Morning, Little Schoolgirl," (+)
Mighty Joe Young, "Guitar Star"

HARMONICA

Luther Allison, "Evil Is Going On"
Jimmie Anderson, "When I Play My Harp"
Little Willie Anderson, "West Side Baby"
Nate Armstrong, "Red Light Boogie"
Billy Boy Arnold, "I Wish You Would"
DeFord Bailey, "Davidson County Blues"
Carey Bell, "Rocking with Chromanica"
Big Amos, "Dog Man"
Billy Bizor, "Tell Me Where You Stayed Last Night"
Blues Birdhead, "Harmonica Blues"
Houston Boines, "Superintendant Blues"
Juke Boy Bonner, "Call Me Juke Boy"
Boy Blue, "Joe Lee's Rock"
Billy Branch, "Billy's Boogie"
Big Leon Brooks, "Blues for a Real Man"
B. Brown, "Rocking with B."
Buster Brown, "Sugar Babe"
Clarence "Gatemouth" Brown, "That's All Right Mama"
Dusty Brown, "Do You Love Me?"
Sylvester Buckley, "She Treats Me So Evil"
Mojo Buford, "Whole Lotta Women"
Jewtown Burks, "Evalena"
Eddie Burns, "Biscuit Baking Mama"
J. C. Burris, "Dead President"
Wild Child Butler, "Harmonica Prayer"
Paul Butterfield, "Born in Chicago"
Clifton Chenier, "Je suis un récolteur"
Chicago Bob, "Call My Landlady"
George Clark, "Prisoner Blues"
Willie Cobbs, "Eating Dry Onions"
Jaybird Coleman, "Man Trouble Blues"
James Cotton, "Laying in the Weeds"

Lester Davenport, "No Peace"
Harmonica Sammy Davis, "1958 Blues"
Bill Dicey, "Scratch My Back"
Driftin' Slim, "Somebody Voodooed the Voodoo Man"
Johnny Dyer, "Overdose of Love"
Easy Baby, "Good Morning, Mr. Blues"
Frank Edwards, "Chicken Raid"
Forest City Joe, "Forest City Jump"
Little Willie Foster, "Crying the Blues"
Frank Frost, "Pocketful of Shells"
Jesse Fuller, "San Francisco Bay Blues"
Jazz Gillum, "Sarah Jane"
Good Rocking Charles, "The Goat"
Good Time Charlie, "Cleaned Out"
John Hammond, Jr., "No Money Down"
Harmonica Fats, "Tore Up"
Harmonica Slim, "Mary Helen"
Alfred Harris, "Miss Darlene"
John Lee Henley, "Knockin' at Lula Mae's Door"
Robert Henry, "Old Battle Axe"
Ace Holder, "Lonesome Harmonica"
Big Walter Horton, "Blow, Walter, Blow!"
Howlin' Wolf, "Smokestack Lightnin'"
PeeWee Hughes, "Sugar Mama Blues"
Cliff Jackson, "Nine below Zero"
Sonny Boy Johnson, "Desert Blues"
Birmingham Jones, "Chills and Fever"
Sam Kelly, "Ramblin' around Blues"
Eddie Kirkland, "Snake in the Grass"
Lazy Lester, "Lester's Stomp"
Alfred Lewis, "Friday Moan Blues"
Noah Lewis, "Minglewood Blues"
Sammy Lewis, "So Long, Baby, Goodbye"
Papa Lightfoot, "Jump the Boogie"
Little Boyd, "13 Highway"
Little Red Walter, "Aw Shucks, Baby!"
Little Sonny, "Wade in the Water"
Little Walter, "Juke"
Long Tall Lester, "Working Man"

Joe Hill Louis, "Western Union Man"
Louisiana Red, "Red's Dream"
Hot Shot Love, "Harmonica Jam"
Willie Mabon, "Worry Blues"
Sidney Maiden, "Eclipse of the Sun"
Jerry McCain, "728 Texas"
Jimmy McCracklin, "It's Alright"
Sonny Boy McGhee, "Bluebird Blues"
Walter Mitchell, "Pet Milk Blues"
Charlie Musselwhite, "Strange Land"
Louis Myers, "Top of the Harp"
Sammy Myers, "I'm Your Professor"
Kenny Neal, "Change My Way of Living"
Raful Neal, "Blues on the Moon"
Hammie Nixon, "Minnie's Blues"
Paul Oscher, "Double Trouble"
Junior Parker, "Sweet Home Chicago"
Peg Leg Sam, "Strollin'"
Polka Dot Slim, "Hey Mattie!"
Jerry Portnoy, with Muddy Waters, "Baby, Please Don't Go"
Snooky Pryor, "Judgement Day"
Eugene Ray, "Grits"
Jimmy Reed, "Odds and Ends"
Rhythm Willie, "Wailin' Willie"
Robert Richard, "Cadillac Woman"
Walter Robinson, "I've Done Everything I Can"
Dr. Ross, "Chicago Breakdown"
Will Shade, "She Stays Out All Night Long"
Shakey Jake, "Hey Baby"
Little Mack Simmons, "Trouble No More"
Slim Harpo, "Moody Blues"
George Smith, "Ode to Billy Joe"
Whispering Smith, "Hound Dog Howl"
Sugar Blue, with Johnny Shines, "Too Wet to Plow"
Taj Mahal, "Leaving Trunk"
Doc Terry, "Doctor's Boogie"
Sonny Terry, "Harmonica Train"
Kid Thomas, "Willow Brook Blues"
Big Mama Thornton, "Rock Me"

Junior Wells, "Chili Con Carne"
Walter Westbrook, "Midnight Jump"
Phil Wiggins, with John Cephas, "Reno Factory"
Oscar Williams, with Frank Frost, "Harp and Soul"
Slim Willis, "From Now On"
John Lee "Sonny Boy" Williamson, "Down South"
Sonny Boy Williamson (Rice Miller), "Don't Start Me to Talkin'"
Al Wilson, with Canned Heat, "An Owl Song"
Johnny Woods, "Three O'Clock in the Morning"
Big John Wrencher, "Maxwell Street Alley"

PIANO

Dave Alexander, "The Rattler"
Albert Ammons, "Boogie Woogie Man"
Archibald, "Shake Shake Baby"
Big Maceo, "Maceo's 32/20"
Boogie Woogie Red, "Red's Boogie"
James Booker, "Doing the Hambone"
Eddie Boyd, "Third Degree"
Charles Brown, "Driftin' Blues"
Cleo Brown, "Cleo's Boogie"
Henry Brown, "Webster's Blues"
Bob Call, "Thirty-One Blues"
Leroy Carr, "Prison Bound Blues"
Ray Charles, "What'd I Say"
Sam Clark, "Sunnyland Train"
Cousin Joe, "Chicken Blues"
Charles "Cow Cow" Davenport, "Cow Cow Blues"
Walter Davis, "Ashes in My Whisky"
Detroit Count, "Hastings Street Opera"
Detroit Junior, "I Got Money"
Floyd Dixon, "Hey Bartender"
Fats Domino, "The Fat Man"
Champion Jack Dupree, "Dupree Shake Dance"
Lavada Durst, "Hattie Green"
Big Joe Duskin, "The Red Rooster"
Billy Emerson, "Zulu"

Bob Gaddy, "Paper Lady"
Cecil Gant, "Playin' Myself the Blues"
Lloyd Glenn, "Chico Boo"
Roscoe Gordon, "Just a Little Bit"
Henry Gray, "Cold Chills"
Roy Hawkins, "The Thrill Is Gone"
Honey Hill, "Boogie Woogie"
Frank James, "Rusty Can Blues"
Skip James, "How How Long"
Gus Jenkins, "Cold Love"
Pete Johnson, "Blues on the Down Beat"
Curtis Jones, "Lonesome Bedroom Blues"
Little Johnny Jones, "Big Town Playboy"
Latimore, "Let's Straighten It Out"
Lovie Lee, "I Dare You"
Meade "Lux" Lewis, "Boogie Woogie Prayer"
Joe Liggins, "The Honeydripper"
Lee Roy Little, "I'm a Good Man but a Poor Man"
Little Richard, "Tutti Fruiti"
Little Sonny Jones, "Going Back to the Country"
Little Willie Littlefield, "K. C. Loving"
Cripple Clarence Lofton, "Monkey Man Blues"
Willie Mabon, "I'm the Fixer"
J. J. Malone, "Old Fashioned Blues"
Jimmy McCracklin, "The Walk"
Jay McShann, "Hootie Ignorant Oil"
Memphis Slim, "Broadway Boogie"
Mercy Dee, "One-Room Country Shack"
Amos Milburn, "Chicken Shack Boogie"
Little Brother Montgomery, "Vicksburg Blues"
Alex Moore, "Neglected Woman"
Elmore Nixon, "Playboy Blues"
Pinetop Perkins, "Pinetop's Boogie Woogie"
Piano Red, "Sober"
Big Walter Price, "Nothing but the Blues"
Professor Longhair, "Tipitina"
Bob Riedy, "Just off Halsted"
Walter Roland, "House Lady Blues"
Clarence "Pinetop" Smith, "Pinetop's Blues"

Thunder Smith, "Thunder's Unfinished Boogie"
Otis Spann, "Marine"
Speckled Red, "The Dirty Dozen"
Victoria Spivey, "T.B.'s Got Me"
Sunnyland Slim, "Got a Thing Going On"
Roosevelt Sykes, "44 Blues"
Montana Taylor, "Indian Avenue Stomp"
Robert "Dudlow" Taylor, "Lonesome"
Henry Townsend, "Heart Trouble"
Tommy Tucker, "Alimonia"
Ike Turner, "Doing It"
Mose Vinson, "Bullfrog Blues"
Johnny "Big Moose" Walker, "Ramblin' Woman"
Sippie Wallace, "Suitcase Blues"
Eddie Ware, "That's the Stuff I Love"
Katie Webster, "Whooee Sweet Daddy"
Peetie Wheatstraw, "Sleepless Night Blues"
Bukka White, "Drunk Man Blues"
Georgia White, "Daddy, Let Me Lay It on You"
Jimmy Yancey, "Yancey Stomp"

▪ INDEX

Bell, William, 235
Below, Fred, 17, 99, 106, 197, 207, 212, 256, 260, 360, 385
Bennett, Alvino, 99
Bennett, Duster, 370
Bennett, Wayne, 23, 126, 156
Benson, George, 156
Benton, Brook, 318
Benton, Buster, 14, 15–16, 95, 340
Bernholm, Jonas, 224
Berry, Chuck, 15, 17–18, 60, 67, 94, 243, 305, 369, 407, 445, 455, 457, 469, 473
Big Crawford, 13
Big Maceo, 18–19, 35, 36, 37, 89, 108, 124, 279, 282, 322, 331, 335, 471
Big Three Trio, 62, 94
Bihari brothers, 152, 186, 234, 276, 349, 435
Billy Always, 236
Binghamton Blues Boys, 117
Bishop, Elvin, 370
Bizor, Bill, 344
Black Ace, 20, 140, 326, 342, 388
Blackwell, Scrapper, 46, 54–55, 99, 124, 253, 286, 440, 458
Blackwell, Willie, 451
Blair, Sunny, 83
Bland, Bobby "Blue," 16, 21, 23–24, 71, 83, 136, 155, 204, 234, 270, 276, 279, 349, 407, 417
Blind Blake, 20–23, 62, 82, 102, 103, 118, 129, 160, 166, 231, 377, 435, 444
Blind Sammy, 231
Block, Rory, 368
Bloomfield, Mike, 257, 258, 259, 333, 353, 370, 371, 408
Blue, Little Joe, 24, 53
Blues Boy King, 234
Blues Boy Willie, 69
Blues Brothers, 473
Bogan, Lucille, 298
Bogan, Ted, 220
Boggs, Dock, 364
Bollin, ZuZu, 156, 343

Bonds, Son, 109
Bonner, Weldon "Juke Boy," 31–32, 51, 290
Boogie Jake, 247
Boogie Woogie Red, 90
Booker, Charlie, 307
Booker, James, 283
Booker T. and the MG's, 235, 320, 450
Borum, Memphis Willie, 85
Bowman, Priscilla, 457
Boyd, Eddie, 15, 18, 19, 36–37, 60, 63, 91, 174, 448, 459
Bracey, Ishman, 165, 176, 249
Bracken, Jim, 63
Bradford, Perry, 113
Bradshaw, Myron "Tiny," 31, 408
Braggs, Al "TNT," 155
Branch, Billy, 65, 95, 135
Brenston, Jackie, 348
Brewer, Jim, 438
Brim, John, 19, 63, 183, 190, 260, 289, 432
Bromberg, Bruce, 78, 353
Bromberg, David, 370
Brooks, Lonnie, 38, 64, 175, 248, 266, 373, 390, 408, 432, 475
Brooks, Skippy, 141
Broonzy, Big Bill, 5, 18, 38–40, 39, 46, 62, 109, 124, 127, 128, 140, 147, 196, 223, 237, 241, 254, 256, 357, 377, 383, 408, 436, 444, 454, 456, 457, 458, 459, 470, 475, 476, 478
Broven, John, 271
Brown, Andrew, 40
Brown, Arelean, 391
Brown, B., 269
Brown, Buster, 204, 269, 455
Brown, Charles, 3, 42–43, 49, 50, 52, 57, 120, 125, 215, 243, 249, 282, 318, 356, 408, 439, 445, 461, 477
Brown, Clarence "Gatemouth," 42, 43, 73, 116, 135, 155, 180, 270, 284, 291, 292, 343, 356, 409, 474
Brown, Cleo, 35
Brown, Earl, 122

Everly Brothers, 156

Fabulous Thunderbirds, 222, 343, 373
Fahey, John, 158, 165, 236, 278, 368,
 375
Falcon, Joe, 395
Fats Domino, 38, 45, 96, 96–97, 244,
 264, 265, 266, 283, 318, 335, 396,
 411, 436, 445
Ferguson, H-Bomb, 31
Ferris, Bill, 236
Fieldstones, 116–17, 237, 466
Firk, Backwards Sam, 236
Five Breezes, 94
Fleetwood Mac, 106, 148, 322, 370
Floyd, Buddy, 248
Floyd, Eddie, 73, 320
Ford, Robben, 259, 260
Forest City Joe, 383
Forest, Earl, 23
Foster, Leroy, 207, 330
Francis, Morris, 398
Francis, Panama, 99
Franklin, Aretha, 235, 320, 378, 391
Frazier, Calvin, 90, 199
Freed, Alan, 60
Freund, Steve, 285, 374
Frost, Frank, 117–18, 290
Fullbright, J. R., 50
Fuller, Blind Boy, 21, 24, 56, 82, 102,
 118–19, 160, 227, 267, 268, 412,
 457, 472, 476
Fuller, Jesse, 119–20, 299
Fuller, Johnny, 49, 120, 137, 147, 355
Fulson, Lowell, 4, 49, 50, 52, 57, 69,
 79, 121, 121–23, 135, 155, 166, 221,
 224, 343, 353, 354, 356, 412, 439,
 440, 447, 465, 467, 470, 475
Fulson, Martin, 122
Funderburgh, Anson, 31, 261, 421

Gaddy, Bob, 230, 271
Gaines, Grady, 155, 156, 412
Gaines, Roy, 155, 291, 303
Gaither, Little Bill, 55, 123–24, 457,
 468
Gallagher, Rory, 370

Gant, Cecil, 124–25
Garlow, Clarence, 247, 344, 372, 396,
 440
Gatewood, Ernest, 14
Gaye, Marvin, 320
Gayten, Paul, 265
Geddins, Bob, 49, 50, 98, 120, 137,
 224, 243, 294
Gentry, Bobby, 290
Georgia Bill, 231
Gibson, Clifford, 169, 203, 304
Gibson, Lacy, 125–26
Gilbert, Shorty, 308
Gillum, Jazz, 29, 39, 40, 60, 62,
 126–27, 178, 256, 358, 454, 457,
 459
Gilmore, Boyd, 281, 354
Gilmore, Gene, 94
Gitfiddle Jim, 11. See Kokomo Arnold
Glenn, Lloyd, 50, 122, 440, 447
Glover, Henry, 214
Glover, Tony, 28, 368
Goldberg, Barry, 258, 370
Goldstein, Kenneth, 27
Goodman, Benny, 185, 315, 367, 454,
 478
Gordon, Jimmie, 303
Gordon, Roscoe, 23, 234, 456
Gordy, Berry, 319, 462
Govenar, Alan, 155
Granderson, John Lee, 258
Grateful Dead, 250
Gray, Henry, 10, 18, 154, 248, 282
Greelee, Bob, 262
Green, Al, 236, 322
Green, Cal, 30, 156, 343
Green, Guitar Slim, 52, 436
Green, Jerome, 93
Green, L. C., 90
Green, Lee, 18, 253, 331, 448, 476
Green, Lil, 39, 115, 128–29, 271, 378,
 478
Green, Peter, 370
Grey, Al, 43
Grimes, Tiny, 30
Grossman, Stefan, 83, 102, 158, 327,
 370

Kinks, 246
Kinsey, Donald, 183, 190–91
Kinsey, Lester "Big Daddy," 190–91,
  417
Kirk, Andy, 181
Kirkland, Eddie, 89, 143, *191*, 191–92,
Kirkland, Frank, 99, 158
Knight, Gladys, 156, 391
Knopfler, Mark, 78
Knowlin, Ransom, 80, 358
Koerner, Alexis, 179, 369
Koerner, Spider John, 368
Koester, Bob, 5, 28, 109, 216, 360
Kooper, Al, 370
Krupa, Gene, 15
Kustner, Axel, 56
Kweskin, Jim, 368

Lacava, Jacques, 190
Lacey, Willie, 127, 358
Ladnier, Tommy, 288, 302
Lane, Sonny, 53
Lang, Eddie, 4, 169
LaSalle, Denise, 168, 175, 320
Latimore, Benny, 320
Laurie, Annie, 265
Laury, Booker T., 237
Lawhorn, Sammy, 83, 256
Lawlar, Ernest "Little Son Joe," 238
Lazy Lester, 66, 200, 246, 290, 417
Leadbelly, 192–94, 199, 227, 342, 369,
  378, 382, 417, 436, 439, 453, 454,
  455, 462, 467
Leadbitter, Mike, 32, 384
Leake, Lafayette, 17, 53, 95, 385, 450
Leary, S. P., 256
Leavy, Calvin, 194–96
Lee, Alvin, 370
Lee, Bonnie, 339, 391, 393, 431
Lee, David, 305
Lee, Little Frankie, 53, 69
Lee, Julia, 181
Lee, Lovie, 90
Lee, Peggy, 128, 367, 448, 478
Lenoir, J. B., 7, 63, 65, 196–97, 305,
  418, 460, 468

Leonard, Harlan, 275
Levy, Ron, 31, 123, 267, 282, 329, 374
Lewis, Alfred, 134
Lewis, Ernest, 52
Lewis, Furry, 197–98, 232, 236, 327,
  379, 442
Lewis, Jerry Lee, 235, 443
Lewis, Meade "Lux," 34, 35, 124, 298,
  431
Lewis, Noah, 134, 233, 383
Lewis, Ramsey, 52
Lewis, Smiley, 97, 266, 283
Liggins, Jimmy, 50
Liggins, Joe, 50, 205, 275, 452, 465
Lightfoot, George "Papa," 101, 134,
  477
Lightnin' Slim, 130, 147, 200–201,
  245, 246, 397, 418, 432, 452, 461
Lil' Ed, 65, 159
Lincoln, Charlie, 13
Liniger, Walter, 48
Lippmann, Horst, 5, 7, 9
Lipscomb, Mance, 27, 178, 193,
  201–3, *202*, 309, 418, 436
Little Charly and Rick Estrin, 53, 374
Little Johnny, 222
Little, Lee Roy, 269
Little Milton, 41, 126, 203–4, 218,
  234, 235, 304, 307, 321, 349, 418,
  448, 453, 456
Little Oscar, 322
Little Richard, 155, 204–6, *205*, 244,
  265, 266, 275, 318, 418
Little Sonny, 89
Little Walter, 7, 14, 15, 47, 60, 63, 74,
  94, 134, 148, 171, 206, 212, 224,
  238, 247, 256, 258, 259, 261, 295,
  304, 311, 316, 327, 330, 360, 370,
  371, 383, 386, 418, 440, 442, 447,
  456, 457, 461, 463, 464
Little Wolf, 95, 154
Littlefield, Little Willie, 42, 51, 215,
  269, 456
Littlejohn, John, 162, 190, 208–9, 392
Locke, Abb, 305
Lockwood, Robert Jr., 162, 207,

Melrose, Lester, 18, 62, 80, 94, 126, 128, 170, 223, 311, 358, 383
Memphis Jug Band, 197, 220, 232, 238, 258, 359
Memphis Minnie, 46, 116, 150, 164, 197, 232, 237–39, 295, 335, 359, 376, 379, 390, 419, 420, 441, 453, 477
Memphis Piano Red Williams, 236
Memphis Slim, 7, 27, 35, 40, 51, 63, 95, *240*, 241–42, 270, 281, 282, 328, 331, 358, 360, 420, 433, 436, 447, 451, 455
Memphis Sonny Boy, 236
Mendel, Harvey, 259
Mendelsohn, Fred, 267
Mercy Dee, 4, 242–43, 420
Meters, 267
Mighty Clouds of Joy, 339
Mighty Sam, 321, 329
Mikofsky, Anton, *112*
Milburn, Amos, 3, 42, 50, 97, 136, 243–44, 318, 343, 353, 420, 464, 465, 478
Miles, Big Boy, 267
Miles, Luke "Long," 52
Miller, J. D., 200, 201, 213, 244–48, 262, 313, 365, 396, 398
Miller, Jay, 432, 435
Miller, John, 368
Miller, Johnny, 13
Miller, Mark, 398
Miller, Tal, 247
Millinder, Lucky, 30
Milton, Roy, 49, 156, 205, 219, 243, 248–49
Mississippi Sheiks, 176, 220, 239, 249–51, 390, 446, 470
Mitchell, George, 47
Mitchell, McKinley, 321
Mitchell, Rose, 437
Mitchell, Walter, 90
Mitchell, Willie, 174, 235, 278, 279, 379
Mitchum, Snapper, 14
Miton, Tall, 172
Molton, Flora, 56, 160

Monroe, Bill, 250, 365
Montgomery, Little Brother, 18, 35, 51, *112*, 113, 250, 251–53, *252*, 264, 331, 449, 477
Montgomery, Wes, 16, 156
Moody Blues, 290, 369
Moore, Alex, 178, 342, 344
Moore, Alice, 11, 304
Moore, Gatemouth, 31
Moore, Johnny, 42, 50, 445
Moore, Johnny B., 65
Moore, Oscar, 50
Morand, Herb, 239
Morgantini, Marcelle, 168, 217
Morris, Blue Charlie, 247
Morrison, Van, 370, 437
Morton, Jelly Roll, 62, 251, 264
Moss, Buddy, 21, 56, 102, 253–54, 377, 467, 476
Muddy Waters, 7, 14, 15, 17, 28, 36, 40, 47, 60, 62, 63, 66, 67, 76, 80, 89, 93, 94, 105, 127, 130, 148, 151, 162, 170, 171, 173, 174, 176, 180, 190, 196, 199, 200, 206, 214, 223, 238, 254–57, *255*, 258, 260, 261, 272, 273, 279, 281, 289, 292, 294, 295, 304, 307, 309, 317, 319, 322, 330, 336, 354, 358, *366*, 369, 370, 372, 373, 383, 385, 391, 420, 421, 432, 438, 439, 442, 447, 448, 449, 453, 454, 456, 457, 458, 460, 461, 462, 466, 471, 477
Muddy Waters, Jr., 24, 53
Muldaur, Geoff, 368
Mullican, Moon, 365
Mulligan, Gerry, 387
Murphy, Floyd, 172
Murphy, M. T., 7, 126, 241, 256
Musselwhite, Charlie, 52, 135, 206, 257–60, 333, 370, 381, 421, 458
Myers, Dave, 14, 15, 207, 260, 360
Myers, Louis, 15, 106, 206, 207, 212, 260–61, 360, 456, 457, 462, 466, 472
Myers, Sammy, 78, 106, 209, 421, 471

Naftalin, Mark, 370

Portnoy, Jerry, 135, 373
Powell, Tiny, 137
Presley, Elvis, 80, 235, 276, 290, 345,
    365, 448, 449, 452, 462, 463, 467,
    474
Price, Bobby, 397
Price, Lloyd, 266
Price, Sammy, 75
Prince Gabe, 237
Professor Longhair, 97, 99, 264, 266,
    282, 283–84, 422
Pryor, Snooky, 63, 95, 164, 207,
    284–85, 330, 384
Prysock, Red, 15
Puckett, Riley, 364
Pullum, Joe, 124, 439

Queen Ida, 397, 422
Quinn, Bill, 135, 161
Quinn, Strozer, 359, 388

Rachell, Yank, 109, 164, 220, 286, 383,
    451
Rainey, Ma, 21, 110, 112, 114, 159,
    236, 237, 287–88, 315, 335, 376,
    392, 439, 469
Rainey, Willie Guy, 104
Raitt, Bonnie, 114, 289, 454
Ramey, Ben, 233
Raney, Wayne, 246
Rapone, Al, 398
Rau, Fritz, 5, 7, 9
Rawls, Lou, 387
Ray, Dave, 368
Ray, Eugene, 135
Raylor, Sam "The Man," 305
Redding, Otis, 57, 73, 78, 122, 139,
    187, 192, 195, 222, 235, 247, 314,
    319, 469
Reed, A. C., 65, 71, 259, 288–89, 305,
    306, 354
Reed, James, 52
Reed, Jimmy, 7, 16, 31, 32, 38, 53, 63,
    117, 134, 174, 190, 196, 213, 214,
    271, 288, 289–91, 314, 336, 343,
    369, 422, 437, 438, 452, 478

Reed, Mama, 437, 438, 452
Reed, Willie, 4, 342
Reinhardt, Django, 169, 211
Rhodes, Sonny, 53, 219, 277, 291–92,
    294, 326, 457
Rhythm Willie, 469
Richard, Robert, 90
Riedy, Bob, 297, 391
Riggins, Richard, 98
Riley, Billy Lee, 290
Riley, Judge, 80, 99
Rivers, Boyd, 48
Robertson, William, 104
Robey, Don, 435, 436
Robey, Milton, 233
Robillard, Duke, 374
Robinson, A. C., 294
Robinson, Bobby, 163, 267, 269, 471
Robinson, Fenton, 83, 292–93, 306,
    422, 437, 450, 464, 471, 472
Robinson, Freddie, 53, 307
Robinson, Ikey, 113, 377
Robinson, Jessie Mae, 439
Robinson, L. C. "Good Rockin'," 116,
    147, 291, 294, 326, 342
Robinson, Smokey, 320
Robinson, Sylvia, 270
Roby, L. C., 91
Rockets, 261
Rockin' Dopsie, 295, 396, 422
Rockin' Sidney, 295, 320, 394, 396,
    423
Rodgers, Jimmie, 160, 230, 249, 364,
    366
Rogers, Jimmy, 15, 60, 63, 80, 148,
    150, 206, 207, 238, 256, 260, 286,
    295–97, 296, 305, 335, 385, 389,
    423, 432, 437, 454, 456, 463, 471
Roland, Walter, 219, 282, 297–98, 377
Rolling Stones, 154, 256, 269, 288,
    290, 314, 328, 349, 353, 360, 369,
    370, 380, 383, 453, 460, 466, 467
Rooftop Singers, 233
Ross, Diana, 155
Ross, Doctor, 7, 212, 234, 299
Ross, Dwight, 69

Smith, "Thunder," 147

Smith, Trixie, 115

Smith, Willie, 99

Smitty, Blue, 63

Smoky Babe, 248

Smothers, Smokey, 370

Soileau, Floyd, 248, 396, 398

South Memphis Jug Band, Jack
Kelly's, 233

Spand, Charlie, 21, 89

Spann, Lucille, 106, 325, 390

Spann, Otis, 7, 17, 18, 35, 63, 171, 212,
215, 256, 279, 281, 282, 317,
322–23, 385, 391, 424, 431

Sparks, Aaron, 304, 348, 447

Sparks, Milton, 304, 348, 447

Spaulding, Henry, 304

Spears, H. C., 165, 176, 277, 278

Speckled Red, 35, 241, 444

Spencer Davis Group, 144, 290

Spencer, Jerome, 370

Spires, Arthur, 63

Spires, Big Boy, 176

Spivey, Victoria, 7, 12, 112, 114, 169,
267, 323–25, *324*, 327, 335, 439,
474

Spoelstra, Mark, 368

Spruill, Wild Jimmy, 271, 369

Stackhouse, Houston, 176, 236, 272,
384, 385, 441, 460

Staples, Roebuck "Pop," 184, 235,
278, 320, 476

Staples Singers, 235, 278, 424

Steel Guitar

Stepney, Bill, 99

Stevie Wonder, 156, 320

Stewart-Baker, Derrick, 315

Stokes, Frank, 116, 197, 198, 232,
326–27, 379, 436

Stone, Henry, 319

Stone, Jessie, 387

Stowers, Freeman, 134

Strachwitz, Chris, 27, 58, 148, 208,
248, 313, 396

Streeter, Big Time Sarah, 330, 392,
431

Strehli, Angela, 374

Strickland, Napoleon, 47, 117, 227

Struck, Nolan, 322

Stuckey, Henry, 165

Sumlin, Hubert, 7, 154, 172, 308, 329,
424, 431

Summer, Donna, 392

Sunnyland Slim, 5, 67, 95, 317,
329–31, *330*, 450, 468; as "Doctor
Clayton's Buddy," 123, 330, 392

Sugar Blue, 95, 134, 312, 325, 327–28

Sun Ra, 126

Supremes, 156

Sweet Papa Stovepipe, 83

Sykes, Roosevelt, 11, 18, 62, 85, 169,
241, 253, 281, 282, 303, 331–33,
332, 347, 444, 445, 448, 452, 454,
463, 476

Sylvester, Hannah, 325

Taggart, Blind Joe, 377

Tail Dragger, 154

Taj Mahal, 108, 333–34, 443, 472

Tampa Red, 11, 18, 19, 36, 60, 62,
104, 163, 170, 181, 237, 272, 288,
323, 334–36, 360, 455, 458, 459,
473

Tarheel Slim, 56, 147, *268*, 268–69,
271

Tarlton, Jimmie, 442

Tate, Baby, 12, 103

Tate, Buddy, 305, 387

Tate, Howard, 322

Taylor, Arthur "Montana," 35

Taylor, Eddie, 14, 65, 143, 150, 217,
278, 285, 289, 290, 317, 330,
336–37, 389, 422, 425, 463

Taylor, Hound Dog, 5, 7, 36, 158, 188,
337–38, 425, 451

Taylor, Johnny, 235, 240, 425

Taylor, Koko, 50, 65, 94, 218, 338–39,
373, 390, 391, 392, 393, 425, 458,
469, 477

Taylor, Little Johnny, 53, 69, 139, 219,
339–40, 465

Taylor, Larry, 14